The Genesis of Modernity

The Genesis of Modernity is the third book in a series, which will lay the foundations of a new understanding of modernity. It reconstructs the ideas of three of the most important social and political theorists of the twentieth century, Max Weber, Michel Foucault and Eric Voegelin, on the distant roots and sources of modernity.

Weber, Foucault and Voegelin each turned to the study of Antiquity at significant moments in their working lives, and when they were expected to deliver an authoritative statement concerning their views on the nature and characteristics of modernity. In recent years an interest in such comparative historical work has emerged and this book presents and compares key ideas including ethical prophecy, philosophy as a way of life, democratic parrhesia, charisma, the link between empires and the city, and the rise of Christianity, leading to the recognition that the modern age of 'globalisation' has its antecedent in another period of 'globalisation' which began two and a half millennia ago. The work of Weber, Foucault and Voegelin is also considered in light of the contribution of a number of historically and anthropologically oriented social thinkers including Norbert Elias, Lewis Mumford, Georges Dumzil, Victor Turner, René Girard and Franz Borkenau.

Drawing upon the conceptual tools of social theory and political philosophy, complemented by approaches based in the fields of anthropology, comparative mythology and the history of ancient philosophy *The Genesis of Modernity* will prove to be a timely and valuable contribution to this developing area, bringing together the ideas of a group of social and political theorists whose work so far has remained largely unconnected.

This book will be essential reading for academics and advanced students concerned with social theory, political theory, sociology, history and philosophy.

Arpad Szakolczai studied in Budapest, Hungary and has a PhD from the University of Texas at Austin. From 1990 to 1998 he taught social and political theory at the European University Institute in Florence. He is now Professor of Sociology and Head of Department at University College, Cork. This book follows his *Max Weber and Michel Foucault: Parallel Life-Works* (1998), and *Reflexive Historical Sociology* (2000), also published by Routledge.

Routledge Studies in Social and Political Thought

1 Hayek and After
Hayekian liberalism as a research programme
Jeremy Shearmur

2 Conflicts in Social Science
Edited by Anton van Harskamp

3 Political Thought of André Gorz
Adrian Little

4 Corruption, Capitalism and Democracy
John Girling

5 Freedom and Culture in Western Society
Hans Blokland

6 Freedom in Economics
New perspectives in normative analysis
Edited by Jean-Francois Laslier, Marc Fleurbaey, Nicolas Gravel and Alain Trannoy

7 Against Politics
On government, anarchy and order
Anthony de Jasay

8 Max Weber and Michel Foucault
Parallel life works
Arpad Szakolczai

9 The Political Economy of Civil Society and Human Rights
G.B. Madison

10 On Durkheim's *Elementary Forms of Religious Life*
Edited by W. S. F. Pickering, W. Watts Miller and N. J. Allen

11 Classical Individualism
The supreme importance of each human being
Tibor R. Machan

12 The Age of Reasons
Quixotism, sentimentalism and political economy in eighteenth-century Britain
Wendy Motooka

13 Individualism in Modern Thought
From Adam Smith to Hayek
Lorenzo Infantino

The Genesis of Modernity

Arpad Szakolczai

Routledge
Taylor & Francis Group

LONDON AND NEW YORK

First published 2003
by Routledge
11 New Fetter Lane, London EC4P 4EE

Simultaneously published in the USA and Canada
by Routledge
29 West 35th Street, New York, NY 10001

Routledge is an imprint of the Taylor & Francis Group

© 2003 Arpad Szakolczai

Typeset in Baskerville by Taylor & Francis Books Ltd
Printed and bound in Great Britain by Biddles Ltd, Guildford and King's
Lynn

British Library Cataloguing in Publication Data
A catalogue record for this book is available from the British Library

Library of Congress Cataloging-in-Publication Data
A catalog record for this book has been requested

ISBN 0–415–25305–5 (hbk)

To Giovi, Tommi and Stefi

Contents

Acknowledgements

Most of the texts contained in this book were written during the 2001/02 academic year, half of which I have spent on a sabbatical leave of absence in Florence. I am particularly grateful to all those individuals and institutions who rendered this possible: Gerard Wrixon, President of UCC, for granting me the leave; Joe Ruane, my colleague at the Department of Sociology, for taking over my administrative duties; the European University Institute in Fiesole and the Università di Firenze for taking me on as external and visiting professor. For their help, I am grateful to Colin Crouch and Leonardo Morlino, and particularly to Emilio Santoro and their Dipartimento di Storia e Teoria del Diritto for their exceptional kindness in procuring me most precious and scarce office space.

Sebastian Rinken read and commented most usefully upon a draft version of the three Weber chapters, while Stefan Rossbach did so with Chapter 4. I thank them heartily.

This book was written in conditions that were particularly difficult for my family, making things only worse. My sincere apologies to all of them. I wish I could promise them 'never again'.

Those who know her will recognise immediately how much this book owes to Agnes. More cannot be expressed in words.

Abbreviations

The following abbreviations are used for major or frequently mentioned books. They are used only in the reference sections, while in the main text a shortened version of the title is given. For book series and collected writings, an attempt has been made to harmonise the demands of simplicity, coherence and compatibility with usage in existing literature on individual thinkers, and also with the preceding two volumes in the series.

For Michel Foucault

CF75   *Les anormaux: Cours au Collège de France (1974–1975)*, Paris: Gallimard/Seuil (1999).
CF82   *L'herméneutique du sujet: Cours au Collège de France (1981–1982)*, Paris: Gallimard/Seuil (2001).
DE   *Dits et écrits*, 4 vols, D. Defert and F. Ewald (eds), Paris: Gallimard (1994). (Texts from this collection are either cited by volume and page number, or by the chronological number given to them.)
DV   *Discorso e veritá nella Grecia antica*, Florence: Donzelli (1996).
HS2   *L'usage des plaisirs*, (Vol. 2 of *The History of Sexuality*), Paris: Gallimard (1984).
HS3   *Le souci de soi*, (Vol. 3 of *The History of Sexuality*), Paris: Gallimard (1984).

For Eric Voegelin

AN   *Anamnesis*, Notre Dame, Ill: University of Notre Dame Press ([1966] 1978).
AR   *Autobiographical Reflections*, E. Sandoz (ed.), Baton Rouge: Louisiana State University Press (1989).
FPP   *Faith and Political Philosophy: The Correspondence Between Leo Strauss and Eric Voegelin, 1934–64*, P. Emberley and B. Cooper (eds), University Park, PA: Pennsylvania State University Press (1993).
HPI   *Hellenism, Rome and Early Christianity*, (Vol. 1 of *History of Political Ideas*), A. Moulakis (ed.), Columbia: University of Missouri Press (1997).
NSP   *The New Science of Politics*, Chicago: Chicago University Press (1952).

OHI   *Israel and Revelation*, (Vol. 1 of *Order and History*), Baton Rouge: Louisiana State University Press (1956).

OHII   *The World of the Polis*, (Vol. 2 of *Order and History*), Baton Rouge: Louisiana State University Press (1957).

OHIII   *Plato and Aristotle*, (Vol. 3 of *Order and History*), Baton Rouge: Louisiana State University Press (1957).

OHIV   *The Ecumenic Age*, (Vol. 4 of *Order and History*), Baton Rouge: Louisiana State University Press (1974).

OHV   *In Search of Order*, (Vol. 5. of *Order and History*), Baton Rouge: Louisiana State University Press (1987).

SPG   *Science, Politics and Gnosticism*, Chicago: Henry Regnery ([1959] 1968).

(The publication of the *Collected Works* of Eric Voegelin is underway by the University of Missouri Press. However, in the book I use the widely available early editions.)

For Max Weber

AJ   *Ancient Judaism*, New York: The Free Press ([1921] 1952).

ES   *Economy and Society*, Berkeley: University of California Press ([1921–22] 1978).

FMW   *From Max Weber*, H. Gerth and C. W. Mills (eds), London: Routledge (1948). (Contains the *Einleitung*, translated as 'The Social Psychology of the World Religions', and the *Zwischenbetrachtung*, translated as 'Religious Rejections of the World and their Directions'.)

GARS   *Gesammelte Aufsätze zur Religionssoziologie*, 3 vols, Tübingen: J. C. B. Mohr (1920–21). (Contains the *Vorbemerkung*, the PE, the essay on Protestant Sects, and the essays collected under the title *Economic Ethic of World Religions* (*Die Wirtschaftethik der Weltreligionen*) – RC, RI and AJ; referred to as *Collected Essays*.)

MWG   *Max Weber Gesamtausgabe*, H. Baier *et al.* (eds), Tübingen: J. C. B. Mohr (1981–). (Roman numeral I is given to the writings, II to the letters. Texts from this collection are cited by volume and page number.)

PE   *The Protestant Ethic and the 'Spirit' of Capitalism*, Los Angeles: Roxbury ([1904–05] 1995). (Also contains the *Vorbemerkung*, translated as 'Author's Introduction'.)

RC   *The Religion of China*, New York: The Free Press ([1920] 1951).

RI   *The Religion of India*, New York: The Free Press ([1921] 1958).

WuG   *Wirtschaft und Gesellschaft*, Tübingen: J. C. B. Mohr ([1921–22] 1980).

WB   Weber, Marianne, *Max Weber: A Biography*, Oxford: Transactions Books ([1926] 1988).

Introduction

This volume is the third book in a series which aims to lay the foundations of a new understanding of modernity by bringing together the ideas of a group of social and political theorists whose work so far has remained largely unconnected.[1]

The book, however, is self-contained. It addresses a single question: why did three of the most important and politically highly active theorists of the past century, Max Weber, Eric Voegelin and Michel Foucault, each turn at a particularly significant moment of their working life to the study of Antiquity? In order to be as precise as possible in defining the way the book poses its question, each element in the statement needs some elaboration.

The significance of Weber and Foucault is widely recognised. They are today considered as *the* most influential thinkers of their generation. Voegelin is also well known and increasingly so, though – like other members of his generation (Elias, Schutz, Borkenau, Dumézil) – he still has not received his due. Concerning political involvement, Weber was passionately interested in politics throughout his entire life, Foucault was the main representative in the 1970s of the politically involved intellectual in France, while Voegelin had to leave Vienna days after the Anschluss in 1938 because of the outstandingly anti-Nazi character of his writings.

Each of the three thinkers turned to the study of Antiquity at a moment when they were at their prime and when they were expected to deliver an authoritative statement concerning their views on the nature and characteristics of modernity. This happened to Weber around 1910, when he was in his mid-forties, after the completion of *The Protestant Ethic*. Foucault was in his early fifties around 1980 when, instead of continuing directly the 'diagnosis' of modern power started in *Discipline and Punish* and the first volume of *History of Sexuality*, he plunged into a study of ancient philosophy. Voegelin was also in his mid-forties around 1945–46 when, instead of completing the chapters on the modern age in his 'History of political ideas', he also turned back to the distant past.

In spite of the enormous literature on Weber and Foucault, this problem has not yet even been posed in a satisfactory manner, not to mention solved it. The reason no doubt lies in the perplexing character of this reorganisation. Since the seventeenth century, the contrast between the 'ancients' and the 'moderns' was a taken-for-granted commonplace in Western thought, and the rise of sociology only reinforced the almost exclusive focus on the last few centuries for any attempt aiming at an understanding of the rise and dynamics of modernity. Within this framework, a turn to such remote origins remained simply unintelligible, an individual idiosyncracy.

It is only in recent years, largely due to the works of Shmuel Eisenstadt on the 'axial age' and on 'multiple modernity', and also to a series of connected publications by Wolfgang Schluchter, that a broader interest has arisen in Weber's comparative historical work.[2] The long-term research project of which this book is a part fits well into this broader field of interest, even though it emerged outside of it, and hopes to bring a specific and distinct contribution to the field. This can be summarised in three characteristics: its comparative nature in the sense of not simply using but drawing inspiration from the work of a series of major thinkers; the complementarity of conceptual tools drawn from social theory and political philosophy with approaches in anthropology, comparative mythology and the history of ancient philosophy; and finally, its reliance on a series of recent publications that rendered accessible for the first time, in a proper manner, some of the most important writings of these three thinkers.

First of all, while the work of Eisenstadt and Schluchter can be situated on a broadly Weberian horizon, and while books taking up the related works of Foucault or Voegelin did so largely independently of the other two thinkers, the aim of this book is to develop an approach that relies equally on the contribution of each of the three thinkers, as well as on that of a number of others with a highly similar research agenda. Such historically-oriented social thinkers include Norbert Elias, Lewis Mumford and Franz Borkenau, but also Philippe Ariès, Alphonse Dupront, Johan Huizinga, Reinhart Koselleck and many others. Unfortunately, within the scope of a single book it is simply impossible to integrate all of them. Furthermore, the book also argues that some of the central conceptual difficulties encountered by these thinkers could be assisted, even resolved, with the help of some of the most innovative and sophisticated works in anthropology, comparative mythology and the history of ancient philosophy. The book will rely especially on the ideas of Georges Dumézil, Mircea Eliade, René Girard, Pierre Hadot, Karl Kerenyi, Jan Patocka, Colin Turnbull, Victor Turner and Arnold van Gennep. The exact discussion of the manifold parallels between social philosophy and the more 'down-to-earth' approach characteristic of these scholars, however, again needs to be elaborated elsewhere. In this book, only some of the affinities can be sketched between Weber and Girard or Dumézil, Dilthey and Victor Turner, or Heidegger and Colin Turnbull.

Finally, the completion of this book was rendered possible by a series of recent publications. This is because many of the most relevant works of Weber, Foucault and Voegelin were left as – often incomplete – manuscripts, or were edited posthumously and in rather questionable manner.

Concerning Weber, the *Collected Essays* remained a fragment, while *Economy and Society* was mostly in manuscript form at his death. Though the critical edition of *Economy and Society* was the single most awaited part of the *Gesamtausgabe*, decisions about editorial procedures were taken quite late and, so far, only two of the planned volumes of the second part of the book have made it into print. Luckily, these were exactly the two most relevant for our concerns, Volume 5 on The City, published in 1999, and Volume 2 on Religious Communities, published early in 2001.

In the case of Foucault, this book will argue that the most important ideas of his last period are contained not in the – written or unwritten – volumes of the *History of Sexuality*, but rather in the lectures he delivered at the Collège de France in the 1980s. Though delivered publicly, the written publication of these lectures was for more than a decade a subject of intense controversy, as Foucault's explicit wish for no posthumous publication was for a long period interpreted as prohibiting the edition of these lectures in book form. The controversy was only settled in the late 1990s, and three carefully edited volumes have already appeared in French. The full publication of all thirteen years, however, would certainly take at least another decade.

Fortunately, the courses relevant for this book have been available, on tape, in the Foucault Archives since the early 1990s. However, the last four lectures of 1982 that proved to be crucial for its argument were missing from the Archives, available only since the written publication in March 2001.

In opposition to Weber and Foucault who both died suddenly, due to illness, in the prime of their life, Voegelin lived until his 85th year. Still, his magisterial 'History of Political Ideas' remained in manuscript for a complex and still controversial set of reasons (see Szakolczai 2001b), not published until 1997–79.

The organisation of this book is straightforward. The ten chapters are divided into three parts, according to the three main theorists discussed in the book. Each part starts with a chapter on the 'historical methodology' of the respective thinker. 'Methodology' should be understood not in the contemporary sense of a 'scientific method', championed by various versions of positivism, but rather as an attempt to come to terms with the approaches of the three thinkers by 'reflecting' and 'meditating' on their works, trying to distil their central ideas and the way in which they used them.

These 'meditative' chapters serve three purposes. First, they play the role of catalyst in the writing of the substantive chapters, literally 'launching' them. This alone, however, would not justify their publication; but they also provide assistance to the reader, by introducing some of the central concepts of the respective thinkers and showing the manner in which they used them. For these reasons, these 'methodological' chapters will contain ample substantive analysis. Finally, these chapters are written to assist those planning to use the works of Weber, Voegelin or Foucault in their research. This is all the more possible as they do not reconstruct, from the inside, the thought of the three thinkers, but instead add two further dimensions: a 'philological' dimension, by paying attention to some minute details concerning the development and use of key concepts; and a 'comparative' dimension, by pointing out parallel or complementary approaches pursued by other major twentieth-century thinkers. This technique will not be restricted to the methodological chapters.

As these comments already indicate, though each of the three chapters is primarily devoted to the approaches of a single thinker, the central aim of the book is to bring out the parallels not only between them, but also between a series of other thinkers; parallels that are neither trivial, nor widely recognised, and that thus could serve the much-needed purpose of reorienting social thought for the twenty-first century, previously dominated by 'Establishment' versions of various kinds of positivism and neo-Kantianism, and the 'outcast' versions of various kinds of critical theory, mostly derived from Marx and Freud peppered with a romanticised or nihilistic Nietzsche.

For this purpose both the methodological chapters, and the entire body of the book, will systematically emphasise the fact that the basic ideas and approaches of these thinkers share fundamental affinities. This is partly due to shared lines of descent, partly to shared experiences. Most importantly, however, the establishment of such connections helps to lay the foundations of an approach that could provide a genuine understanding of the problems of our age, without the opposite but much related escapisms of official optimism, ignoring the gravity of the 'situation' and playing academic games with words, models and numbers; and the excesses of cultural pessimism and revolutionary mobilisation, manifested recently by the 'no global' movement.

The central methodological principle of this book is the building of these bridges, and their systematisation and interpretation, following a purely inductive method. This is not the book of a Foucauldian, trying to demonstrate that Weber or Voegelin said the same things; or a follower of Victor Turner, translating everything into the language of liminality. The manifold connections between the various thinkers were built up gradually, eventually approaching a 'whole picture'. It is true that after a time the approach gained a dynamic on its own, and for example the generational identities and divisions, related to the experiences of the two World Wars, gained a systematicity that almost defies belief.

Weber, Voegelin, Foucault, Dumézil, Hadot, Turner or Girard did not say exactly the same thing. But they were touched by the same problem. Furthermore, a book must use a coherent and frugal terminological language. It is not possible to list every single time all the terms employed by the various thinkers in order to capture a phenomenon. To give an example, Foucault talks about 'techniques', 'technologies' or 'practices of self', Hadot about 'philosophical' or 'spiritual exercises', Voegelin about 'anamnetic experiments' or 'meditations', while Elias and Turner use the language of reflexivity. The problem is even more acute for the central analytical concepts in the book, and the parallels one can draw here between the various thinkers and approaches. As a solution the book will 'prioritise', for every basic conceptual field, one particular term developed by one author, and will establish the parallels by tracing all the others to this term. Such terms include the 'genealogical method', developed by Foucault on the basis of Nietzsche's work but close to the reading of Nietzsche by Weber, and then Elias, Borkenau or Voegelin, as well; 'problematisation', developed again by Foucault, but capturing a similar hermeneutical–historical interest by many other thinkers; and 'liminality', taken from Victor Turner; while the concept 'experience' will be understood in the sense attributed to it by Voegelin.

The sequential order of the substantive chapters was established on the basis of three basic principles: the internal logic of the respective work of each thinker, the comparability of their works, and the need to establish a coherent line of meaning running through the book. The two Weber chapters are based on a genealogical line of reasoning. In his historical sociology Weber started, in terms of both substance and method, on the trail of Nietzsche, more specifically of *The Genealogy of Morals*. In *The Protestant Ethic* he investigated the 'other', less visible, undercurrent thread of modernity, the inner-worldly asceticism characteristic of the Protestant sects, which constituted the 'spirit' of capitalism, as opposed to its more visible and self-evident 'formal' or 'structural' characteristics like finance, accounting and banking, that were derived from the Italian city states, especially Florence and Venice. He then planned to investigate the medieval monastic roots of this asceticism, but ended up instead, in the essays of the 'Economic Ethic of World Religions', moving further back in time as far as ancient Hebrew prophecy.

 This new orientation can again be traced to the *Genealogy of Morals*, this time the theme of *ressentiment*, and its connection with modern nihilism and rationality. Using this extended historical perspective, Weber planned to connect, still in this thread, ancient prophecy to Protestantism through a study of early Christianity, and completed a draft of the other thread, studying the rise of the Italian city states out of the background of the ancient city. At this moment, however, there intervened first war and then the influenza epidemic and death, and his project remained in fragments. The second and third chapters of this book will reconstruct, separately, the two basic threads identified by Weber in his genealogy of modernity, (ancient Hebrew) prophecy and the (Occidental) city. The tension set up between these two poles is still a resource for social theory.

 Voegelin took up the task of completing and complementing this task in the 1940s, by studying the interlacing of monastic asceticism and apocalyptic sectarianism in the medieval cities in the form of an inner-worldly eschatology. The best-known and most important segment of the manuscript on the 'History of Political Ideas', on the 'People of God', was devoted to the heart of this theme. If Weber's interest was the rise of capitalism, Voegelin wanted to diagnose the nation state, especially its totalitarian tendencies. However, instead of finishing this project, Voegelin also ended up shifting the time horizon of his work back to Antiquity. Simplifying things, one could say that this was because he realised that Weber omitted a crucial element of the picture, Greek philosophy, relevant both in terms of the complement and contrast it provided to prophecy, and as the dominant form of reflection in the ancient city. Thus Chapters 5 and 6 of this book reconstruct the two basic threads of Voegelin's 'genealogy' of modernity, dealing with Hebrew prophecy and Greek philosophy.

Foucault also started his 'History of Sexuality' in the footsteps of Nietzsche's diagnosis of the ascetic ideal, focusing on the field of sexual asceticism. Planning a short background study of Christianity, he ended up fully devoting the last period of his work to Antiquity, especially to Greek and Roman philosophy. Foucault did not study prophecy, only philosophy, identifying in his Collège de France courses two basic threads: the care of the self, lying at the heart of ancient philosophy, according to him; and parrhesia, or the frank and courageous telling of the truth, which emerged in Athenian democracy. A genealogical design would require analysis of these two threads separately. However, partly because of the highly unfinished character of Foucault's-related works, partly the quick joining of the two threads in Socratic philosophy, it was not possible to follow this way of proceeding. Instead, the discussion was divided into three chapters, following a chronological order.

Part I

Max Weber

Charisma and the world of the city

1 Weber's historical method

Weber's historical method of proceeding can be reconstructed from prominent places in three of his most important writings on the sociology of religion: the first pages of the relevant chapter in *Economy and Society*, the *Einleitung* and the *Zwischenbetrachtung*. These texts were written in sequential order, representing a subsequent summary and reflexive elaboration of the enormous historical material that went into the twin projects of the years 1911–13, the 'Economic Ethic' essays and the second part of *Economy and Society*.

Just as Nietzsche's 'genealogical method' bracketed the substantive issues of religion and morality, focusing instead on the conditions out of which the main religions grew and their lasting (secular) effects, in the first paragraph of the 'Sociology of Religious Communities' Weber also defers any definitions, adding that his concern is not the 'essence of religion', rather 'to study the conditions and effects of a particular type of social action' (ES: 399). Similarly, in the *Einleitung* the emphasis is on the 'psychological and ethical contexts of religions' (FMW: 267), while the *Zwischenbetrachtung* starts by clarifying the 'motives from which religious ethics of world abnegation have originated, and the directions they have taken', thus 'their possible "meaning"' (*ibid*.: 323).

This simple point about conditions and effects may seem trivial in itself, but it is not quite so. It is definitely not just another way of talking about 'causes' and 'effects'. It is closely related to the central diagnostic concern, the identification of long-term hidden effects – in the concrete case of Weber, of religious factors on the economy. The idea is that the specific historical conditions out of which a certain phenomenon develops determine the way in which the phenomenon may possess hidden, long-term lasting effects, even when it ceases to exist in its original form. Thus, in the case of religion, it is not the elements of dogma, theology, religious beliefs – those that are usually considered the most important elements, the character, the 'essence' of a particular religion – that define the manner in which this religion exerts its long-term social effect; rather it would transmit to the future the conditions of its 'birth'.

The question is to capture the exact mechanism of this transference. How do such 'conditions of emergence' define exactly the most persistent, lasting characteristics of a phenomenon? It is here that Weber made a series of major steps towards methodological clarity, most importantly in the *Einleitung*.

Conditions of emergence

Weber first of all distinguishes between two types of such conditions: the external or objective situation, and its internal, subjective aspects. Identifying them with Marx and Nietzsche, he starts by criticising the respective positions of these two thinkers and then – combining what is valuable from both perspectives – presents his own account.

External–objective factors

Weber recognises the special importance of two external factors, social stratification and settlement patterns, alluding to Marx. But clearly he is opposed to the idea that such external interests define the content of ideas (FMW: 269–70). This point is further elaborated in the famous 'switchmen' metaphor: 'Not ideas, but material and ideal interests, directly govern men's conduct. Yet very frequently the "world images" that have been created by 'ideas" have, like switchmen, determined the tracks along which action has been pushed by the dynamic of interest' (*ibid.*: 280).[1]

Weber's resistance to Marx's position, and the exact meaning of the metaphor, can be understood by one of the most important, though strangely ignored, conceptual tools of Weber, the distinction between 'ordinary' and 'out-of-ordinary' situations, or even their degree of ordinariness.[2] Under ordinary, ordered, routine, normal conditions, external, structural factors and interest situations indeed play a dominant role. However, when the normal business of everyday life is upset through sudden, unforeseen *events*, structures become suspended, thus objective factors cannot play a decisive role. There is need for a different kind of explanation.

Internal–subjective factors

It is here that Weber turns to the other side, the internal–subjective factors, to the way in which events are lived, or the side of *experiences*.[3] In contrast to the previous, 'Marxian' side, this brings in the perspective of Nietzsche. However, beyond simply combining the two opposite perspectives, he immediately revises Nietzsche's position. Though referring to the *Genealogy of Morals* as 'Nietzsche's brilliant essay', he points out that the idea that Christianity is rooted in a feeling of *ressentiment* is untenable.

Weber's references to ressentiment are central for understanding the entire thrust of the work, as they indicate most clearly the profound impact the ongoing dialogue with Nietzsche had on it. Though critical of Nietzsche's position, his argument is based positively on this criticism of Nietzsche. This can be seen in three main areas: the specification of the basic underlying psychological motivation of salvation religions in suffering, not ressentiment; the treatment of Buddhism; and the differentiation between Judaism and Christianity.

 Laing

Weber is not denying completely the insight, and acknowledges that feelings of ressentiment and vengefulness indeed played an important role in religion. But he argues that ressentiment is only one particular aspect of a much broader and more important complex of problem: that of *suffering*. According to Weber, the experience of suffering is the decisive factor underlying the most important religious developments. Thus Weber follows Nietzsche by identifying the roots of nihilism, or the questioning of the world, in an overwhelming negative life experience, but changes the central concept from ressentiment to suffering.

Weber introduces here another crucial dichotomy, the contrast between the theodicy of suffering and the theodicy of the fortunate (*ibid.*: 271–2). The argument again closely follows the *Genealogy of Morals*, agreeing with Nietzsche even regarding the claim that it is only the religious ideas of the 'less fortunate' that are more complicated.[4] Though this conceptualisation is not elaborated fully, by evoking a war-conflict model, it traces the rise of religion to another case of 'out-of-ordinary' situation.

The second point concerns Nietzsche's claim that Buddhism as a religion is also based on ressentiment, central for Nietzsche's general theoretical case. For Weber, Buddhism as a religion has nothing to do with ressentiment (ES: 494–9, 935). It did not even grow out of socially deprived groups. It is rather a religion *par excellence* that *abnegates* the world. Following Nietzsche by locating the source of comparative theoretical generalisation in the case of Buddhism, Weber changes the central concept from ressentiment to world rejection.

Finally, with his theory of ressentiment Nietzsche argues for a profound continuity rather than a break between Judaism and Christianity. This makes it evident that his main adversaries are not at all the Jews but rather the Christians, in particular his contemporary anti-Semites who vehemently denied this continuity. Weber, however, has a different problem, the problem of rationalisation and universalism, so he returns to put the differences between Christianity and Judaism at the centre. These differences can be situated exactly with respect to the other departures from Nietzsche's theoretisation of ressentiment. On the one hand Weber acknowledges that, under special conditions in the history of Judaism, the religion of suffering did turn into ressentiment. The quest for vengeance is present in various places in the Old Testament, particularly in the Psalms (*ibid.*: 495), and a 'hope for revenge…suffused practically all the exilic and postexilic sacred scriptures' (*ibid.*: 96). Though '[t]o interpret *ressentiment* as the decisive element in Judaism would be an incredible aberration…Nevertheless, we must not underestimate the influence of *ressentiment* upon even the basic characteristics of the Jewish religion' (*ibid.*).

These characteristics would be analysed in detail at the end of *Ancient Judaism*, where – through the prophecies of Deutero Isaiah and the figure of the 'suffering servant' – Weber elaborates on the continuities between this aspect of Judaism and Christianity. Still, for Weber, such continuities are by no means central to Christianity. Quite on the contrary, he argues that the central message of Jesus is not ressentiment, not even release from suffering or an active abnegation of the world, but rather 'an absolute indifference to the world and its concerns' (*ibid.*: 633).[5]

Responses

The out-of-ordinary conditions identified above, lived and experienced (literally 'suffered through'), both individually and collectively, call for a response. Weber's ideas in this respect will be reconstructed along a continuum, related to the time elapsed (from immediate to more delayed), and the amount of reflexive thought involved.

Immediate response: natural charisma

The suspension of the ordinary course of life, whether in the form of drought, illness, or armed conflict, is experienced as a traumatic event, requiring an immediate solution. There are only a few individuals who manage to rise up to the challenge, manifesting extraordinary powers. It is in this context that Weber introduces one of the central concepts of his sociology, 'charisma' (ES: 400). While here Weber emphasises religious charisma, in his other works he also acknowledged the importance of military charisma. Indeed, the warrior hero and the religious saviour are the two main archetypes of the charismatic person.

Just after introducing the concept, a methodologically central distinction is made by Weber between 'primary' and 'artificially produced' charisma in the very first pages of the relevant chapter (*ibid.*). 'Primary' charisma is a 'gift', a natural endowment or a personal quality, fully outside thought (*ibid.*: 241).[6] 'Artificial charisma' refers to the production, through stimulations or techniques, of the state in which 'out-of-ordinary' actions become possible. With this distinction we move from the immediate level to the next three steps of the process, each characterised, to varying degree, by the work of reflexive thought.

In his entire work Weber had a fundamental interest in the effective role played by ideas in reality.[7] In this respect, he again followed Nietzsche, and exactly in the way Foucault would later thematise Nietzsche's concerns with the genealogical method.[8] He did not attribute an exclusive role to the force of ideas, claiming only that far from simply 'reflecting' real processes and structures ideas did have an effective impact in history. But a successful diagnosis of modernity depends on the identification of the exact chain in which ideas played a central role in launching the dynamics of the kind of development that today looks inexorable.

After the level of immediate response, dominated by the sudden irruption of charisma, the role of thought can be followed through at three levels: the transformation of temporary charisma into a permanent holy state, through the application of ascetic techniques; the more-or-less parallel but more extensive and lasting process of 'permanentisation' or 'routinisation' (*Veralltäglichung*) of religion in the form of sacrificial priesthood;[9] and the work of reflexive thought proper that incorporates an interpretation of these responses, and the overall situation created by them.

These three steps are all present in Weber's work, though they are not explicitly systematised. In the *Einleitung*, Weber continues with the analysis of permanent holy states (ascetics, saviours etc.), and of the highest concepts corresponding to such holy states, 'rebirth' and 'redemption', characteristic of the various salvation religions (FMW: 279). In the *Zwischenbetrachtung*, the discussion moves to the level of the establishment of religious community, but only in the sense of focusing on the new kind of religious communities and their 'tension with the world', as a prelude to the discussion of the modalities of this tension in the various autonomous 'spheres', the central concern of the essay. More important for our purposes, however, are the relevant sections of *Economy and Society*, where Weber discusses the rise of religion out of magic (ES: 422–39). In between magic and the salvation religions, the magician with his tribal cult and the prophet with his community of the saved, there are the priests and the religions of sacrifice. The point is important not simply for concerns of exhaustivity or sequential order, but for reasons fundamental to the central thrust of Weber's sociology. Between the occasional tricks performed by the magician and the renewal preached by the prophet, there lies the long-term process of religious routinisation or *institutionalisation*, of which priests are the main agents, and cults of sacrifice the main tools. As the essays of the 'Economic Ethic' make it clear, prophets always arose in the context of heterodox sects, formulated against institutionalised forms of religions.

Though these ideas seem to be well entrenched in standard sociological wisdom, this is not quite the case. The context of the argument is the interlocking of dual conceptual pairs, between ordinary vs 'out-of-ordinary', and temporary vs permanent. 'Institutionalisation' or routinisation in this context does not simply mean the gradual transformation of customary, informal, personal relations into something more stable and formal, but the transformation of fleeting, temporary phenomena into permanent ones.

At this point it should be recalled that 'religion' belongs to one of the two main categories of 'out-of-ordinary' events and charismatic actions, the other being warfare. A proper systematic treatment of the 'permanentisation of the temporary', in the sense of routinisation, should therefore cover these two spheres together.

This has important implications for the relationship between the various 'spheres', central to the discussion of the *Zwischenbetrachtung*. There is a difference between the formal institutionalisation of regular everyday relations and activities, and the routinisation of the responses to such temporary situations. While the logic of conventional social theory corresponds to the former, the thrust of Weber's discussion privileges the latter. According to this, the two major driving forces of institutionalisation are in the spheres of religion and warfare. The field of magic develops into the ritualised forms of cultic and religious practice, performed by the priests; while the temporary dispositions of war are turned into the permanent arrangements of the court and its politics.

The historical record shows that power in the early civilisations was based on the institutionalisation not of everyday relations and conduct, but of these two 'out-of-ordinary' spheres, with the central question being the relationship of these two poles of power.[10] This question took up a central place in Weber's discussion of Antiquity, the crucial issue being whether these two sources of power were kept in independent hands, or were united. Weber considered the latter case, whether in the form of hierocracy or caesaropapism (see *ibid.*: 1159–63), as a main reason underlying 'Asian despotism', and as being in fundamental contrast to the European separation of these two powers.[11]

Further systematisation: Dumézil and the three functions

This line of analysis can be complemented and further systematised using the classic works of Georges Dumézil on the tri-partite conceptualisation of sovereignty characteristic of Indo-European people (Dumézil 1958, 1995).[12] Through a comparative study of mythology Dumézil established that in all Indo-European cultures it is possible to identify a three-fold partition of functions, or 'the three fundamental activities that groups of human beings must assume – priests, warriors, producers – so that the collectivity survive and prosper' (Dumézil 1958: 18). There is a strict hierarchical order between these three functions, with the priestly function being the highest, the warrior coming second and the artisan third.

The best-known example corresponding to this arrangement is the rank order of the three 'clean' castes of India, the *brahmana*, the *ksatriya* and the *vaisya*, that indeed provides the starting point of Dumézil's work (*ibid.*: 7). Using the line of argument presented so far, this means that the Indo-European way of thinking, as evidenced in its mythology, both assigned clear priority to the two spheres that were institutionalised on the basis of 'out-of-ordinary' concerns, and furthermore placed an emphasis on the separation of all three of them. The case of the Indian caste system also shows that the fourth, the 'unclean', caste can also be traced back to the 'out-of-ordinary', mostly to the results of warfare, or to the permanentisation of the results of warfare in the sense of a conquered population which is kept in a permanently subjugated, deprived state.[13] Dumézil gained his insight when perceiving the parallels between the Indian stratification system and the main divine functions in Roman mythology.

At this point we need to move beyond Weber, by further systematising the relations between the ordinary and the – permanentised or routinised – 'out-of-ordinary' spheres. The central point is to draw the consequences of the fact that the process of institutionalisation progressed not through the formalisation of the normal, everyday practices of social interaction and relationships but through the routinisation of the irregular, temporary, 'out-of-ordinary' spheres. Whether in the form of illness, drought, violence or warfare, the 'out-of-ordinary' always represents a threat to the normal everyday business of life of the community. Charismatic individuals are esteemed because, by their proven record, they manage to alleviate such situations. This is what Weber means by arguing for the original 'this-worldly' orientation of magic and religion. The 'world image' (*Weltbild*) of human beings becomes fundamentally coloured by the eventuality of such events, but, exactly because and to the extent that they remain rare, extraordinary, they do not fundamentally and continuously influence the ordinary business of everyday life. This could be considered a degree of 'naivety' or 'innocence'.

However, once magic and warfare become permanent in the institutionalised forms of (priestly) religion and (courtly) politics, the situation becomes different. While originally aiming only to defend the community in the eventuality of a threat, priests and warriors continuously need to give proofs of their own useful-ness and functionality, and therefore would exert a permanent 'mobilising' and 'repressing' control over the population under their control. This eventually gives rise to a new 'image' of the world: a much more solid, unshakeable image – certainly less 'innocent', and perhaps even more threatening. The crucial aspect, at any rate, is closure: to the extent that these permanent spheres develop, the openness full of threats is replaced by a world in which the promise of a better control from external danger is 'compensated' by a closure created by perma-nent control.

Role of ideas: charisma produced

The distinction between 'genuine' and 'artificial' charisma sounds strange, rhetorical. Yet, it is crucial for Weber as it introduces the second conceptual dichotomy, between 'temporary' and 'permanent', and especially the transfor-mation of a temporary situation into a permanent state. Out-of-ordinary situations are by definition temporary, emerging due to unforeseen events. Once the situation is solved, the emergency ends and it is possible to return to the regular state of affairs. There is no longer any need for charismatic acts or persons. However, the stimulating exercises can be performed continuously, producing permanent holy states.[14]

Weber is analysing the phenomenon of religious 'virtuosi' under three aspects: the use of ascetic techniques, the ability to produce ecstatic states and, finally, the continuous proving of the self.

We must start the reconstruction with the fundamental characteristic of charisma, the genuine–artificial, authentic–inauthentic, spontaneous–forced, gift–product dichotomy. Charisma is the sudden rise to a challenge; it is not a permanent state, cannot be maintained continuously. This is only possible for artificially induced charisma. The major means of inducing such charismatic states are the tricks-of-the-trade of all magicians and shamans: the various kinds of ascetic exercises. The underlying mechanism of these techniques is artificially to incite, through various deprivations of the body and regulations of the mind, the kind of excited, frenetic, frenzied, unconscious states of trance that usually accompany genuine charismatic acts. Though it implies a reversal of causality, this is typical of magical thinking. At any rate, ascetic techniques infallibly produce *real*, psychological states of trance, and also prepare for otherwise impossible performances. In this sense they are the remote sources of all contem-porary forms of physical or spiritual exercises.

The constant application of ascetic techniques and the production of ecstatic states are two of the three central aspects of the way in which artificially produced charisma becomes permanent. They also go closely together, both for religious and military charisma. However, they are not the most important element. Ascetic techniques are central as a stage of preparation. Ecstatic states are important and unavoidable, both as signs of virtuosity and accompaniments of ascetic exercises. But ultimately any kind of charisma must demonstrate its usefulness by succeeding. The charismatic war hero must win the war, the medicine man must cure, the rain maker must bring clouds to end the drought. In the case of a *permanent* holy state, this implies a continuous 'proving' of oneself, in front of others but also oneself, and the subsequent transformation of the 'world' by the religious virtuoso into a 'theatre of God-willed activity in one's worldly 'calling' (FMW: 291). The terminology closely recalls Weber's essays on Protestantism, indicating how direct a thread leads, for Weber, from shamanistic techniques to the economic ethic of Puritanism. Not surprisingly, ascetic and ecstatic warriors and diviners would lie at the origins of Hebrew prophecy as well.[15]

Before we go further, however, we need to systematise this discussion. This will be done using an anthropological perspective, this time the analysis of rites of passage by Turner and van Gennep (Victor Turner based his ideas on the work of Arnold van Gennep).

Further systematisation: van Gennep, Turner and rites of passage

The three main aspects of the artificial production of charisma can easily be brought together as corresponding to the three stages of rites of passage. Various forms of deprivation (food, shelter, clothes, sex), closely corresponding to ascetic techniques, are central for the first phase of rites of passage, the rite of separation. This phase, just as ascetic techniques, can be considered as preparatory, a period of training for the performance. The second stage, the 'liminal period' proper, is the moment of trial and testing, where the candidates must 'prove' themselves by passing the ritual test. The third phase is the celebration of the successful performance and the return to order, usually accompanied by ecstatic states of 'collective effervescence' like feasts, festivals or orgies.

All this has an important corollary. The 'routinisation' of the 'out-of-ordinary', or the 'permanentisation' of the temporary, so central for Weber's analysis, can be translated in the language of 'permanent liminality'.[16] The crucial question concerns the large-scale social impact of the phenomenon.

Role of ideas: sacrificial priesthood

Already the permanentisation of holy states contained elements of thought, in the sense of the purposeful deployment of techniques to produce the ecstatic states that accompany charismatic deeds. However, the permanent institutionalisation of religions employed reflexive thought in a much more clear-cut and systematic manner.

cf Gellner

The basic idea is the same as in the previous case: to start from the successful performance of charismatic deeds, and to ensure that a systematic, regular, reliable performance of these measures can be achieved. Thus, permanent institutionalisation can be situated on the side of the 'theodicies of good fortune' (*ibid.*: 271), or the 'priestly aristocracy' (Nietzsche 1967: 32).

This implies two basic characteristics that move – in spite of the identical origin in the attempt to 'copy' charismatic success – in opposite direction from that of holy states. In both cases this implies a tight link between the agents of success *other than* the religious virtuosi. First, it implies a close and hierarchical relationship with the other instances of the 'out-of-ordinary', especially its routinisation in the form of warfare. Heroic deeds in warfare are the least ambiguous success stories, little connected to the work of reflective thought. The permanentisation of religion involves more thinking, including reflection on the success of military endeavours, and thus has a distance from the military and the court. In terms of their fundamental aims, priestly religions in most cases indeed became apotheoses of the established, and militarily-based, socio-political hierarchies.

Second, concerning the major modalities of priestly religions, Weber emphasises prayer and sacrifice, finding the origins of both in magic, in attempts to coerce the gods (ES: 422–3). Such attempts to force supernatural powers are close to the efforts of religious virtuosi to produce holy states and thus enable themselves to perform unusual deeds, but fail to account for a key element of priestly religions, sacrifice – an aspect that represents an important, and different, lesson learned from pure charisma. Charisma is a force that comes as if 'from outside', over which the community has no control, thus it is a *gift* freely provided by the gods. It is either 'given' or not given – to a certain individual; in a given moment. The idea of forcing the gods to give gifts is profoundly paradoxical if not outright absurd.

This indicates that there is something in the link between magic and charisma, taken for granted by Weber, that is not worked out properly, and that ultimately has serious consequences for his thought. This appears in the ambivalent use of concepts like demagification, disenchantment and the impossibility of charisma in the modern world – terms that Weber handles as synonyms, but that carry very different meanings and connotations. It is in connection with this magical coercion that he discusses the two main means used by priestly religions, prayer and sacrifice. According to Weber, prayer has an ambivalent relationship with the use of force, the boundaries between coercion and supplication being fluid (*ibid.*: 422). Sacrifice, however, has a direct relationship to gift. It represents a consistent attempt to 'learn the lesson' of charisma.

If charisma is a freely given divine gift, if solving unusual difficulties lies beyond human reach and requires the clemency of 'gods' (on whom 'genius', 'talent', 'heroism' and other superhuman faculties depend), then the only possible effort humans can make to stimulate such goodwill is to offer gifts themselves.[17] This solution has indeed been almost universally reached, as the performance of sacrifice is a feature of all institutionalised religions, just like the performance of ascetic exercises by religious virtuosi.

At this point, we should turn to Weber's theoretisation of sacrifice. However, Weber did not discuss the theme in depth.[18] His short comments on sacrifice only summarise contemporary ethnological wisdom.[19] According to this, the original source of sacrifice is magic, an attempt to coerce the gods. This is possible because the gods also draw part of their force from humans. Eventually, however, non-magical elements would appear and even come to dominate. Central of these is the sacrifice of animals in the context of a *communio*, or a common ceremonial meal. With further rationalisation, this leads to an exchange-like interaction between gods and humans, where '[t]he pervasive and central theme is: *do ut des*' (*ibid.*: 424): give so that you may be given.[20]

It is after this short and inconclusive discussion of sacrifice, strangely uninte-grated into his general discussion of charisma and its routinisation,[21] that Weber makes a crucial and sweeping general reference to a 'special evolutionary process' by which religion moves away from worldly concerns into two main directions: to an 'ever-broadening rational systematisation of the god concept', and to a 'recession of the original, practical and calculating rationalism' (*ibid.*: 424). In other words, this was a move towards an ever more powerful god, or towards monotheism, and a move from worldly to other-worldly aims.

Significantly, these remarks were at a strategic place in the work, at the end of the first section of the chapter, entitled 'The Origin of the Religions', and before the second section, differentiating the magician and the priest. Though this would indicate the significance of these considerations, the point remained unex-plored. Here Weber's related comments will be systematised through a recent work inspired by both anthropology and comparative mythology, the ideas of René Girard on the sacrificial mechanism and the role of prophecy.

Further systematisation: René Girard and the sacrificial mechanism

The central points singled out for attention above are the conception of sacrifice as a form of gift, the idea that sacrifice is universal and is closely related to the institutionalisation of religion in the form of cultic rituals associated with priest-hood, and that this entire set is associated with the 'religion of the fortunate'. Missing from the discussion, except for a passing reference (*ibid.*: 400), is the question of human sacrifice (see also AJ: 91). The work of René Girard takes off at exactly this point, incorporating all the major points identified above in a full and rounded discussion.

Just as Weber's argument started with the problem of the 'out-of-ordinary' situation, Girard takes as his point of departure a specific crisis situation, one that lies outside Weber's entire conceptual framework: the internal collapse of social order. Such situations can't be solved by a charismatic hero. The Weberian perspective assumes a stable reference point, a clear-cut division between us and them, the friend and the enemy, health and illness, well-being and poverty. In the case of a 'civil war' such a shared and self-evident reference point is missing. No hero can emerge to defeat the enemy, as the enemy is inside. The aim is to re-unite the community, but this cannot be done through any of the fighting factions. The only solution lies in the highly paradoxical idea of *creating* an enemy, by designating somebody as a scapegoat and unifying the community against this new target. This is what the sacrificial mechanism sets out to accomplish.

Girard launches his work through a set of paradoxes and mysteries. In a number of rituals, sacrifice has a double character: it is the most sacred of things, while at the same time it is considered as something almost criminal (Girard 1972: 9). This led Hubert and Mauss in their famous work on sacrifice (Hubert and Mauss 1968 [1902]) to come up with the strange idea of the sacred character of the victim. This indicates that there is a 'mystery' at the heart of sacrifice, in the link between violence and sacrifice, the violence and the sacred – a mystery which is increased to the second power by the fact that standard theories simply fail to take the bloody, violent aspect of sacrifice seriously.

Central to such theories is the idea that sacrifice implies some kind of 'mediation' between the gods and humans, the same '*do ut des*' motive accepted even by Weber, and that therefore it belongs to the realm of the imaginary and is quite harmless (*ibid.*: 17–18). As exceptions, Girard mentions the works of Godfrey Lienhardt and Victor Turner. Taking up their hints, Girard proceeds to uncover the real function of sacrifice. Through an analysis of rituals, myths (both classical and ethnological) and tragedies (both classical Greek and Shakespearian), he comes to the idea that sacrifice does fulfil a real function, even a central one: this is the prevention of violence in societies lacking a judicial system.

The universe of these societies is dominated by the attempt to prevent the outbreak of violence, as the smallest conflict can provoke disastrous consequences. In Weberian terminology, the 'world image' of these societies is based on fear: the fear of conflict and violence.[22] This is because violence is mimetic and highly contagious.[23] Once conflict breaks out, a spiral of violence escalates through acts of vengeance and this endangers the very survival of the entire community. The role of the sacrificial mechanism is the prevention of this violence.

Here we encounter another series of mysteries. First, the question of the origin of sacrifice usually is not even posed in the literature. Girard again returns to the classic work of Hubert and Mauss to illustrate his point. As they start by claiming that sacrifice is the origin of religion, the origin of sacrifice is a question they can't even pose (*ibid.* :135). The answer to the question, however, according to Girard, is not hopeless. He starts by noting that there is an amazing uniformity in rituals around the globe, indicating that these rituals are not at all imaginary and false, but rather very technical and real. In the simplest sense of 'technique', rituals – of which the prototype, according to Hubert and Mauss, is sacrifice – are the technical solution to a problem. The problem is violence, the escalation of a mimetic conflict within the community; and the solution is the exteriorisation of violence by the designation of a single individual as a sacrificial victim. This mechanism, Girard claims, is not only the source of all rituals, but the origin of culture as well.

Surprising as it may sound, Girard simply follows here Freud and the idea that culture is derived from an original murder. Girard's interpretation of Freud, however goes completely against received wisdom. In general, it is Freud's psychoanalytic works that are considered valuable and classic, with the visionary discovery of the Oedipus complex lying at the heart of the work; while his excursions in the fields of anthropology (in *Totem and Taboo*) and Biblical criticism (in *Moses and Monotheism*) are usually countered with a benevolent but dismissive nod. Girard, however, does not simply dismiss but in the strictest sense of the term 'deconstructs' the Oedipus complex (*ibid.*: Chapters 3 and 7), while he claims that the real value of Freud's work is contained in his ethnological incursions (*ibid.*: 317), even though Freud himself did not recognise the real significance of his discoveries (*ibid.*: 322).

Freud realised that culture is not based simply on violence, but on murder. However, blinded by his misreading of the Oedipus myth, he argued that this murder was the murder of the father. Girard accepts that there was an original murder, but argues that this was the murder of a scapegoat, a designated victim (*victim émissaire*),[24] and it was this murder that universally founded culture by externalising violence from the community.[25]

The universality of this mechanism is due to a 'blind spot' in human societies; this is the collapse of social order, due to the elimination of all differences. This has not been realised so far by social scientists due to another mystery – the universal adherence to the idea that social differentiation is the main source of conflict. Here Girard quotes Victor Turner as a particularly clear representative of this view (*ibid.*: 79, quoting Turner 1969). However, for Girard, it is exactly the *collapse* of social differentiation that is the cause of the escalation of mimetic violence. As a source of support, he both refers to anthropological literature, in particular the case of the Kaingang Indians, studied by Jules Henry in his classic *Jungle People* (Girard 1972: 83–5), and quotes from Shakespeare's *Troilus and Cressida*: 'O, when Degree is shaked/Which is the ladder to all high designs,/The enterprise is sick!' (*ibid.*: 80–1).[26]

This is because when all difference is erased in a community, nothing can stop the whirlwind of mimetic violence. The spiral of revenge escalates, violence begets more violence, until the entire community becomes united in the designation, expulsion and murder of an innocent victim, the scapegoat. This sacrificial victim then becomes the foundation of the new order and the origin of all structure (*ibid.*: 141). The unanimity, self-abandonment and collective ecstasy characteristic of all rituals, theorised by Durkheim as 'collective effervescence' and by Turner as 'communitas', is nothing else for Girard but a staging of the original, frightful event in which the fear and the rage of the entire community is turned, in a moment of 'violent unanimity' (*ibid.*: 152–3), against the sacrificial victim – murdering him, but at the same time enabling the community to end violence and return to normality. This explains the paradox with which the book started: at the moment of his death, the innocent victim, executed as a criminal (but in reality murdered because innocent), becomes revered as a sacred figure, indeed as a god, for the 'services' he rendered, with his innocent death, for the community.

Rituals are based on double substitution: the (invisible) substitution of all the community into one by the designation and killing of the innocent victim; and the substitution of the original victim with the sacrificial victim in the actual ritual (*ibid.*: 154). The characteristics of the victim and the details of the scape-goating mechanism are discussed by Girard in a later, much more concise book (Girard 1982). Girard argues that the mechanism does work, but it is based on a lie, the unpunished murder of an innocent, and that it can only work in so far as this lie is not exposed.

There is, however, one more mystery to be solved: this is the 'mysterious immunity' of 'Western civilisation' to this sacrificial mechanism; an immunity that renders it unable both to understand the mechanism as it works in other cultures, and to understand itself (Girard 1972: 54–5). Girard traces this immunity to prophecy and especially the Gospels, the fact that the innocence of Jesus – executed as a sacrificial victim *par excellence* – was maintained by the disciples and then became the foundation of Christianity.

Returning to Weberian terminology, in the case of the implosion of order, the charismatic hero – a god-like figure – is substituted by the sacrificial victim, another sacred figure (*ibid.*: 443). The personal and social characteristics of the two, however, are fundamentally different. Both of them are 'out-of-ordinary', but in a different way. The hero is exceptionally strong, powerful, beautiful, attractive and successful. He is exceptional in the sense of possessing to the utmost degree all the positive human characteristics; he is the best in everything. The proper sacrificial 'hero', however, is exceptional only in the sense of being the furthest possible away from the norm or the average. In social terms, it means that he can be either a king or a prince, but also a foreigner, a vagabond, a beggar or someone from the lowest rungs of society. In personal terms, he can indeed be exceptionally beautiful (the death of a charming, attractive person is always particularly memorable), but more often than not ugly, or at least possessing visible signs of handicap. He might have committed, or might be charged with, all kinds of deviations, especially of the more horrifying kinds – parricide, incest or treason. In one of the most striking and convincing parts of his work, Girard presents a reassessment of the story of Oedipus, showing how this figure, whose guilt has been taken at face value by Freud, presents an almost perfect case of the sacrificial victim, incorporating most of the characteristics attributed to sacrificial victims, even those that seem to be mutually exclusive (foreigner but also king, so both lowest and highest in social status; accused of incest and parricide at the same time; of royal origin, but then cast out and raised by shepherds, so of both low and high birth).

Girard's work cannot be ignored in any account of the Nietzsche-inspired Weber, as it gives a fundamental correction to the positions held by these two master thinkers.[27] Through his doctrines of the eternal recurrence, the will to power and the 'Superman', Nietzsche identified religion and morality with ressentiment, with the 'slave revolt' of the weak and the lowly, incapable of any positive performance. Through his concept of charisma and the theodicy of suffering, Weber made fundamental corrections to Nietzsche's scheme, but did not provide a comprehensive discussion of priestly-sacrificial religions, thus ignoring problems posed by the dissolution of order and sacrifice. By calling attention to the problems posed by the internal implosion of order and a full-scale discussion of the problem of sacrifice, Girard showed, beyond Weber, that the Nietzschean glorification of the strong and of the eternal return is histori-cally and sociologically untenable.

Girard's discovery can perhaps best be characterised as an almost inevitable dead end in the process of evolution. Human societies are not simply threat-ened by natural disasters, illnesses and plagues, and wars waged with other societies, but they are also threatened by the internal collapse of their own arrangements. As such an internal dissolution destroys all stable values and structures, usual solutions fail, and the situation converges to the sacrifice of an innocent victim. The result, eventually, is a world of dissimulation, oppression and lies.

Role of ideas: reflexive thought

The following discussion will commence from three general considerations, linking up with the previous sections. First of all, it is necessary to re-state the conventional wisdom that, partly as a polemic against Marx(ists), Weber consid-ered the effective role played by ideas in history of fundamental importance. This line of interpretation is only mistaken when understood in an exclusive and causal sense. Second, a long tradition in the history of thought assumes that ideas, especially reflexive thought, come after events, exemplified by Hegel's famous 'owl of Minerva'. Without fully questioning this point, Weber inserts another temporal dimension, the dimension of the temporary as opposed to the permanent, and this changes the thrust of the entire account. According to the standard logic, 'real' events, structures and interests produce lasting results, while reflexivity, coming after everything is settled, can only relate, in its precarious-ness, to whatever has already been solidly put on the ground. From the perspective of the Weberian dimension of transitory vs permanent, however, 'real' solutions are elaborated by agents who possess temporary existence and produce lasting results exactly because they are compelled by the (liminal) circumstances.

Finally, rationality, thought and reflexivity so far meant a relationship towards the *solution* of the 'out-of-ordinary' (the crisis), and were connected to the perma-nentisation of the temporary. Now we need to move to a broader time horizon, the even more encompassing activity of reflection, in which the object of thought is the results of the entire process: the events, the immediate responses, the long-term permanent institutions based on these responses, their relationship to the normal business of everyday life, or the entire 'world' as such. More than anything before, a central place in these reflections will thus be played by the respective attitudes towards existence, or the various 'world images' (*Weltbild*) produced by different forms of reflections.

The 'world'

The term 'world' plays a prominent place in Weber's works most relevant for this book. In the expression 'religious rejections of the world', it is in the title of the *Zwischenbetrachtung*. It is there in the title of the last two (in the English edition, the last four) sections of the chapter on religion in *Economy and Society*. It is contained – in the form of the term 'world image' – in the single most widely quoted passage of the *Einleitung*. Yet, not only has this not received much attention in the secondary literature,[28] but even Weber failed to devote explicit attention to it. This is because – another proof of Weber's fundamental concern with the *diagnosis* of the roots of modernity and not the search for theoretical systematicity as the central moving force of at least this part of the work – almost all his related attention is devoted to the religious *rejections* of the world, its origins and sources.

However, if one is interested in the (religious) *rejections* of the world, one must start by clarifying what it is that is actually rejected. Weber indeed places a huge emphasis on the conditions out of which the religious rejections of the world developed. This is at the heart of his historical method. But he does not work out explicitly the relationship between these conditions and the 'image' of the world. As a result, in the term 'religious rejections of the world' the word 'world' gains the same overall, taken-for-granted meaning of implying 'everything', the entire universe, as in Nietzsche, which greatly impairs the potential uses of the diagnostic term 'religious rejections of the world'.

There is, however, an exception to this rule, where Weber does provide an explicit discussion of the meaning of the term 'world', as understood by the salvation religions. This is furthermore at a rather significant place in *Economy and Society*, just at the point where Weber is introducing one of his most important conceptualisations, his typology of asceticism as 'world-rejecting' or 'inner-worldly'. The passage is worth quoting in full: 'The "world" in the religious sense, i.e. the domain of social relationship, is therefore a realm of temptations' (ES: 542). The sentence is short, but complex and ambivalent. First of all, it is not really a definition, rather an 'on-the-spot' clarification of meaning. Second, 'world' is identical with the complex of social relationships. Weber here simply means the entire gamut of social life that develops through ordinary everyday life, without any reference to the 'out-of-ordinary'. The reference is also to *social* relations, thus no emphasis is given to the objective external world.

This becomes particularly important when we turn to the last part of the sentence, when the meaning of the world from the perspective of salvation religions is given. It is here that the 'out-of-ordinary' enters the picture and the revaluation of the world emerges: the normal, daily business of social relations becomes transformed and transvalued as temptations, because they turn the faithful away from the devout performance of religious duties. The tension between *this* concept of the world and *this* type of religion is clear – but the problem is that it takes for granted the existence of certain kinds of religions, failing to give an account of their *raison d'être* and to give a characterisation of this 'image' of the world related to the fundamental conceptual pairings of ordinary and out-of-ordinary, of temporary and permanent, lying at the centre of Weber's work.

It is therefore necessary now to give a more sustained discussion of the term 'world', partly bringing out Weber's implicit meanings, and partly taking the analysis further.[29]

Weber's starting point is asceticism on the one hand, and the existence of established (priestly) religions on the other. These were precisely the components discussed in the previous two sections, except that while in those sections reflection was directed at the successful result, now it is directed at the consequences. The question is not simply: 'how to assure that these responses to crises, given by charismatically gifted persons, are performed in an unfailing, regular manner?', but rather: 'what is this world in which events happen in this way; that has a like "nature" or "essence"?'

Let's start from the ordinary vs 'out-of-ordinary' dichotomy. Corresponding to this conceptual pair, there are two contrasting images of the world; or, the world has a Janus-faced character. The world is, on the one hand, the world of regular human ties and interaction, the world of family, kinship, household and subsistence economy. On the other hand, the world is also full of potential threats of disaster — of flood or drought, of illness and death, of violence and warfare. Fear, a fear from *this* world, therefore becomes a fundamental aspect of the 'basic' human condition, at least in societies dominated by the dichotomy established above. The actual character of a given culture much depends on the exact mixture established therein between these two aspects.[30] The reflections on the immediate responses discussed in the previous sections, and the ensuing 'permanentisation of the temporary', aim precisely at this dual-faceted image of the world, having as their objective the elimination of permanent fear, the prevention of the potential threats, with all the ambivalence in their effects.

From the perspective of the Weberian diagnosis of the religious rejections of the world one can recognise that in this dual-faceted world image there was no possibility for the emergence of the religious rejections of the world; or, in Weber's own words, religion, in the sense of magic, had an 'original this-worldly orientation'.[31] This is because in the world image described above, none of the sides of this world can be rejected. One's own world, the network of social relationships, is impossible to reject, as this is the taken-for-granted world in which one is living. The idea of rejecting this is inconceivable, and at any rate would only leave one at the mercy of the hostile, threatening world outside, or certain death. But one cannot reject the external world either. Such an idea is again inconceivable, as whatever one does or thinks about it, it remains there, fearful, forever threatening. The only thing to do with it is to perform properly the magical acts and rituals, to appease the unknown and unpredictable spirits and gods who populate and animate this world.[32]

The religious rejection of the world becomes possible only in a completely different set-up. For a proper reconstruction of the 'world image' that made it possible, and short of presenting a full-scale philosophy of history, we need to bring together the two key developments we indicated above, relying on Weber's ideas. On the one hand, the major line of development in the sphere of regular, ordinary, everyday relations is traced to settlement patterns.[33] The transformation of hunter-gatherers into villagers, then the rise of cities and finally the much more ambivalent process of the emergence of large-scale socio-political entities, is indeed an irresistible, evolutionary process that has been going on for the last 13,000 years (Diamond 1998), and incorporates one of the major meanings of civilisation, 'urbanisation'. The 'world' of the city, and especially the 'world' of an empire, in the sense of the horizon of regular everyday activities, is fundamentally different from the 'world' of a small village or a tribe. However, even a city, and most certainly an empire, is not simply the product of the gradual, peaceful expansion of everyday activities, but inextricably incorporates the other main line of development, the permanentisation of the temporary, of religious and military activities; including – possibly even at the centre of the process, at the interweaving of internal transformations and the incorporation of responses to external threats, or properly at the 'foundational' level – the Girardian sacrificial mechanism, the idea that not only external threats but the implosion of the previously taken-for-granted social order is central for the emergence of stable institutionalised cultures, or that order is produced out of disorder.

In very sketchy terms, resuming the previous line of analysis, this unity (which could be called 'ancient civilisation', and whose best examples are Egypt and Mesopotamia, India and China, the Maya and Aztec empires, but to some extent also Rome and Greece) has the following characteristics:

- In terms of settlement patterns, a considerable part of the population is living in large, overcrowded cities, which together compose a large entity, an empire. These cities are the centres of the entity, with one of them serving as the capital, or the location of the court, the residence of the emperor. The majority of the population still live in villages, but compared to the cities they have inferior status.
- In terms of social relations, the entity is highly stratified. This stratification is based on kinship, both at the lowest and highest levels (the position of king is usually hereditary), but the complex web of lineages characteristic of small communities is replaced by a rigid hierarchical system that is fundamentally organised *not* along divisions of everyday activities, but rather in line with the permanentised functions (military and religious). This means, on the one hand, privileges (high position) granted to the priestly and the warrior classes, that can be completely separated or more or less closely integrated, depending on particular cases and conditions; on the other, the subjugation and subordinate position of the conquered people, the immigrants or guests. In other words, social stratification should be best conceived of as a process that, as always, starts not from the top or the bottom, not from the beginning or the end, but from the *middle*: from the position of those who perform

the regular everyday activities. Taking again as the 'archetypical' model the case of Indian castes, so closely corresponding to the Indo-European model, this is the third caste, the producers, or the lowest of the clean castes. Above them we find the priests and the warriors, corresponding to the two 'out-of-ordinary' functions; and below them the pariahs, the conquered 'guest' people.

- At the level of religion, we find the performance of ritualised sacrifices as being at the centre of religious activities, with religious ideas serving basically the role of presenting this type of order as eternally given and just, or the role of apologetics.
- Finally, concerning military activities or warfare, we find the uprooting and limiting of sporadic conflict, the centralisation and institutionalisation of the use of violence, but at the price of the emergence of a highly centralised repressive machinery (that can be mechanised in the form of a standing army or can remain in the hands of a class of warlords and warriors), that is closely integrated with the sacrificial priesthood and that exchanges temporary fear for permanent oppression.

In fact, it is from this perspective that we can start to reconstruct the 'world images' that correspond to this new state of affairs, and especially the way in which this state of affairs was lived and experienced.[34] First of all, we should recognise that the previous, more or less 'unified' experience of the world in small-scale tribal societies becomes widely differentiated.[35] In a small community, everyday life, just as the external threats and fears, was shared by everyone. In the new entities, everyday life became very different from the perspective of the warlord and the peasant, the priest and the artisan, the prince and the outcast. However, a full reconstruction of these various views of the world should not concern us, as – according to Weber – only a few of them gained religious significance: these are the views of the intellectuals (priestly or secular); the views of the city dwellers, especially those city dwellers *par excellence*, the artisans and commerciants; and the views of the outcasts, the pariahs.[36]

With these differences, we arrive at a central point in Weber's historical methodology: the 'carrier strata' of various religions, the way in which social aspects and religious experience mutually condition or 'stamp' each other, and the role of reflexive thought, largely through the mediation of various intellectual strata, in changing reality.

Stamping and carrier strata

Though the term 'stamp' (*Gepräge*) or 'stamping' is widely present in Weber's writings, its most intensive use is in the *Einleitung*. The importance Weber attributes to the term is shown both by the frequency of its application and the contextual location. It is used five times in the first few pages (FMW: 268–70), thus at precisely the point where, according to our general line of interpretation, Weber situated his methodological comments; and on two further occasions, close to each other, at a crucial juncture in the text, just after the theoretisation of the transition from temporary to permanent holy states and before the famous 'switchmen' metaphor (*ibid.*: 279–80).

In the introductory pages of his major theoretical statements Weber attempted to elucidate the specific characteristics of his historical method. At the beginning of the *Einleitung*, this is contained particularly in the following statement: 'under the term "economic ethic" one should understand…not the ethical theories of theological compendia…rather the practical impulses for action which are founded in the psychological and pragmatic contexts of religions' (*ibid.*: 267; GARS I: 238, trans. modified). The sentence repeats, in a different form, the message of the starting sentence of the chapter in *Economy and Society*: the aim of Weber's study is not religion *per se*, but rather the 'psychological and pragmatic' conditions out of which a certain religious doctrine emerged and the practical, or non-religious effects of this religion.

The question now concerns the exact link between these 'original' conditions and the eventual effects: how does a certain religious ethic operate this transformation? It is here that the concept of stamping comes into play.

On the one hand, this means that 'the directive elements' in the life-conduct of the social strata significant for a particular religion leave a stamp on the practical ethic (FMW: 268). This implies a 'stamp [received] primarily from religious sources', among the 'directive elements' the most important being the content of the 'annunciation' and 'promise' of the respective religions (*ibid.*: 270). On the other hand, this religious content is itself stamped, as, argues Weber, 'the type of a religion, once stamped, has usually exerted a rather far-reaching influence upon the life-conduct of very heterogeneous strata' (*ibid.*). Thus, a particular religion can only exert lasting effect, outside of its own sphere, on practical life due to the fact that it has itself been 'stamped' – by the conditions out of which it emerged.

The previous passage also implies a close link between 'type' and stamping. It is a religious 'type' which is stamped. The connection is not accidental. 'Typing' is the same word as 'stamping', only their etymological roots are different. Weber's 'typological' and 'historical' concerns, already connected in the 'ideal type' as a 'historical individual', are closely interwoven.

These comments receive further clarification from the two subsequent passages containing 'stamping'. While the first set of usage put the emphasis on the way religious content stamped conduct, here the emphasis is reversed. In the first passage, Weber is talking about the 'various religious or magical states that have given their psychological stamp to religions' (*ibid.*: 279); while in the second he talks about the way in which the 'character' of the social stratum that 'carried' a certain religion had its theoretical or practical rationalism stamped by its conduct of life, and how this subsequently exerted a significant 'effect' (*Wirkung*) on religious behaviour (*ibid.*: 280).

Taking these passages together, it becomes clear that the word 'stamping' is applied to various aspects of a complex dynamic process. Both external conditions, especially the manner in which the social strata significant for a particular religion (its 'carrier'), conduct (its daily life), and psychological 'states' associated with religious practices, do stamp the specific content of a religion, but this religious content on its own stamps the 'practical ethics' guiding the conduct of life of these strata and the others that accept these religious values. One is tempted to use the term 'dialectics' to capture the modality of this dynamics, but this would be a mistake. The logic of interaction is different. Instead of the Hegelian triad, it has to do with connections made between internal and external factors under temporary, fluid conditions, and the subsequent lasting, persisting effect of the transitory.

Though central for Weber's methodological concerns, the term 'stamping' is not sufficiently defined and elaborated, remaining hardly more than a metaphor. Two aspects are missing in particular: the specification of the exact character of the 'conditions' under which stamping experiences occur, and the elaboration of the exact work of reflexive thought at the moment of experience. A proper systematisation of these two elements would require its contrast with Weber's conceptual framework, especially the two key dichotomies (ordinary vs out-of-ordinary and temporary vs permanent), and with more recent conceptual innovations like Turner's liminality.

Lasting effects: reflections on the experience of suffering

The content of religions – most importantly, of the religious rejections of the world – are therefore stamped, under particular, out-of-ordinary conditions, departing from various psychological–ecstatic states and influenced by aspects of the everyday conduct of life of the strata particularly sensitive to these religious values. The question now concerns the manner in which religion 'mediates' certain 'conditions of emergence' into 'lasting effects'.

For this, we need to reconsider the way in which the world was lived and experienced in an early empire. First of all, cutting across all social groups, wherever they were settled, was a shared perception of the monolithic solidity of the world, replacing the earlier flimsiness and dualism. Previously, at the level of the small village, the internal order of the community, the criss-crossing network of kinship ties, was perceived as stable in a taken-for-granted manner but rendered unstable by all kinds of sudden, external threats. It was a combination of a thoughtless, carefree regularity with sudden, fear-stricken moments of panic. This was replaced, through the process of 'permanentisation', by a stable, hierarchical social structure that seemed inalterable, impenetrable, solid, eternal.[37] This solidity was proclaimed as a virtue and an achievement by those who stood at the top of the hierarchy; was taken for granted in a matter-of-fact way, including its inconveniences, by those for whom this provided a stable framework for their regular everyday activities; but was lived as an all-but-intolerable, permanent pressure by those who happened to be at the bottom.

Here we reach the experiential basis of the religious rejections of the world: the experience of *suffering*. Weber closely follows the footsteps of Nietzsche. The central argument of the *Genealogy of Morals* concerns the link between warfare and religion, the aristocrats as opposed to the common mass, the religions of the fortunate and slave morality, leading Nietzsche to the doctrine of the ressentiment. However, though recognising the merits of Nietzsche's approach, Weber claimed that the basic experience out of which the religious rejections of the world grew was not ressentiment, but suffering (FMW: 271).

But what exactly is new in this experience of suffering? In itself, the experience of suffering is universal, part of the human condition, just as unavoidable as death. The novelty lay in its modality, its transformation from a temporary state into a permanent condition. In the previous world order, suffering was associated with natural disasters, bad weather, illness, grieving, but – unless the irrevocable was involved – things eventually returned to the normal state. However, in the new world order, whoever was 'harmed' – oppressed, exploited, abused – by his/her superiors, given the timelessness and solidity of the new order, could never hope for a better turn of fortune. Suffering was turned into a permanent state.

The lasting significance of this new experience depended on a variety of factors: social factors, the absolute and relative numbers of those who were permanently suffering due to the 'new' institutional order and the compactness of this group of people; or 'subjective' factors, the extent and depth of suffering. However, a review of the historical record would show that the 'purely' quantitative aspect of suffering does not explain the character and especially the success of the eventual response.[38] This depended rather on the intellectual force of presenting a comprehensive, coherent 'image' of this world, by gathering arguments to reject it and substituting with an alternative; and on the motivational force of mobilising a number of people to orient their life towards this 'other' world.

How could such an enormous and unlikely feat, the realisation of a successful 'stand' in the 'face' of the entire 'world' be possible? Weber's answer is simple: this was due to the emergence of a new human type, – the *prophet*.

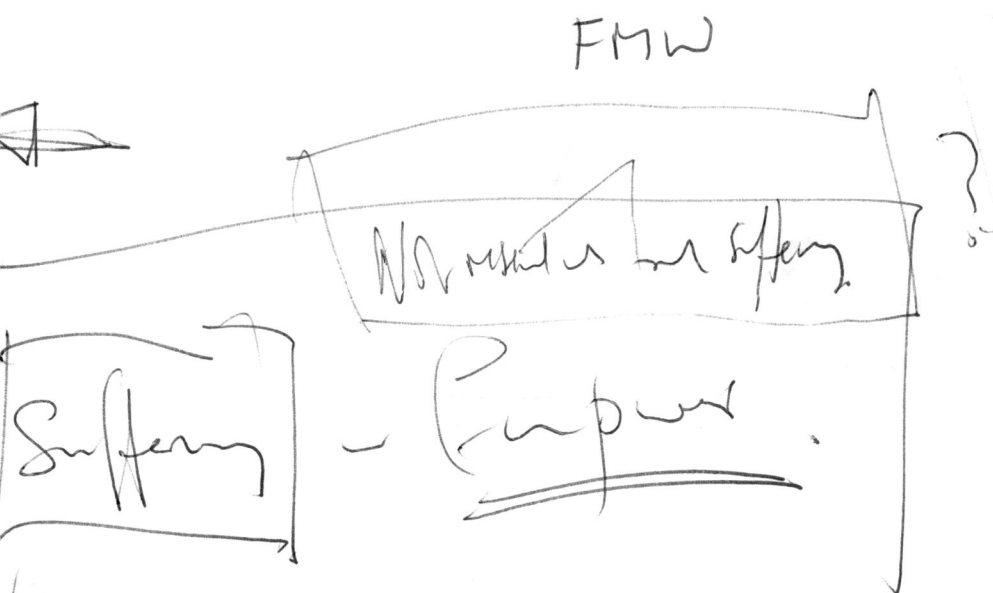

2   Ethical prophecy

Weber's views on the characteristics and effects of prophecy are central to his entire work, playing – among others – a fundamental role in his distillation of the concept of charisma. Still, his discussion of prophecy rarely receives sustained attention in social theory. This is no doubt partly due to the intrinsic difficulties of the subject matter. Prophecy is not a topic that intellectuals and academics in our age are happy to discuss. There is also a methodological difficulty involved. Weber followed a straightforward work method: first the digestion of the material in long draft historical papers, and then the successive theoretical elaboration and systematisation of the material. For his writings on religion this means that he started with a draft of the essays that eventually were published in the 'Economic Ethic'; then wrote the conceptual chapter for *Economy and Society*; and then came the two, subsequent, reflexive-summary essays, the *Einleitung* and the *Zwischenbetrachtung*, in that order. However, in the case of *Ancient Judaism*, more specifically the chapter on classical prophecy, the order was different. Weber's first draft of *Ancient Judaism*, dated by 1913 focused on the prophets of the Exile period, not on the classical prophets. This has a corollary: that the theoretical work, strangely enough, does *not* incorporate these later sections; and this might have contributed to puzzlement about what Weber had to say about prophecy.

Thus, in this section we have to reverse the order of procedure, starting with the theoretical essays and concluding with *Ancient Judaism*.

Prophecy in the theoretical summaries

As Weber's discussion of prophecy did not change between the three theoretical pieces, they will be reconstructed together.

The conceptualisation of prophecy is straightforward and closely based on the theoretical and methodological foundations reconstructed above. The prophet is considered as a type,[1] and is contrasted with other types, especially the magician and the priest. These contrasts are inserted in the general process of 'routinisation'.

The emergence of the prophet as a type is presented in contrast with these two other, more 'archaic' types. These two types are situated in a sequential order: the priest represents the 'routinisation' of the temporary charisma of the magician in the form of the sacred rituals, especially sacrificial offerings. This does not mean the replacement of magic with priestly rituals. Quite the contrary: while sacrificial priesthood was concentrated in the cities, belief in magic, especially in the more remote and rural parts, continued almost unaltered. Such a surviving belief in magic assured the regular emergence of holy men, figures who gained prominence through personal charisma. While official religion perceived this as a challenge to its monopoly of power, it never succeeded in eradicating such popular beliefs fully, and thus learned to live with them, often turning the phenomenon to its advantage.

The emergence of prophets, as a type, though related to magical performance and often relying on popular beliefs, was something altogether different. Prophecy was a much more serious challenge to priesthood than any magician or holy man; it created a fundamental break. This is because the performance of extraordinary acts was not for prophets an aim in itself, only a way to present visible proof of their authority and mission (ES: 439–40). Their purpose was to proclaim a doctrine or a divine commandment. The central aspect of prophecy is the unique combination of a 'personal call' on the one hand, the 'purely individual' possession of charisma, and the claim of providing ultimate truths and definite revelations on the other. It is the force of this combination – at once concrete, direct, individual, and yet claiming to lean on the highest possible authority – that enabled prophets to inaugurate a break, to challenge existing, priestly or kingly authority.

In spite of the purely individual character of prophecy, prophets only emerged in certain kind of time periods. Even the prophetic tradition reflected on this phenomenon, claiming that only specific times are conducive to the appearance of prophecy. In the language of modern social science or history, such periods were conceptualised as '*Sattelzeit*' (Koselleck 1985), 'times of trouble' (Toynbee), the 'axial age' (Jaspers, Eisenstadt), the 'ecumenic age' (Voegelin); or they can be identified as real-world, large-scale 'liminal' periods (see Szakolczai 2000).[2] But prophets are not the only figures that made their appearance in such periods. Apart from comparing prophets to the previous types, magicians and priests, Weber also contrasts them with three other figures that, in one respect or another, resemble prophets: the lawgiver, the mystagogue and the teacher (ES: 442–7).

After individuating the type 'prophet', Weber turns to the features of prophecy. Here we need to alter slightly the order of presentation, as Weber continues with the internal typology of prophecy, but we will first examine the common feature of all prophets. According to Weber, the core of all prophecy can be captured in a single expression: giving a 'unified view of the world' (*einheitlichen Aspect des Lebens*), which is based on a 'consciously integrated meaningful attitude towards life' (*bewusst* einheitliche sinnhafte *Stellungnahme zu ihm*) (*ibid*.: 450, WuG: 275). We must start with a terminological discussion. Though the English translation first uses 'world' and then 'life' to translate 'Lebens' here, this is not contradicting the spirit of Weber as in this passage he is indeed using the two words *Welt* and *Leben* interchangeably. *Stellungnahme*, however, is not simply 'attitude', but a 'position', a 'stand' taken with respect to the world, and recurs at significant places in Weber's work; for example just before the appearance of the 'switchmen' metaphor. The technical term 'world image' (*Weltbild*) is still missing from Weber's vocabulary at this stage, appearing later in the *Einleitung*. We have here instead the rather imprecise expression *Aspect des Lebens* which the translator almost 'rectified' into the expression 'view of the world'.

With these in mind we can now identify the core of prophecy, the break which prophecy represented at the intellectual level, as an attempt to capture the entire world, the 'theatre' of human life, in a singular 'image' derived from an existential 'stand' regarding this world and life, which leads to the position that the world as a whole has a 'meaning' – even a 'systematically unified meaning' (*ibid.*, *ibid.*, trans. modified).

The significance of this passage can be recognised if we shortly turn to the three consequences Weber draws from this prophetic 'core'; three claims that summarise the main thrust of Weber's entire investigation. First, this unified world image, the 'religious conception of the world as a cosmos', producing a ' "meaningful" ordered totality' (ES: 451), did not remain a doctrine, but developed into an attempt to systematise all manifestations of life, including the organisation of practical behaviour into a conduct of life (*Lebensführung*). The adjective 'methodical' is missing here, but is implied in the context, just as is the term 'rationalisation'. But this is clearly a formulation of the rationalisation thesis, and precisely in the Hennisian sense of the rationalisation of the 'conduct of life'. This direction can also be resumed under the concept of 'inner-worldly asceticism', Weber's central suggestion for analysing the dynamics of modernity.

Second, the consequence of this attempt is the emergence of a tension within the human being and in its relationship to the world. It is this tension that will then be systematically elaborated in the *Zwischenbetrachtung*, and which is the background for the Weberian diagnosis of the religious rejections of the world. This direction can be summarised under the concept of 'inner-worldly eschatology', a concept Weber did not elaborate systematically, but that was taken up by some of his most important followers like Karl Löwith, Eric Voegelin and Shmuel Eisenstadt.

Finally, the passage is concluded by one of the strongest formulations of the 'secularisation' thesis by Weber. He acknowledges that similar questions have indeed been posed by secular philosophy as well. However, though claiming that the link between philosophy and religion would be an important topic for analysis and promising such in the future (though it was not delivered), he subordinates the former to the latter, claiming – in a striking metaphor – that '[t]he religious problem of prophets and priests is the womb from which non-sacerdotal philosophy emanated, where it developed at all' (*ibid.*).[3]

Given the significance of this characterisation of prophecy, we need to analyse these passages further. First of all, if the unified world image of prophets is central for Weber's diagnosis, the root of the religious rejections of the world, then we must inquire about Weber's sources. The shadow of Nietzsche and the diagnosis of nihilism is not far away: 'A nihilist is a man who judges of the world as it is that it ought *not* to be, and of the world as it ought to be that it does not exist…*In summa*: the world as it ought to be exists; this world, in which we live, is an error – this world of ours ought not to exist' (Nietzsche 1968:No. 585). The thesis is formulated with particular force in the fifth book of *Gay Science*, where it becomes evident that Nietzsche's problem is not reduced to the explicit questioning of the world but includes the very idea of having a 'stand' with respect to the world, or even of having a single, all-encompassing 'image' of the world: 'The whole pose of "man *against* the world," of man as a "world-negating" principle, of man as the measure of the value of things, as judge of the world who in the end places existence itself upon his scales and finds it wanting – the monstrous insipidity of the pose has finally come home to us and we are sick of it. We laugh as soon as we encounter the juxtaposition of "man *and* world," separated by the sublime presumption of the little word "and"' (Nietzsche 1974: No. 346).

Nietzsche traced this 'world negation', this 'hostility to life', to ressentiment and slave morality. Weber would thus turn – after a discussion of the congregation that will be covered later – to the 'religious propensities' of the various social classes. There, though recognising the elective affinity between prophets and the lower classes, especially those in a 'pariah' situation, he also draws parallels between the prophets and the urban strata, especially the intellectuals. The three threads would be brought together in the concluding chapters of *Ancient Judaism*, on Deutero Isaiah.

Though Weber corrected Nietzsche's account in many ways, the question still remains whether Weber does not after all remain too close to the Nietzschean problematic. The core of Nietzsche's diagnosis is that, in order to be able to talk about the 'world' and 'life', one must gain an external position to it – otherwise one can only discuss aspects of it. The consequence is that any metaphysics, any general philosophy, any overall discussion of the meaning of the world or of life, must be based on a prior experience of alienation; therefore, it must be ultimately world-rejecting or world-hostile. In searching for the possibility of gaining such an outcast position, Nietzsche and Weber both came to the same conclusion: on the one hand, this can be a 'real' socio-political situation – not simply the 'poor' or the 'lower parts of the system of social stratification' (they are still *inside* the 'world'), but the outcast, the exile, the conquered, the pariah, the unclean; on the other hand, it can be an intellectual stand, the result of a 'mental' game. Nietzsche attributes this to the priests, while Weber emphasises the special role of the prophets. It is precisely here that the problem lies. It is revealing that, while much of the earlier discussion centred on the difference between prophets and priests, where the definition of the core of prophetic revelation is concerned Weber ends on a point shared by prophets and priests.

Two aspects of prophecy are missing in the description summarised above. The first is covered elsewhere by Weber, even centrally, but is omitted here: this is the personal aspect of prophetic revelation. The second aspect is also discussed at length in *Ancient Judaism*, but its theoretical significance is not assessed even there: this is the prophet's hostility to sacrifice. Taken together, these two aspects have a series of implications for the previous discussion. First, prophecy is indeed based on a 'stand', but this stand is not simply an intellectual separation from the world, but rather a tearing away from one's own existential ties. The prophet, in opposition to the priest or the philosopher, is not simply abandoning himself to the free flow of speculation in an environment assured by his institutional position.

Second, however, the previous passage must immediately be corrected, as the prophet in fact gets 'torn away' from his world, by a call. The passivity of prophets, their character as 'servants' or 'vessels' of their god, is fundamental to their type. And if this is opposed to the Hegelian self-consciousness of the spirit, it is also opposed to the Heideggerian 'thrownness'. A prophet is not thrown into 'the' world; he is rather suddenly torn away from *his* world.

This leads to the third point. A prophet is not rejecting 'the' world. Rather, he leaves the world in which he lived before, which he took for granted, following a sudden 'illumination' or 'call'. He suddenly perceives this world as intolerable, unliveable, alien; most importantly, as devoid of meaning. The search for an all-encompassing meaning, if ever, only comes afterwards, later, by others – starting with the prophet's disciples.

The crucial element in all three points discussed above is the concreteness of the prophetic gesture. This concreteness appears both in the relationship of the prophet to the world from which he was torn away, and also in the matter-of-fact reality, the authenticity of his personality. It is here that we touch another crucial issue, the question of true prophets vs false prophets, or the genuineness of prophecy. Weber repeatedly states that the correctness of prediction is not the crucial aspect of genuine prophecy. He places the emphasis instead on the effect of prophets, in the sense of producing ethical conduct. However, no matter how important ethical conduct is, it does not solve the inner problem of authenticity. There is something intrinsically valuable and convincing in genuine prophets; and this is the truthfulness of character – a theme discussed by Nietzsche (Nietzsche 1974: No. 344);[4] and by Foucault, in his lectures on parrhesia. The prophets are believed, not because of the possibility of an external confirmation of the truth of their 'propositions'; rather, what they say is accepted as true because of the way they say it: because it is perceived as a personally believed and even suffered truth, and thus authentic, significant, possessing meaning.

If concreteness, in the sense of both real existential stand and genuine personality, or personal authenticity, are central to prophecy, then the separation of ethical and exemplary prophecy can also be traced here, to the *modality* of this concreteness. The exemplary prophet remains at this level of concreteness, and exerts an effect directly by the example of his own life (ES: 447). The ethical prophet, however, considers himself an instrument for the revelation of truths that a personal god transmits through his mediation with the world, and therefore 'transcends' concrete time and place. This contrast between the concrete and the transcendental is clear enough, but it is misleadingly simple. The point is not only that all real prophets demonstrate aspect of both (ethical prophets must lead exemplary lives and exemplary prophets must have some kind of doctrine).

It is rather that the effect of prophecy depends on the modality of transcendence that can be attributed to the different types (and concrete cases) of prophecy.

The significance of the difference between exemplary and ethical prophecy, however, is best visible in the effects of the prophets, especially concerning the difference in the simple 'evolutionary' line from the magician to the sacrificial priest. These effects can be summarised in three sets of concepts: recognition by followers, the 'routinisation' of prophetic charisma, and the rationalisation of the conduct of life.

The concept of recognition is central to Weber's sociology of charisma, even though this has been rarely made the object of sustained attention.[5] The relative difference between the two types of prophets is to be attributed to the difference between recognising exemplariness in conduct and genuineness of prophecy. This has an especially important consequence concerning the differential significance of laic followers amongst the two types (*ibid.*: 454–7).

The central difference between ethical and exemplary prophecy, however, lies in the way they modify the routinisation process culminating in sacrificial rituals and priestly power. It is indeed this discussion that directly follows in *Economy and Society* the typology of prophecy and the capturing of the prophetic 'essence', and which has been further theorised in the relevant passages of Part One (*ibid.*: 246–8). This discussion, however, should be complemented and slightly modified in light of the previous reconstruction.

Both types of prophet represent a radical challenge to the existing order of things. This challenge is concrete and personal, addresses the world in which they live, and is contained in their entire existence: in what they do and what they say. Thus, in opposition to the temporary charisma embodied in the tricks of the magician, it is lasting, durable, permanent, embodied in a mission. However, after the death of the prophet, carrying on the mission becomes the task of the disciples. Though in some cases even charisma is directly transmitted, at least for some generations, through 'routinisation' it leads to the eventual emergence of priesthood within prophetic religion.

This presents a fundamental problem. Prophets emerged in the context of an existing sacrificial priesthood which already routinised charisma. Unless they are able to maintain their difference, prophetic religions are threatened with becoming swamped by the existing priesthood. Maintaining difference becomes the fundamental testing of the new prophecy, in terms of the spread and the durability of its influence. It is here that the difference between exemplary and ethical prophecy comes to the fore.

This can be pursued by assessing the relevant attitudes with respect to the two pairs that characterise the two earlier 'stages', temporary magic and permanent priesthood: magic and ritual on the one hand, and prayer and sacrifice on the other. Both kinds of prophecy are opposed to the performance of magic, though some prophets, in order to validate their charisma, did not shy away from performing miraculous cures. While tolerating rituals, they place emphasis on the inner side of behaviour, on motivations and intentions. They similarly share an opposition to sacrifice and accord preference to prayer as the proper way to address the godhead. Their opposition to sacrificial priesthood and popular magic is thus shared. The difference lies in the means at their disposal and therefore in their relative effectiveness.

Exemplary prophecy focused on an ideal way of conduct and the demonstration of a personal example as an aim on its own. This resulted in excessively high demands on the followers, which hindered the development of an extensive mass following. Ethical prophecy, however, proclaimed concrete commands required by the godhead and promised salvation for those who followed.

The consequences should be pursued alongside both dimensions singled out above for attention: magic and sacrifice. Weber, however, does so only for the first. Because of its 'elitism', the combat of exemplary prophecy against magic remained inefficient. In spite of the spectacular spread of Buddhism in cities and courts, the countryside remained largely unaffected. Not surprisingly, popular belief in magic became a major source for the established priestly religions to attack and drive back Buddhism. The result could be called a 're-magification' process, or the 'transformation of the world into a magic garden', that, according to Weber, characterised both India and China (see RC: 200 and RI: 255).

The opposite development took place in the lands of ethical prophecy.[6] This was due to the existence of a revealed message, and of its lasting effect on the regular conduct of the laic population. This in itself is paradoxical at first sight, as one could expect it to be exemplary prophecy that gives guidelines for conduct, while dogmatic revelations remain the esoteric property of the priesthood. This is, in fact, what happened in the case of Zoroastriansm, the only major case where the prophet happened to be a priest. The difference was due to the preoccupation of ethical prophecy with dogma. Entirely absent in Asia, in Christianity this preoccupation was due to the influences of the priestly concern with the education of youth in Judaism and with Greek philosophy, also much concerned with the education of youth. This resulted in an unprecedented concern with the general education of the laity, systematised in two main ways: preaching and pastoral care (ES: 464–7).[7]

Preaching, or the 'collective instruction concerning religious and ethical matters', is specific to prophecy (*ibid.*: 464). This is, however, the less important of the two, declining with routinisation only to gain importance in times of charismatic renewals, like Protestantism (or like the Crusades).

Pastoral care is the 'religious cultivation [*Pflege*] of the individual'.[8] It has its source in oracular consultation,[9] and in the identification of the magical transgression committed by the individual – which is also the source of the confessional. Weber gives here the sketches of a genealogical analysis *par excellence*. The confessional and ethical conduct became joined through prophecy, under the particular conditions of 'times of inner or external distress' (*ibid.*: 464), which led to the emergence of pastoral care, or the provision of 'care of souls' (*ibid.*) that were affected and disheartened by these times.

Weber now turns to his central concern, the 'practical influence on the conduct of life [*praktischen Einwirkung auf die Lebensführung*]' of these two factors. Concerning preaching, he only reasserts what he stated before about its loss of importance due to routinisation. Pastoral care, however, is 'the priests' real instrument of power', having a particularly strong influence over the 'workaday world' and the daily 'conduct of life' (*ibid.*: 465). This was especially strong in Western Christianity where the routinisation of prophetic demands happened under the aegis of the casuistry of Roman law, resulting in a rationalised system of penances.[10] However, this development also resulted in the mechanisation of religious duty, leading to a 'loss of that unity which the prophet had introduced into the ethics', or the basing of the conduct of life on a 'distinctive "meaningful" relationship to one's god' (*ibid.*). This results, even in the context of ethical prophecy, in a compromise with traditional views and a partial return to magic.

While this implies an unavoidable decline of prophecy, Weber considers ethical prophecy as a force of permanent renewal, always able to reassert itself and break away from traditionalised and institutionalised forms. This is the dynamics of prophecy in ancient Judaism, continued in Christianity up to Protestantism, that Weber reads as a charismatic revival. This dynamics only ends with modernity, where further charismatic renewal seems to have become impossible – though Weber leaves a question mark (PE: 182).

The second aspect, the successful eradication of sacrificial rituals by ethical prophecy, however, is not discussed by Weber at all. This is surprising, if only for the fact that this was exactly the 'chief' priestly instrument of power that was replaced by pastoral care in the churches of prophetic religions.

Here again we have to call attention to the fact that Weber's aim was not systematic and comprehensive but diagnostic. It was to give a definite formulation to the Nietzschean diagnosis of nihilism and meaninglessness. Weber traced this to the loss of magic (and charisma), and the opposition to the sacrificial mechanism in this respect was not his problem. However, and here we must agree with Blumenberg (1983), modernity not only needs a diagnosis, but also a certain kind of 'legitimation'. To a large extent this is to be traced back to the eradication of the sacrificial mechanism. What we need in this regard is not simply a legitimation of modernity, but a reassessment of Christianity. This task, however, was accomplished not by Blumenberg, but by René Girard.

Prophecy in *Ancient Judaism*

Weber's discussion of prophetic charisma contains a main paradox. In everyday terminology, by 'prophet' we usually mean Mohammed and the classical Hebrew prophets. Given that Weber wrote *Ancient Judaism*, one would expect that Weber's theorisation of charisma is based on the classical Hebrew prophets. Yet, this is patently not the case.

This can be seen from the previous summary of the discussion of prophecy in *Economy and Society*, which does not apply to classical Hebrew prophecy. After all, the standard line of discussion of Weber is in the direction of the recruitment of disciples and the eventual establishment of a lay congregation, tailor-made for Christianity and Islam. Consulting the index of *Economy and Society* or *Wirtschaft und Gesellschaft* one can immediately realise that the names of the great prophets are virtually absent from the book, while prophecy hardly appears under the entry 'Judaism' – the index sub-entries focus rather on legal, economic and dogmatic aspects. However, one finds ample references to Jesus, Paul or Mohammed, those figures who were to be discussed in the fourth and fifth volumes of the GARS, supporting the point that the theoretisation of prophetic charisma in *Economy and Society* is modelled mostly on Christianity and Islam.

The background to prophecy

Ancient Judaism starts with the social background factors, focusing, like the other essays of the 'Economic Ethic', on settlement patterns. Here Weber moves beyond the level of the village culture foundations of higher civilisation – as he did for China and India – to unsettled, nomadic people, where contemporary literature located the Patriarchs (see also Zeitlin 1984).[11] Weber places all this in the context of another, even more important factor: the region out of which Judaism grew had a markedly in-between and marginal character. The ancient region of Canaan is situated in between the two main civilisational centres of the period, Egypt and Mesopotamia; the territory of the Hebrew tribes lay in between the mountainous region of the North and the more fertile agriculture of the South; and though the tribes took up their residence close to major cities, for a long time they did not reside inside. Thus, the Patriarchs were not simply nomadic, but were rather 'semi-nomadic stock breeders', standing '[m]idway between the settled population of the city patriciate and the peasantry, on the one hand, and the free Bedouins on the other' (AJ: 37).

Even further, this peculiar in-between social background of ancient Judaism was explicitly theorised by Weber. At a significant juncture of the work, when moving to the intellectual rationalisation of the religious foundations, Weber returns to these characteristics, claiming that '[r]arely have entirely new religious conceptions originated in the respective centers of rational cultures'. These were, rather, formulated in 'marginal regions', listing as examples – apart from Jerusalem and Galilee – the more recent cases of North Africa (at the time of Augustine), Assisi, Wittenberg, Zurich, Geneva, the Netherlands, Frisia and New England, and adding that this, of course, 'never occurred without the influence and the impact of a neighboring rational civilisation' (*ibid.*: 206). In other words, marginality, remoteness and isolation in themselves only lead to sterililty. Potential fecundity assumes the interaction, the creative tension between marginal areas and the centre; in other words, it requires a liminal situation.

Weber even gives an explanation of why this is so: 'prerequisite to new religious conceptions is that man must not yet have unlearned how to face the course of the world with questions of his own', which is not given to '[m]an living in the midst of the culturally satiated areas' (*ibid.*). The discussion ends with one of Weber's most striking, and oft-quoted passages: 'The possibility of questioning the meaning of the world presupposes the capacity to be astonished about the course of events' (*ibid.*: 207).

This is not even the last word concerning 'out-of-ordinary', in-between situations at the sources of ancient Judaism. Weber's entire related discussion is compatible with the language of liminality. This continues with the overwhelming importance played by warfare on the very constitution of ancient Judaism. According to Weber the origins of Hebrew prophecy lay in war prophecy. Yahweh was originally the saviour god of a military federation; the oldest Judaic institutions can be traced back to an oath-bound military confederation; while the prophets to the ecstatic oracles of this military federation who played a fundamental role in mobilising for 'holy wars'.

Let us review these points in more detail. The origins of Israel as a political community lay in an oath-bound war federation (*ibid.*: 75, 77, 81, 93).[12] Yahweh was a 'war god' (*ibid.*: 130) or a ' "man of war" ', full of wrath, with a thirst for the blood of enemies, and with unlimited passion (*ibid.*: 127). Weber compares him to Indra, the Indian god of war. His fearful appearance was also increased by the fact that he resided on a mountain top, was a ' "god from afar" ' (*ibid.*: 124), and his appearance was accompanied by thunder and lighting, a common characteristic of warrior gods from Zeus to Thor.[13] But he was first and foremost the god of the extraordinary as opposed to the ordinary. This can be seen in his character of a saviour god of war emergencies (*ibid.*: 81, 85), or as 'a god of the great catastrophes of nature' (*ibid.*: 128). But perhaps the best example is the persistent, acute, relentless opposition between Yahweh and Baal, accompanying the history of Israel. Baal was not a bloodthirsty, hostile, menacing god. On the contrary, he was the god of the good harvest, of fertility, of nature – in other words he was the god of ordinary life. For Henri Frankfort, it was the radical transcendence of Hebrew religion, rooted in prophecy, which supported this position (Frankfort 1948: 342–3). In our terminology, Yahweh could be considered as the god of liminality – embodied originally in particularly tight links between warfare and religion.

There is furthermore a special religious type corresponding to the war federation as a political organisation and the warrior–saviour god: this is the oracle prophet, the 'Nabi'. The fundamental role of the Nabi was to mobilise for holy war, or a war in which the entire federation participated together (AJ: 91), both by providing oracles about the outcome and by showing example in warfare. He was a 'professionally trained ecstatic' (*ibid.*: 101), originally not different from similar figures found elsewhere (*ibid.*: 96). Through various ascetic techniques these figures produced in themselves psychological states in order to acquire magical force (*ibid.*: 97). Their main function was not prediction, but rather 'the incitement to crusade, promise of victory, and ecstatic victory magic' (*ibid.*). It is only with the pacification of Israeli society that a different type of prophet emerged, the 'Roeh' or 'seer' (*ibid.*: 103) who was not a prophet of warfare but of the spirit, and who did not employ 'orgiastic frenzy and mass ecstasy', but rather 'had his visions in solitude' (*ibid.*).[14]

Apart from the '*nebiim*', the federation included a body of ascetic professional warriors, trained for war ecstasy, who were called 'the "Nazarites", the "separated ones" ' (*ibid.*: 94). The role of war prophets was originally to help the preparation of these warriors, to provide the magical force, helping them to reach full physical power in the moment of performance, military battle. It was only with the later pacification that the Nazarites were transformed into ascetics of mortification, leading ritualistically exemplary lives (*ibid.*: 95). It needs little effort to show that the short summary of the Nazarites exemplifies, as if in a condensed essence, the stages of a rite of passage: the 'ascetic' exercises characterising the rites of separation, leading to the 'magical force' of the 'performance' in the liminal phase, and culminating in the 'ecstatic frenzy' of the rites of reaggregation.

From all perspectives the original social context of ancient Judaism was characterised by the out-of-ordinary, the unusual, the in-between, the liminal, with the 'images' of the godhead closely mirroring the actual unsettled, in-between condition of the people itself. It is therefore no surprise that the subsequent history of ancient Israel gives, up to a degree, a textbook picture of the process of 'routinisation' or 'permanentisation'. Over the centuries the semi-nomadic cattle-breeders became settled, the ascetic and ecstatic warriors were transformed into peaceful ritualistic ascetics, the place of the frenzied war prophets was taken by the ritualistic sacrificial priesthood, the charismatic war hero was replaced by hereditary kingship, and the patriarchic chiefs of the war federation were replaced by the courtiers and the army generals. All this led to the emergence of an Israelite 'court society',[15] but with two crucial differences – two instances of permanent lasting effects that in significance go way beyond the straightforward process of 'routinisation'. First, the prophets did not disappear completely, integrated into the priesthood, but kept returning, reappearing, being a permanent source of criticism within the court, giving considerable trouble both to kings and high priests, and thus becoming a permanent source of renewal (*ibid.*: 112–13). This is a most striking fact in itself, as on face value it is not easy to understand why the all-powerful courts were unable to get rid of these figures – seemingly isolated, lonely, powerless outside the force of their words. Indeed, in other courts, whether in Egypt or Mesopotamia, India or China, such prophets did not appear, and would certainly have been crushed, without mercy, if they had. The persistent recurrence of prophecy is for Weber therefore a problem to be solved. The second issue, touched on by Weber but pursued more vigorously by Voegelin, is that within the mere logic of routinisation the story of Israel should have ended with the fall of Jerusalem, the destruction of the Temple and the following Exile, or the collapse of the independent Jewish kingdom. The standard storyline allows, of course, a charismatic revival; the emergence of a new charismatic military hero who liberates the people. This, however, did not happen; the main prophets lived before (or during) and not after the Exile; and they, furthermore, did not lead the people out of exile, but rather proclaimed a catastrophe and even argued that this was deserved. There is clearly something to be added to the picture.

This other aspect for Weber is a 'special event in religious history' (*ibid.*: 78), or a 'very unique historical event' (*ibid.*: 118) – the encounter between Moses and Yahweh.[16] Being a sociologist and not a theologian, Weber qualifies the claim by saying that Yahweh 'was said to have concluded' this covenant with Moses, and that this event was 'assumed' by the entire Israelitic tradition (*ibid.*). But, exactly as a sociologist would be, Weber is interested in the precise effect mechanism of this (supposed) event. So we have to pursue him cautiously in this extremely precarious terrain.

The first religious event: the berith

In spite of the singular importance Weber attributes to this event-experience that stamped the entire course of Jewish history, he is remarkably unclear about its exact specification – partly due to the delicacy of the issue, but no doubt even more to the (perceived) requirements and limits of a properly *sociological* perspective. The 'event' is a complex set of happenings, consisting of three main parts:

- the original 'encounter' between Moses and Yahweh, that resulted in the all-important 'promise', the leading-out of the enslaved people into Canaan, the 'promised land';
- the Exodus, the successful escape from Egypt, 'proving' the genuine charisma of Moses, and therefore the veracity of his encounter with the godhead, involving the miracle of the crossing of the Red Sea with dry feet; and
- the conclusion of the promise at Mount Sinai with the Covenant, or the annunciation of the *berith*, a singular contract drawn between a god and his chosen people.

Weber is not giving either a systematic treatment to these three aspects, or an equal attention to its parts. Not only is the – 'assumed' – encounter between Moses and Yahweh not covered at all, but the 'promise' is simply taken for granted in its content. Similarly, there is only passing reference to the 'Exodus', again taken for granted in its meaning as a kind of 'proof', a 'token of God's power' (AJ: 118). This is to be understood in a double, 'experiential' and 'existential', sense. According to the first, it was the common experience of living through the miraculous escape (whether the term 'miracle' is to be meant in a real or a metaphyorical sense), reconfirming what Moses had said and done before, that gave originally cohesion and force to the Jewish people. The second, on the other hand, alludes to the fact that these people still exist, in spite of being unknown for a long period and much harassed after.

Apart from the more-than-sketchy character of Weber's treatment of these two important elements, there is a further omission: both the promise and the idea of leaving, of a civilisational exit, can be traced back to the figure of Abraham. Of course, if the historical reality of Moses is still a highly controversial issue among experts, Abraham is generally assumed to be a mythical figure. The point is not to enter into this discussion, but rather to stress the significance of the Abraham tradition. It has two crucial elements for Weber's perspective. First, Egyptian and Mesopotamian civilisation, society and religion are generally considered to be the background to Judaism. Putting the two 'exits' together, one reaches the – symbolically highly significant – conclusion that Judaism emerged as the direct rejection of the two most important ancient civilisations. It represented, therefore, in this respect an actual, existential, and not simply a theoretical or mystical 'religious' rejection of the 'world'.[17] The second point is closely related: while in the story of Moses the promise precedes the exit, the case of Abraham is the opposite. It is his father, Terah, who leaves the city of Ur first, and the promise only arrives later, in Haran, after the death of Terah, indicating the primacy of the act of leaving.

Of the three aspects of this first event-experience, for Weber without any doubt the *berith* is the most important. This is the experientially-based substance of Judaism, that distinguishes this religion, and the ethical monotheistic religions that derived from it, from all the other religions, whether 'primitive' or sophisticated, ritualistic or spiritualised.

This can be seen first in the special modality of ritualisation in Judaism. The unique specificity of Judaism concerns the relative downplaying of sacrifice. Yahweh is a god of action, of power, of the gratuitous performance of extraordinary deeds. He has no need of sacrifices (*ibid.*: 135). Even further, in some of the best-known episodes of the Bible, he expressly rejects sacrifice. Instead of offering sacrifices, the faithful are, rather, required to show boundless loyalty and keep the revealed commandments. The single, omnipresent, personal god must be served by unconditional faith and obedience to his commands as a 'permanent obligation [*dauernde Verpflichtung*]' (*ibid.*: 118, GARS III: 127) and not by the offer of sacrifices.

This had consequences for the distinguishing character of Levite priesthood. While in certain periods the priesthood did manifest developments in the direction of ritualised sacrifice (AJ: 165), its main feature was the systematisation of the codes of conduct required by Yahweh, especially the provision of guidelines for the education of the youth, leading first to the Decalogue and then to the Torah (*ibid.*: 176, 235–43).

The main opponents of sacrifice, however, were always the prophets. This can be traced back to Moses and his hostility to the adoration of idols, to the story of Abraham and Isaac, or even – according to the interpretation proposed by Girard – to Cain and Abel. It was also reasserted, forcefully, by the prophets of the classical age, like Amos and Jeremiah, who 'presented any and all sacrifices as ultimately quite indifferent to Yahweh' (*ibid.*: 136).

Concerning the evaluation of sacrifice, there has been a persistent relative conflict between priests and prophets. Like any priesthood, the Levites were inclined to increase the role played by ritualisation and sacrifice, while the prophets kept opposing this 'priestly evaluation of sacrifice' (*ibid.*: 284). However – and this should be understood as a partial correction of *Economy and Society* – this conflict in the case of Judaism remained relatively minor, as ultimately even priestly ritualisation centred on ethical and not ritual issues. In sum, ritualisation was subordinated to ethics, ethics was based on revelation, and the most authoritative persons in matters of revelation were the prophets.

The other standard direction of the permanentisation of charisma was towards 'spiritualisation', the abstract sublimation and depersonalisation of the divine forces, characteristic especially of Asiatic intellectualism. The path of Judaism was completely different. Because of the *personal*, direct character of the link between the God and his people, sealed by the *berith*, the anthropomorphic character of the original god was never lost. The prophets were again central in establishing and maintaining a direct, personal contact.

Another special feature of Judaism, to be traced to the *berith*, was the inclination towards universalism. This seems paradoxical on a first look for the saviour god of an oath-bound military federation. However, Weber traces the roots of this potential universalism back to the semi-nomadic character of the original tribes, and thus the relative lack of localisation (*ibid.*: 133–5). Furthermore, even though the *berith* was concluded exclusively with the people of Israel, it had the character of a contract, and thus others could join in. The most important reason for this relative universalism, however, according to Weber, lay in the character of the *reception* of the religion, which was due to the proven powers of the god, and thus – again – the lack of interest in sacrifices (*ibid.*: 135–6).

A further consequence of the *berith*-event is the unique modality of 'world rejection'. Salvation religions, as a rule, downvalued worldly involvement in favour of a reward in the next life, the 'other' world. The promises of Judaism, however, offered not the hope of an individual salvation in the beyond, but a *collective* salvation in *this* world (*ibid.*: 145). As a consequence there was no flight from the world in Judaism; or rather, it was a world-accommodating and not a world-rejecting religion.[18] Just as the source of this promise was prophetic, these were the prophets who kept up this hope over the times.

The fifth and last characteristic resumes and concludes the previous four. The mere logic of routinisation moves in the direction of permanence, rigidity, ossification, eventually rendering the particular culture impermeable to change, except for the impact of an external charismatic movement.[19] Judaism, however, not only showed a remarkable persistence over time, against all the odds, but it was also able to renew itself (at least up to a point) periodically, to generate, internally, 'revolutionary' change. The main agents of this renewal, again, were the prophets.

This propensity could on a first level be attributed to socio-political background factors, to the origins of the prophets in the warrior *nebiim*, an attempt to shake up Israeli court society by calls for a return to the less 'decadent' good old days (*ibid.*: 111). This, however, only scratches the surface, as the main reason for the propensity for renewal must be sought again in the characteristics of the *berith*.

This can be traced at the level of both ends and means. At the level of ends there is the promise of collective salvation in *this* world, the unique hope of Judaism. At the level of means this required indeed a return – not to the old days of war fraternities, but rather to a life led according to the revealed commandments. This was the message of the prophets, and it was due to this message that they were in constant, relentless struggle with Hebrew 'court society' and its lapses.

The second event-experience: the fall of the Temple

The dynamics of this internal struggle within the court, the persistent presence of voices of dissent, was in itself unique. The strength of the prophets, however, gained an even more surprising reinforcement in the next experiential moment, the collapse of the state of Israel.

In order to gain a fresh look, we have to start again with the trivial. Because the Hebrew people and religion still exist today, it is easy to take this persistence for granted, overlooking its truly extraordinary character. The period under discussion, the seventh and sixth centuries BC, was a period of utter turmoil, with countless tribes and local kingdoms disappearing without a trace in history, or surviving only in name. The compact survival of the Hebrews is little less than a miracle.

Historical events only increase the puzzle. The status of the court was unusually precarious in ancient Israel, but only due to the existence of the Covenant, the promise of this-worldly collective salvation. The collapse of the kingdom and subsequent Exile evidently gave the clearest possible refutation of this promise.

Weber attempts to solve the problem by reconstructing not just the socio-political but also the experiential context, focusing on the figure of the prophet. Prophecy and promise are inextricably linked, and not only in Judaism. But Judaism included the unique feature of collective salvation in this world, and this forced the prophets to devote a careful attention to reality. This implied, first of all, the close monitoring of the political–military events in the surrounding region, making them 'experts' in 'international relations'. They had to realise that – unless a spectacular divine intervention happens – the days of the independent kingdom are numbered.

Such an intervention may seem unlikely to us, but it was part of the *berith* experience in ancient Israel. However, the *berith* was a contract between two sides, and the question became whether the people fulfilled their obligations. The answer of the prophets was a resounding 'no'.

This, in itself, was not a novelty. The recurrent dynamics of prophecy in Israeli court society was the exhortation of the kings and the people to return to the true path of Yahweh, ending the various forms of devious conduct such as idolatry and paganism, or the taking of foreign wives. The novelty lay in the context: no longer the inexorable ritualisation and re-magification of Hebrew court society, but rather its imminent collapse due to the international situation. This increased stress: '[t]he typical prophet apparently found himself in a constant state of tension' (AJ: 291); the 'men of most passionate temper produced by Israel lived in a constantly tarrying mood' (*ibid.*: 327). This led to the unique phenomenon of the *prophecy of doom*.

If prophecy is all about promises, then it is about promises of the *good* life. 'Prophets' (diviners, augurs, oracles) were remunerated,[20] and nobody is willing to pay for bad news. It is to overcome this dilemma that prophecies are often couched in uncertain terms, leaving open the possible interpretation – like the famous story of the oracle of Delphi's legendary advice to king Croesus before his battle with the Persians. As Judaism is based on the promised land of Abraham and Moses, a prophecy of doom seems even more implausible. Yet this was exactly what was pronounced, under the enormous tension produced by the impending political catastrophe, especially by its main representative, Jeremiah, who becomes the main figure not simply of the respective chapter of *Ancient Judaism*, but of Weber's entire account.[21]

Here we reach the core of Weber's analysis of classical prophecy. The political existence of Israel was based on a singular prophecy, the unique idea of a contract made between a people and its god. At the moment of political collapse, however, it should only have rendered the catastrophe even more complete and irrevocable. But *before* this event could happen, based on an assessment of the international situation combined with a diagnosis of the moral corruption of Israeli court society, classical prophecy (and in particular the prophet Jeremiah) succeeded in reversing the argument and preaching a prophecy of doom and not victory. This voice, at first silenced and repressed as blasphemy, once it proved to be true became the new foundation of existence for ancient Israel. In Weber's words, '[i]t is completely inconceivable that without the profound experiences of a confirmation of the prophetic word of doom uttered in public and still remembered after a hundred years (Jer. 26:18) the belief of the people was not only unbroken by the fearful political fate, but in a unique and quite unheard of historical paradox was definitely confirmed. The entire inner construction of the Old Testament is inconceivable without its orientation in terms of the oracles of the prophets' (AJ: 334).

The third religious experience: Exile

The new phase of Judaism is situated in a novel socio-political and experiential context. After the conquest of Jerusalem and the destruction of the Temple, the elite of Israel was captured and taken into exile in Babylon. It is with this event that the experience of *suffering* came to leave a lasting stamp on Judaism. In this chapter, arguably written before the previous one, Weber attempted to take up and correct the Nietzschean diagnosis of ressentiment.

In assessing the stamp left by the new experiential context, we have to start by understanding the way in which those who had undergone this experience have interpreted it. It is at this level of interpretation that the 'revaluation of values' can be captured, in a series of successive steps. First of all, Jewish history had so far been lived under the aegis of promises, interpreted as a reward for the faith of Abraham and then of the Patriarchs. Now that the promises became untenable, emphasis shifted to the opposite side, the side of *punishment*. Classical prophets like Isaiah and Jeremiah consistently threatened the people with punishment for their sins; and among the most important of these sins was the sin of overconfidence, conceitedness, *hubris* (*ibid.*: 320), or pride.[22]

The catastrophe was read as a punishment for these sins, to be met by the opposite conduct: an ever stricter adherence to the revealed commandments and the rules of conduct upon which they are based. This led to an increased importance being placed on the correct performance of rituals, highlighting the importance of priestly rationalisation and systematisation.

This, in turn, had major social consequences, having to do with the increased separation driving a wedge between the Jews and other cultures, enhanced by the requirement to preserve identity in the multi-ethnic context of the capital of a major empire. Weber discusses these in two sections, entitled 'The Development of Ritualistic Segregation' and 'The Dualism of In-Group and Out-Group Morality'. The crucial element, however, is again related to sacrifice. It was the 'refusal to participate in any sort of sacrificial meal [that] was unique in Antiquity and, indeed, decisive for the political pariah situation of Jewry' (*ibid.*: 358). As a result, the community of Jews became a 'ritualistically distinct confessional congregation' (*ibid.*: 362).

The replacement of complacent this-worldly eschatological expectations with the suffering of the punishment for sins was in itself a major change. The real 'revaluation of values', however, required an additional turn that found its prophet in Deutero Isaiah. This was due to a social factor, the increasing economic differentiation within the exiled community. While the upper strata of the exiles was better accommodated to the new conditions, only exchanging one type of 'court society' for another and tending towards religious indifference, 'the resentment of the pious poor mounted' (*ibid.*: 367). For them, the idea of being punished for the sins committed by previous generations was less and less tolerable. This experience received full elaboration in exile prophecy, especially that of Deutero Isaiah, which 'produced the most radical and one may say the only truly serious theodicy of Ancient Jewry. It represents at the same time an apotheosis of sufferance, misery, poverty, humiliation, and ugliness which in its consistency is not even second to New Testament prophecy' (*ibid.*: 369).

Reviewing the various attitudes held in Judaism with respect to suffering and poverty, Weber emphasises a diversity of views and the absolute novelty of the idea of the 'positive soteriological meaning of suffering per se', especially of innocent suffering, that became 'valued in sharpest contrast to pre-exilic prophecy' (*ibid.*: 373).

This new theodicy did not simply remain as mere words, but exerted manifold and lasting effects, stamping the future course of history. Most directly, it had major theological consequences. The 'revaluation of values' goes first of all directly to the heart of Judaism, reassessing the *berith*-experience. Deutero Isaiah 'places less weight on the breach of the old *berith* than others', as '[h]is problem is neither the promises nor the *berith*, but the theodicy of Israel's suffering in the universal perspective of a wise and divine world government' (*ibid.*: 375).

While this poses the problem of the potential universalism of exilic and post-exilic Judaism – a problem Weber does not pursue – it also brings forth a fundamental reshaping of the links between theology and the people. While the old promises and the *berith* were easily intelligible, the new theodicy of the positive value of suffering was only accessible to the initiated (*ibid.*), resulting in a turn towards esotericism. Finally, and still at the theological level, Weber alludes

Isaiah

to the apparent links between the suffering servant Deutero Isaiah and the New Testament, especially the Sermon on the Mount and the prescription to 'resist no evil' (*ibid.*: 376).

Concerning the social effects, Weber's comments can be summarised in two ways. On the one hand there persisted, and indeed became decisive for daily conduct, the 'mood of Deutero Isaiah, the worm feeling (Isa. 41:14) and the positive evaluation of self-abasement and ugliness' which, according to Weber, had a major impact on Christianity, up to Pietism (AJ: 376). Even further, this can be traced in the even broader overall underlying attitudes, in the 'weary and waitful (*harrende*) pathos of the pariah situation and the alien eyes with which the Jews walked in the world' (*ibid.*: 377, GARS III: 395, trans. modified).

The other major aspect of Deutero Isaiah, the 'conception of the innocent Servant of God offering himself voluntarily for the sins of others' (AJ: 376) was almost immediately dropped – most probably due to changes in the political situation. It did not become the starting point of Messianistic hope – at least, up to the times of Christianity (*Ibid.*: 377).

Conclusion

Weber's work was based not on an idea, nor on a hypothesis, but rather on a double existential stand with respect to the times and the world in which he was living; a two-fold diagnosis. On the one hand, this was a sense of meaninglessness, the loss of values and the emptying of life, best captured in Nietzsche's term 'nihilism', to which Weber attempted to give a more precise meaning. On the other hand, it was a feeling that this state of affairs, though inevitably leading to further loss of meaning, was inexorable and unalterable, best captured in Kierkegaard's term 'resignation'.

The results of the search for a better diagnosis, and an analysis of the reasons why this state of affairs came to be, led Weber to the formulation of a number of important terms, such as 'rationalisation', 'disenchantment' and 'routinisation', but the broadest and most central of all these terms is the religious rejection of the world. Weber's 'vision' can be summarised in the idea that there is a fundamental 'affinity', but also a direct, 'causal–genealogical' connection between the contemporary state of affairs and the religious rejections of the world.

This leads to a number of paradoxes. The first of these is the following. On the one hand, there is an evident affinity between the stand of Weber (or that of Nietzsche, Kierkegaard, Marx, or other critiques of their society) and the stand of the old prophets recognised by Weber for example in the way he identified himself with Jeremiah. On the other hand, the thrust of Weber's diagnosis is that contemporary problems are *precisely* due to the lasting effects of these earlier stances. This result in itself could lead to a 'meta-resignation', as it implies that resistance to or criticism of the contemporary state of affairs is not simply doomed to failure, but could only make things worse if successful.

The second point, though attenuating this paradox, is no less puzzling. This is the methodological guiding idea, underlying the second part of the previous point, that contemporary secular developments can be directly rooted in earlier religious phenomena. This implies that everything is not hopeless; one only needs to identify these 'secularised', undercurrent tenets properly. This, however, is not so simple, as the 'world' in which we live, the world of 'globalisation', is so thoroughly impregnated with these 'secularised' ideas, with inner-worldly asceticism and eschatology, that their 'rejection' would arguably be even more impossible, more 'nihilistic' than the original religious rejections of the world.

The crux of the matter, however, lies in the various meanings that were attributed to the term 'world', or 'world images [*Weltbild*]'. What was exactly the 'world' that came to be opposed not only by the prophets, but also the philosophers, sages and mystagogues, etc.? And how precisely did they perceive this world? Such questions must be answered so that the manner in which prophets and the like altered the characteristics of the 'world' can be individuated and analysed.

This also shows the enormity of the task, and that – in spite of the amount of work that Weber did in the 1910s, relying on much of his earlier knowledge – he could do no more than sketch the central issues. He managed to reconstruct some of the most important religious rejections of the world and their dynamics, and to sketch the 'images' of the world that underlay these attempts. But he did not ignore the study of the characteristics of the 'world' the prophets lived in. He could partly rely on the knowledge he possessed, having written his Habilitation thesis on Roman property law, and also three different versions of an 'agrarian sociology' of Antiquity, *before* he started to study ancient religion. Furthermore, he did write considerable segments of *Economy and Society* on the politics and history of Antiquity, from the perspective of his *Fragestellung*. Most important, however, for our purposes, is the manuscript he wrote on 'the City'.

3   The city

Weber's work on the city is connected to his historical–religious sociology in a threefold manner. First, in all the essays of the 'Economic Ethic', the main social background factor to the rise of the world religions was settlement pattern and not social stratification. Second, the affinities between prophecy and the city were recurrently mentioned, though the connection was not worked out explicitly and in detail. Finally, together with (ethical) prophecy, the (Occidental) city was for Weber the other main source of modernity, to a large extent independent of the first. Though this idea is worked out even less in the extant texts, 'prophecy' and the 'city' were Weber's way of re-posing the problem of the dual, Judeo-Christian and Greco-Roman sources of modern Europe.

The status of the manuscript

The large manuscript on the 'city' found in the *Nachlaß* is one of Weber's most controversial texts. Such a chapter did not feature in the outline plans of *Economy and Society*. Marianne Weber published it first in 1921 in the *Archiv*, and then inserted it at the end of the third volume of *Wirtschaft und Gesellschaft*, published in 1922. Since then controversy has raged about the proper title of the work; whether it belongs to *Economy and Society* at all; and in general about its relationship to Weber's oeuvre. Increasing the confusion, the manuscript of the piece has subsequently been lost. The critical edition of the text, published in 1999, helps to settle at least some of these issues.

Concerning the title, in 1921 Marianne Weber added the subtitle 'A Sociological Study' to Weber's simple term 'The City'. The fourth edition of *Wirtschaft und Gesellschaft*, edited by Johannes Winckelmann, changed this to 'Non-Legitimate Domination: A Typology of the City', following Weber's 2 June 1914 suggestions for an outline plan (MWG I/22, 5: 46). The English edition of *Economy and Society* followed this suggestion, though reverting the title–subtitle order. The critical edition, finally, restored the simple title 'The City' and published it as the last volume of the first (1911–14) version of *Economy and Society*.[1]

Another problem concerns the proper place of the piece in Weber's oeuvre. The June 1914 letter would seem to be a clear enough indication of Weber's intentions to locate it at the end of *Economy and Society*. However, in autumn 1919

Weber made two important statements that would seem to indicate that he had come with a different idea. In the leaflet published on 25 October 1919 concerning the forthcoming volumes of the *Collected Essays*, sent to the publisher on 24 September, Weber is talking about two further pieces of work that would better situate his essays on the sociology of religion. One would be a short study of Egyptian, Mesopotamian and Zoroastrian religious ethics, while the other, more important, piece is a 'sketch devoted to the rise of the social singularity [*Eigenart*] of the Occident, i.e., an essay on the development of the European bourgeoisie [*Bürgertum*) in Antiquity and the Middle Ages' (Schluchter 1989: 425; MWG I/19: 28). Furthermore, just a few weeks before, in a letter Weber wrote to his publisher on 11 September 1919 (thus, at precisely the time he was working on the *Vorbemerkung* – see *ibid.*: 46), he claimed that he also had in mind a study of the 'basic grounds of the unique path of Occidental development [*allgemeinen Grundlagen der occidentalen Sonderentwicklung*]' (MWG I/22, 5: 48). Though it is not absolutely certain that Weber refers here to this manuscript, the probability is high.

It might be, however, that the problem posed by the exact position of this text is more apparent than real. It only appears if we consider *Economy and Society* and the *Collected Essays* (or the 'Economic Ethic' essays) as completely different projects. This, however, is not the case, as the two projects only represent a different way of elaborating and putting into a published form the same basic historical material. Hesitations about its proper place, far from indicating marginality, rather underline the central importance of the piece, the connecting role between the two aspects of the project.

This can be illuminated by considering it jointly with the other problematic piece of the 1911–14 manuscript, the chapter on the sociology of religious groups. These are the two chapters of *Economy and Society* that clearly have nothing to do with the original aim of the work, which was an update of Schönberg's *Handbook of Political Economy*. The other texts, about the economy, the law, the social communities or politics and power, have all grown out from various planned chapters of the *Handbook*, and relate to the development, function and context of the economy. It is by incorporating these two 'outlier' chapters that the '*Handbook*' project became close to Weber's heart;[2] but the addition of these two pieces also ensured that the project went in a direction quite different from a conventional handbook, and thus became unfinishable and – in its planned form – unpublishable. The two unplanned parts of *Economy and Society* define the centre of Weber's project and identify the unique specificity of the Western line of development, which can be resumed in the two central terms of these two manuscripts: the (ethical) prophet and the (Occidental) city.

The second main comment is related to the structure of the piece. It is clearly unfinished, the last (fifth) section's title only being added by the editor, giving the impression that the text was written continuously from the beginning to the end. However, in light of Weber's general style of work, the first version had to be the long historical sections (ES: 1266–1367), resumed from the perspective of the 'diagnostic' interest in the specificity of the Western line of development, resulting in the current second section 'The Occidental City' (*ibid.*: 1236–62), and finally the first section entitled 'Concepts and Categories of the City' (*ibid.*: 1212–34, esp. pp.1212–26; the subsequent pages, as usual, digress into illustrations and special cases). This would explain a number of repetitions in the text.[3]

Settlement patterns vs social stratification

The three-fold thematisation of the social affinities of prophecy

Weber repeatedly asserted that prophecy as a religious phenomenon manifests affinities with three different kinds of social group: those who are living in a 'pariah' or outcast situation; the urban middle classes; and the intellectuals (see FMW: 274–84, and ES: 468–517). In contrast to Nietzsche's analysis of ressentiment, Weber emphasised that salvation religions did not grow out of a slave or outcast situation, but acknowledged that once such religions developed, they showed affinity and sympathy with the plight of the downtrodden and the suffering. The affinity with the urban middle classes was due to the common interest in systematic rationality, though in one case it was due to the attempt to translate the revealed commandments into rules guiding everyday conduct, while in the other to the rational calculations inherent in daily activities. Finally, the affinity with intellectuals is similarly due to the rationality inherent in prophetic religions, the search for meaning in the world.

While all three factors can be considered as 'social' in the classical sense of social structure, they are more related to settlement patterns than to what is usually understood by a system of social stratification. The central characteristic of pariahs is that they are not part of the system, being 'out'-casts. More often than not this status is rooted in a previous instance of warfare and conquest, not a consequence of the ordinary daily life of a community. Even further, there is a general difference between the urban and rural consequences of conquest. A conquered rural population usually does not mix with the conquerors, and thus eventually becomes integrated in the social order at the lowest rungs, as serfs or bondmen. A permanent outcast status is maintained much more in urban areas, where shared living and interaction between the conquerors and the conquered leads to a more permanent differentiation. The civic strata are by definition an urban phenomenon, while intellectuals similarly live in cities, and in cities only.

The social background chapters in the 'Economic Ethic'

All three series of essays of the 'Economic Ethic' start with one or more sections on sociological background factors, focusing on settlement patterns, especially rural–urban differences. Thus the first sentence of Confucianism and Taoism contrasts China, a 'country of large walled cities', with Japan (RC: 3), though later in the book Weber adds that the city in China remained a princely city, lacking any political autonomy (*ibid.*: 13–14). The internal organisation of city life remained subordinated to kinship relations and the ancestor cult. Hinduism and Buddhism starts similarly, by contrasting India, a country of villages, with China (RI: 5–6).[4]

In *Ancient Judaism* special attention is given to the rural–urban differences between the north and south of Palestine, and the unique situation of semi-nomadic stockbreeders who were considered as aliens to the city (*gerim*) (AJ: 39). This prompted Weber to draw connections between the situation of the pariahs in India and the Hebrews in the Middle East.

'Stamping' and 'carrier strata'

The thrust of the previous discussion seems to be contradicted by the third factor, the manner in which the life conditions of those social strata that became the 'carriers' of certain religions left a lasting stamp on these religions. This is at the centre of the relevant discussion in the *Einleitung* (FMW: 268–70), and it is from precisely this point of view that the emphasis on settlement patterns in the 'Economic Ethic' essays was striking. However, more careful analysis reveals the contrast to be more apparent than real. Prophetic religions are 'stamped' and leave a lasting 'stamp' under 'out-of-ordinary' conditions. Such situations of distress, however, are also conditions of 'anti-structure' (Turner) or structural 'undifferentiation' (Girard). It is therefore less the 'social structure' and its stratification that matters at those times, 'determining' the content of religions in a Marxist or a 'class' sense, than the specific living conditions of various strata, in so far as such living conditions have some affinity with the emerging religions.

'Out-of-ordinary' conditions only underline the significance of settlement patterns, if only for the trivial reason that any moment of distress increases the value assigned to the 'home'; or, coming from the other direction, that the most significant possible threat is against one's life and one's home.

The nature of the city

The city has three major external distinguishing features: it is a closed, dense and large settlement. Such an 'objective' description, however, fails to give justice to the most important experiential aspect of city life. A city is a settlement in which many people who live relatively close together do not know each other person-ally; a place where the meeting of strangers, otherwise a most 'out-of-ordinary' and often threatening situation, becomes an everyday experience. This experi-ence has a significant impact on all aspects of city life.

From this conceptual definition Weber turns to the origins of the city. He identifies two main sources. One is in the regular order of everyday activities, in exchange and the market. He is sketching here an entire 'philosophy of history', contrasting the city to agriculture and the village (ES: 1217–18) and situating the 'urban economy' as a 'stage of economic development' (*ibid.*: 1218–20). Weber's other source is warfare, leading to the emergence of the court, which is residing in a citadel or fortress, usually on the top of a mountain or a hill.[5] The genealogical design is visible even here, in the language of the 'fusion' (*Einheit*) of 'fortress' and 'market'.

The short conceptual exposition contains three puzzling features. Just after the 'definition' of the city, Weber gives a typology of cities, the 'consumer city', the 'producer city' and the 'merchant city', which were never to be used. Furthermore, strangely missing in this section is any reference to the other 'out-of-ordinary' sphere, religion. Religious functions were certainly central to the rise of the city, whether in Greece or in ancient Mesopotamia. Weber, however, does not discuss religion or prophecy explicitly here.[6]

The final remarks concern the relationship between commerce and the city. In Weber's short sketch it appears as if the rise of commerce would be an almost 'natural' development, growing out of the ordinary activities. However, in the differentiation between 'ordinary' and 'out-of-ordinary' activities, commerce takes up a special position. In opposition to religion or warfare, commerce is not concerned with the solution of emergency situations but evolves directly from regular, everyday activities. However, it is still markedly different from the simple business of daily life. Less interestingly, it deals with surplus product. Most importantly, it assumes regular contacts between strangers. While this establishes clear affinities between commerce and city life, it also implies a continuous movement between the 'home' and the 'world at large'. This meant that wherever kinship ties dominated social life, commerce as an activity was either down-valued (as in China), or was left to strangers (Jews, Armenians, other religious or ethnic minorities). So in many respects commerce can be considered as a third major type of 'out-of-ordinary' activity, to be contrasted with the other major activity of dealing with strangers, or warfare.[7]

The Occidental city

The perspective of Weber's 'sociology of the city', just as of his 'sociology of religion', was a concern with the unique historical path that eventually resulted in the rise of modern capitalism, and of modern culture in general. In the manuscript Weber first shortly summarises the distinguishing features of the Occidental city in the last paragraph of the conceptual section. The central message is contained in two words: the 'Commune' and the 'Burgher'.[8] The first means that the entire city as a whole constituted an autonomous legal body. The second refers to its members, implying both that membership within the city, or citizenship, was a legal right given to all (qualified) inhabitants, and that it was possible to acquire this right outside personal (or blood) ties; and that on the other hand the city was an association of its members.

The next large section of the manuscript (ES: 1236–62) elaborates this short description, mostly by retracing the sources of the Occidental city. Weber's account is based at a first level on a clear differentiation between legal and non-legal sources. Concerning the first, the two fundamental rights identified above are traced to, and complemented by, a series of legal characteristics that, according to Weber, are specific to the Occidental city: the real estate law, especially the alienability of urban landed property, or the fact that houses could be sold without restriction (*ibid.*: 1237); the absolute legal status of the person, or the fact that outsiders (aliens) could gain citizenship rights (*ibid.*), resulting in the possibility of an 'ascent from bondage to freedom' (*ibid.*: 1238; emphasis in original); the existence of a special law applicable solely to citizens, or the 'quality of the *polis* or *commune* as a special status group [*Stand*]' (*ibid.*: 1240); and the right of the city community as a whole to own property (*ibid.*: 1241). But in the same pages Weber also claims, elaborating on the enigmatic planned subtitle, that at the same time 'urban citizenry...usurped the right to dissolve the bonds of seigneurial domination', and that 'this was the great – in fact, *revolutionary* – innovation which differentiated the medieval Occidental cities from all others' (*ibid.*: 1239). This claim is reinforced and elaborated later: the 'real origins [of the Occidental city are] to be found in what is from the formal legal point of view a revolutionary usurpation of rights' (*ibid.*: 1250).[9]

In this way the clear distinction turns into a paradox: the origins of the city were evidently both legal *and* non-legal at the same time. The problem seems to lie outside Aristotelian logic. The solution requires a genealogical approach, in the sense of opposites having the same origin (see Nietzsche 1966: No. 2), but not before our perplexity increases further. Beyond this first paradox, Weber shows that the legal peculiarities can be traced back to non-legal sources, while the non-legal aspect is profoundly tied to the law.

The second point is the easier of the two to substantiate. Though in strictly formal legal terms the rise of the Commune established a non-legitimate domination, the aim of these actions was not to overthrow the law, establishing a purely substantive type of government, but rather to assert the autonomous right of the city to establish and administer the law within its boundaries. This struggle was waged against two main enemies, the temporal and the spiritual powers, the two main sources of authority in the medieval world, that can be traced to the two upper echelons of the Indo-European tri-partite ideology and the two 'out-of-ordinary' instances, the religious and the military: the bishop (ES: 1251–2) and the landlord (*ibid.*: 1253–4). The non-legal, revolutionary struggle was therefore waged strictly in, and not against, the spirit of the law. This is central for the evaluation and the assessment of the potential implications of this revolution.

The unique legal features can also be traced to non-legal origins. The most important of these, tying the account directly to the legal foundations of the non-legal aspect, is the existence and significance of fraternal associations, the oath-based confraternities of Occidental cities. The central element is the military character of these confraternities. Weber would call this the 'ultimate basis' (*ibid.*: 1260) for the specificity of the Occidental city, and the resulting '*military* check on the city lord' and the presence of '*armed* strata' in the cities the 'decisive difference' (*ibid.*: 1262). This entire development again has its economic and sociological bases on its own.[10]

Part of this basis is purely negative, which can be summarised in two factors. One is the absence of magical religious cults, due to the dissolution of clan or kinship ties in the West (*ibid.*: 1242–3, 1260). Here a central role is played by the universalism of Christianity, which prevented the formation of religious and kinship segregation within the city (*ibid.*: 1244, 1286). Second, also absent from the medieval city was the large-scale bureaucratic administration that developed in all parts of Asia due to the needs of river regulation and irrigation policy (*ibid.*: 1261).

For such a development to take place, however, there was need for some positive grounds as well. An important background part was played by the legacy of Roman law, ensuring that the development of the Commune was the strongest in Italy.[11] Weber attributes special importance to the foundation of new towns, especially frequent in inland as opposed to coastal areas (*ibid.*: 1238), as in these cases 'the burgher joined the citizenry as an individual, and as an individual he swore the oath of citizenship' (*ibid.*: 1246).[12] The third aspect, most directly relevant for military confraternisation, was the right (and duty) to bear one's own arms, or the 'principle of *self-equipment*' that prevailed in the West since the time of the Roman Empire (*ibid.*: 1261).[13]

After the negative and positive background forces, the task is to analyse the emergence of the phenomenon of confraternities. The transformation of a 'temporary' phenomenon into a permanent one, a recurrent analytical tool of Weber, was spelled out explicitly in his analysis of the Italian *coniurationes* (*ibid.*: 1254). The question concerns the exact conditions under which this development happened, and the lasting stamp it has left. Broadly speaking, this context was the struggle of the cities with the ecclesiastical and feudal powers. This, however, was a very long process, rendering difficult the identification of the moment of breakthrough, a central methodological concern of Weber.

The manuscript mentions a decisive moment, the last decades of the eleventh century. Up to this time, the bishop and the landlord retained their position, and 'the great transformation was felt only in the existence of the burgher assembly' (*ibid.*: 1253). It was only then that the institution of annually elected *consules* appeared, which 'completed the revolutionary usurpation by seizing all or the major part of judicial powers and the supreme command in wartime' (*ibid.*). This same moment has been identified as decisive in the more recent literature (Waley 1969). The reasons for this breakthrough, however, are not explained. Without going into details, let us just mention that the last decade of the eleventh century was the decade of the Crusades. Beyond military emergency, it was also a moment of extreme enthusiasm and mobilisation, largely through the force of preaching.

These developments were not identical in all parts of Europe, and in the historical chapters Weber duly discusses the differences. The 'model case' is Italy. In a crucial passage of Confucianism and Taoism, Weber would claim that of 'the five great revolutions that decided the destiny of the Occident' the first was 'the Italian revolution of the 12th and 13th centuries' (RC: 62).[14] The contrast case is England (ES: 1276–81). There, due to the strong power of the king and

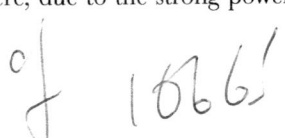

the central administration, the privileges of the city developed within the context of feudal and patrimonial rights, and were not derived from autonomous association. As a consequence the burghers did not possess independent military powers, and thus 'the notion of the commune as a territorial institution never arose in England' (*ibid.*: 1279). This resulted in the domination of the 'gentry', in opposition to the 'at least relative democracy developing in Continental cities' (*ibid.*: 1280).[15]

The consequences of this unique development of military confraternities in Occidental cities were numerous. First, it allowed a specific kind of 'democratisation', especially in Italy.[16] Through the rise of military confraternities, in the Italian city-states the 'popolo' managed to break the power of the patriciate (*ibid.*: 1296, 1301). In contrast to the *demos* of the Ancient polis, the *popolo* was not simply an economic but also a political category, with not only independent finance but also military organisation. As a result, the popolo was '[i]n the truest sense of the word...a "state within the state" – the first deliberately nonlegitimate and revolutionary political association' (*ibid.*: 1302). The end of this line of development is the 'rise of the "Estates" in the Occident – and only there' (*ibid.*: 1261), in opposition to the emergence of a central bureaucratic apparatus.

This dynamics was the result of ongoing struggles against both main medieval powers, occasionally leading to full-scale insurrections (*ibid.*: 1305), based on the existence of autonomous military associations. Still, just as the aim of the usurpation of power was to establish an autonomous system of law, similarly the chief consequence of this development was not in the field of military undertakings, but in that of business activities, and especially commerce (*ibid.*: 1352). Even in this respect the development of the medieval city passes through full circle, again in contrast to the city of Antiquity. The foundation of medieval cities, especially inland cities, was 'primarily a business undertaking' (*ibid.*: 1332). The defence of economic interests was central to the search for military autonomy, which again further promoted economic development. The 'medieval commercial inland city' therefore constitutes a 'direct antithesis' (*ibid.*) to the coastal polis of Antiquity that was typically a guild of warriors (*ibid.*: 1238, 1285, 1332, 1352, 1359).

The third point concerns the last, unfinished section of the manuscript, on impediments to empire formation (*ibid.*: 1263–6). Though the discussion is inconclusive, given the theoretical and political significance of the question of 'Empire' it should be mentioned nonetheless.[17]

Part II

Eric Voegelin

Metaxy and the order of the soul

4   Voegelin's historical method

Introduction

The central concern of Voegelin's work was an attempt at the self-understanding of contemporary society. The last sentence of the long middle section of the Preface to the first volume of *Order and History*, explaining the nature of the epic undertaking, speaks for itself: the work 'should be read, not as an attempt to explore curiosities of a dead past, but as an inquiry into the structure of the order in which we live presently' (OHI: xiv).

This work was first of all driven by an epochal consciousness. The age in which Voegelin's work was rooted belonged to a specific type of historical period. The modality of the work, furthermore, was diagnostic. Voegelin wanted to analyse the origins and the dynamics of those mass movements and ideologies that provoked the outbursts of violence that marked the twentieth century. Putting the epochal consciousness and the diagnostic aim together, Voegelin's work was based on the premise that the age in which he was living was an age in which the very ordering structures of society were collapsing.

The diagnosis of such a situation requires analytical, even 'clinical' tools. And it is at this point that the more interesting, complicated, but also questionable part of the work starts. Voegelin firmly asserted that the most important turning point in his research was the reading of Husserl's *Crisis* and the ensuing correspondence with Schutz in 1943, culminating in the 'anamnetic experiments' and the first sketch of his theory of consciousness. The central element of this radical reorientation was the shattering recognition that the modern forms of thought attempting to diagnose the situation, and of which – not the least due to his friendship and correspondence with Schutz – he considered Husserl as its prime exponent, shared the exact same form of thought which they intended to diagnose. This Socratic recognition of ignorance, that occurred just at the stage when his own work had reached a 'dead end', implied a need to search for possible tools of analysis, beyond the 'mental' horizon in which he himself was so far situated (AN: 3).

This eventually led to the recognition that the analytical framework within which he had worked so far, centring on 'sentiments' and the ideas they 'evoked' (HPI: 228–9), had to be substituted by 'experiences' and their 'symbolisation'.

The search focused on the proper analysis of 'experiences', and was only put to rest with the discovery of 'metaxy' (AR: 72–4) that did not take place until 1962 (Hollweck and Caringella 1990: xvi–xvii, fn. 4). The reconstruction of this symbol will be the central aim of this chapter.

Though the term 'metaxy', as we will soon see, was central not only to Voegelin's thought but also for its relevance for the genesis of modernity, this does not mean that the work done between 1943 and 1962 was rendered obsolete. In the writings of this period, and in fact, to a large extent, in the entire *History of Political Ideas*, there is a continuous struggle to find the proper linguistic expression of the way in which thoughts do not simply 'reflect' and 'categorise' events, but are themselves parts of the historical process, as representing ways in which the thinkers who lived through certain historical events attempted to make sense of their own experiences and the dynamics of the events shaping the world in which they lived. Voegelin's thoughts, step-by-step, crystallised into a few insights that only gained further clarity through the discovery of 'metaxy'.

'Experience' means at its limit the living-through of a period of earth-shattering events; events in which the surrounding world order, formerly taken for granted, collapses, falling to pieces. At the same time, beyond reflecting on the meaning and consequences of the events, thinkers were also searching for ways to resist the processes of decay and dissolution, to provide ways out of the crisis. Central in this search was an opposite type of experience, the 'experience of order', based on a sense of participation; participation in the 'mystery of being'. Finally, such an experiential perspective was also highly reflexive, implying that the thinker had to consider the relationship between his experiences and his appropriate role as well. In spite of the carefulness with which Voegelin tried to tackle this issue, it is here that the problems of the undertaking can be rooted.

Such problems become visible by taking a simple glimpse at the basic coordinates of the work. A project whose aim is to diagnose the present, analysing the roots of modern mass ideologies and revolutions, and that furthermore is based on the premise that even the dominant forms of thought share the same premises, eventually should substantiate such claims by giving a detailed account of such links – between past and present, and between various contemporary forms of thought. The central problem of the works of Weber and Foucault was that their authors died before they could reach and draw the consequences of their historical work for the present. Voegelin, in contrast, lived and worked for four decades after the insight of 1943. However, not only did a conclusive analysis of modern thought never come to light, but Voegelin hardly published anything that did more than touch upon not just modernity, but even the Middle Ages. There is surely a puzzle to be solved here for anybody arguing about the contemporary significance of his work.

The details of the perpetual postponement of the promise to deliver the analysis of modernity are intriguing. By the summer of 1943, the manuscript of the *History of Political Ideas* was finished basically up to the nineteenth century, and the long part on the Middle Ages would never be touched again after summer

1944. In correspondence with editors, Voegelin repeatedly assured them that the manuscript was ready up to the 'modern' period, and the analysis of the latter would also be finished shortly. However, this never happened. Instead of moving ahead in time, Voegelin again and again returned to Antiquity. Related publications made allusions to the imminent follow-up of the volumes on modernity, promising two such volumes in 1956 and one in 1974. These, however, were never delivered.

Beyond the analysis of modernity, there is the all-but-missing analysis of Christianity. Here again, the problem is caused by Voegelin's own claims. Voegelin repeatedly charged modern thinkers, among others Weber, that they failed to engage in a study of Christianity, 'jumping over' the two thousand years separating classical Greece and the Renaissance. The problem is that Voegelin, after all, ended up by almost repeating the same fault – except that he stayed with Plato and Aristotle. In his writings one repeatedly gains the feeling that, after his insightful and convincing analysis of the Greek thinkers, the moment at which Christianity or modernity came up as themes, Voegelin lost both his confidence and his calmness at the same time.

All this leads back to the crucial year of 1943: what exactly happened at this moment with Voegelin's project? What is the reason that – in a truly Nietzschean fashion – both the assets and the liabilities of the later period of the work can be rooted here?

1943 revisited

What happened to Voegelin when reading and discussing Husserl's essay can be described as a simple and typical case of a 'vision' experience – an intellectual insight that, through a reorganisation of the structure of identities and differences in the very mental framework of an individual, alters the way the world is seen by the person who has undergone the experience. *Before* the experience, Husserl and the proponents of 'murderous mass ideologies' belonged, for Voegelin, to a completely different part of the intellectual landscape. *After* the experience, they shared a common field. Aspects of Voegelin's reading of Husserl, provoking this vision experience, are also of considerable importance. They include the charge that Husserl rejected transcendence; the attempt to 'erase' Christianity, neglecting the period between classical Greece and the Renaissance; and, perhaps most interestingly, taking exception to Husserl's self-characterisation as a functionary of humanity (FPP: 23).[1]

Of course, in spite of these and other similarities, Husserl and the Nazi or Communist ideologists did not say *exactly* the same things. Though the experience redraws the intellectual map of differences and identities, it should have been followed by a careful analysis of the exact links in the new landscape. The problem is that this is precisely what Voegelin failed to do for over forty years. Instead, and very strangely, whenever the theme of modernity came up, he remained, as if petrified, at the level of playing with identities, and moreover, in an emotionally charged and dismissive invective. This requires explanation.

First of all, the problem should be re-stated to render its perplexity even more visible. The Husserl reading experience for Voegelin strangely remained an unhealed wound. This would indicate an absence of reflexivity. However, quite to the contrary, the experience was followed by intensive meditative exercises. This indicates that something has gone wrong in the process of reflexivity, or at the level of the interpretation of the experience.

The first thing to note here is related to this term 'experience'. The 'ultimate' consequence of the experience-insight was the discovery of the conceptualisation of experience as metaxy; and the language of experience and symbolisation was already present in the late 1940s. However, and very significantly, it was not immediately identified and analysed as an experience. Instead, Voegelin interpreted his own experience in two seemingly opposed ways that constitute a tight interpretative framework. On the one hand, the event-experience led him to realise that he needed to develop a *theory* of consciousness; on the other, this was to be done through an analysis of one's *own* consciousness.

The claim about the need for a theory of consciousness as the answer to the experience was very emphatic. It is the title of the theoretical piece of 1943 (AN: 14), and it is repeated in the very first paragraph of the 1977 Introduction to *Anamnesis (ibid.*: 3). Thus, this idea was the basic positive response to the question marks posed by the reading experience. This is important for several respects. First, because this response misidentified the 'field' in which the response was supposed to be thought. Voegelin did not reflect on the experience *as* an experience, but rather directly on the entire 'mental structure' which was altered by the experience, as 'consciousness'. Second, even the modality of the undertaking was flawed. By searching for a 'theory' of consciousness, Voegelin simply fell into the almost stereotypical German error of trying to reduce intellectual endeavour to the development of a general theory, an error attacked relentlessly by Nietzsche, and identified by Voegelin as the Gnostic search for a system.

This problem was to some extent balanced by the way in which Voegelin decided to search for a theory of consciousness, the focus on the concrete consciousness of the individual thinker. To some extent, this compensated for the missing thematisation of 'experience', and kept the undertaking away from abstract theorising. However, it led to serious imbalances of other kinds. The first problem concerns the very idea of such a self-analysis. Voegelin's repeated claims that the structure of individual consciousness holds the key to the study of consciousness is a very strong claim, difficult to accept fully.

The exact link between individual biography and the condition of possibility of understanding is in fact a crucial problem. It was at the centre of Dilthey's work.[2] By focusing on 'experiences' and not 'consciousness', the problem would disappear. But this is not Voegelin's way here, and the content of 'Anamnetic experiments' (*ibid.*: 36–51) does not help to accept the claim. Such a meditative exercise could have been relevant for Voegelin in his own work, but reading the twenty scenes causes more perplexity than understanding. Only the last one is illuminating, but it ends in a gnomic way. The text therefore says too much and too little at the same time.

Perplexities multiply if we add the name of Freud to the picture. Reference to self-analysis through childhood experiences would immediately bring to mind Freud for anyone. Voegelin was growing up and maturing in Vienna at exactly the time and place in which and for which Freud developed his theories. Thus the fact that Voegelin never even alludes to Freud in the context of his 'anamnetic' method is rather perplexing, as Gilbert Weiss has rightly pointed out (Weiss 2000:129, fn.73). This puzzle indeed holds the key to the problem with Voegelin's self-interpretation of 1943.

The first problem concerns the general value of such a self-analysis. Much of the criticism voiced against Freud holds true for anamnetic exercises as well. Such a self-analysis is extremely dangerous, as the search for one's own 'true self' on the one hand produces the very self it is supposed to discover, while on the other it can easily lead to the drying up of creative energies. It seems that the proper target of self-reflexion, following Hadot and Nietzsche, is not the 'self', but the work.

Such general question marks are only rendered more acute by a second problem, relevant to Voegelin's own case: the fact that this self-analysis coincided with a generalised 'self-rejection'. The concrete experience was due to a reading of Husserl, but by implication it included the entire landscape of modern thought. Using the Nietzschean idea that only a nihilist can identify nihilism, the experience should have led to the realisation that Voegelin himself was part of the landscape he was distancing himself from. But the anamnetic exercise turned to exactly the opposite direction: the discovery of the structure of one's own consciousness as the positive ground for a proper theory of consciousness. This meant a fundamental conflict and incompatibility between the meditative turn and the analysis of modernity. The more Voegelin progressed in his meditations, the more it helped him to analyse and understand the Greek classics, especially Plato who had an affinity with such an undertaking; but also the more impossible it became to analyse properly the modern period, as that would have implied a coming-to-terms with the part that he was rejecting from himself.[3]

This leads to the problem of the exact place of the author with respect to a 'diagnostic' work, including the link to his predecessors. The Voegelinian approach emphasises the self-analyses of past and present thinkers. It starts with the idea that the theories of past thinkers were based on the analysis of their own consciousness, and thus self-analysis becomes a privileged access to their thought. The problem is that, in this way, the work is bound to be distracted towards and short-circuited by those thinkers who had affinities with the type of analysis suggested. This is exactly what happened with Voegelin: after 1943, figures like Rousseau, Hegel or Kant all but disappeared from the *History of Political Ideas*, while Bodin, Vico and Schelling gained a special position.

This had two very serious consequences, highly detrimental to the original enterprise of Voegelin, as transgressing two central limits of a diagnostic inquiry. First of all, any philosopher or historian of ideas has a degree of freedom of choice. Such freedom, however, does not apply for a general textbook survey, the work that Voegelin originally started; and it does not apply for a work tracing the history of the present. The central concern of such a work should be the *effective* history of thought, or the real impact exerted by different modes and systems of thought. This was a central concern of Voegelin's work, and his methodological angle, the focus on meditations and transcendence, allowed him to re-pose at the centre of attention the question of the effective impact of spiritual movements.[4] However, it was precisely this angle that remained inconclusive in his later work. Even the exact break-point can be identified here, with remarkable precision: this was the figure of Plato. It was with Plato that his ideas had the greatest affinity; thus, according to the anamnetic methodology, Plato had to take up a central point in his own work. The problem, however, is that Plato's thought had little direct effective impact; to make matters even worse, this impact was strongest on the various 'Gnostic' systems of thought. This implied, on the one hand, that Voegelin could not pose properly the question of the effective impact of Christianity, in other words why and where did Christianity succeed where Plato did not; and, on the other hand, starting from Plato as the measure, it became impossible to diagnose properly those elements of Plato's thought that showed affinity with Gnosticism.

As a consequence, Voegelin's work remained unfinished, and below its promised potential. Nevertheless, even as a fragment, and especially in so far as his analyses of Antiquity are concerned, it stands up to and complements the works of Weber and Foucault.

Metaxy

The most important discussion of metaxy is in Chapter 3 of *The Ecumenic Age*. Both the context and the exact dynamics of the discussion are of utmost importance.

First of all, it is the opening discussion of the first substantive chapter of the book. This may sound difficult to maintain for what is in fact the third chapter of a book; even more so if we add that it is preceded by a long Introduction and two other long chapters which together take up 170 pages. But Chapter One, 'Historiogenesis', sketches the historical background; Chapter Two, 'The Ecumenic Age', sets up the historical context; so it is only on p. 171 that the argument of the book starts. The relevant chapter title and the two section titles also indicate the significance of the discussion; they are, respectively, 'The Process of History', 'The Process of Reality' and 'The Dialogue of Mankind'.

The theme is metaxy, or Voegelin's conceptualisation of experience. It centres on philosophers, on those thinkers who – according to Voegelin – contributed most to the clarification of the meaning of experience, or the development of this tool of analysis, Anaximander and Heraclitus, and especially Plato and Aristotle. But almost as important a role is played by questions of history. The title of the chapter, after all, is 'The Process of History', setting the fundamental context for the analysis of experience; and section two, 'The Dialogue of Mankind', contains four subsections titled by the names of Plato and Aristotle and the two historians, Herodotus and Thucydides. Though the discussion of the philosophers is significant, the point concerning the tight connections between philosophy and history is forcefully made. Though the subject matter of thought is experiences, these experiences are reflected upon by those human beings who lived through the events, and thus the story of events and the symbolisation of experiences are interconnected. This is authoritatively stated in the very first sentence of the chapter: 'The men living in the Ecumenic Age were forced by the events into reflections on the meaning of the course' (OHIV: 171).[5] Reflection on experiences, in certain kinds of time period, is not a free choice but a matter of fate.

The significance of the piece, and the type of links established between philosophy and history, events and experiences, is also reinforced by the basic structure of the argument. The first sentences of both the first section and the first sub-section of the chapter identify an identical concern: 'The issue that appeared to take precedence over all the others was the problem of identity' (*ibid.*). The epochal character of the historical events of the ecumenic age forced reflection upon the level of being, which, for human beings, involves a question of identity, whether at the personal or the collective level. For the latter case, the issue becomes the identification of the collective subject that is undergoing the events, and it is in this context that Voegelin quickly ran through the related ideas of St Augustine, Hegel and Toynbee. These names are highly significant, as they are *the* paradigmatic representatives of reflections on the course and meaning of history, the central concern identified by Voegelin in the first sentence, in three highly significant time periods – Christianity, modernity, and the contemporary era. However, in this short discussion Voegelin emphasised their similarity and not their difference. This is the extent to which each of them came to adhere to the 'historiogenetic pattern' of progressive, 'unilinear' history (*ibid.*: 172–4). It is in opposition to this fatal error that Voegelin introduces the treatment of experience in Greek philosophy, through the first steps in the works of Anaximander and Heraclitus, and then the culmination in Plato and Aristotle at the height of the chapter (*ibid.* 184–91). These seven pages are without any doubt among the most important Voegelin ever wrote.

The remaining pages of the chapter, however, are just as significant in indicating the endemic problems Voegelin encountered in covering developments of thought after Aristotle. After concluding the discussion of metaxy in Aristotle, he first jumps to the twentieth century, reflecting on the omission of Aristotle in contemporary debates on the meaning of history; then he goes on to utter the usual diatribes against Hegel, Comte and Marx; and he finishes the section on Aristotle with a cryptic and unreferenced quote from a letter of Aristotle on his liking of myths in his last years. It is followed by a final, very succinct and sharp concluding statement on modern thought, about arrogance and revolt, and the need for humility. But then, at this point, at the bottom of p. 192 the argument, already disturbed by the emotional outburst against modern thought, instead of picking up the line of development on experience digresses into the – certainly highly important – reflections of Burckhardt on history, only to return to a series of contemporary reflections, not on experience, but on the symbol '*oikoumenē*'.

It is very risky to second-guess the work of great thinkers. Nevertheless, the perplexity caused by the tailing-off of the argument at its height is considerable. The crucial discussion of metaxy is interrupted with Aristotle, implying that after Aristotle there was no thinker who had anything substantial to add to the analysis of experience. There is indeed a decisive moment showing the problems of this chapter, and this is Voegelin's treatment of St Augustine. If there was a Christian thinker whose conceptualisation of experience was fundamental for the later developments of both history and philosophy, it was certainly him. Yet, in this chapter, Augustine is only discussed as the source of a deviation leading up to Hegel and Toynbee. If already Augustine's approach to experience was deemed irrelevant, then one can understand that Voegelin did not waste much time on Dilthey's renewed efforts, after Nietzsche (together with Weber) and before Gadamer. But this does not make it more acceptable.

Anaximander and apeiron

Voegelin traces metaxy back to the famous fragment of Anaximander, in which he wrote ' "The origin (*archê*) of things is the Apeiron...It is necessary for things to perish into that from which they were born; for they pay one another penalty for their injustice according to the ordinance of time" ' (OHIV: 174). This text is considered as the very first word of philosophy, 'this famous *dictum* that we have analysed so many times and on which we shall never finish to meditate' (Patocka 1983: 70). The fragment, furthermore, is concerned precisely with the conceptualisation of origins. One could not even dream of finding a better pedigree; and in his efforts, Voegelin follows closely the footsteps of Plato and Aristotle.

Voegelin's analysis gives a perfect illustration of both the merits and the shortcomings of his approach. It is based on two principles, defining the external and internal correlates of the development of thought: thoughts are engendered by reflections on events experienced, and they progress from the more compact towards the more differentiated symbols. Thus the Ionian beginnings of philosophy are based on a first-hand 'opportunity to experience the violence of the Ecumenic Age' (OHIV: 174); the fragment only 'happens to be the earliest extant pronouncement by a philosopher on the process of reality and its structure'. Furthermore, later advances in thought do not falsify this statement, only giving a more differentiated symbolisation of the experience (*ibid.*: 177–8).

This has two corollaries. The fragment, or rather this novel form of thought of which it is the extant representative, becomes something like a zero point in history, an utterance resembling a revelation that breaks new ground with no links to previous forms of thought. On the other hand, in this quality the statement is practically impossible to analyse; it only states what it states. The statement captures an original experience, and one cannot do much more than use other words to express this same experience.

Voegelin's analysis is therefore very short. According to him, the fragment captures an experience of reality as a cosmic process, focusing on the 'apeiron', the 'limitless', which is not a substance comparable to the water of Thales, but rather the ground out of which things appear and to which they return. Using a fragment of Heraclitus (*ibid*.: 174), it is furthermore identified as the ground which is in between existence and non-existence, life and death, the mortals and the immortals. It is to this idea that the conceptualisation of metaxy as the divine–human in-between situation will later be traced. The short analysis is concluded forcefully: 'Thus far one can go in an analytical elucidation of the texts, but no further; any attempt at paraphrasing their meaning would destroy their compactness' (*ibid*.: 175).

This, however, does not seem acceptable. First of all, it is rather perplexing that Voegelin, whose entire philosophy is based on the centrality of meditation, argues about the fragment that – according to Patocka – is the eternal source of philosophical meditation, that its claim is self-evident, and one can only turn to its elaboration in the thought of Plato and Aristotle. Voegelin, of course, does not say that we cannot meditate on these texts, but that their 'analytical elucidation' is not possible. However, this is simply not the case. With the help of the guides that have already served well in this book, Turner, Dumézil and Girard, the meaning of the fragment can be illuminated in the context of previous forms of thought. This analysis, furthermore, helps to shed crucial light on the value of Greek philosophy.

Turner, Dumézil and Girard on 'liminality'

The first point is etymological, made here by Turner and not Dumézil. The term 'apeiron' is derived from 'peras' (limit), which contains the Indo-European root 'per'. This root, with the meaning of 'going through' or 'passage', is at the origin of a number of terms expressing danger (like peril, fear, perish, German *Gefahr* (danger)), passage (port, French *porte* (door), German *fahren* (travel) – from which comes *Erfahren* (experience)), or testing, proving (experience and experiment) (Turner 1985: 226). Even further, Turner also points out that etymologists trace to this complex three further Greek words, *peira* (experience), *peirao* ('I try'), and *perao* ('I pass through'). This etymology helps Turner to reinforce his vision insight that Dilthey's attempt to conceptualise experience, and his own concept, liminality, developed on the basis of rite of passage, capture the same thing.[6] Thus, though Turner did not refer to the fragment of Anaximander, it certainly would give him much amusement to know that 'liminality' can be identified as the first concept of philosophy.

The previous line of argument receives further support from Dumézil's analysis of the Roman god Janus (Dumézil 1970: 327–33). Etymologically, the word 'Janus' is traced to an Indo-European root meaning 'passage', in the precise sense of a 'ford'. It is still visible in the Gaelic *áth*, present in the name of Dublin (Baile Atha Cliath, or the 'town of the ford of the hurdles').[7] It is also close to the word 'rite' in two different Gaelic languages.

In accordance with his comparative method, Dumézil assessed the specific functions associated with Janus in contrast with three other main figures of the Roman Pantheon, Vesta, Jupiter and Juno. While Vesta (the goddess of both hearth, or family life, and the state as a community, attended by six virgins) is the last (*extrema*) in the offerings and prayers in the Roman ritual order, Janus is always the first (*prima*). The second contrast establishes the significance of this position. The highest Roman god (*summa*) is Jupiter; he is the king and the carrier of sovereignty. Janus, however, came first in the order of being. Here Dumézil moves to the third contrast.

There are two ways of conceiving beginnings in Roman mythology: origin as a birth; and origin as a passage or transition.[8] The first belongs to the realm of Juno, the highest female god in the Pantheon, the consort of Jupiter. Her field of activity, however, is rather limited. Janus is the god of passage, and he rules over a vast field of activities. Spatially, Janus is located at the threshold of houses, at the door, symbolising two beginnings, the entry and the exit. A close colleague of Janus is Portunus,[9] and both are often depicted with keys in their hands. Temporally, Janus rules the beginnings of the year, still preserved in the word 'January', but – shared with Juno, the female god associated with the moon – he also rules the first day of every month, and even the dawn, the first moment of the day, belongs to him.[10] In historical times, Janus was the first king of Latium, of the 'golden age' in which men and gods still lived together; and the name was also used to translate the Greek idea of Chaos, Janus being the oldest god in time. Finally, Janus was also associated with natural beginnings, opening the way for the reception of the seed. He was a great inventor, introducing metal coinage, and was the founder of religion, being the constructor of the first temples and instituting the festival of Saturnalia.

At this point Dumézil revisits the two best-known aspects of the god. Janus is represented as having two faces (thus the expression 'Janus-faced'), as each transition implies two sides, an end and a beginning. Similar two-faced gods also exist in India and Africa, and Dumézil also evokes the Greek representations of the 'double Hermes'. The other well-known fact is that the doors of his temple could only be closed when the city of Rome was not involved in warfare. The interpretation of this fact, however, is perennially controversial, as it is not clear whether the closed doors are supposed to maintain peace, or to contain warfare. At any rate, the meaning of the open doors was always the same.

In conclusion, Dumézil turns to the question of originality. Strangely enough, in his *Metamorphoses* Ovid asserted that Janus is a particularly Roman god, not known even by the Greeks, and even in Latium, except perhaps for the Etruscan Ani, no neighbouring tribes knew about his existence. Dumézil questions this assertion, points to the ancient, Indo-European origins of the god, and mentions as a similar figure the Scandinavian Heimdallr, the watchman of gods, the ancestor of humanity and the founder of social order. Heimdallr was subordinated to Odin, like Janus was to Jupiter, as he was not the first king, only the one who created the royal function and who set up the first king.

Though Dumézil questions the claims about the special originality of Janus, he does not go nearly far enough. After this review we can safely state that Janus was the Roman god of liminality and, as such, is a member of the family of one of the largest and most universal of mythological figures. A comparison of Kerenyi's analysis of Hermes, to be discussed in Chapter 9, would make evident for example the close links with Hermes. Still, this comparison also demonstrates indeed a unique peculiarity of the figure. In opposition to his 'family relatives', Janus is not a trickster. Though the ambivalence of liminality is well captured by the figure, instead of evoking playful tricks or the darker recesses of the human spirit, Janus keeps his sobriety and directs the liminal energies into two sole endeavours: intellectual and military.

Anaximander's fragment is also analysed by Girard (1972), who reaches at once the same and radically different conclusions. In line with the analyses of Vernant (1990 [1965]), he takes this passage as indicating the tight links between early philosophical thought and the mythical way of thinking, and perceives in the injustice lying at the origin of things a trace of the original violence, the expulsion of the scapegoat, lying at the heart of all culture. The lifting of boundaries and limits expressed in Apeiron does not only allude to innocent rituals, marking the change of seasons and the renewal of nature, using only the metaphorical language of life and death and thus violence, but refers to the actual process of undifferentiation and the escalation of the mimetic conflict of violence, resulting in the expulsion and annihilation of the innocent victim. The Girardian reading of liminality as undifferentiation and confusion is also supported by the etymological meaning of confusion (*aporon*) as the loss of limit (*peras*), or the forming power.

Girard, therefore, agrees with Turner and Dumézil that the first statement of philosophy expresses transitionality and liminality, the identity of all beginnings and ends, and thus the eternal recurrence of the same. This eternal recurrence, however, also implies a resignation to the inevitability of the endless circle of violence.

In light of this analysis, it is now possible, *pace* Voegelin, to identify the exact experience expressed in the first philosophical statement. The 'reaction' of the first 'philosophers' to the sudden, and unprecedentedly massive, eruption of violence was a reassertion of the eternal recurrence of the same. In the terminology of Eliade, their reaction to the experiences of 'history' was the same response as that performed by all myths and rituals of the past: an attempt to deny and reject history, to pacify events into the timeless pattern of the eternal recurrence (Eliade 1954 [1949]).[11] The reality of the new events, the novelty and scope of violence, however, could not be denied. The logic was the same as before, but the scope much worse. The 'pacification' and 'enchantment' of the playful world of gods could not longer be maintained; the tragic character of the eternal recurrence of violence became more pronounced.

Put into the proper context, the reading of the fragment thus identifies the two central concerns of Greek thought, disenchantment and rationalisation on the one hand, leading to the rise not only of philosophy, but also of the scientific and legal spirit; and the tragic world view on the other, as expressed in the other key, eternal aspect of Greek culture, tragedy.

Thus, in this way, we have identified the second source of the 'great process of disenchantment', traced back by Weber to Hebrew prophecy, in Greek philosophy. This idea in itself, of course, is not surprising, but rather commonplace wisdom. It is very unfortunate that Weber never got to study the rise of philosophy in Greece, though he alluded to such a need (ES: 451). Applying to Anaximander, one might argue that this was because Weber never managed to escape his origins, out of which his project was born, the *economic* ethic of world *religions*, and the (Marx-inspired) diagnostic concern with the roots of capitalism. But the results of the previous section do not simply re-state the truism that modern reason was born also out of Greek philosophy and not solely Hebrew prophecy, rather they show that rationality and disenchantment had dual sources, traceable to the same experiential setting: to liminal regions situated at the margins of the convulsive events of the emerging Ecumenic Age: the south-western margin of Palestine, a passage towards Egypt; and the north-western margin of Ionia, a passage towards Europe. The two great prophets of the first phase of the axial age, Jeremiah (who had his call between 626 and 587 BC) and Ezekiel (his call was between 597 and 570 BC), and the first two Ionian philosophers, Thales (624–546 BC) and Anaximander (610–546 BC), were exact contemporaries.

Towards Plato and metaxy

From the discovery of Anaximander, Voegelin traces two roads to Plato's metaxy: the road of philosophers, and the road of historians, both advancing the 'field of noetic consciousness' (OHIV: 177). Concerning philosophy, in the next great generation, centring around 500 BC and thus at the 'height' of the axial age, reflections on events and experiences led to the questions of identity and being, the two representative figures being Parmenides and Heraclitus.[12] More attention is devoted to the reflections of the two great historians, Herodotus and Thucydides.[13] For Voegelin, they were first of all historians of the convulsive events of the period, and they saw Greek history as a 'subprocess in the larger process of the Ecumenic Age' (*ibid.*: 178). For Herodotus this led to the discovery of tight links between exodus and conquest, or 'the problem of a concupiscential exodus from reality under the apparently realistic surface of ecumenic conquest' (*ibid.*: 181), a theme Voegelin would discuss in detail in Chapter 4. It is also not difficult to perceive here the Weberian concern of world-rejection. Thucydides was led to much the same insights, recognising the 'daimonic senseless' (*ibid.*: 183) of the endless violence of the ecumenic age. In his texts the 'blackness of [the] extreme despair' (*ibid.*) that would surface in the apocalyptic and Gnostic views of the later 'Ecumenic Age' is already visible.

The discussion of the historians is short but most significant for the logic of Voegelin's argument. Yet it raises two perplexities. The first concerns the novelty of such insights. Once the endless circle of violence is traced to age-old ideas about the eternal recurrence, the question of what exactly is novel in these insights must be posed again. The second is related to the way in which Voegelin subordinates Greek history to the global trends of the ecumenic age. Voegelin's global approach is insightful, as it is opposed to the nationalistic reading of the *Histories* as solely concerned with the internal developments of Greece. However, Voegelin takes the point to excess by treating Greek history as *all but* a sub-process of the ecumenic age, deprived of independent value on its own. Though this is not argued explicitly, it is clearly visible in the way Voegelin fails to refer to Athenian democracy. Here Voegelin's de-mythologisation has clearly gone too far.

Bringing in the problem of democracy also shows how the two slips support each other. The fundamental novelty of the Greek experience, *pace* Nietzsche and Voegelin, was not the discovery of the eternal recurrence, but rather the democratic experiment. Ionian thought, formulated at the 'limen' of the ecumenic age, contained crucial insights, but could not move beyond the 'limit' between myth and philosophy. This only happened in Athens and in the aftermath of the experience of democracy. It was in the context of the Athenian experiment that nascent philosophical thought was struggling to escape the logic of the eternal recurrence.

Plato and metaxy

Voegelin derives the concept of metaxy in Plato from two passages in *Philebus* (16c–17a and 30c–e) and one in *Symposium* (202a–203a). The context in both cases is similar, being related to pleasure and love.

Philebus

Voegelin considers the two passages in *Philebus* as an interpretation and further differentiation of the compact insight of Anaximander, a kind of 'revised edition of the Anaximandrian dictum' (OHIV: 185). Socrates introduces his point by making three comments: that this insight is a very old tradition; that it was a 'gift of the gods'; and that it was brought down by Prometheus, 'together with a fire exceeding bright' (*ibid.*: 184). Voegelin ignores the issue of old age, while he identifies the new Prometheus with Plato (*ibid.*: 187). However, given the emphatic antiquity of the statement, the associations of Prometheus with sacrifice should not be forgotten; all the more so as the Greek word for sacrifice is derived from that for burnt offering. The central question, therefore, is the extent to which the Platonic reinterpretation of the statement escapes the logic of the eternal recurrence.

Plato thematises the Anaximandrian circle between the origin and the end of things in the apeiron through the use of two conceptual pairs, the one–many and the limited–unlimited. Things that exist 'spring from One and Many', which themselves have 'inherent in them Limited and Unlimited' (*Philebus*, 16d). The first pair is one of the standard tools of Platonic thought, while the second pair makes the etymology of apeiron, the link between the limit and the unlimited, explicit. Between these two pairs Plato sketches a series of complex movements, reaching the infinite from the one through the many, by use of the forming powers of the limit, and also in the opposite direction. The more important of the four terms are 'one' and 'unlimited', the two opposite poles. This allows Plato to make two central points. First, through the identification of these end poles Plato isolates the concept of in-between, or metaxy, interpreted by Voegelin as the tension between them. Second, it is immediately used as a diagnostic device, to separate serious thought (dialectics) from mere speculation (eristics). The latter makes the connections in a haphazard way, reducing the space between the one and the infinite, and eventually eliminating the in-between, or the metaxy.

Through this symbolisation, according to Voegelin, 'Plato recognizes the philosopher's role in history as that of the man who is open to reality and willing to let the gift of the gods illuminate his existence' (OHIV: 184), while the discovery of the in-between represents the 'truth of man's existence' (*ibid.*: 185). Central is the additional level of reflexivity gained by Plato. While the Anaximandrian statement only 'expressed a philosopher's experience of the reality' (*ibid.*), the Platonic reading incorporated the noetic consciousness of the philosopher, and identified the metaxy as its tensional centre.

However, this analysis can be rendered more precise if we recognise the ancient component in the Anaximandrian statement, and return to a more detailed analysis of the Platonic interpretation, using again the tools developed by Turner and Girard. First of all, it can be shown that the reference to the archaic nature of the tradition on which Anaximander drew was not merely a rhetorical device. Plato rather provided in *Philebus* (16c–17a) a perfect mapping of liminality and the sacrificial mechanism. All things that ever existed, all the artefacts of human culture, have as their source the opposition between the one and the many, the situation in which society is split into this singular constellation opposing one with all the rest; and it is this constellation that carries in itself the 'limit' and the 'unlimited', in the sense of responding to the liminality of the situation of undifferentiation by the setting up, through a specific kind of 'limiting', the exclusion of the scapegoat, a new ordering principle, a new form or structure.

Thus, the Platonic differentiation has only rendered the archaic substance of Anaximander even more visible. But it was exactly the archaic character of this statement that rendered it novel in its effects. It was a wake-up call, an invitation from the contemporaries to look at their world just as it had lost its relatively pacified and civilised face and returned to a cycle of violence that it had thought to have escaped; and precisely this 'wake-up' character would become even more visible in the similar re-statements of the eternal recurrence by Heraclitus. And it is here that both the novelty and the self-conscious, self-reflexive character of the new form of thought becomes visible; or becomes conscious of itself.

Symposium

After differentiating the structure of the apeiron, accomplished in *Philebus*, Plato captures in *Symposium* the exact movement that this happens in the metaxy, or the 'symbolisation of the erotic tension in man's existence as an In-Between reality' (OHIV: 185). The key words are 'tension' and 'erotic'. 'Tension' is a word not used by classical thinkers, where 'Eros' stands for the concrete symbolisation of this moving force. The text emphasises that Eros is only one of the various 'spiritual forces', but its centrality is emphasised, both by Plato and by Voegelin, in using this spiritual force to capture the movement of the soul that takes place in the metaxy. In these passages the 'In-Between' is still characterised as being in between knowledge and ignorance, but the emphasis definitely shifts on the identification of the two poles as the human and the divine. The 'spiritual man' (*daimonion aner*) is somebody who is 'in between' the merely human and the divine; who mediates between the two poles; or who possesses the spiritual forces that enable communication between the two spheres.

The capturing of the nature of this 'in-between' situation of spiritual forces is fraught with difficulties. Voegelin emphasises this through the roundabout way in which this information is conveyed. Plato's weariness to reduce true knowledge to the simple notion of verifying propositions is characteristic of his entire work, preferring to transmit his own insights through the figure of Socrates. But in this piece, and this piece only, and exactly at this crucial juncture, recognised since millennia as one of the most importance pieces of Plato, mediation has gone to extremes. The story of Eros was told to Socrates by Diotima, who re-told it at the Banquet, where Aristodemus was present, who told it to Apollodorus, who was now telling it to his friends (*ibid.*: 186). According to Voegelin, all this inter-mediacy serves a definite purpose. It indicates that the truth that is gained in the metaxy is not information received about facts, but rather it has the character of 'an insight arising from the dialogue of the soul', which is 'the exegesis of the erotic tension experienced'. This erotic tension is not a pre-existing object that is simply there to be discovered: '[t]he subject–object dichotomy, which is modelled after the cognitive relation between man and things in the external world, does not apply to the event of an "experience-articulating-itself"' (*ibid.*). The in-between reality is to be experienced; but this experience is not 'subjective', but rather formative: it alters the mode of being of those who enter the liminal state. These entities are therefore not simply 'subjects' but 'spiritual beings', in the sense of being able to undergo the transformation of their mode of being. We can see that this Voegelinian conceptualisation of experience is profoundly compatible with both the Turnerian concept of liminality and the Foucauldian attempt to treat spirituality as the formation and transformation of one's mode of being.

Thus, after further clarifying the exact meaning of apeiron in *Philebus*, Plato identified in *Symposium* a fundamental dimension of the 'unlimited', or the 'liminal', alongside the violent origin and end of things, and also the spiritual tension of love. The realm of the divine depth is not only the merciless turning of the spinning wheel of history, but also an opening in which humans can receive divine gifts, and in which their existence can suddenly be illuminated by an experience of participation and order. Two questions, however, still remain to be solved. The first concerns the exact link between this new interpretation of the unlimited as metaxy, and of the apeiron as the violent and unjust origin and end of all things. The other is the identification of the exact condition of possibility of this insight.

Let us start with the latter. The emphasis of Voegelin is on the self-consciousness of the philosopher, and he sees a direct line from Anaximander through Heraclitus to Socrates, Plato and Aristotle. But the identification is too quick, and the link between self-consciousness and Eros remains unexplored. The first is due to the absolutisation of the Ionian starting point, already analysed in detail. The second overlooks the exact nature of the shift of the centre of philosophy from the 'periphery' (Ionia and Sicily) to the 'centre' (Athens), and requires some further clarification. It is by no means trivial that the discovery of self-consciousness leads to a thematisation of the erotic tension. Quite on the contrary, it can lead to disillusionment, alienation and cynicism. The question concerns the exact carriers of self-consciousness – and it is here that the fundamental difference between the Ionians and the Athenians lay. The basic Ionian experience was the threat of violence and chaos, without being able to rely on a strong sense of participation, togetherness and community. As a consequence, most of the ancient philosophers turned out to be homeless, wandering teachers, going from town to town. They were the Sophists, the Cynics and the Stoics, whose ideas indeed expressed more a sense of alienation than an erotic tension with reality. The difference of the Athenians was not due to a more sophisticated analysis of their own consciousness, but rather to their closeness to the heroic Athenian experience, the successful resistance to the Persians and the resulting, reverberating experience of democracy. Democracy was based on *philia*; and though Athenian philosophy emerged out of the collapse and not with the rise of democracy, in their thought Socrates, Plato and Aristotle managed to transfer and spiritualise this experience and memory of democracy and *philia* into their formulation of the erotic tension. Voegelin's rediscovery of this phenomenon is indeed an event in thought, and the neglect of his ideas is largely due to the fact that our own age finds many more common points with the experiences of the Stoics, but especially with the Sophists and the Cynics. The problem with Voegelin is his strange overlooking of the democratic experience as being central to Athenian philosophy – a point where his ideas can be complemented by the related work of Foucault.

Concerning the second point, the link between the old and new interpretations of apeiron, it is necessary to go back to the text in some more detail, by looking especially closely at passages that Voegelin omitted, and terms where he did not indicate the original words. The first point concerns the exact characterisation of the human–divine metaxy. Love is introduced as a 'great spirit' by Diotima (202e), and Diotima gives a comprehensive answer to the question of Socrates to identify the exact power possessed by this spirit. This still reproduces the logic of the ancient ideas concerning the sacred. The mediation is first of all described by the word *hermeneuon*, alluding to the figure of Hermes, the great messenger, the trickster-figure conversing between humans and gods, a fellow of Prometheus in more ways than one.[14] The substance of this mediation is sacrifices coming from below, and ordinances (not gifts) coming from above. And the specific nature of spiritual power is described as the knowledge of sacrificial rituals and incantations, sooth-saying and sorcery (the term used is *goéteia*, meaning witchcraft and sorcery, but also suggesting juggling, cheating and charming through spells, an inventory of the Hermesian trickster characteristics). Diotima concludes this description of spiritual power by saying that '[m]any and multifarious are these spirits, and one of them is Love' (*ibid.*: 203a).

At this stage, the dialogue turns to identify the specific nature of this type of spiritual power, *Eros*, gaining dominance in the thought of Plato. The discussion progresses through a 'genealogy' of *Eros*, the identification of its parents and the exact conditions under which it was conceived (*ibid.*: 203b–c). The parents of Love are identified as *poros* and *penia*. Now, *Penia* is indeed 'poverty', or lack, but *Poros* is not simply 'riches' (OHIV.: 185), and even more than 'resource'. In this word we can again capture the root 'per'. The original meaning of *Poros*, closely related to both *peira* and *perao*, analysed by Turner (see Turner 1985: 226), is 'passage-way', especially where a river can be crossed, or a 'ford'. The word is therefore identical with the etymological root of 'Janus'. Love is the child of the successful completion of the passage; is conceived of liminality, in the sense of the successful 'passing through', the finding of the solution (through skilful art and wisdom, as *Poros* is identified as the son of *Metis*, or wisdom, skill, craft, counsel). Furthermore, it is also conceived *in* liminality, but of a different kind: the old liminality of trickstery. After the banquet held to celebrate the birth of Aphrodite, *Penia* managed to conceive a child from *Poros* when he was asleep and drunk, and this child is *Eros*. The scene is extremely dense with meaning. It starts with another self-referential allusion, to (another) banquet. *Penia* is characterised as 'resourceless' (*aporos*; a word that recalls at the same time the *apeiron*, the unlimited depth, but also the *aporia*, or the puzzle and the question mark of Platonic philosophy), thus the exact opposite of *Poros*; but at the same time possessing an important 'resource' or 'device', which is playful creativity. The word used is *paidiou*, referring both to culture and to play.

The consequence of being born from liminality as successful passing through (performance), and liminality as a lack and absence combined with playful trickery, is that the child, *Eros*, is an embodiment of liminality itself (Siotima: 203d–e). She embodies both key aspects of the metaxy identified by Plato, being neither mortal nor immortal, thus in between man and god; and being 'midway betwixt wisdom and ignorance'. In the same day she is flourishing and alive at one hour, dying at another, but reviving again 'by force of his father's nature'. She is poor, even homeless (*aoikos*), thus embodying another of the most extreme characteristics of the liminal; but at the same time searching for the beautiful and the good, and possessing a number of crucial and interesting characteristics, being brave, a good hunter, always thinking strategically and possessing wisdom (*phronesis*). The list of characteristics ends with four traits (one general and three particular) that, in this combination, and in light of the previous discussion, are particularly striking. She is a philosopher, and for his whole life; but she is also a *goés* (a trickster); a *pharmakos* (not just performing witchcraft but also a potential scapegoat); and a Sophist.

Thus, Love, for Plato, is not just one of the spirits that reside in the metaxy, or in liminality, but is the very embodiment of liminality. *Eros* takes upon herself all the characteristics of the liminal, not only the new tension of the philosopher, but also the old concepts of apeiron and sacrifice. The characterisation therefore is profoundly ambivalent, as the extent to which the various aspects of Love gain dominance remains unclear in the Socratic formulation. In fact, as the end of the description makes it clear, *Eros* is just a 'new and improved' version of the apeiron; an uncontrollable force of change, moving from upside down, from plenty to nothingness. The way in which Voegelin completes the chapter, by referring to a famous fragment by Heraclitus on the burning fire (OHIV: 187), gives much support to this argument. Apart from the question of the large-scale social effect of Platonic philosophy, it seems that the conceptualisation of *Eros* as the embodiment of liminality also leaves things to be resolved.

Perhaps the two points are fundamentally intertwined. Can Platonic *Eros* offer any way out of the concupiscential conquest and the exodus from reality, characteristics of the Ecumenic Age, if it is only a 'new and improved' version of the underlying moving force of the eternal recurrence of the same?

Aristotle on metaxy

Plato developed the term 'metaxy' by elaborating on the Anaximandrian dictum in three directions. The first was spiritualisation, in the sense both of reading the 'unlimited' as the space of the man–god encounter and of identifying the 'spirits' as the 'agents' of this interaction. This 'spiritualisation' was also a pacification of the violence of the return of the eternal recurrence, especially given the role attributed among these 'spirits' to Love. The second dimension was reflexivity and self-consciousness; while the third was the importance attributed to knowledge. Both were developed by reflecting upon the path-breaking works of the Ionian physiologists. Aristotle developed further the ideas of Plato along all three dimensions, while integrating them in an even tighter interpretive framework.

Aristotle starts by reinterpreting the apeiron. From the origin of all things it is transformed into a beginning (*ibid.*: 189). This is because, though the apeiron still remains identified with the Divine, it is 'no longer the unquestioned presence of the Divine in the compact experience of the process', but rather it must be 'argumentatively deduced', advancing the later need for proofs for the existence of god. This leads to a duplication of the apeiron: the 'first' apeiron is reduced to formless inertia, or matter, needing a 'second' principle of origin, the divine intelligence (*nous*) that acts formatively on the first.

This change is mirrored by a similar reconceptualisation of the human side. The existential and experiential anxiety caused by traumatic violence is transformed into the experience of 'an existential unrest to escape from ignorance' (*ibid.*: 190), into an urge to ask questions in a state of doubt. Aristotle is struggling here to put into words the same problem that, according to Foucault, troubled both Socrates and Plato, but also the later Stoics of the Roman Empire: how to awaken in human beings the recognition of their ignorance? The solution of Aristotle is to 'characterise this unrest through the…terms *diaporein* or *aporein* which signify the asking of questions in a state of confusion of doubt. "A man in confusion (*aporon*) or wonder (*thaumazon*) is conscious of being ignorant (*agnoein*)" ' (*ibid.*). The human side of the divine aporein is thus *aporon*. The near identity of the words, with the root signifying 'passage' and 'limit', could not be more evident.

On the human side, this state of anxiety and confusion leads to a 'desire to know', or a 'restless search (*zetesis*) for the ground of being' (*ibid.*). In the next step, through the desire for knowing and the object of knowledge, Voegelin elaborates the inherent affinity between the divine aporein and the human aporon, as not merely a search of the human subject for knowledge-objects, but as mutual attraction. 'The search from the human side, it appears, presupposed the movement from the divine side' (*ibid.*), in the sense of a pull or attraction. This mutual involvement is further elaborated through the concept of participation (*metalepsis*).

This meditation on Anaximander by Aristotle, according to Voegelin, concludes in the recognition of the fundamental affinity between the human and divine *nous*, much like the Platonic idea of the soul as being the divine element, and the further claim that the area of reality in which this encounter and dialogue takes place is the noetic consciousness (*ibid.*: 189–90). This allows Aristotle to discover the 'relation of equivalence between symbolic forms' (*ibid.*: 188), implying that not only the different philosophical schools, but even the 'mythopoets' like Homer or Hesiod 'express the same reality' of the search for the divine ground, only 'in various modes of compactness and differentiation' (*ibid.*: 191).

Thus, though not using the word 'metaxy', Aristotle further developed the reflections of Plato on the Anaximandrian *apeiron*, and gave a systematised and unified reading, but at a considerable price. In his account the two main in-between situations (man–god and ignorance–wisdom) became the same, the desire for knowledge was identified as the main spiritual moving force of human beings, and knowledge became a goal in itself. In this way the reality of the divine–human interaction was reasserted, but as only taking place in consciousness and subordinated to the search for knowledge. In this way the conflict between the old and new understandings of spirituality, and the conflict between various kind of 'spiritual' powers, was simply ignored, as the relationship between existential experiences and the external reality, not reducible to a question of knowledge, was similarly omitted from the perspective. As the search for knowledge became a goal in itself, at once the sole significant field of spirituality and a proof of its existence, the question of the direct effect of various spiritual forces of reality was not addressed.

Athenian philosophy grew out of reflections on the polis and the fate of democracy. By the time of Aristotle, however, democracy was definitely lost. It is of more than symbolic relevance that the first real founder of an ecumenic empire, Alexander the Great, was educated by none other than Aristotle. In a world where the possibility of a political life organised on the basis of *philia* was lost, the inside of consciousness and the search for knowledge became the only possible experiential bases of spirituality. This, however, implied that *outside* the consciousness of the ruler, there was no possibility of having an effect.

5 *Israel and Revelation*

Introduction

The problem to which Voegelin tries to give an answer in the first volume of *Order and History* is simple, and is identified at the start of the substantial discussion of the history of order in Israel, after the introductory chapters (OHI: 116–21). Furthermore, this is a problem that goes beyond the volume, and has a fundamental relevance to Voegelin's entire project.

The concrete problem is the intriguing contrast between 'pragmatic' and 'spiritual' history that can be gained by comparing tables about the internal history of Israel, as preserved by the Bible, and various attempts by archaeologists and historians to reconstruct the history of the region of Syria/Palestine, or in general the Middle East. In pragmatic histories, the Hebrews are all but absent, and the assignment of a place to Moses in such historical narratives is still problematic. In this light the most impressive twentieth-century effort for a panoramic overview of world history, the work of Arnold Toynbee assigns a marginal place for ancient Judaism at the periphery of the 'Syriac civilisation'. According to Voegelin, however, such a view is unacceptable, as 'Jews and Christians have a disconcerting habit of outlasting the rise and fall of political powers', so 'we cannot eliminate Judaeo-Christian spiritual history without making nonsense of history in general' (*ibid.*: 121). The Weberian inspiration is clearly visible here. The point is not simply that, in the history of ideas, once one reaches beyond a certain historical point, purely 'theoretical' ideas cannot be separated from 'religious' or 'theological' thought; it is rather that such formulations, as symbolisations of crucial experiences, exert a profound and lasting effect on the course of history.

In order to identify the difference this impact made, however, one must start by sketching the context. In *Israel and Revelation*, Voegelin does so with the term 'cosmological empires'. However, it is precisely here that some of the central discoveries of the later work would lie. Central to this is the concept of 'historiogenesis', in which Voegelin captured the specific 'world-image' characteristic of the empires, conflict with which resulted in the Exodus. The most wide-ranging reorganisation of the project, however, happened between the publication of Volumes One and Two, due to a major reading experience: the recognition of the significance of the 'axis time' or the 'axial age' – emphasis being on *re*cognition, as the work was already discussed earlier (NSP: 60, 79).

The axial age

Though Weber and Foucault both followed Nietzsche in the sudden backward reorientation of the time horizon of their work, none of them managed to reflect on this fact and come up with a proper reason. Whatever other reasons may have played a role, they simply had no time. This was accomplished by Karl Jaspers and the concept of 'axis time' (Jaspers 1953 [1949]).

Both the person and the time period are of particular significance. Jaspers was *the* closest personal disciple of Max Weber, the one most faithful to his spirit;[1] and the book was written shortly after World War Two.[2] Furthermore, Jaspers was particularly prepared for reflecting at that moment on the broader context and significance of the events, as he had a long-standing concern with 'crisis' experiences and situations. He started his 1931 book on 'The Spiritual Situation of the Times' with the following formulation: 'For more than a century, the problem concerning the situation of mankind has been growing ever more urgent' (1951 [1931]: 9).[3] The term 'situation' was used as a technical term, and would be taken up as such later by Gadamer (1975 [1959]). It has to do with a sense of crisis, but also with a reflection on this perception, resulting in an 'epochal consciousness'. In 'The Spiritual Situation of the Times' Jaspers traced the emergence of this 'epochal consciousness' to Kierkegaard, who 'was the first to undertake a comprehensive critique of his time' (Jaspers 1951 [1931]: 17), and to Nietzsche, who diagnosed the advent of European nihilism. Just after World War Two, when he was intensively preoccupied with the significance of the events posed in the form of the problem of 'German guilt', and involved in vicious controversies concerning the appropriate attitudes under Nazi times, he gained the 'vision' of the unity of the 'axis time' in history, and its parallels with the contemporary situation.

The axial age thesis rests on the recognition that, within a relatively short time span in between 800 and 200 BC, more specifically focusing around the year 500, there occurred a series of parallel spiritual outbursts that fundamentally altered the cultural shape of the planet and the course of world history. 'The most extraordinary events are concentrated in this period' (Jaspers 1953 [1949]: 2), with Lao-tse and Confucius in China, the Buddha and Jainism in India, the great ethical prophets (Amos, Hosea, Isaiah, Jeremiah, Ezekiel and Deutero Isaiah) in Israel, and the rise of philosophy in Greece. As a particularly striking illustration, the Buddha (c.560–483), Confucius (551–479), and Heraclitus (c.550–480) were born and died within a very few years of one another.

From the very first pages of his book, Jaspers is quick to emphasise three crucial characteristics of his thesis. First of all, the thesis is empirical. It is not a speculative construction, a competitor to Hegel's philosophy of history, but simply highlights the fact that practically all major forms of spirituality and thought, religious or philosophical, with a contemporary significance in our world can be traced back directly to this relatively short time period. Second, Jaspers calls attention to the universal significance and scope of the thesis. He is especially keen to point out that it overcomes the limitations of the classical Western philosophies of history that started – following Hegel – with the uniqueness of Christianity. Finally, the recognition of the unity and significance of the period puts on a stable, at once empirical and universal, basis the 'spiritual' history of mankind, as opposed to the view that an empirically-based universal history can only be written on the basis of a 'materialistic', economic or technological explanations.[4]

Jaspers offers fundamental insights into the period, including striking formulations. 'What is new about this age, in all three areas of the world [that is, India, China and the West], is that man becomes conscious of Being as a whole, of himself and his limitations. He experiences the terror of the world and his own powerlessness. He asks radical questions. Face to face with the void he strives for liberation and redemption. By consciously recognising the limits he sets himself the highest goals. He experiences absoluteness in the depths of selfhood and in the lucidity of transcendence' (*ibid.*). The result was the emergence of personality as we know it: '[h]uman beings dared to rely on themselves as individuals' (*ibid.*: 3). This was accompanied by a new wakefulness, consciousness and reflexivity: '[t]his movement reaches consciousness. Human existence becomes the object of meditation, as *history*. Men feel and know that something extraordinary is beginning in their own present' (*ibid.*: 5). Thus, it was not simply the occurrence of spiritual outbursts but the 'quality of reflection which transformed mankind' (*ibid.*: 52).

These developments opened up unforeseen possibilities, especially the promise of freedom (*ibid.*: 152–71). But they also increased, beyond the limits of tolerability, the tensions of existence. The figuration of key words in the previous passages immediately evokes, and on a grandiose scale, the Turnerian concept of liminality. Indeed, the language of Jaspers is unequivocal, not just combining Kierkegaard and Nietzsche but also as if anticipating Turner: 'As a result of this process [that is, the beginnings of the world religions], hitherto unconsciously accepted ideas, customs and traditions were subjected to examination, questioned and liquidated. Everything was swept into the vortex' (*ibid.*: 2). Through the discovery of personality, reason and the individual, '[t]he whole of humanity took a forward leap' (*ibid.*: 4). The 'axis time' is 'a ferment that draws humanity into the single context of world history' (*ibid.*: 51).

The situation is unmistakably liminal; but with the axial age, we have to do with massive, global, almost planetary liminality. According to Jaspers, the period of spiritual outbursts was also a period of unrest, even of 'spiritual chaos' (*ibid.*: 2). The sense of chaos and collapse was not restricted to the realm of spirituality and thought, but was extended to every single aspect of human existence. At the very moment of spiritual awakening, participants were 'conscious of belonging to a late or even a decadent age'. As a result they saw themselves 'faced by *catastrophe* and [felt] the *desire to help* through insight, education and reform' (*ibid.*: 5).

The emphasis put on practical urgency makes it evident that, in spite of putting the emphasis on spiritual outbursts, Jaspers did not fail to extend his scope to political or sociological factors. In sociological terms, he points out the analogous conditions of three main regions, implying India, China and the West (*ibid.*: 4–5). The political aspects received an even more detailed treatment, as the immediate answers to the 'situation' lay there. 'The *conclusion* is at first of a political character. Mighty empires, made great by conquest, arose almost simultaneously in China (Tsin Shi hwang-ti), in India (Maurya dynasty) and in the West (the Hellenistic empires and the *Imperium Romanum*). Everywhere the first outcome of the collapse was an order of technological and organisational planning' (*ibid.*: 5). He even suggests a 'sociological parallel' between the respective failures of Plato and Confucius at the courts, and of their schools (*ibid.*). And still, at another level, the success of the great prophets and philosophers proved to be more lasting, as they provided 'the *questions* and the *standards*' to apply to what happened both before and after them (*ibid.*: 8; my emphasis).

This passage also helps to bring out with particular clarity the central perspective of this captivating historical panorama. Jaspers was not interested in a philosophy of history, but in a history of the present. Though admitting that the axial period ended in a failure, he concluded the crucial first chapter with the following words: 'Only this much seems certain to me: Our present-day historical consciousness, as well as our consciousness of our present situation, is determined, down to consequences I have only been able to hint at, by the conception of the Axial Period irrespective of whether this thesis is accepted or rejected. It is a question of the manner in which the unity of mankind becomes a concrete reality for us' (*ibid.*: 21).

In spite of all its groundbreaking significance, *The Origin and Goal of History* is not a good book. The problems start with the overdrawn title that evokes the worst Hegelianism and only served to turn away from the book those people who could have had an interest in its content. Jaspers was also not able to express his insights concisely and in clear analytic terms, and the style and language of the book is often irritatingly obsolete. The thinkers who nevertheless took up the thesis had to differentiate and systematise his insights before they could be further developed.

A simple and unambiguous explanation of the axial age seems to be beyond the reach of the human intellect. There is no way one could 'explain' why it happened that the birth and death dates of the wisest persons who ever lived in China, India and Greece were practically identical. Under the omnipresent impact of a linear view of history, the first persons who recognised the parallel spiritual outbursts came up with an explanation along the lines of diffusion theory. This, however, soon proved to be untenable. As a consequence, today even the attempt to come up with an explanation has been all but given up. Still, several thinkers produced insights that offer at least some degree of rationalisation for the events.

This required, first of all, a tightening of the time horizon. Jaspers designated the period between 800 and 200 BC as the 'axis time', spreading the events across six centuries and rendering any coherent account impossible. His followers focused attention on the sixth and fifth centuries BC (Mumford 1956: 59; OHIV: 310), and introduced concepts like 'secondary breakthroughs' (Eisenstadt 1986), in order to trace subsequent developments. This enabled them to better characterise the period of spiritual outbursts. Thus, according to Mumford, '[t]he axial religions often took form during a period of social disintegration, when the normal satisfactions and the normal securities of civilized life no longer seemed possible', or, using an expression of Arnold Toynbee, in 'times of troubles' (Mumford 1956: 65). Eisenstadt also connected the axial age to 'specific processes of social change', especially the 'disintegration' of previously existing territorial units (Eisenstadt 1986: 19). Similar formulations by Voegelin are even more frequent and precise. Spiritual outbursts can only be rendered intelligible by taking into account that they responded to a 'disturbance of social order' (OHIV: 328), which came about because 'the spirit of the early order had disintegrated' (*ibid.*: 299), resulting in a general state of confusion or doubt (*ibid.*: 190).

Given that *Order and History* was about the historicity of experiences of order and disorder, Voegelin's interest in the 'axis time' is not surprising. The manner in which this happened, in the context of the oeuvre, however, is worthy of more detailed attention.

The axial age in Voegelin's work

The term 'axis time' is discussed in three significant places in Voegelin's work: in the Introduction to *The World of the Polis*; in the major unpublished essay 'What Is History', intended as the Introduction to the planned fourth volume of *Order and History*; and the published Introduction and the last chapter of *The Ecumenic Age*.

The first time Voegelin discussed the term indicates both its significance and its paradoxical place. The discussion takes up four of the last five pages of the Introduction to *The World of the Polis*, and can thus safely be taken as a conceptual device central to the work. Its place at the start of Volume Two and not Volume One is therefore slightly puzzling. This is all the more so as the original plan was to publish the three volumes in quick succession, and much of the discussion in Volume One is relevant to the axis time (or the 'axial age', as the epoch is called in recent discussions).

Voegelin's explanation for the seventeen-year delay between Volumes Three and Four is also relevant here. He argued that the original plan for *Order and History* was still too much imprisoned in the image of a linear view of history, and it was only in the early 1960s, through the development of the symbol 'historiogenesis', that he managed to overcome this problem (OHIV: 2). However, in the Introduction to Volume Two, parallelism, as opposed to the linear reading of history, was already emphasised.

The problem can be solved by the hypothesis that Voegelin recognised the significance of the thesis only after the publication of Volume One. The result was that after the publication of the first three volumes, instead of proceeding with the writing of the remaining three volumes, and driven by the need to understand the 'nature' of parallel spiritual outbursts, he started a major series of reflections of the conceptual scheme of his work. This led to the discovery of the symbols 'historiogenesis' and 'metaxy', and eventually to the publication of Volume Four more as a revisitation than a follow-up to the previously published material.[5]

This hypothesis can be supported by a careful reading of the three discussions of axiality, which also help to appreciate the significance of the Voegelinian advance in the understanding of the axial age.

In The World of the Polis

Though the work of Jaspers is not introduced until page 19, the entire Introduction is devoted to the problem of parallel spiritual outbursts.[6] The central issue, for Voegelin, is the appearance of a universalistic conception of mankind. In this, the central place is attributed to Christianity, at the level of both historical events (the letters of Paul) and the philosophy of history (Augustine's *City of God*). The Augustinian vision of the singular event of Christ and the ensuing linear vision of history was held to be valid up to Bossuet. The recognition of the existence of parallel histories, however, undermined the validity of this view, leading to three major revisions, signalled by the works of Voltaire, Hegel and Jaspers.

This setting marks both the significance and the modality of the 'Jaspers reading experience'. The axial age fits into the central line of reflection on the course of history, as identified already in the *History of Political Ideas*. The interpretation, however, is different. The shift from Bossuet to Voltaire is no longer read as an 'apostasy', but rather as a revision due to shortcomings.

Jaspers tried to address the problem of the uniqueness of Christianity. While Hegel still accepted the birth of Jesus as the turning point in history, Jaspers argued that such an idea was not acceptable for other civilisations, so there was a need to search for a different 'axis point' in history.

The discussion of the consequences and effects can be summarised in three points. Voegelin gives short shrift to the criticism voiced by Toynbee. Toynbee wanted to extend the axis time from the tenth century BC to the thirteenth century AD, and questioned the significance of the clustering around 500 BC, but in this way the specificity of an epochal change would have been lost. The second point concerns the main advances and the limits of the idea. The central asset, according to Voegelin, is that the recognition of parallel leaps helps to overcome the 'eurocentric, unilinear constructions' of history (OHII: 21). The main limitation, however, is not only a certain arbitrariness in inclusion and exclusion,[7] but the relativism and resignation implied in the Jaspersian perspective. In an almost Nietzschean language Voegelin reasserts an order of rank: the respect for the search for order in different societies 'must not degenerate into a tolerance which disregards the differences of rank, both in the search of truth and the achievement of insights' (*ibid.*: 23). At the philosophical level, Voegelin reasserts the position of Western standards.

The last paragraph of the Introduction goes a step further. For Clement of Alexandria, Hebrew prophecy and Greek philosophy were the resources to draw on; as '[t]he origin and historical structure of Western order were better understood by the men who created the form than by their late successors who live in it without remembering the conditions of tenancy' (*ibid.*: 24).

In 'What Is History'

Compared to this reading, the unfinished essay 'What Is History?' contains a number of major differences (Voegelin 1990). The piece is situated between Voegelin's two great conceptual discoveries of the early 1960s: 'historiogenesis' and 'metaxy'. Moreover, it is a major operator in the process. It documents the shifts in thought, up to the point of the discovery of 'metaxy'.[8] The essay starts by introducing the term 'historiogenesis', and concludes with the idea of 'eternal being in time', the eventual title of the meditation in which metaxy will first appear (AN: 116–40).

The discussion of axis time takes up a significant part of the concluding part (Voegelin 1990: 39–47). It starts by summarising the position Voegelin had reached just before the discovery of metaxy. First of all, Voegelin defines his way of posing the problem in almost Nietzschean–Weberian genealogical terms: the two central variables of the work were the 'context in which an experience of transcendence occurs' (or the 'conditions of emergence'), and the 'degree of actualization achieved by the experience' (or the 'lasting effects') (*ibid.*: 33). Concerning the former, Voegelin puts the emphasis on the 'unexpected' result that the 'context in which the experience of transcendence was supposed to appear turned out to be not a rigid set of institutions, customs, and beliefs but a medium that could be softened by unsettling disturbances to the point of receptivity', later characterised as a 'ferment in the setting previous to the outburst' (*ibid.*). This is as close to describing liminality as possible without naming it. The lasting effect, on the other hand, is identified as the conditions of possibility of further such experiences, or the making of the expressive symbolism 'part of the setting, thereby increasing its receptivity for future and more articulate experiences' (*ibid.*). The analysis leads to the introduction of the concept 'configurations of history'.[9]

This discussion also takes up an in-between place with respect to the two published discussions of axis time and, in a certain way, the most interesting part is what is missing from it: either not yet, or not fully discussed. Gone are the references to Christianity, and not yet present is the three-fold symbolisation of the axial age as a period not only of spiritual outbursts, but also of imperial expansion and the emergence of historiography. The latter concerns, just as the conceptualisation of experience, are lurking in the background, but not yet integrated and given a final form. The questions of empire and the 'pragmatic history' of ecumenic expansion, and the idea that the purpose of 'world domination' is comparable to eschatology, are there (*ibid.*: 31–2), just as is the allusion to the link between parallel outbursts and the rise of historiography (*ibid.*: 34). They only needed to be pulled together with the discovery of metaxy. The omission of Christianity, however, represents a fundamental reorganisation of the entire project, as it started by questioning the omission of Christianity from the history of political ideas. The two phenomena together indicate a decisive shift by Voegelin in this period from prophecy and Christianity to Greek philosophy.

Compared to these two great absences, the actual content of the discussion contains few points worthwhile mentioning on their own. Most important is the claim that the concentration of spiritual outburst was the wrong way of posing the problems. Instead, Voegelin suggested a 'theory of dominant constants'. This theory was not elaborated in detail, but the language represents steps toward 'eternal being in time' and the discovery of metaxy.

In the Ecumenic Age

The third and last, and in several ways decisive, discussion of axis time takes place in Volume Four, and at two prominent places. The first is in the opening pages of the book, in a subsection of the Introduction entitled 'Linear Time and Axis Time', in the context of explaining why the publication of Volume Four did not proceed according to plans. In these self-critical remarks Voegelin argues that reorientation was necessary as the earlier work was still caught in a vision of history arranged along a linear time dimension. In this reorganisation the debate between Jaspers and Toynbee on axis time is identified as the 'problem', while the concepts 'metaxy' (OHIV: 6) and 'historiogenesis' (*ibid.*: 8) were seen to be the central tools for the solution. The second term is introduced at the start of the second subsection, whose title ('The Beginning and the Beyond') also helps to identify the rhythm of meditations and substantive-historical volumes in Voegelin's oeuvre. 'What Is History' was planned as the Introduction to Volume Four, but – through the reflection on the axis time – it developed into the meditation 'Eternal Being in Time', and the discovery of metaxy. This shifted Voegelin's interests away from finishing *Order and History* and publishing the meditative *Anamnesis*. With the help of these 'conceptual' findings Voegelin returned to *Order and History* and completed Volume Four, whose title reflected the basic result of Voegelin's rethinking of the concept of axis time; but then, instead of continuing with Volume Five on the study of 'the contemporary problems which have motivated the search for order in history', as promised (*ibid.*: 58),[10] he took off from the meditation 'The Beginning and the Beyond', which eventually, through the meditation 'Wisdom and the Magic of the Extreme', resulted in the posthumous and meditative Volume Five (see OHV).

If the first discussion of axis time indicated the role of the Jaspersian problematics in the dynamics of Voegelin's work, the second gave a conclusive interpretation. There was indeed something epochal in the period Jaspers identified as the axis time, or the period lasting from about 800 to 200 BC, with a 'concentration about 500' (*ibid.*: 310). It was, however, not 'the' absolute epoch. Its exact significance can be recognised by adding to the spiritual outbursts the rise of the ecumenic empires and the emergence of the consciousness of history (*ibid.*: 312),[11] thus identifying the epoch through 'the triad of ecumenic empire, spiritual outburst, and historiography' (*ibid.*: 308). The discussion starts with a striking and strongly Foucauldian formulation: in the epoch, the 'divine mystery' surrounding human existence 'has been opened up by the concupiscence of power and knowledge' (*ibid.*: 312–13). This way of thematising the problem led to the reformulation of axis time into the 'ecumenic age'. We need to specify here what exactly Voegelin meant by this term, the title of the work, proposed to render obsolete the Jaspersian 'axis time'.

The ecumenic age

The term 'ecumenic age' has three main characteristics. It gives a very simple and empirical definition of a historical epoch; far from claiming the status of novelty, it is traced back to the first comparative historian, Polybios; and it allows Voegelin to analyse the tight interconnections between pragmatic and spiritual histories of imperial conquests and spiritual 'exits' from reality. A systematisation of the results, however, again brings out a series of puzzles.

Concerning exact periodisation, the ecumenic age is defined as the period starting with the rise of the Persian Empire and ending with the Roman Empire, the two being connected by the Macedonian Empire and the Hellenistic period (OHIV: 114, 133). This immediately poses two problems: the comparison of this new type of empire with the early empires, and the link between pragmatic and spiritual history in the ecumenic age. Concerning the first, Voegelin convincingly argues the difference. The second problem, however, is more tricky. The issue is central, because in a book arguing for the effective significance of spiritual history one cannot simply return to the landmarks of power politics. The solution offered is not satisfactory: Voegelin argues that the 'epochal events' that made the creation of the concept necessary were 'the fall of Israel and Hellas to the power of empire' (*ibid.*: 114). Instead of clarifying the relationship between the two histories, Voegelin dissolves the problem into two identities: the ecumenic age is identical with the series of three empires, but also with the fate suffered by both societies in which the decisive spiritual outbursts happened.

The puzzle is only deepened further by the way the spiritual outbursts are discussed in the context of the chapter entitled 'The Ecumenic Age'. Though started on a Jaspersian problematic, in this chapter Voegelin is only interested in the cases of Israel and Hellas. Furthermore, within the chapter three major spiritual figures are discussed, Paul, Mani and Mohammed, without much attention being given to the figures of the axial age – though, argues Voegelin, the new concept should replace the old idea of an axis time. Finally, the chapter tails off, without even attempting to conclude the argument, into the fate of Greek rule in India (*ibid.*: 170).

Voegelin's reading of Polybius (201–120 BC) offers a step towards the solution. Polybius was motivated by the recognition of 'the extraordinary character of events' which he lived through, 'the unprecedented constellation of power that was gaining shape before his eyes' (*ibid.*: 123). In his magisterial work he attempted to explain the success of Rome, in contrast to the fate of Hellas, from the perspective of a victim (*ibid.*: 125). The word 'ecumene', originally meaning the inhabited world, gained in the vocabulary of Polybius a technical meaning referring to the peoples that became subjects of imperial expansion (*ibid.*: 124, 132). For Voegelin the fact that the term was used by the 'contemporaries of the events' (*ibid.*: 132) has methodological significance, as 'the self-interpretation of a society is part of the reality of its order' (*ibid.*: 121). But it is at this point that the link between Hellas and the empires becomes a crucial problem. Voegelin argues that Hellas, whether in resistance to the Persian Empire or as a part of the Macedonian and Roman Empires, was all the time part of the ecumene. This, however, ignores key aspects of 'pragmatic history', such as the question of victory or defeat at Marathon or Salamis, and is clearly untenable.

The contrast between these two hypotheses, the axial age and the ecumenic age, needs to be revisited.

'Axial age' vs 'ecumenic age'

The starting point is that there *was* indeed a period of spiritual outbursts, and this focused around the year 500 BC, when spiritual events of epochal significance happened in several major parts of the world that were not directly related. The period, however, instead of being extended, as Toynbee wanted, should be restricted. The axial age only extends to the sixth and fifth centuries BC.

First of all, any placing of the axial age before the sixth century BC can safely be discounted. One can trace antecedents to any intellectual and spiritual movement. But the early *Upanishads*, just as do Homer and Hesiod, clearly belong to the realm of mythopoesis, and not to experiences of transcendence. The first figure of the axial age is the prophet Jeremiah – the only personage of the axial age whose activity started in the late seventh century BC.

The figure of Jeremiah is also of exceptional significance in identifying the events that led to the explosion of spiritual outbursts. The international constellation, so central to prophecy (Neher 1961, Zeitlin 1984), was marked by the power vacuum generated by the collapse of Assyrian rule (612 BC) and the rise of the Babylonian Empire (604 BC). These events had a triple significance. Assyria, whose rise to power started in the eighth century BC, was a very special type of empire; the first entity which could be characterised as being 'not organised societies at all, but organisational shells', driven by the will to 'expand indefinitely' at the expense of existing, substantive societies (OHIV: 117), the description used by Voegelin for 'ecumenic empires'. In this respect Assyria differed fundamentally from Egypt or the earlier Mesopotamian empires. Second, due to geographical proximity, Israel became one of the first targets of this new type of empire. In the first documented period of Israeli prophecy, Amos, Hoseah and Isaiah were pronounced in the new context of the threat represented by the rise of Assyria to imperial power. Thus, in this sense it is not surprising that Hebrew thought and spirituality was particularly well disposed to react to the sudden escalation of violence and 'concupiscential conquest'.

The third point is that the collapse of this 'new experiment' created an enormous 'power vacuum' (OHIV:117), leading first to a major reorganisation of the Mesopotamian region and its surroundings, and then, with the rise of the Persian Empire, creating waves involving truly the entire ecumene, as it was then understood to be.

If the starting point of the axial age can be defined with such precision, the same holds true for its end. Socrates died in 399 BC, and with his death the period of parallel spiritual outburst can be said to draw to a close. No more major prophets survive in Persia or in Israel, and spiritual movements in India or China follow the normal logic of internal renewal or impact through diffusion. The only region in which the axial age seems to continue, convincing Jaspers to extend the period to the second century BC, is Greece. This indeed remains a problem to be solved, and it will be revisited in the next chapter.

Provisionally, the discussion can be summarised in the following way. The axial age was a large-scale, real-world liminal period of unrest marking the transition to the age of ecumenic empires, characterised by spiritual and political–military resistance to the new empire. The ecumenic age started with the rise of the Macedonian empire when, after the demise of the 'spirit' of Athenian democracy, effective resistance collapsed. Classical prophecy and philosophy were then replaced by the spiritual movements characteristic of the Hellenistic period: Stoic, Cynic, Sceptic and Epicurean philosophical schools, and apocalyptic and Gnostic religious sectarianism.

Historiogenesis

While the axial age provides the general context for the analysis of Hebrew and Greek developments in thought, classical prophecy, especially through the figure of Moses, reaches way back in time. Hebrew self-consciousness, uniquely in the world, was rooted in a rejection of the value and even the reality of the world of early empires and civilisations (Frankfort 1948). The exact character of this 'world rejection' was a central concern of both Weber's and Voegelin's investigations, and its analysis must be started by presenting the main characteristics of the world-view that came to be rejected, with lasting consequences, in Hebrew thought and spirituality.

Relying on the path-breaking works of Henri Frankfort and his associates in the Chicago Oriental Institute, and of Mircea Eliade who followed Frankfort as head of the Institute, Voegelin called this the 'primary experience of order', characteristic of 'cosmological empires', first of all Egypt and Mesopotamia, or entities in which the existing socio-cultural order was derived from and legitimated by the very structure of the cosmos (OHI: 16–45).[12] Later, however, Voegelin changed his account, reaching eventually the position that such a cosmological symbolism can be traced back at least 20,000 years before the ancient Near-Eastern empires (AR: 82). Specific for the ancient civilisations of the Near East was the conflation of these mythologies and actual historical events into a form of speculation that Voegelin called historiogenesis.

With the term 'historiogenesis' Voegelin identifies the emergence of the idea of a unilinear vision of history. 'Historiogenesis' designates those speculations on the course of history that locate the origins of one's own society in relation to the original creation of the cosmos, and then trace a linear and continuous line of development from the earlier times to the present. In this way Voegelin radically extends the historical scope of the linear view of history. The idea of progress is usually traced to Christian, Greek, or at most Hebrew sources, while Voegelin argues that it was precisely the basic ideology of the empires *against* which the Judeo–Christian system of ideas emerged. Taking this idea a step further, a truly significant insight arises: the linear philosophy of history, as exposed by Augustine, was not a specifically Christian or even Hebrew idea, but rather a certain 'return of the repressed': it was in this way that discredited forms of ancient imperial thought managed to 'infiltrate' and transform from the inside the system of values that defeated it.

While the origins of the cosmological myth are lost deep in ancient times, the emergence of historiogenesis can be reconstructed in recorded history. This form of speculation emerged not with the rise of the ancient empires, but with the first major, life-threatening crisis they underwent. It is a symptom of 'times of troubles', a reaction to traumatic experiences, of which the paradigmatic example is the case of Egypt in the First Intermediate Period (OHIV: 94–5).[13] Though this trauma is comparable to the disorder experienced by the first prophets and philosophers, it did not lead to a comparable spiritual out-burst. Instead, the experience resulted in a hybrid product, an amalgamation of myths, traditions and recent history into a single teleological narrative, tracing the line of descent of current rulers to ancient kings, eventually to the foundation of the world, with the aim of creating the image of an unshakable, eternal order, as if the power of such words and genealogies could serve as magical forces to ward off any potential source of disorder.

The Egyptian term '*ma'at*' can be considered as the representative embodiment of this idea of an eternal order, underlying cosmological empires, while the law-book of Hammurabi was the first attempt to lay down the legal and institutional frameworks of such an order. *Ma'at* was a supreme value of Egyptian civilisation. According to Voegelin, it is a complex symbol that cannot be translated in a single word: 'As the Maat of the cosmos it would have to be rendered as order; as the Maat of society, as good government and justice; as the Maat of true understanding of ordered reality, as truth' (OHI: 79). In sum, *ma'at* is a term combining in a single symbolic form order, justice and truth. Norman Cohn has also emphasised the crucial importance and wide range of meaning of the term. Though originally meaning 'base', the word *ma'at* soon 'acquired a far wider significance', and 'was used to indicate a principle of order so all-embracing that it governed every aspect of existence' (Cohn 1993: 9; see also Assmann 2001 and Zeitlin 1984: 5). Most important of all, it came to represent 'the base on which the ordered world itself rested' (Cohn 1993: 10). The fruits of *ma'at* included justice, abundance, fertility, rightfulness and good government (*ibid.*: 14–15). The intellectual and bureaucratic elite was to play a particularly strong role in

maintaining *ma'at*: '[t]he heart of the good official was supposed to be so pene-
trated with *ma'at* that he could not possibly contravene the divinely appointed
order' (*ibid.*: 15–16). Significantly, *ma'at* was a female deity, daughter of Re, the
sun god.

Living in such a world, however, had its own shortcomings in our eyes. This is
because our view of the world has been fundamentally shaped by that form of
thought and spirituality that first questioned the taken-for-granted world of the
empire.

Israel and the modalities of Exodus

The main line of Voegelin's argument can be summarised in a few sentences.
The uniqueness and world-historical significance of ancient Judaism lies in the
fact that the very existence of the Hebrew people is based on a rejection both
real and symbolic of the cosmological order. This rejection took place well
before the power vacuum created by the collapse of the Assyrian empire, and
therefore rendered Jewish thought and spirituality particularly predisposed both
to reflect upon the experience and to propose a way out. The possibility of such
a rejection was rooted in a unique experience of transcendence that happened to
Moses, the 'thorn-bush episode', and its repetition, at the collective level, with
the covenant experience at Mount Sinai. Such experiences, however, pose
formidable problems of (self-reflexive) interpretation. The experience had potentially universal implications, both at the level of Moses as an individual, and at
the level of a community created by participation in a shared experience of the
divine. In the concrete case, however, it was derailed into the particularistic interpretation of the Hebrews as chosen people, and the ensuing conquest of
Canaan. The build-up of the Jewish Kingdom was a misreading of the experience and prevented the spread of the potentially universalistic message. These
potentials were liberated only with the changing international configuration and
the collapse of the independent state of Israel. By rendering expectations about
the particularistic reading of the promise impossible, these events opened two
possibilities: a further deflection into eschatological expectations, an exit from
reality; and the performance of a major step towards the realisation of the
universalistic potential by an 'exodus of Israel from itself'. The former step was
taken by the prophets of 'metastatic faith', starting with Isaiah, while the second
was taken by Jeremiah and Deutero Isaiah.

Existence in revolt

The rejection of the cosmological empire is a genuine revaluation. Though the
term is Nietzschean, the content is quite different. It does not imply a rejection of
the 'world', only the image and reality of the world of the empire. It is not based
on a rejection of good and bad, rather on a diagnosis of life under the empire as
an existence in revolt. Voegelin supports his point by an ingenuous interpretation
of the first chapters of the Book of Genesis (OHI: 16–17). These contain three

major revolts against God: the Fall, punished by the expulsion from the Garden of Eden; a somewhat obscure crisis of licentiousness, punished by the Flood; and the Tower of Babel, punished by the fragmentation of language.

This interpretation of the Exodus as a rejection of the revolt establishes a series of links and analogies. The first link is with the Decalogue cast in stone, and thus with Moses. In another insightful account (*ibid.*: 424–7), Voegelin reads the Decalogue as a diagnosis of rebellious existence, with a key role being played by the first and the last Commandments, identifying the 'injunctions against the antitheistic rebellion of pride and the antihuman rebellion of envy' (*ibid.*: 427). The episode supports Voegelin's characterisation of Moses not as a lawgiver, nor the founder of a religion, but rather as a simple mediator of God (*ibid.*: 383–4).

It also immediately brings to mind parallels with the ancient Greeks and modernity. Concerning the Greeks, the combination of the rebel and the mediator recalls the Prometheus and Hermes of Aeschylus, in *Prometheus Bound*. Prometheus embodies the Greek version of the rebellion against the gods, while Hermes the messenger is the Greek mediator *par excellence* between the humans and the gods. The Hermes–Moses parallel is important in helping to identify the various 'trickster' aspects still present in the Mosaic figure. Concerning modernity, Voegelin's analysis draws on his reading of *L'homme révolté* of Camus.

Most important, however, is the figure and the story of Abraham, immediately following in the Old Testament the story of the Tower of Babel.

Abraham, exit, sacrifice

The first, symbolic exit from the early empires and their cosmological order is associated with the leaving of the city of Ur by Abraham, the wandering Aramean. Voegelin's interpretation focuses on Genesis 14–15. Chapter 14 gives a realistic account of the power struggles taking place in Canaan. The situation is disappointing for Abraham: he had left the cosmological order of Babylon in vain, finding again the same world of *Realpolitik*. In the next chapter, however, the hesitations are transformed into a solid faith. The chapter describes a first transcendental experience, a genuine leap in being, the voice of Yahweh giving reassurance, protection and the promise of wealth and offspring, followed by the Covenant symbol. It is with this symbol that Canaan became transvalued, and '[t]he symbol of bondage has become the symbol of freedom' (*ibid.*: 194). According to Voegelin's experiential method, the trustworthiness of the story must be judged by the authenticity of the experience, and this cannot be in doubt, as 'nobody can describe an experience unless he had had it, either originally or through imaginative re-enactment' (*ibid.*: 195). Later writers only gave literary form to the 'spiritual sensitiveness of the man who opened his soul to the word of Yahweh', possessing the 'trust and fortitude required to make this word the order of existence in opposition to the world', which made his experience into 'one of the great and rare events in the history of mankind' (*ibid.*).

The experience, however, was compact, undifferentiated, leading to two possible readings: the military–political reading, that would lead to the conquest and the establishment of worldly rule, and the pacific–spiritual interpretation, that would eventually be taken up by the prophets (*ibid.*: 183, 185–7, 210). The conflict between the two principles first broke out between Saul and Samuel, laying down the paradigmatic foundations of the struggle for 'spiritual control over temporal rulership' (*ibid.*: 245).[14]

The story of Abraham contains a number of elements central for the argument of this book. The first concerns the gap between the physical exit and the eventual promise, already analysed in Chapter 2. The second is the long period of childless wandering with a beautiful wife. This aspect, emphasised recurrently in the narrative, is central, as it connects the exit and the promise, underlying the difficulties of the context out of which the experience of the promise, together with the experience of transcendence, has grown. The 'questioning soul' written of by Thomas Mann was actually walking and wandering between Egypt and Mesopotamia, recalling the Foucauldian etymology of Oedipus as the 'knowing foot', and during all these times his homelessness was rendered even more acute by his childlessness in an age where tribal clans and dynasties were all-important, especially for somebody on the road. All this contributed to the build-up of the tension in the background of the experience of transcendence.

The Old Testament contains no sudden appearance of a hidden God to Abraham comparable to the thorn-bush episode. There is, however, a singular and most significant episode that at the same time is a fascinating proof of the compactness of this early experience, the famous story of the sacrifice of Isaac. The story of Abraham willing to sacrifice his first-born son is almost incomprehensible to modern ears, whether from the perspective of divine command or human obedience. Through the reflections of Kierkegaard, it has also become one of the founding paradoxes of modern philosophy. Yet, the perspective of the charisma–trickster separation does provide a simple explanation. The god-experience of Abraham was a compact one, and he had few tools at his disposal to discriminate between its aspects. In sudden and compact spiritual experiences, the various types of spiritual powers are strongly intertwined. Abraham interpreted the inner voice as testing his faith, by first commanding him to sacrifice his only son and then, in the last minute, to pull back. Tempting and testing, however, are typical features of trickster gods. Characteristic of the experience of Abraham, and of later Jewish thought, is the unity of these features with other aspects of Yahweh. This perspective can also shed a new light on the appearance of the Devil in Christianity, a major innovation in contrast to Judaism. The decisive point here concerns the staunch rejection, by Jesus, of the central trickster features: testing and tempting on the one hand, and joking and laughing on the other. Starting from the great scene of the three temptations, just at the start of his public career, after forty days in the wilderness (Matt. 4: 3–11), he would assign any attempts to test him, whether by spirits or by the Pharisees, as the work of the Devil; while on the other hand he would never use jokes, comic turns or even ironic language in his speeches and, as was observed by perceptive writers like Nietzsche, it is inconceivable to imagine Jesus laughing (Hadot 1995b: 85).

This means that, in the figure of Jesus, there was a complete separation between the charismatic and trickster-like spiritual modalities. Jesus *is* the ideal type of charisma, exactly in the Weberian sense, implying the – practical – impossibility of the actual embodiment, in a concrete being, of an ideal type in its full purity. But this also means that, at the opposite end, the ideal type of the 'trickster' also became similarly crystallised in the figure of the Devil. This figure was not embodied in a concrete person, but conceptualised by the Church fathers as a force internal to every human being.

The Abraham episode reveals the profound ambivalence of the transcendental experience at its founding moment. Abraham is the first realistic figure in the Old Testament to whom the experience of a personal god is attached, who is in continuous contact and conversation with the divine. Yet, this divine figure also turns out to be a trickster who repeatedly makes promises but postpones delivery; who plays jokes on Abraham's wife Sarah, first by denying her a child and then by allowing her a child when she is so old that the neighbours are laughing at her; and even submits Abraham to the ultimate test of sacrificing his first-born. This episode, one of the most memorable in the entire Old Testament, also points to another major ambivalence, the presence of the motive of human sacrifice as still representing, in the mental–spiritual horizon of Abraham, the ultimate way of establishing contact with the divine. Finally, the conclusive consequence of the transcendental experience is not universal human redemption, but rather the securing of a tribal promise, the promise of a homeland and numerous offspring for the individual who was wandering for so long in the desert, homeless and childless.

Moses and the thorn-bush episode

We can now return to Voegelin's analysis of Moses and the thorn-bush episode, situating it in the context of the Abraham figure as sketched above.

First of all, and in a methodologically most important way, Voegelin argues for the existence of the figure of Moses through the reality of the experience; and this is based on the continuous existence, up to the present day, of Jewish religion and society. The facts are indeed impressive: while the traces of most of the great empires of the period only exist at the level of archaeological evidence, and the link between ancient and modern Egyptians, Persians and Greeks is precarious at best, the Jewish people still exist, and with a definite identity, in spite of the historical fate they have suffered. Such persistence in spite of adversity must be based on a source, and this, according to Voegelin, can be traced back to the thorn-bush episode and the ensuing Covenant made on Mount Sinai.

The next question concerns the exact meaning of the experience. Focusing on the meaning of the famous tetragrammaton YHWH, 'I am that I am', Voegelin dismisses the etymological interpretation as irrelevant, arguing that it can be summarised as the sudden *presence*, or revelation, of a *hidden* God, who is also a *helping* god. Moses experienced a benevolent divine presence, an experience that empowered him with the strength to collect a people and lead them out of their captivity. After this escape, a second, and just as important, experience happened on Mount Sinai, where the entire people, together, had a similar transcendental experience related to the Covenant.

Given that the experience happened, twice even, the next question concerns the actual interpretation of the experience, both by Moses and by the people. And here Voegelin identifies, in Hegelian terminology, a difference between the universalistic potentials of the two experiences, and their actual derailment. The potential of the experience is the rise of a new type of man and a new type of society, a 'people living under God', animated by a new spirit and a genuine revaluation. This potential universality, however, was derailed into the formation of a concrete political entity, a concrete nation, with the self-proclaimed promise of a power among other nations; with a right to conquer their 'promised land', and then gain precedence among nations.

The covenant experience with the potentially universal consequences, according to Voegelin, happened in the hearts of those who participated in it. This explains why this event hardly left more than a trace in the Bible. Such a paucity is not even surprising, as ' "And they beheld God, and ate and drank" is the perfect formula for an event in which divine order becomes established in history, while externally happens nothing at all.' (OHI: 423–4, referring to Exod. 24:9–11). Its 'derailment' into the imperial ambition of Israel, apart from jeopardising the universalistic message, also presents a testing point for the secular claims. In so far as the original experience stimulates military undertakings, earthly success confirms the interpretation of the transcendental experience, with secular rulers like David and Solomon becoming carriers of the divine message, in spite of their more-than-questionable behaviour. At the moment in which success is replaced by defeat, however, a fundamental problem of interpretation emerges.

It is at the level of this problem that Voegelin locates the figure of prophecy.

The prophets

The differentiation between these two readings, the rise of secular power and the restoration of the original spiritual experience of 'people living under God', became the organising principle of the book, Part III being devoted to the first aspect and Part IV to the second (OHI: 187). For our purposes, only the second aspect will be relevant, though it will be necessary to refer to segments of the discussion in Part III as well – all the more so as the organisation of the material is somewhat perplexing.[15]

The prophets gave a more differentiated understanding of the berith experience, by identifying the 'foundation of the Kingdom' as 'the specific crisis that revealed the demonic derailment of the Mosaic foundation', and waging 'the struggle of the spirit for its freedom from encasement (alluding possibly to Weber's famous *Gehäuse*) in a particular social organization' (*ibid.*: 183).

The '*ruach*' of Yahweh (*ibid.*: 222), the spiritual force that came alive in Abraham, also animated the various military and prophetic figures of the Old

Testament – a quality for which Voegelin recurrently used the word 'charisma' (see, for example, *ibid.*: 265). This 'spiritual formation of character...was unique in its time', and represented a 'new type of man on the world-political scene' (*ibid.: 222*). Between the carriers of military and spiritual charisma there was a definite shift over time. At the beginnings of the foundation of the kingdom, the two are closely connected, as in the struggles between Saul, the military hero, and Samuel, whose theocratic intentions make him more a priest than a prophet, or the military–prophetic sects analysed by Weber. In the early period of the kingdom, from Saul through David to Solomon, the most lively figures were the royal personalities. This changes, however, after Solomon, as – due to the rise of the prophetic movement – 'the kings had ceased to be representative of the spiritual order of Israel' (*ibid.*: 223).

The first figure who could be called a prophet was Elijah. Though half legendary and lacking a clearly drawn picture, the figure of Elijah is central for capturing the prophetic experience. The pages devoted to him are among the most captivating in the book.

Elijah

Voegelin starts his attempt to recover the experiential basis of the Elijah figure through an anonymous fifth-century prophet called Malachi (the name meaning simply 'my messenger'), who first pronounced the return to Elijah (*ibid.*: 336). Elijah was widely considered as a 'first' prophet, the prototype of a voice in the wilderness, but it was Malachi who transformed him into the symbol of a 'recurrent call to restore the order' (*ibid.*). Even more importantly, the content of Elijah's prophecy was identified as the Day of Yahweh transformed into a symbol of divine punishment.

Taking into account recent work on the cultic character of the Davidic Psalms, this last point contains a crucial clue. Far from being post-exilic, the Psalms were rather incorporations of standard Egyptian and Canaanite New Year's Eve rituals into the Jewish Kingdom. In this context the Day of Yahweh was a popular feast, a further sign of derailment due to secular success, a 'chauvinistic, cosmological defection from Yahweh' (*ibid.*: 343). Such voices became even stronger in the ninth century, when the weakening of secular power only contributed to the even greater spread of the Baal fertility cult in Israel. This was the context in which the revaluation of this positive, triumphant symbolism into a negative Day of Yahweh as a Day of Judgement can be situated (*ibid.*).

At this point, before further analysing the experiential bases of the Elijah figure, Voegelin resumes the stages of eschatological symbolism. The problem is traced back to the ambivalence of Canaan. In order to overcome this ambivalence and realise the full universalistic implications of this transcendental experience, three components had to be eliminated from the compact symbol: reference to a particular ethnic group as the carrier; the idea that this kingdom could be realised by a mundane organisation; and the idea of a continuous line of history. Due to the presence of these three components, actual Israeli history took up the rhythm of defection and a call for a restoration of order, eventually crystallising in the figure of the prophet, transforming the Day of Glory into a Day of Judgement. The new stage is reached by Amos, who came up with the new idea that not only the kings but the people themselves are guilty of defection. At this point, Voegelin returns to the fifth century with Malachi, where the centre of the eschatological experience became visible as 'the eternal present in which the divine–human drama of history was enacted' (*ibid.*: 345), thus announcing the appearance of Jesus, with whom '[t]he Law and the Prophets were now "fulfilled"' ' (*ibid.*).

These 'intermediate reflections' allude to the concluding section of Part IV. However, at this stage, the major prophets of the sixth and fifth centuries BC were not yet discussed, and the last chapters, introducing the terminology of 'metastatic faith', unfortunately do not return to the eschatological problem.

In its concluding section the chapter gives a convincing rendering of the Elijah experience. At the heart of Elijah's attacks is the Baal cult,[16] and the main adversary is the king. The account contains many gaps, but for Voegelin these only confirm the validity of the story, as they show an 'author in search of literary devices to convey the inexplicable suddenness of a spiritual outbreak' (*ibid.*: 347). Elijah challenges and eventually defeats the prophets of Baal in a spectacular public contest, where he successfully ends the drought by making rain.[17] The mission, however, still ended in failure, as the power of the Baal cult was not broken and at the end even Elijah's life came under threat. He escaped to the desert and sat under a tree in order to die. According to Voegelin, 'Elijah in the desert is one of the great scenes in the history of mankind' (*ibid.*: 350). It was a reversal of the Exodus theme, in the soul of the prophet: a lonely exit from Canaan, into death. But this was still not the end. Yahweh first made him walk forty days and nights, and then he appeared to Elijah, in a highly elaborate and significant way. First, and in three different modes, all the great divine tricks of the trade were displaced: a mighty wind, an earthquake and a fire. Yahweh, however, did not come in any of these garbs, only with a 'sound of gentle stillness'; and when finally appearing, he only posed a most simple question: ' "What are you doing here, Elijah?" ' (*ibid.*). And then Yahweh cared little about the sulking complaints of the prophet, but rather sent him back to his task, the establishment of prophetic succession.

An intermediate summary

With some help from the Girardian theory of sacrifice, the argument so far can be summarised in the following way. The Mosaic experience had the character of a 'leap in being' and had potentially universal validity, but – like the Abrahamic wandering and quest for God – it was ultimately sidetracked by an adherence to the ritual of sacrifice and the pursuit of a particularistic worldly power. The main figures of institutional power, the kings and the priests, indeed became strongly caught in the framework of these ancient practices, thus jeopardising the universal potential. The spirit of the original experience, however, was preserved and carried forward by a special type of personality, peculiar to Judaism: the prophet. The main message of prophets was a call to restore order and to return to the original experiences.

The contrast between the prophets and the priests was drawn more starkly by Voegelin than by Weber. Using the later terminology, the prophets kept alive the tension of metaxy, while the priests and the kings prioritised one of the poles. At one point Voegelin even compares the contrast between the prophets and the priests with that of Plato and the Sophists (*ibid.*: 436). The parallel could be extended to the other key term Voegelin applies to the prophets, the effort to awaken the consciousness of the people (*ibid.*: 428).

The prophets were able to exert an impact because neither the realities of the worldly kingdom, nor the strictures of the law, erase completely the memory of the earlier experiences. Even more importantly, the changes in the political constellation that rendered the pursuit of independent kingdom impossible only reinforced the message of the prophets.

Voegelin argues that this message was dual-faceted, offering a new path. In the Weberian interpretation, reinforced by Zeitlin, the major dividing line lay between the true and the false prophets. The latter continued to predict worldly success, in order to please the people and especially the kings, while the former argued that as the people and their leaders failed to live up to the Covenant, such a success was increasingly unlikely.[18] According to Voegelin, however, at this point even the 'genuine' prophets can be divided into two major groups. There were those who argued that through a return to the true ways of Yahweh the Israeli nation could become victorious even in the new situation, with Yahweh destroying all its enemies. The representative figure of such apocalyptic expectations and metastatic faith was Isaiah.

The opposite position would be taken by Jeremiah and Deutero Isaiah, the two main prophets of the axial age who made major steps toward universalism by recognising that the struggle against the realities of the external world was hopeless, but who, far from being resigned, used their experience to develop new symbols. The decisive breakthrough happened at the heart of the Messianic expectations, which were still tied to the political existence of Israel (*ibid.S*: 472–3).

Jeremiah

The rejection of the external manifestation of the spirit, like the rituals of sacrifice, and the turn towards the inside, the internal order of the soul, occurs with Jeremiah (*ibid.S*: 446, 467, 484). Voegelin shifts the focus from the more famous predictions to those containing a 'new form of prophetic expression', what can be considered as 'pieces of spiritual autobiography' (*ibid.*: 485). In these pieces the emphasis shifts from mediating the Word of God to the person of the messenger, in the sense of 'the order of personal existence under God. In Jeremiah the human personality had broken the compactness of collective existence and recognized itself as the authoritative source of order in society' (*ibid.*).

Voegelin's discussion of Jeremiah is difficult to reconstruct as it forms part of a huge chapter on prophecy, integrated with the discussion of other prophets, and partly leading to the climax of the argument, Deutero Isaiah. The central part of the discussion is contained in two sections: one is devoted to the analysis of the prophetic call, and the other to the vicissitudes of the public mission.

The short passages in which the call (received in c.626 BC) is introduced define, in three oracular steps, the central elements of the new symbols, using the method of transfer (*ibid.*: 467). The first oracle evokes powerfully the original call of Yahweh: 'Before I formed you in the womb, I knew you' (Jer. 1:5). Jeremiah is therefore defined as the Son of God, transferring to him the ancient Egyptian symbolism applied to the Pharaoh and taken over by the Near-Eastern Kings. This transfer also represents a major advance in the 'Messianistic problem', with the royal symbolism being transferred to an 'institutional outcast' (OHI: 467).

The second oracle is a reply to the protests of Jeremiah, repeating the call and reassuring support (Jer. 1:6–8). The hesitation and the confirmation together establish a parallel with Moses, who similarly protested against his being called. These two transfers in themselves condense an extraordinary symbolic charge, combining the highest possible authority of the 'world' and Hebrew history. They are reinforced by the third oracle in which divine authority itself is transferred to Jeremiah (*ibid.* 1:9–10). The transfer is affected by a touch of the mouth, so the nature of this authority is to speak with a specific power. The parallels with the similarly charismatic parrhesia are evident.

As a representative example of the public mission of prophecy, Voegelin selected the Temple Address of 609/8 BC (Jer. 7; OHI: 431–4). Jeremiah was instructed to deliver his address at the liminal place of the Temple door, in contrast with the substance of the message, targeting the very heart of the creed of the people. Its content can be defined as a general problematisation of the everyday conduct of life. Jeremiah shouted to the people entering the Temple that they can only consider it as their home if they properly mind their behaviour. The disorder of the contemporary state of affairs was 'measured by the comprehensive order of the Decalogue', focusing especially on the first and tenth Commandments, the sins of self-assertiveness against God and man (OHI: 433; see also 440). The charge was not about 'morals' or the law, but the order of the soul, the guiding force of conduct.[19] Jeremiah threatened the people that if they did not change, the Temple would be destroyed.

As the audience was predictably incensed, prophecy immediately caused serious problems both of legitimation and of public order. The words were offensive to the highest degree, invoking the charge of treason, but they also evoked supreme authority, the word of Yahweh. The consequences can be followed through in its sequel, the trial of Jeremiah (Jer. 26). The priests and the (false) prophets wanted his death, but the princes and the people were impressed by the references to Yahweh's authority and let him go free.

The next set of prophecies were not proclaimed at the Temple door, but rather delivered by his scribe, Baruch (Jer. 36:1–7; OHI: 435–6). After its reading, the scroll was confiscated and read to the king, who immediately threw it into the fire. As a consequence Jeremiah was imprisoned until the fall of Jerusalem.

At this point Voegelin draws further parallels: '[t]he trial of the prophet and the mutual death sentences when the order of God is about to disengage itself from the order of man form an aggregate of symbols that recurs, at a distance of two centuries, in the Hellas of Socrates and Plato' (OHI: 436). These parallels are not due either to contingent events or to mysterious laws, but rather to 'essential processes of experience and symbolisation'. The symbolisation is similar, as it expresses a comparable experience of the relationship between the divine and the humane order, or metaxy. The central issue, alluded to in this paragraph, is how this experience would become 'a force in community life' (*ibid.*). It is in this regard that a decisive advance would be made by Deutero Isaiah.

Concerning the symbolic expression of the experience of transcendence, Jeremiah presents two major novelties. In line with the unique exploration of interiority, Jeremiah is not only the first prophet who appears to us as a clear personality, but he also avoids the short-circuiting of particularism. However, this separation between external, worldly aims and the order of the soul also opposes him to the people and leads to a type of persecution that brings out certain not-too-positive character traits. The loneliness of the prophet leads to an almost paranoid sense of persecution, witnessed in notices about a conspiracy against his life (Jer. 18:18) or plots to murder him (Jer. 11:21; OHI: 485). These notices are always followed by pleas of vengeance for the proper punishment of his enemies. Though Voegelin is quick to absolve the prophet, at this point the Weberian analysis showed much greater sensitivity to later problems.

Deutero Isaiah

The prophet whose utterings are contained in chapters 40–55 of Isaiah and whose period of activity is assigned to the period just around the conquest of Babylon by Cyrus in 539 BC closed the period of classical prophecy and, according to Voegelin, indeed brought this line of development to a conclusion. His work was the third and final Exodus, the 'Exodus of Israel from itself' (OHI: 491), solving the ambiguity derived from the particularistic reading of the covenant experience.

This was again based on personal experiences: the Exile in Babylon, the conquest of Cyrus, the expectations tied to this conquest and the disappointment of these hopes. Beyond these general facts, however, no biographical information is available on the personal experiences of the prophet, rendering analysis particularly difficult.

Voegelin starts by looking for lines of descent. Given that the prophecies, together with the ensuing collection, attributed to Trito Isaiah but written by various authors, were all collected under the name of Isaiah, it had to represent some kind of continuous tradition (*ibid.*: 482). This tradition is usually associated with eschatology, which Voegelin thematised by the concept 'metastatic faith'. However, in between Isaiah and Deutero Isaiah, there was Jeremiah, and Voegelin primarily interprets Deutero Isaiah as a successor to Jeremiah. The problem is that the leaving-out of the eschatological component not only renders the reading partial, but would have consequences for Voegelin's ability to diagnose the eschatological–apocalyptic elements of modernity.

Though relying on the advances of Jeremiah, Deutero Isaiah did not use the technique of telling a series of experiences. Instead, the author constructed an entire drama out of his experiences, indicating that the 'Exodus has happened in the soul of the author, and his work is the symbol of a historical event' (*ibid.*: 495). With this symbolism a novel type of prophecy was created. The prophet is no longer the mouth of god, but rather the recipient of heavenly voices, which do not call for a return to order, but rather have an existential appeal.

The novelty, however, had to be inserted into existing forms of symbolism, and it was done as a message of salvation. Though Voegelin does not spell out the point, his interpretation implies that this is the reason why the message (of Jeremiah) was misread by the compilers of the sayings, as just another Isaian call and promise just as did those modern scholars who read him as an eschatologist. The meaning of salvation, however, was different with Deutero Isaiah: it was no longer a divine act assuring the victory of the people and the Kingdom, but rather a shift 'from the order of the Chosen People under the Sinaitic Berith to an order under the Redeemer God' (*ibid.*: 500).

Voegelin's interpretation of this shift, contained in the next pages, is of extreme importance, and can be highlighted using his later conceptual tools. With Abraham and Moses, ancient Judaism emerged through an Exodus from the cosmological empire, through certain flash-like transcendental experiences that represented a leap in being. The new experience, however, was not yet properly differentiated, leading to a continuous tension between submerging in a new mundane kingdom and the struggle to return to life under Yahweh. The collapse of the kingdom rendered the cosmological myth of Israel impossible, opening up the universalistic potentials of the message as an order of the soul through the works of Jeremiah and Deutero Isaiah. With this, the 'movement from the order of the concrete society toward the order of redemption was…completed', implying 'that the order of being has revealed its mystery of redemption as the flower of suffering' (*ibid.*: 501). This completion, however, was put into the terminology of Messianic salvation that, through the priestly codification of the doctrine that happened around the same time, meant that the historiogenetic constructions of the empire were taken over in the form of a salvation postponed from the present into the future. Thus, the form which Deutero Isaiah selected in order to render the message intelligible partially overtook the message, explaining the fact, already emphasised by Weber, that the prophet remained without followers, and that his real succession was Christianity, where the 'participation of man in divine suffering' (*ibid.*), already thematised by Jeremiah (*ibid.*: 486–8), would encounter the opposite move, 'the participation of God in human suffering' (*ibid.*: 501).[20]

Voegelin substantiates his reading of Deutero Isaiah by a careful and detailed commentary, centring on the four songs of the 'Suffering Servant', the figure who became the main protagonist of the drama. The Prologue immediately announces the central message. As long as the Sinaic revelation was interpreted in the context of effective military empires, part of the truth remained veiled. However, now this God is 'revealed as the God of all mankind' (*ibid.*: 506). The fact that Israel perished 'as a concrete society in pragmatic history' does not cancel the revelation, but rather renders it available for the entire mankind. This defines the 'task of the Servant' in the following way: 'From the center of its reception in Israel, the news of Redemption must be spread over the whole earth' (*ibid.*). This difficult missionary enterprise should be driven by the prophet, surrounded by disciples, who would 'move into the position of a Jeremiah, who enacts the destiny of the Servant as Israel's representative' (*ibid.*: 507).

The analysis of the Prologue is followed by the four songs.[21] The First Song (Isaiah 42:1–4) evokes a powerful royal symbolism, so much so that it is not clear whether it actually refers to the prophet as representative or the entire people. Indeed, the next passages indicate that the Servant who is to 'open blind eyes and bring the prisoners out of the dungeon' (OHI: 508) is still blind and deaf, thus it represents Israel before its liberation by Cyrus. With the victory of Cyrus, redemption is indeed accomplished, but only applies for the prophet as a representative (OHI: 508–9). This is pronounced in the Second Song (Isaiah 49:1–6) at the start of Part Two (Isaiah 49–53). The model for the figure in this song is clearly Jeremiah who, even though apparently failing, received the even larger task of 'becoming the light to the nations' (OHI: 509). The problems of performing such a mission in the marginal situation of Israel were enormous, thus the Second Song is followed by words of comfort. This is the context for the Third Song (Isaiah 50:4–9), with its expression of trust and obedience in God. Central in this Song is the (self-)characterisation of the prophet as *limmud* or 'one who is taught', meaning (but only in the context of Isaiah, according to Martin Buber) a 'disciple' (OHI: 511), and here specifically meaning 'being taught by Yahweh'. Thus, here Deutero Isaiah moves 'his' Suffering Servant beyond the figure of Jeremiah.

This prophetic self-definition is followed by action, exhortations and threats, concluded by an exhortation to go out of Jerusalem and bring the news of salvation to the world (Isaiah 52:8–12). After this call comes the Fourth Song where, just as in the First Song, Yahweh is speaking again. The Song is an apotheosis of the Servant's story as 'the mystery of representative suffering' (OHI: 514), thus completing the 'Exodus from the cosmic-divine order' (*ibid.*: 515). Though this vision had hardly any effect for almost five centuries, it would 'break to the historical surface again in Christianity' (*ibid.*).

Voegelin finishes the book by evoking a passage from Luke (Luke 2:29–34). Just as important a conclusion can be reached, however, especially in light of the events of the last century, from the side of the pragmatic history of Israel, that explains the long latency not simply by the survival of the imperial tradition but by its gaining of potential within the new, Messianic–eschatological–historiogenetic context. The crucial passage is in Ezra, describing the way in which the high priests, coming back from the Exile, stood in judgement over the people who had remained (Ezra 10:3; see OHI: 172). The interpretation of this 'new' *berith* was the exact opposite to the promise of Deutero Isaiah: instead of bringing the news of Redemption to the world, it was concluded with the dismissal of all foreign wives and their children. The scene was truly gripping: the entire people was convoked into Jerusalem and, sitting in the rain, waited for the judgement to keep or dismiss their family.[22] The Book of Ezra ends with the long 'shame' list of those who took foreign wives, concluding with the following sentence: 'Some of them had begotten children by them' (Ezra 10: 44). This indeed could not have been further from the spirit of Deutero Isaiah.

6   Plato and the order
of the soul

Introduction

According to the original design of *Order and History*, the parts relating to Israel and Greece were to constitute two separate threads that were to be joined, through the rise of Christianity, in a basically genealogical design. Though the 'discovery' of the axial age presented a blow to this organisation, it was not possible to incorporate this development into the two volumes on Greece, already in the process of publication. This chapter will attempt to incorporate this finding into the web of argumentation, in the same way as the later conceptual discoveries of metaxy, the ecumenic age and historiogenesis.

While at the start of *The World of the Polis* Voegelin introduces the specificity of ancient Greece through its internal history, it is just as important to underline its relationship to the hydraulic or cosmological empires, as was the case with ancient Israel. The Aegean area, especially Ionia, similarly to Palestine in this respect, took up an at once marginal and liminal position. While Palestine was at the borderline of the zone of influence of both Egypt and Mesopotamia, lying on the road connecting them, Greece was situated on the north-western margins of the empires of the Near East, being connected across the sea. A crucial role was played in this regard, first by the island of Crete, and then by the Ionian coastline.

Crete

Crete mediated Egyptian influences to the mainland, while not itself developing into an empire. The central role played by Crete as the 'homeland' of Greece was established in mythology. Crete was the birth-place of Zeus, with the Dictean cave and Mount Ida competing for the honour. This was also the place to which Zeus, in the shape of a bull, took Europa from the city of Tyre,[1] and it was here that the first 'Greek' lawgiver, Minos (son of Europa) reigned. The Delphi oracle, the *omphalos* of classical Greek culture, derived its origins from Crete; and even Plato, who in his last period was much concerned with the links between Greece and Egypt, had set his ultimate work, *Laws*, as a walk in Crete, from Knossos up to the cave of Zeus (OHII: 44).

Though, after a flowering of about half a millennium, from 1400 BC on Crete declined as a cultural centre, its achievements were not lost, as first it became incorporated into the rising Mycenean culture; and even after the collapse of the entire area in the thirteenth and twelfth centuries its memory was kept alive through the 'dark age' of the next three centuries, to resurface in the Homeric epics of the eighth century BC.

Taken together, this represented at least three major assets upon which Greek culture, starting from the eighth century, could draw: negatively, the lack of an imperial past; positively, the presence of a rich cultural and mythical heritage of an advanced town culture; and the memory of the experience of a profound, traumatic crisis and the subsequent disorganisation of the background culture,[2] resulting in the reflections on these experiences in the form of a pathology of passions. These experiences of order and disorder are summarised in a section of Chapter 3 (*ibid.*: 76).

As a particularly important aspect of the tradition of constitutional order derived from the town culture, Voegelin reviews the famous council meeting of the *Iliad* (II: 1–52; OHII.: 80–2). The description has four main elements. The meeting is opened by the senior king, Agamemnon, who presents the case. More than just outlining the issues, the king uses the occasion in order to ' "try" (or "put to a test")' (*ibid.*: 80) his soldiers. The language of Voegelin and its tentative character are both of significance here, as they show that the well-known 'agonism' of Greek culture should be complemented, and at the very same point, by its 'proving' or 'testing' character, which – though it only presents another aspect of the same field of liminality – has not received enough attention so far. It is only after this first discourse of the king that the elders enter the scene. Finally, at the end, the decision must also be confirmed by the army – indicating that this early Greek assembly was still close to the simple forms of military 'democracy', identified with the early history of Mesopotamia (Frankfort 1948: 215–21) or of Judaism (AJ: 79).

The experiences of crisis and their symbolisation in Greece, just as in Israel, grew out of the interaction of internal developments, referring back to Crete and Mycene, and changes in external relations, the rise of the field of international power politics. This explains the central role played by Ionia in this change in Greek culture.

Ionia

This external setting was similar for Ionia, the eastern coastline of Anatolia, now in Turkey, as it was for nearby Palestine, both geographically and through the ever greater waves provoked by the sudden rise and fall of Assyrian power in a series of steps in the eighth and seventh centuries BC. The two cases differed in that the Assyrian power expansion was transmitted to Ionia through the formation of and struggles between a series of smaller empires: Phrygia, Lydia and Media.

As a result, Ionia played a central part in the formation of the poleis (through the colonising activities of refugees from the mainland areas of the Mycenean world) and was at the same time most subjected to conquest by the successive empires (OHII: 114). Given that the physical and political geography, the history and the contemporary situation of the region was liminal in multiple regards, it is understandable that the main mythopoets (Homer and Hesiod), the first great philosophers (Anaximander, Anaximenes, Pythagoras and Heraclitus), the founding figures of historiography (Herodotus), geography (Anaximander again, inventing the *gnomon*) and medicine (Hippocrates) all came from there (*ibid.*: 35).

The foundation of the poleis, however, was not simply a civilisational advance, but a painful process in its own right. In evaluating this process, Voegelin is strongly influenced by a Nietzschean position. With great powers of empathy and imagination, Nietzsche described in the *Genealogy of Morals* the painful aspects of the process through which a warrior aristocracy is forced to live inside the closed area of a walled city. This process, arduous even in early modern Europe,[3] had to be especially painful in the formation of the Greek polis, as there, after the 'dark age' (in opposition to the High Middle Ages), the warrior aristocracy did not opt for a life in rural castles and manor houses but moved directly into the city. The civilisational benefits of such a move were enormous, just as in the case of the medieval Italian city states, especially Florence, as analysed by Weber. Voegelin, however, following Nietzsche, argues that the experience of a crisis in the eighth century was rooted in a perceived decline of aristocratic standards, arguing for the primacy of 'a decline of the old aristocratic order' before a 'strong conscious-ness of the polis' could emerge (*ibid.*: 118). The dynamics of the process was therefore given by a struggle between the upper and lower classes in this specific sense: '[t]he pathos of the polis was the pathos of a dynamic participation of the people in a culture that originated in the aristocratic society' (*ibid.*: 120). In this process a crucial importance was played by the establishment of the Olympic games, serving the purpose both of maintaining the unity of the polis world and at the same time of taming the warriors.

Early diagnoses

The rise of the polis in the eighth and seventh centuries in the areas impreg-nated with the legacies of Minoan and Mycenaean cultures, coinciding with the first signs of the outburst of a new age of imperial violence, resulted in works of exceptional and in certain respects almost timeless quality, driven by the will to understand the causes of disorder and the possibility of order.

Homer

While the epic poems of Homer are usually considered to sing the deeds of the heroes, Voegelin – following some path-breaking hints from Shakespeare in *Troilus and Cressida* – rather calls attention to the pathology of its heroes. The portraits drawn of two of the main protagonists of the *Iliad*, Achilles and Paris, demonstrate the exaggerated passions to which they fell prey: the excessive wrath of Achilles, the warrior (see OHII: 84–92, with his recovery being a striking 'psychological masterpiece'; *ibid.*: 92); and the woman-chasing Paris, 'handsome but without spirit or valour' (*ibid.*: 95), later characterised as possessing 'refined rascality' (*ibid.*: 106). The analysis, however, is not psychological, as the pathological syndromes of these heroes only reflect the general corruption of the social order of which they are a part. Voegelin argues that, under normal conditions, the cause of the Trojan war, the seduction of Helen, could have easily been smoothed. But as conditions were different, the fateful development of the final climax could not have been avoided.

Homer, however, was not satisfied with a poetic description of the symptoms, but was searching for the causes of the illness, giving an 'aetiology of disorder' (*ibid.*: 101). The suggestion that all this is due to the gods, which could be identified as a typical purifying and scapegoating ritual, is not accepted as sufficient (*ibid.*: 98, 101), and later is characterised as a sign of civilisational disorder (*ibid.*: 107–8). The question at stake is to discover the cause of evil: '[e]vil is experienced as real; and the evil forces which disrupt order certainly are disturbing enough to invite exploration of their nature and source' (*ibid.*: 101–2). As Homer did not yet have at his disposal the symbol of the 'soul', he had to use cruder analytical means, and this evil source was identified with the 'blindness' of 'passions'. Voegelin elaborates both terms in detail. The centrality of 'blindness' as a diagnostic tool for social disorder is based on the double meaning of the word 'oidos',[4] standing for both knowledge and seeing, and contributes to the belief in the instant transformative value of knowledge, present in Greek thought through Socrates to Aristotle and beyond. The idea of Homer is that, once this blindness, caused by a certain god, is removed, the individual can again assume responsibility for his deeds. This idea of a 'new' and true sight gets close to the later philosophical discovery of the noetic consciousness, or the 'true self' (*ibid.*: 105).

The heart of Homeric insight, however, lies in the analysis of the passions as the source of evil. Without using the word 'psyche', Homer describes its 'internal organization through a center of passions and a second center of ordering and judging knowledge' (*ibid.*: 108). These two centres stand in a state of tension. The passions play 'tricks' with reason, thus rendering humans blind. Ordering action, centring on the discriminating or discerning ability, needs standards for measure, and these standards are defined by conformity with 'transcendent, divine order' (*ibid.*: 108–9). This implies that troubles start with a 'toying and tampering with fate', when the hero tries to satisfy his 'childish desires', while the solution, the unveiling of blindness, comes 'when the burden of fate and responsibility is accepted with humility' (*ibid.*: 105).

Hesiod

Following standard accounts, Hesiod is considered by Voegelin as standing halfway between Homer and philosophy in terms of disengagement for the myth. Only three parallels drawn by Voegelin will be mentioned here. Two are interesting from the perspective of the axial age. The famous fable about the 'Ages of the World', that introduced the myth of the Golden Age and diagnosed its author's present as the 'Iron Age',[5] is compared to the myth of the four ages of Krishna in the Jainist tradition (*ibid.*: 145–6).[6] The similarly striking apocalyptic vision that in *Works and Days* follows on from the fable of the ages, is contrasted with a series of passages from the classical prophecies of Hosea, Isaiah and Micah (*ibid.*: 159–61) who were Hesiod's close contemporaries. In both cases Voegelin emphasises that the point is not direct diffusion, but rather the equivalence of symbolisation. Even more striking is the third parallel, where Voegelin compares this apocalyptic vision to the *History of the Peloponnesian War* by Thucydides. Though not formulated in the language of prophecy, in light of later events the 'visions' of Hesiod could be considered as realised. This presents in as clear a form as possible the problem Voegelin wants to address with his entire life-work: 'If the visions engendered by the anxiety of annihilation can become the structure of society – what is reality?'; or, 'What status of reality has a society that could be created by an apocalyptic vision?' (*ibid.*: 164). In the last sentence of the chapter, Voegelin even hints at his answer: if the reality of power politics and its support by intellectual sophism and cynicism is understood as the product of an 'apocalyptic nightmare', then Plato's ' "idealism" ' can be understood as 'the attempt to overcome a nightmare through the restoration of reality' (*ibid.*).

Hellenic historiogenesis

In Volume Two, Voegelin moves directly to the break with myth and philosophy. However, this might be the point to insert his later identification of the historiogenetic threads in Greek thought (OHIV: 101–6).

After alluding to the differences from Near-Eastern historiogenesis, due to the absence of indigenous empire and the consequent universalistic advances, Voegelin briefly discusses the cases of Hesiod and Herodotus. About the first, little more is done than to summarise the previous analysis of the 'Ages of the World'. The possibilities opened up by this work, however, were realised by Herodotus.

The short analysis of Herodotus as being not just the father of historiography but also the 'importer' of historiogenesis into 'empirical science' is of exceptional significance. Herodotus (c.485–c.425 BC) was an exact contemporary of the last of the great playwrights, Euripides, and the first generation of Sophists, Protagoras and Gorgias. Being born in Halicarnassus, one of the largest cities of Ionia, in the period between the Greek victories of Marathon and Salamis, he was well disposed to deal with the theme of the Persian Wars. The 'motivating experience' of the book was 'the threat to the existence of Hellenic society and the restoration of a precarious balance of power' through the two victories (*ibid.*: 104). While such a motivation can be identified in any imperial historiogenesis, the Greek situation was different, as the problem was not the apology of empire and its order but the struggle against imperial domination. This enabled

Herodotus to break the horizon of the city-states and bring out the truly universal characteristic and significance of the events. Even further, this was not even a radical innovation, as '[f]rom the very beginnings of Hellenic civilisation, it is present in the Homeric epics as they conceive the Achaean–Asiatic conflict as a disturbance of universal human order' (*ibid.*). This aspect gives the centrality of the achievement in a positive rather than a merely negative sense. In the absence of empire, Herodotus does not need to trace the origin of Hellas back to the foundation of the world; rather he reconstructs the 'European–Asiatic conflicts' as a 'chain of violations of justice' from mythic origins, through the Trojan war, up to the present day (*ibid.*: 105).

Though influenced by the ideas of the main philosophers of neighbouring Miletus and Ephesus, Anaximander and Heraclitus, the experiential perspective of the heroic struggle prevents Herodotus from envisioning the story of the events as just another gigantic turning of the wheel, and can even appreciate the wonder of the great spectacle (OHII: 339). This is visible even in his treatment of the rise and fall of the empires of Asia Minor. A chronicler was supposed to tell of the feats of emperors, just as a myth had to have as its heroes the gods or the ancestors. The Greek poleis, however, did not have such heroes after the Mycenean period. Thus, in a perplexing but understandable manner, the heroes of the early parts of the *Histories*, and to some extent even of the Persian Wars, became the enemy emperors.[7]

At this point, however, we should recall that the construction of Herodotus was still historiogenetic, even if it was a 'new and improved' version. This had two grave consequences, the first more axiological and the second analytical. Though the heroic resistance against empire permitted a universalistic touch,[8] a historiogenetic perspective does not allow a revaluation of position, the identification of the moment when the former heroes are metamorphosed into villains. The second point concerns the fact that, in this way, the historiogenetic construct managed to be carried over into the heart of 'science'.[9]

The Golden Age of Athens

Herodotus, the father of both historiography and of the incorporation of historiogenesis into the techniques of 'rational' thought, and one of the last great figures of Ionia, serves as a perfect figure of transition from the early period dominated by Ionian thought, developed out of the experience of the threat of Near-Eastern imperial politics, to Athenian thought, dominated by reflection on the experience of politics as developed out of the successful resistance to this threat and the unforgettable experience of democracy, but also its quick collapse. By this time the pioneering cities of Ionia, under Persian rule, had been transformed into the 'sleepwalkers' of Heraclitus. The 'Great Awakening' was the feat of classical Athens, 'with consequences for the history of mankind which have not been exhausted to this day' (OHII: 241).

The most importance consequence for Voegelin, however, was the creation of the philosophies of Aristotle and especially of Plato. Voegelin is not talking from the perspective of a historian of philosophy, but as a person interested in the effective history of thought. Emphasising the parallels with Israel, he is talking about the 'transfer of authority' to Plato and Aristotle (OHIII: 36–9). Living in a 'knowledge society', it would be more than a little premature to label this as pure idealism. However, the position of Voegelin does raise serious problems, as both his 'Platonism' and the downplaying of the democratic experiment seem excessive. The path opened up by Foucault with his study of parrhesia provides a way out of this impasse. This question will be revisited in detail in the general conclusion.

The discussion that follows will proceed in a slightly different order than the sequence of *The World of the Polis*, partly reflecting the methodological implications of the later discoveries of metaxy and historiogenesis.

Institutional and legal background

As we have seen earlier, the 'crisis' of the polis in the seventh century BC was indeed due to an endemic struggle between the upper and lower social groups. Far from being a class struggle, however, it was due to the conflict between a former warrior aristocracy and the common people, within the enclosed space of a small city. The two main constitutional reforms of Athens, by Solon (594 BC) and Cleisthenes (508 BC) became of exceptional relevance, partly because of their own inherent merits and partly because they enabled Athens to gain ascendancy among the Greek poleis just at the moment of the Persian challenge, and even to fight it successfully. As a result Athens, a 'politically rather insignificant town' before the war, was first 'propelled into political leadership', and then 'became the expanding, wealthy capital of [the] new political structure' (OHII: 267).

Solon

While in institutional histories of democracy primacy is given to the reforms of Cleisthenes, Voegelin puts the emphasis on the 'spirit' of Solonian legislation. Solon was considered as one of the mythical seven sages and, according to Voegelin, could even be credited with the rare feat of creating a new personality type in history, that of the 'lawgiver' (*ibid.*: 199). His wisdom lay in the recognition that, under the new conditions of city life, the pursuit of the ancient values of excellence became impossible (*ibid.*: 196). The agonistic lifestyle of the charismatic military hero, who is only pursuing his own ideas in search of victory and fame, became unacceptable hubris in the new world: '[i]f everybody wants to play Agamemnon or Achilles, the result will not be an aristocratic culture but a war of all against all and the destruction of the polis' (*ibid.*). Magnificence is a 'gift of the gods', not an aim to be realised (*ibid.*: 197). Hubris results in the enclosure of every individual in his own doxa, or private illusion, and the main form of this illusion is the pursuit of wealth, a delusion all the more dangerous as the strive towards wealth knows no ends.[10]

The main aim of Solon's reforms was to set up precisely the right boundaries (*peirata*) (*ibid.*), by an appeal to the unseen measure. It is only through the balance provided by such limits and measures that the right order (*eunomia*) can be attained. While the tension between (human) passions and the (divine) measure cannot be eliminated, and is even the animating force of human life, it needs to be moderated, pacified by an appeal to balance and restraint. Here Solon does not have in mind only the restrictions and sanctions of the law, but rather the 'spirit' underlying these laws. In his meditative prayer, by setting up the opposition between the doxa and the unseen measure, Solon evokes the 'experience of a truth, gained through the differentiation of the soul, in opposition to the delusions of commonly accepted opinion' (*ibid.*: 202), which thus cannot be the result of a 'collective process'. The formulation closely recalls the interpretation given by Foucault, following Dumézil, of the last words of Socrates (see Chapter 8 of this book). And, indeed, Voegelin turns immediately to the *Apology* of Socrates, to underline the experience of isolation to which the mediators of the truth are subjected. The chapter closes by evoking the memorable lines of the Sermon on the Mount, 'But I say unto you…'.

Cleisthenes

In contrast to the detailed and substantial discussion of Solon, the constitutional reforms of Cleisthenes receive not much more than a cursory treatment (*ibid.*: 106). The evident reason is that Voegelin holds mere 'institutional tinkering' in high contempt (see, for example, *ibid.*: 257). The point, however, is unnecessarily polemical, as significant changes require a proper mix of institutional reforms and the right spirit, as shown exactly by the example of Athens.

In this respect the reforms of Cleisthenes, closing the period of tyrants, served their purpose admirably. They were based on two congenial insights. On the one hand, through a territorial reorganisation based on strict arithmetic, they managed to break the powers of the old tribal organisation, coming up with a homogenous concept of citizens' rights. The reform, though, was not complete, as citizenship was still not merely a legal act but was based on blood relationship within the new basic unit, the demos. The second aspect was perhaps even more important. By substituting the new, relatively uniform and universal territorial citizenship in place of the previous order of aristocratic privileges, Cleisthenes effectively 'extended aristocratic…status to every Athenian citizen' (*ibid.*: 106). This had the crucial consequence of homogenising a population through an ascending movement, and not a downward nivellation that is always the threatening flipside of the modern democratisation process, from the Levellers of English history, through the Jacobins, and realised in full with the general proletarisation accomplished by the Communist regimes of Eastern Europe. Even this reform, however, had its limits, as the generous extension of rights had to be met with a similarly generous and spirited awareness of duties, posing the problem of 'democracy' vs 'ochlocracy', as analysed by Plato and Aristotle.

The new democracy of Athens immediately had to go through the 'baptism of fire' of the Persian Wars, and it performed extraordinarily well. The impact of the victory was tremendous, liberating and channelling the spiritual force that animated the 'Golden Age' of Athens. The exact balance of the new constitutional experiment, between the risk of letting the military leaders develop into new tyrants and the deprivation of the city of its best citizens by the practice of ostracism, was, however, precarious. The question of 'education' became a primary concern. It was met through two basic channels: theatre, with the public performance of tragedies; and education, where the Sophists gained an increasing role. These channels are discussed in the first two chapters of Part III.

Tragedy

Athenian tragedy is considered to be of fundamental relevance for political thought for Voegelin, almost comparable to philosophy. In this respect as well, among contemporary thinkers Voegelin's work is closest to that of René Girard, Victor Turner or Foucault. More than anything else, however, it brings out the strong formative impact of the thought of Nietzsche, who in *The Birth of Tragedy* emphasised the extent to which tragedy captured the Greek spirit. Just as had Nietzsche, Voegelin considered Aeschylus to be the genuine representative of this spirit, and Euripides little more than a symptom of decadence. Just as had Nietzsche, Voegelin hardly spent more than a few remarks on Sophocles.[11] And finally, the common root of this is a shared aristocratism, and the – only partly justified – suspicion of the Athenian democratic experiment.

Tragedy was the main form of expression of this 'new consciousness' of Athens, based on an awareness of historical role, and best represented in the funeral oration of Pericles, where '[p]ower and spirit were linked in history for one golden hour through the inseparable events of the Athenian victory in the Persian Wars and the Aeschylean creation of the tragedy' (*ibid.*: 243). Apart from being an expression of this spirit, however, and in line with the Periclean characterisation of Athens as the 'school' of Hellas, tragedy also played the role of educating the people.

In his analysis Voegelin focuses on two plays by Aeschylus, *The Suppliants* and *Prometheus Bound*. The dilemma of the first play cannot be more actual, underlined by the talking names. Following the defeat of their father at the hand of his brother Aegyptus, the Danaïds, the fifty daughters of Danaus, arrive at the island of Argos, asking for asylum. If their request were to be granted, the king and people of Argos would have to be resigned to the inevitable war with the powerful Aegyptus. By refusing asylum, however, they would commit an unjust act. In dramatising reflection on the options, the play combines the two main advances of the Greek world: the nascent discovery of philosophy (of the soul), and (democratic) politics. First, the indecision of the king is presented in a masterful psychological description, the descent to his soul and the decision to grant asylum. This decision is then presented to the assembly of the people, where the king no longer uses tricks to test the people but presents his true counsel arrived at after careful consideration. The people, after a similarly careful discussion, decide to support the position of the king.

The great instrument of order in the play is persuasion (*peitho*), a concept that would also play a central role in Platonic thought. While the play serves to evoke the spirit and the institutional order of Athens, it also makes it clear that Athens is only an 'island of order' in a 'very disorderly world', being surrounded by 'demonic evil' (*ibid.*: 253). This problem is addressed in the second play analysed.

Prometheus Bound presents numerous difficulties, partly because it was probably the first part of a trilogy, still undated, and partly because of the modern, romantic imagery that has developed around it.[12] The diagnosis of the forces of evil proceeds at two levels. At the first level, the inevitable precariousness of all inner (spiritual or psychological) forces is emphasised. The order of the soul is not something that can be safely and for ever secured.[13] The same forces of the soul that can 'create social order when they are properly balanced' would 'destroy this order when the balance is disturbed' (*ibid.*: 255). Thus, just as in the case of Solon a century before, the emphasis is on measure, distinction, discrimination and discernment.

Prometheus, however, is not simply a lost or wandering soul, but is in explicit and conscious revolt against the gods. When identifying the exact sources of this revolt, Voegelin again warns against romantic misunderstandings and quick analogies, pointing out that Prometheus himself was a Titan, thus he cannot be simply represented as the revolt of man against the gods. Instead, Voegelin suggests a return to the original words. The key term identifying the nature of this 'divine–demonic force' motivating Prometheus is his characterisation as a *sophistes*. This does not mean a 'Sophist' in the later sense of the professional itinerant teachers of a successful life, the key opponents of Socrates and Plato, since the first such Sophists only came to Athens in the mid-fifth century.[14] The word, however, was indeed a linguistic innovation of the early fifth century. Its meaning was first 'wise man', and in this positive sense it was used widely to characterise sages and statesmen. However, it very soon acquired a more negative connotation, suggesting the making of something like a special job out of wisdom. It is in this sense that Liddell and Scott (1961) refer to the two passages of *Prometheus* quoted by Voegelin (OHII: 258). Thus, Aeschylus might well have been the inventor of the word, or at least the person who gave a different spin to a relatively new word.

What, then, is the main characteristic of Prometheus as a *sophistes*? He is first of all a man of skills and knowledge, a person who furthermore performed a positive, civilising mission by transmitting his knowledge to human beings, especially the knowledge of mathematics, the '"chiefest of sciences"' (*ibid.*). But *sophisma* also means 'plan, device or trick', incorporating the playful elements of inventiveness, together with its clownish and trickster aspects. This already indicates that the question of the right balance or measure would be particularly necessary in case of the figure. This, however, is precluded by a further, indeed a crucial characteristic, captured in the Greek word *authadia*, 'a term that cannot be translated by a single word, but may be circumscribed as a brazen, shameless, conceited, self-reliant self-satisfaction' (*ibid.*). Authadia represents the smug pride of the self-righteous civiliser. The 'revolt against the gods' is thus based on this specific kind of hubris. In the Nietzsche–Eliasian terminology used earlier, one can say that with Prometheus Aeschylus transferred the diagnosis of hubris, applied by Solon to the pursuit of an aristocratic warrior ethos inappropriate within the walls of city life, to the very performers of the successful taming mission. It also has an important corollary. Though having the 'objective' characteristic of a revolt, this is not a conscious action. Those who commit this act are just as 'responsible', at least in the level of original intentions, for their acts as the previous warrior heroes were when trying to continue their old way of life under the new circumstances. This absence of intention, not always heeded by Voegelin in his diatribes against modern thinkers, becomes visible in the next two steps of the analysis: the concern with pity and philanthropy, and the diagnosis of madness.

Prometheus was diagnosed as being possessed by a demonic force, but Voegelin calls attention to the ambivalence of the character. The civilising mission performed is real, and Prometheus even has a degree of moral scruple about his own excess of pride. Self-exuberance and indulgence are compensated for by sentiments of pity. The link between the two main characteristics of the *sophistes* is perfectly circular: the civilising mission is rooted in a sense of pity, and further philanthropy is performed in order to attenuate the sense of guilt and bad faith due to a dim awareness of excess of pride, and also that the entire mission was rooted in a 'demonic drive' of 'self-assertion and expansiveness' (*ibid.*: 261). Using the later terminology of 'exodus' and 'conquest' (OHIV: 212), Aeschylus came close to identifying the motivational centre of the movements of the ecumenic age. This terminology also helps to tie here with the later development of the Sophists. The Sophists as itinerant teachers, mostly refugees from Ionia, indeed played a crucial role both in 'civilising' and in 'corrupting' Athens, in the sense of transforming the spiritual forces derived from the Persian Wars, always on the brink of exploding out of balance, into full-scale power politics.[15] The net result, at any rate, is the grief produced by the joint 'indulgence of *philantropia* and *authadia*', expressed in the words ' "See now, my friend, how unblessed are your blessings!" ' (OHII: 261).

But Prometheus, indeed, does not see. Here the analysis of Aeschylus, in a scene between Prometheus and Hermes, elaborates on the Homeric diagnosis of blindness. When threatened with the harsh punishment, the very excess of which indicates unbalance even on the side of the 'gods', Prometheus pronounces the memorable lines: ' "I hate all the gods" ' (*ibid.*: 259).[16] The reply of Hermes is that Prometheus is simply mad. Madness here stands not for a diagnosis in the modern sense, bringing exoneration from any possible responsibility, but a disease in the spiritual sense that absolves Prometheus from the charge of willingly committing evil, but justifies even more the need for punishment, as the previous calls for humility and the application of the Delphic maxim 'know yourself' went unheeded (*ibid.*: 261). Prometheus thus had to suffer his agonising punishment. At this point the play offers a final surprise. Prometheus would have ' "no end of [his] agony, until a god appear[s] to take upon himself your suffering, who willingly descends to unlighted Hades and the dark depths of Tartarus" ' (*ibid.*: 260), bringing out astonishing parallels with the words of Deutero Isaiah, pronounced only a few decades earlier.

Voegelin concludes his analysis on a Nietzschean note, though again on a difference. Tragedy as a genre was restricted to Greece. It was a reflection on historical experiences. Similar experiences were symbolised in different ways in Israel and in China. The Greek development was rooted in the presence of specific public rituals, the cult of Dionysus. This source, however, far from being the reason for the unique achievements of the Greeks, rather precluded the 'irruption of a divine revelation' (*ibid.*: 264)

Voegelin's discussion of Euripides, in the section entitled 'The End of Tragedy', is very short, but contains a few significant points, not least because of the parallels with modernity. The plays of Euripides were not a 'cause' of the rising corruption, no more than the inquiries of Socrates, but rather a faithful reflection of the disintegration of Athenian democracy.[17] Voegelin only evokes a few striking images: the self-debasement of Hecuba, who takes revenge on the murderer of her son by blinding him after setting him up in a cunning trap, but not before killing his two innocent children; the madness of Heracles who, after killing the tyrant, continues to kill and murders his own family, but when coming to his senses lets himself be convinced that the gods did not do much better either, and settles for a quiet retirement. The climax is reached in *The Women of Troy*, where 'finally, Euripides holds up the mirror to Athens herself' (*ibid.*: 265). The existing play is the concluding piece of a trilogy whose second, lost, part was interpreted in the fourth century BC as a prediction of the fate of Socrates in Athens. The piece – not analysed in detail – represents the 'suicide of the Greek soul in the hour of victory. What began as an heroic adventure, ends in the vulgarity and atrocity of the conquest' (*ibid.*). With this play we reach again the decisive date in Voegelin's interpretation of Athenian history, the slaughter at Melos, as the play was performed in the very same year.

The three plays are listed in sequential order, from c.425 through c.421 to c.415 (though some of this dating is still controversial), indicating the deepening of the process. This can be contrasted with the Foucauldian analysis of parrhesia in Euripides, starting with the first, positive occurrence in 428, the culmination with *Ion* in c.418, and the negative connotation appearing in 408 BC.

The Sophists

The conflict between Socrates and the Sophists was central for the philosophy of both Plato and Voegelin. The argument was also already hinted at in the analysis of *Prometheus*, and there we also identified a slight lack of precision in Voegelin's argument. This could be safely taken, as usual, as an indication of an unsettled disturbance of autobiographical origin. The clarification of this issue at the start helps to see the entire argument. The point is not to dismiss the argument as an autobiographical idiosyncrasy, but rather to render it even clearer and more useful by excising a slight but not insignificant perturbation.

In characterising the Sophists, Voegelin repeatedly presents an argument that seems disturbing, both intellectually and in a sense even morally. The Sophists are presented not simply as professional teachers, who can be charged with exchanging truth for money, but as homeless foreigners. Some of these descriptions border on the 'xenophobic'. This seems to present an especially perplexing dilemma, given that Voegelin himself was an exile from Nazi Austria. This shows that the point cannot be taken at face value, but rather as a strong and personally felt position concerning what is and what is not a proper way of behaving in a foreign country. It also indicates that he had in mind a definite group of people whom he considered as failing to live up to his standards.

We get closer to the problem if we recall an obscure but not unimportant part of his personal itinerary. Like every refugee from Central Europe to the United States, Voegelin first arrived at the East Coast. However, after a short period, and in opposition to his friend Schutz, he decided *not* to stay there, but rather take up positions in the American hinterland, such as in Georgia and Louisiana. The respective careers of Voegelin and Schutz showed how much he was right. Though considered in these areas to be a continental eccentric, he managed to establish a reputation based on his erudition and his work habits. Schutz, however, staying at the centre of European emigration becoming marginalised there, never managed to secure an academic position. The question now becomes how to find the nature of this centre; and it is not difficult to identify it in the exiled Frankfurt school.

Short of a proper non-hagiographic history of the Frankfurt school, and taking up suggestions by Dick Pels (1993), only two comments will be stated here. The first is that all those major figures of social theory of the 'great generation' who failed to receive proper recognition, like Elias, Borkenau, Voegelin, Schutz or Mannheim, suffered marginalisation by the sophisticated techniques of exclusion practised by the official bastion of 'critical theory', that filled and monopolised the space left by official academic theory. The second point is that this autobiographical episode, which adds further colour to the Voegelin–Schutz correspondence, goes a long way towards explaining the excessively and self-defeatingly polemical tones of Voegelin in the confrontation with Hegelianism and Marxism, both in the USA and in Germany.

With these strictures in mind we can now turn to Voegelin's analysis.

The issue addressed is the same as it was for tragedy: the education of Athens. As a source of support, Voegelin refers to a passage of Aristotle evoking the Athenians' sudden urge to know more that became evident especially after the Persian Wars, and immediately adds a comment on the role played by foreigners in this process, identifying them as Sophists (OHII: 268).

There are three problems with this characterisation. The first is that there is no trace in Aristotle of the second part of the comment, the reference to foreigners. Second, Voegelin applies some caution in the characterisation, claiming that to these foreigners the term 'Sophist' 'may be applied'. However, as 'Sophist' is a technical term, the conditional is not really applicable. Third, between the Persian Wars and the arrival of the first Sophists in 442 BC, there is a gap of three or four decades. In the period of history right after the Persian Wars there is no reference to 'foreigners' being involved in the teaching of Athenians, and the term *sophistes*, as shown above, had a different meaning. In fact, it is even unlikely that there was a lack of relevant evidence here, as Anaxagoras, who came to Athens in 462 BC, thus just at the halfway point between the battle of Salamis and the arrival of the first Sophists, was evidently the first of his kind, and was emphatically not called a Sophist.

In fact, Voegelin perceives that the argument is not watertight here, as he proceeds on a double legitimating strategy. On the one hand, he dismisses the relevance attached to the history of the term. This, however, is highly dubious, partly because terminologies, especially related to the self-understanding of a society, do have their importance, as he knows all too well, and because his general assessment of the Sophists very much relies on their perception by their contemporaries, especially Socrates and Plato. On the other hand, he attempts to widen the circle, in space and time, trying to draw into the orbit older philosophers like Zeno and Anaxagoras, members of the Pythagorean school, with an ambivalent formulation ('we hesitate to...'), even involving Herodotus, Democritus or Thucydides.

This blurring of the chronology had grave effects on Voegelin's argument, reinforcing the exact blind spot in properly assessing the period that, with all its shortcomings, is considered to be the 'Golden Age' of Athenian democracy. The generation which was born just before the Persian Wars and was coming of age in the aftermath of Athenian victory and glory, the generation of Pericles (c.495–429 BC) and Sophocles (c.496–406 BC), all but ignored by Voegelin, was educated by the heroes of the wars like Aeschylus and in general by the spirit of the times, defined by victorious war and the democratic experiment. It was only the main protagonists of the next generation, Euripides and Socrates, who started to notice the emerging problems of education, not so much in their own generation, but in the next, the epigones who took the achievements of their predecessors for granted, were born into prosperity and power, and after 442 BC became increasingly educated by the Sophists. This means that the impact of the Sophists can indeed be tightly identified with the Peloponnesian War, or the decline of Athens, and not much before.

In resuming Voegelin's analysis of the main ideas of the Sophists, use will again be made of the later discoveries, such as metaxy and the ecumenic age. As the analysis of *Prometheus* already indicated, Voegelin does not ignore the positive, civilising achievements of the Sophists. The emphasis, however, is on the fact that theirs is a pathological form of existence, based first on the loss of the centre of one's existence, the experience of home, and then on the resulting systematic neglect of the traumatic formative experiences and an escape into the speculative, abstract manipulation of symbols, deprived of their experiential setting and content. In its most pathological forms, this leads to the denial of the very meaning of terms like 'home' and 'centre', and the radical idea that symbols are to be treated purely on their own terms, as they bear absolutely no relation to reality. In such ideas one can identify the Heraclitean sleepwalkers, the *idiotes* closed into their private worlds, but at the same time claiming, with sophistication, that nothing else exists both in Antiquity and in modernity.

Such a loss of an experiential centre first of all leads to the dual combination of encyclopaedic, even eclectic empiricism,[18] and the pursuit of logical antinomies. Thus, Hippias was boasting of his book that it was assembled on the basis of all the relevant information gathered from a whole series of related books (OHII: 279), thus 'substituting empirical generality for the universality of transcendence' (*ibid.*: 281), while the anonymous collection *Dissoi Logoi* took pleasure in a lengthy catalogue of contradictory opinions and valuations on the same matter (*ibid.*: 296–7). At the second, interpretive level, such pastimes gave rise to another tight figuration of nihilistic relativism on the one hand, and malevolent universalism on the other. Based on the various and contradictory evidence of encyclopaedic compilations, the view emerged that all customs are relative and one is just as good as the others (*ibid.*: 306), giving rise to the 'conservative sceptic' who does not believe in the validity of any values, but is willing to adhere to the customs of the country in which he happens to live (*ibid.*: 307–8; see also OHIII: 372). This relativism is supported by the attribution of universal, but egoistic and animalistic motives to every single human action, formulated paradigmatically by Polus in Plato's *Gorgias* that, by not admitting the validity of his arguments, Socrates must perforce lie, as ' "surely you must think as I do" ' (OHII: 164).

Moving on, this combination of relativism and universalism poses the problem of the constraint of human behaviour by repressive laws. In this account, laws evolve out of an original state of all-encompassing violence (*ibid.*: 320). A particularly telling representative of this argument is the myth of Sisyphus as told by Critias, that emphasises the role being played by a 'false tale' about the existence of gods, which instils the fear of god into humans and thus renders social control more effective (*ibid.*: 320–1). The wise men, the Sophists, of course, do not need such modes of restraint, which partly maintains their sense of superiority and partly enables them to do as they please with good conscience. This perspective is summarised in a triple argument: the gods don't exist; if they do, they don't care about humans; if they care, they can be bribed by sacrifices (*ibid.*: 274).

The fundamental part of Voegelin's argument, however, concerns the interconnected questions of the right measure, as seen by the Sophists and Plato, and whether virtue can be taught (*ibid.*: 285–91). The claim of Protagoras, that man is the measure, is countered by Plato's 'unseen measure' that is God,[19] while the latter question is the central theme of Plato's dialogue *Protagoras*. These issues are crucial for identifying the precise difference between the two positions, as the teachability of virtue is usually considered to be a central argument of Platonic–Socratic philosophy, while the position of Plato on measure is ignored by those who consider him as a founder of 'rational' thought. It is, however, Protagoras who argues that virtue can indeed be taught, and who invokes a version of the myth of Prometheus as a source of support. Socrates first convinces Protagoras to give up the technique of making speeches, in order to focus on the argument, and then reaches the well-known argument that erring can only be involuntary, guided by ignorance. This would seem to support a purely cognitive–rationalist position. However, Socrates–Plato then qualifies the point. The central issue in ignorance is not factual knowledge but a question of *misjudgement*. This identifies the central problem as a question of the measure. Thus, concludes Socrates, the only way virtue can be taught is as an art of measurement – but the dialogue is inconclusive, it is not clear whether such an art can be taught at all. At this point, Voegelin 'feel[s] justified in extrapolating the Socratic art of measurement into the Platonic counter-formula of God as the Measure' (*ibid.*: 291). This problem of the teaching of the measure is also close to the Weberian problem of exemplary as opposed to ethical prophecy.

Historiography

While the tragedists and the Sophists were performing their role in the education (and miseducation) of Athens, the historians registered the events that served as the background to philosophical reflections. Just as importantly, through their interpretations they helped to generate a new historical consciousness. Such an interpretation, however, had to rely on existing analytical tools, which included Ionian philosophy, including cosmological and historiogenetic constructions; tragedy, especially the vision of Aeschylus, itself a philosophy of history, according to which wisdom is born out of suffering; and also the Sophists. The division of labour between the two key figures was very simple. Herodotus was the historian of the glorious Persian Wars, while Thucydides documented the self-destruction of Athens in the Peloponnesian Wars.

Herodotus

Strongly influenced by the ideas of Anaximander and Heraclitus concerning an inescapable cosmic dynamism of eternal return and the will to power, with warfare (*polemos*) being the principle of all, Herodotus transferred the principle to the field of human history. Being especially interested in the study of human motivation, he developed the technique of putting speeches into the mouth of protagonists. An example is the speech of Queen Atossa to Darius, inciting him to war against Greece by identifying the 'expansionist drive' as the 'essence of man' (OHII: 338). Voegelin uses two further sets of speeches to illustrate the point. One is the deliberation of the royal council held by Xerxes about action against Hellas. The king proposes war, but some of his elder councillors are opposed to the idea, even evoking the charge of hubris. The king is incensed and opts for war, but later reflects on the counter-arguments and reverses his position. In his dream, however, he receives a vision inciting him to warfare, a vision that recurs the next day to his elder councillor when he sleeps with the royal garb. The argument of Herodotus is not for divine intervention in sleep, but rather it recalls the Heraclitean contrast between the voice of reason, given after reflection and a searching out of the soul, and the behaviour of the sleepwalkers who act on the fancy of their dreams. Though not pointed out by Voegelin, the episode has the further, almost Goffmanian insight about identity (as the 'essential' drive to power) being rooted in the socio-political role (dresses). The insight of Herodotus is therefore particularly sharp: the expansionist drive, the 'will to power' in this sense, is due to a combination of private fancy and sleepwalking, and resignation to the fulfilment of social role.

The second set of discourses renders the parallels with the present even more pointed. This is the famous deliberation on the best form of government. The first argument, in favour of democracy and against monarchy, focuses on the inevitable abuse to which the rule of a single man can lead, as in this case the hubris of the tyrant would know no limits. The second speaker, however, counters the argument. A mob rule would not necessarily be better, as '[t]o change the hubris of a despot for the hubris of a demos would be unbearable' (*ibid.*: 342).

Thucydides

Though Herodotus is called the 'father of history', this designation, according to Voegelin, should be reserved rather for Thucydides. The feat was accomplished by the recognition of the unity of the Peloponnesian War through the symbol *kinesis* (movement or upheaval; one could add the adjective 'frenetic') (*ibid.*: 351, 358). Contemporaries had no idea that they were living in the 'Peloponnesian War'. They made a distinction between the ten years' war of 431–21, followed by an in-between period of relative peace, and finally the Ionian war of 414–404 BC (*ibid.*: 350). It was the great vision of Thucydides to recognise the unity of the entire period, and the establishment of historiography, according to Voegelin, was based on this vision.

The recognition of this unity and the development of the concept of 'kinesis' form a tightly knit circle. Thucydides could recognise this unity as he understood that the two wars are part of the same 'movement'; but one could argue that the concept was developed out of the vision of the unity. Thucydides even had an inkling that this movement was not restricted to Greece, but encompassed the greater part of mankind. In pinning down the exact causes of this frenetic movement, Thucydides discards the Miletian philosophical ideas of the turning wheel and the eternal recurrence and turns instead to medicine for conceptual tools (*ibid.*: 353–7). Relying on the recently developed methods of the Hippocratic School of Cos, also in Ionia, Thucydides argues that kinesis is a disease (*nosos*). Moreover, this disease is an epidemic one.[20] In order to characterise its extent, he uses the word '*metabole*', meaning disturbance, revolution or upheaval. Voegelin is critical of the excessive reliance on empirical medicine, calling it an immanentist speculation. The disease on which the frenetic movements of warfare and conquest were based, was not a material disease, a substantive essence, but a disease of the soul. The analysis of the disorder by Thucydides prepares the way for the Platonian search for the sources of disorder.

Thucydides could develop his vision and method by making use of the distance gained through exile.[21] Still, his involvement remained strong, shining forth in the 'deepest stratum' of his kinetic analysis, which is 'despair' (*ibid.*: 362). Athens became involved in the kinesis, in the frenetic movements, and thus his 'brilliant expansion is self-destructive', both in the political and the moral sense (*ibid.*). Still, though dissecting this process with the acuity of an anatomist, at this point the mind of Thucydides shows some hesitation, as if unwilling to draw the necessary conclusions of his own ideas. The point of Voegelin here is so important, also due to the parallels with the Foucauldian analysis, that a lengthier quote is justifiable: Thucydides 'could not or did not want to see that a society and its political system was doomed if it could maintain itself in existence only by the miracle of a succession of Periclean personalities; nor would he admit that with progressive corrosion of ethos another Pericles could hardly emerge from Athenian society'(*ibid.*:363).

Kinetic theory yielded two further insights. Under the weight of events, beyond recognising the unity of the Peloponnesian Wars, Thucydides later extended the investigation even to the period of the Persian Wars. Furthermore, this allowed him to capture the long-term historical significance of the events in the metamorphosis of his main hero, Athens, telling 'the story of the death of the hero who once represented the order of Zeus against the disordering hubris of power' (*ibid.*: 364). This, at the same time, represented the death sentence for the entire order of the polis.

The last section of the book deals with the main literary device of Thucydides, the use of speeches. Though already employed by Herodotus, the device gained a new meaning in Thucydides. The speeches were not a literal transcription of what was actually said, which would not have been possible anyway, but rather the reconstruction of the drama of the events at the level of consciousness, focusing on the manner in which the speakers were mobilising their audience (*ibid.*: 366–7). Voegelin emphasises that this device has fundamental links both with tragedy and with the theory of kinesis. At this point Voegelin gives long excerpts from the speeches, focusing on the 'Funeral Oration' of Pericles, in order to convey the 'pathos' of Athens, 'a manifestation of pride in existence' (*ibid.*: 370–1). At a political level, it is difficult to avoid taking pride in the achievements; but there is a direct continuity between this pride and the later atrocities of the Wars, culminating in the conquest of Melos, where 'all men were butchered, and the women and children were sold into slavery' (*ibid.*: 373).

Within the logic of the Ionian view of the world, the world of Anaximander and Herodotus, the atrocities committed by the Athenians should be followed by their suffering a similar fate. This is, in fact, what the inhabitants expect after the news of the loss their last fleet (*ibid.*). Such a fate was avoided only because the

Spartans, the arch-enemies, recalled the services of Athens in the Persian Wars. The heroic myth of the freedom fight against the empire was an effective force as early as 404 BC. The close escape of Athens also meant that classical philosophy could emerge out of the ashes of Athens's glory days.

Philosophy

In giving an account of the way (Athenian) philosophy, in contrast to (Ionian) physiology, emerged, it is necessary to overcome the historiogenetic constructs of Aristotle and Hegel and replace them with a 'genealogical' method. Instead of representing the achievements of Socrates, Plato and Aristotle as the culmination of a linear development that started with Thales, one should rather reconstruct the way in which Ionian physiology was inserted into the framework of Athenian experience.

Such a perspective must be generational, focusing on common formative experiences, including displacements suffered. Of course, a proper generational analysis cannot be performed for thinkers for whom we often do not even know the exact dates of birth. Still, the broad outlines of four basic generations can be identified with reasonable confidence.

The first is the 'founding generation' of the Miletian thinkers, Thales, Anaximander and Anaximenes. Strictly speaking the three belong to three different generations, as tradition considers them pupils of each other. Thales is usually considered as the 'first philosopher', but the fact that not even a fragment of his ideas survived always created perplexity. It seems that the problem can be resolved by the idea of 'predecessor selection' (Camic 1992). Thales came to be considered as the first philosopher simply on account of being the teacher of Anaximander, who can truly be considered as conceiving, in his famous fragment, the first genuinely philosophical idea. The gap between the primary experience of the world of Thales, for whom the universe is still full of gods, and of Anaximander's apeiron, cannot be greater, opposing an 'unreconstructed' experience of the myths with an attempt to come to terms with the whirlwind of history. This is also supported by the contrast between the original principle of Thales, water, and the Anaximandrian infinite. The same contrast is present in their respective views of nature, one focusing on cosmology, the other on geography.[22] Anaximander used the tools of his master, Thales, a conventionally trained priest and astronomer, not to study the stars (in order to help the harvest), but to study the space that became relevant for the current warfare and conquest, confirming Foucault's observation, based on seventeenth–eighteenth-century material, that geography is rooted in military strategy (DE169). Both Thales and Anaximander died in the same year (546BC), in the year of the Persian conquest of Ionia, though this fact did not seem to have merited comment even from Diogenes Laertius.

The second generation of philosophers is comprised of those who were already grown into a world marked by the Persian conquest of Ionia, the main representatives being Heraclitus and Parmenides, the great 'mystical philosophers' and discoverers of the soul, whose dates of birth are not known with exactitude but are assumed to be roughly between the years 550 and 540 BC. The crucial transition figure between the two generations is Xenophanes (580/ 70–475/65 BC), who lived through the Persian conquest as an adult in his thirties, migrating from Colophon (a small town near Miletus) to Sicily and founding the Eleatic school, and who died around the time that Socrates and Democritus were born.[23] A similar role was played by the more enigmatic figure of Pythagoras, born on the Ionian island of Samos.

The third generation is transitional in a different sense: it involves the shift of the centre of Greek culture and thought from Ionia to Athens. It thus includes not only thinkers, but even (charismatic) political figures. The unity of the generation is rooted in the formative experience of the Persian Wars of 490–479 BC, coming just after the decisive suppression of the attempts to liberate Ionia, led by Miletus, resulting in the complete destruction of the city in 494. Typical members of this generation were born in the early decades of the fifth century BC, thus just growing into adulthood in the period of the glorious victories of Athens. Representative figures include Sophocles (c.496–406), Pericles (c.495–429), and Anaxagoras (500–428), while the limits are marked by Aeschylus (c.525–457) and perhaps Euripides (c.484–c.406). The first thing to note is the centrality of tragedy for the generation, as its upper and lower limits, just as its centre, are defined by the three great figures. Aeschylus is the oldest of this great generation, belonging there by virtue of taking part in the battles of both 490 and 480, and then putting the experience into a definite form; Sophocles was becoming a young adult in the first years of Athens's glory, while Euripides closed the great generation by documenting, in his best-known plays, the symptoms of its decline.[24]

The generation, however, has another key figure, at once central and marginal. He is a lifelong friend of Pericles who only arrived in Athens in 462: Anaxagoras, native of Clazomenae in Ionia, the 'first philosopher' of Athens. Anaxagoras was not a Sophist, though he was a pioneer of independent, detached investigation, and this indeed created problems in Athens. His trial in 430, when he was only saved from execution due to the personal intervention of Pericles, foreshadowed the trial of Socrates. Not being an innovative thinker, his great role was to transmit the concept of '*nous*' (intellect) from Ionia to Athens.

There are two further points to be mentioned about this 'great generation'. The first is that belonging at its later end are the two great Sophists, Protagoras (c.490–c.420) and Gorgias (c.485–376). Though they only arrived in Athens in the 440s, political events no doubt were defining their upbringing as well.[25] Though, with the benefit of the knowledge of twentieth-century intellectual history, with the two great generations born between 1895 and 1900 and 1920 and 1927 followed by the two generations of modern 'Sophists' born around 1902–1905 and 1929–1930,[26] one could risk arguing that the ancient Sophists can also be defined as being epigones in the Nietzschean–Weberian sense, having being born just a little too late.

The second point concerns the curious absence of the 'great generation' in Voegelin. Sophocles is not discussed, Pericles only as a manifestation of excessive Athenian pride, while Anaxagoras is mentioned in the highly questionable, but revealing, manner as a typical Sophist (OHII: 293–4, 6–7). It seems as if Voegelin would simply blur the distance between this great generation and the Sophists, repeating the anachronistic identification of the *sophistes* of Aeschylus with the later Sophists.

In fact, this suspicion is reinforced by Voegelin's treatment of the next crucial group of thinkers, the main figures of transition between the third and the fourth generation. If the third generation can be defined by the heroic events of the Persian Wars, the fourth generation was formed by the (or in the aftermath of) the Peloponnesian Wars and the death of Socrates. The great transitional figure between the two is of course Socrates (469–399 BC), whose period of activity is more or less identical with the Peloponnesian Wars, but others are Democritus (c.470–c.370) and to some extent Euripides, standing on the borderline. Now, the treatment by Voegelin of these figures is particularly scarce and problematic as well. Socrates takes up a mere eight pages at the start of a book-length treatment of Plato. Democritus is discussed in the chapter upon Sophists, and in *Plato and Aristotle* he is only mentioned – though widely considered as an important predecessor of Plato – as being engaged, together with Anaxagoras, in 'the topical transformation of Parmenides' Being' (OHIII: 277).[27]

The identification of the four generations, with the figures of transition, also helps to bring out the internal logic of Voegelin's presentation. Stripped to its bare structure, and ignoring the diagnostic parts, Voegelin first briefly discusses Xenophanes, then in greater detail Parmenides and Heraclitus; then, again shortly, Socrates, and in great detail Plato and Aristotle.

Xenophanes

Xenophanes attacked two of the main pillars of the traditional Greek social order, the myths and agonistic culture as manifested in the Olympic games. His main charge against Homer and Hesiod was that their accounts were 'unseemly', and that their image of the gods was anthropomorphic (OHII: 172–7). However, as he failed to provide criteria of truth, Xenophanes was found wanting by Heraclitus (*ibid.*: 173). Concerning agonistic culture, his main charge was that the Olympic games promoted a false vision of virtue. The games do not contribute to the good order of the polis, as the victor is just another version of the Homeric hero (*ibid.*: 185).

Such attacks against conventions could be considered as nihilistic, indeed as advancing the later Cynic charges against agonistic aristocratic culture, but Xenophanes has a different agenda. He attacked aspects of Greek culture because of their parochial character, from a transcendental and universalistic perspective: '[b]ehind the critique of anthropomorphism there appears the experience of divine and human universality as the motivating force' (*ibid.*: 178).

Developing further the ideas of Anaximander, Xenophanes argues about the unity and the universality of the divine, even though the argument that he was already a monotheist cannot be accepted (*ibid.*: 179). Thus, his attack on the myths was not in the direction of the 'secularisation' of the Sophists: '[t]he universality of transcendence discovered by him did not abolish the old gods; it only improved their understanding' (*ibid.*: 180).

Parmenides

Parmenides developed further the critique of Xenophanes against mere fancy and opinion by developing the symbol of the 'way of truth' in his didactic poem of c.485 BC. Though the work of Parmenides in many respects stands parallel to classical prophecy, this symbol did not exist in the orbit of Hebrew thought until the coming of Jesus.[28]

The main work of Parmenides is organised into a Prologue and two parts entitled 'Truth' (aletheia) and 'Delusion' (doxa). The Prologue defines the 'way', the first part the 'truth of being', while the second part diagnoses the false ways of delusion.

The Prologue describes the 'way' as a mystical 'transport' or out-of-body experience, which the author has undergone in his younger years. Emphasis in the first step is on the immediacy of personal experience as the way (*hodos*), and in the second step on the transcendence of this immediacy towards the idea of the immortality of the soul.

It is reflection on this experience that gives rise to the development of two crucial 'methodological' terms (terms which describe the progress 'according to the way', *meta hodos*), the *Nous* and the *Logos*. 'The *Nous* is discovered as the organ of cognition that will bring nonsensual, intelligible reality into the grasp of man' (*ibid.*: 208). For the actual articulation of the content that is approached through the *Nous*, Parmenides uses another term, the *Logos*, which 'appears on this occasion for the first time…in the narrower sense of logical argumentation' (*ibid.*: 209). We can thus conclude that in the 'way of truth' Parmenides established, almost out of nothing, the central conceptual apparatus of the rational methodology and logic of inquiry.

In light of more recent investigations on the origins of philosophy, however, we can even say more. Using the works of Vernant (1990 [1965]) and Eliade (1969 [1954]), the 'transport experience' and the concept of the immortality of the soul can be traced to the influence of shamanism or yoga, probably transmitted through the travels to the East of Pythagoras.

The method of Parmenides laid the foundations of method and logic, but at the same time it was a visionary philosophy, leading, in a cathartic way, 'from the Night of the mortals…to the Light of eternal truth' (OHII: 207). The core of this visionary experience is the exclamation 'Is!', or the discovery of existence itself as a problem, leading to the symbol 'Being'. Here, just as at the level of method, Parmenides broke new ground. Voegelin argues that 'Parmenides has no predecessors, and his concept of Being has no prehistory' (*ibid.*: 208). The result of the methodical and logical elaboration of the transcendental experience 'is not only a truth *about* Being; it is the Truth *of* Being voiced through the "knowing man"' (*ibid.*: 213). Due to this, Parmenides should be considered, along with Plato, as the founder of philosophy.

The second, and much more fragmented, part of the poem deals with delusions. *Doxai* does not mean false views or mere opinion in the later sense of the term, only another kind of experience: the experience of the alternation between day and night, life and death, end and beginning, or the view of the world as the place of the eternal return (*ibid.*: 216).[29] Parmenides here revalues the entire cosmological view of the early Ionian philosophers, not as an error, but as a type of truth inferior to the truth gained by the transcendent experience and the recognition of the immortality of the soul, still caught in the experience of a 'delusionary dualism' (*ibid.*: 217).

Given the importance attributed to Parmenides in *The World of the Polis* and the evident link of this analysis to crucial concepts like the 'leap in being' and 'metaxy', it is somewhat perplexing that Voegelin would not return later to this analysis, not even in the revalorisation of the Anaximandrian *Apeiron*.

Heraclitus

While Parmenides discovered the way of Truth and the truth of Being, Heraclitus can be accredited with the discovery of the depths and the true order of the soul. This is accomplished through setting up three basic tensions. The first is between the human and the divine, and is best defined in one of the most famous and enigmatic of the fragments, '*ethos anthropos daimon*', read by Voegelin to mean that the specificity of the human type of 'spirit' is character, or personality (Fragment B 119; OHII: 224). Humans are spirits, and in this respect similar to the gods, thus capable of transcendental experiences, but they should beware of eliminating the tension through self-divinisation. Voegelin traces the discovery of Heraclitus to Pythagorean sources, and argues that Heraclitus here seems to advance a warning not heeded by the other thread of mystic philosophers, that lay from Pythagoras through Parmenides to Empedocles. Empedocles, in fact, claimed to have recalled the experiences of his previous lives, made in public the claim that '"I go about among you, an immortal god, no longer a mortal"' (OHII: 223), and allegedly ended his life by jumping into Etna.

The discovery of the immortality of the soul for Heraclitus is not an occasion for self-divinisation, but rather renders possible a search, alongside the tension opened up between the human and the divine. Human knowledge does not have the character of a possession. Only the divine possesses wisdom, and are able to have visionary insights (*gnomê*).[30] Humans can only embark on a search, starting with themselves, by exploring the depths of the soul (see ibid.: 227–8).[31] The argument is concluded in Fragment B 115: '"The soul has a logos that augments itself"' (*ibid.*: 228). This, however, identifies a crucial problem with Heraclitus, a potential short-circuiting of the soul and the logos, without exteriorisation.

This search for truth through, though not in,[32] the depth of the soul sets up the second tension with the world of flux and appearances. In the world of nature and life everything is in constant flux, where one ' "cannot step twice into the same river" ' (*ibid.*: 236–7), permanent change renders the days indiscriminate, as ' "[o]ne day is like every other" ' (*ibid.*: 237), and even the tight links between death and life are established in a striking formulation recalling Anaximander: ' "The name of the bow [*biós*] is life [*bíos*], but its work is death" ' (*ibid.*). Most human beings resign themselves to the illusion that this is all there is in the world, and thus become sleepwalkers: ' "This Logos here, though it is eternal, men are unable to understand before they hear it as well as when they hear it first....it escapes their notice what they do when awake, as it escapes their memory what they do when asleep" ' (*ibid.*: 230). This order of the Logos is common to all men, and to follow it is a duty: ' "But though the Logos is common, the many live as if they had a wisdom of their own [*idian phronesin*]" ' (*ibid.*: 232).[33] This chimerical pretence of living in one's own individual world identifies the sleepwalkers: ' "Those who are awake have a world one and common, but those who are asleep each turn aside into their private worlds" ' (*ibid.*).

The task of the soul is to overcome delusion and find this common order of the logos under the chaos of the apparent world, as ' "[t]he invisible harmony is better [alternative trans: greater, more powerful] than the visible" ' (*ibid.*: 228). The reaching-out for this order requires a special kind of attitude or attunement, a combination of faith and hope: ' "If you do not hope, you will not find the unhoped-for, since it is hard to be found and the way is all but impassable" ' (*ibid.*); and ' "Through lack of faith (*apistie*) the divine [?] escapes being known" ' (*ibid.*).

This struggle, however, is rendered even more difficult as the realm of the divine is itself divided between the serene order of the cosmic logos on one side, and its more playful, cunning and joking aspects on the other. The one common order of the logos bears a divine imprint, as ' "all human laws nourish themselves from the one divine" ' (*ibid.*: 232). But, as Voegelin argues in a crucial piece of re-translation, the real meaning of Fragment B 52 is Zeus 'is a child playing draughts; the royal rule is a child's' (*ibid.*: 235). If, however, the divine spirit is itself divided, one cannot expect that it would be different for the world of humans; thus, ' "war [polemos] is of all things the father" ' (*ibid.*: 233).

The sorting-out of the inner tension between spiritual forces is beyond human capability. The soul who has awakened from its sleepwalking, from a mere swimming in the eternal recurrence of the ebbs and flows of passions and desires, can only hope to restrain excess: ' "Hubris must be put out, more than a fire" ' (*ibid.*: 238).

Conclusion

The appearance of the mystic philosophers, as opposed to the Ionian physiologists, gives a new answer to the problem of the disorder of the times. The restraining of the kinesis, the frenetic movement that is about to tear apart all existing societies, can only be restrained if order is restored in the inside of individual souls. At a collective level, this can only happen if a proper space and role is given to those individuals who attained such an order in their soul: 'the new order of the spirit is socially an aristocratic achievement of charismatic individuals' (*ibid.*: 240). This sets up a fundamental opposition between the mass of sleepwalkers refusing to wake up and the problems involved in the 'authoritative self-assertion of the charismatic souls' (*ibid.*). This is the problem to which Plato attempted to give a solution; and this will also be the problem addressed by Christianity. The big question, which Voegelin, in opposition to practically every modern thinker, dared to pose, but which even he failed to try to answer, is to study the reasons why Christianity succeeded at precisely the point where Plato failed. Nietzsche's claim, that Christianity was 'Platonism for the people', is in fact almost on target.[34] But to what extent, and exactly why? This question will be revisited in the Conclusion to this book.

Plato

Introduction

Voegelin reads Plato as the thinker who gave a definite formulation to the problem first posed by Parmenides and Heraclitus, the true order of the soul, as a source of resistance to societal corruption. This was no doubt due to the fact that Plato did not simply revisit and deepen the idea of his predecessors, but posed the problem anew, on the basis of a novel type of experience. Plato did not fully belong to the axial age. His problem was not annihilation through military conquest by empire, but rather the collapse of Athenian democracy that at first promised to counter the threat successfully.

In Voegelin's reading, Plato did not give *the* answer, in the sense of a definite body of doctrine, a truly scientific method, or the basic principles of logic; but he formulated an approach, a mode of philosophising that was basically unsurpassable. No attempt will be made to assess the interpretation in its full complexity. Focus will be on two questions: was the solution of Plato fully balanced, and was it effective?

The diagnosis

Plato's work is based on a diagnosis of the situation of Athens, and in general the Hellenic polis, after the Peloponnesian Wars and the legal murder of Socrates. Plato identified the times in which he was living as a period of corruption and cultural disintegration (OHIII: 24, 160, 261). The gravity of the situation is only worsened by the fact that its contemporaries are 'reluctant to recognize the magnitude of the problems' (*ibid.*: 161). The Heraclitean problem of the sleepwalkers returns a century later in Athens (*ibid.*: 67), and Plato would devote much attention to the question of the proper technique of 'awakening', on the basis of the experience of Socrates. Such a task is all the more difficult as corruption extends to the entire society. Athens is a corrupt society through and through.

Against such a society a philosopher must declare warfare (*ibid.*: 24). Plato, however, is careful to avoid any semblance of incitement to acts of violence. Struggle means resistance against this corruption (*ibid.*: 5, 62), a search for the restoration of order and not the provocation of further disorder.

After this uncompromising diagnosis of the state of affairs, Plato moves on to penetrate to its source. This is done with the help of a series of conceptual pairs, like justice vs injustice, philosopher vs philodoxer (the lover of mere opinion), truth vs falsehood or lies, developed in the *Republic* (*ibid.*: 63–70). These pairs establish a close analogy between the order of society and of its members. The dichotomies are used in order to allude to the agonistic stand against the corrupt society, a duel that is impersonated in the debates between Socrates and his Sophist interlocutors. The pairs also help to identify a series of opinions, or *doxai*, held by the multitude, as influenced by the Sophists.

This allows Plato to pin down the nature and source of the crisis. A society is corrupt when it exerts power over the individual who does not follow accepted standards of truth and justice, and thus 'the fate of the individual will on the whole depend on his conformity with the standards that are socially recognised' (*ibid.*: 79). Though the tension between truth, justice and reality and the widely-held and thus profitable opinions are felt by many, those living for a sufficiently long time under such conditions eventually lose their sense of judgement and discernment. As a result, 'the accent of reality shifts from truth to the socially overpowering appearance – the dream tends to become reality' (*ibid.*). Thus, the 'primary source of the crisis is…the shift of what we called the "accent of reality" under social pressure' (*ibid.*).

In the third part of the *Republic* the analysis of social decomposition is complemented by a perspective of philosophical anthropology, an analysis of the decomposition of the soul. For Plato the balanced order of society and of its individual members assume one another. When a society has become corrupt, it means that its members are no longer able to maintain inside their soul the right balance, letting its components loose 'until the passions without a higher ordering principle range freely without restraint' (*ibid.*: 126).

This, however, does not mean a simple chaos and confusion of passions. Rather, it means that the previous order of the soul will be replaced by 'a new order of evil' (*ibid.*). In the next two pages (*ibid.*: 126–7) Voegelin's summary of Plato's diagnosis is particularly powerful, indeed passionate, and one can only wonder which aspects of his personal experiences with the various 'social experiments' of the twentieth century, and their Sophist programmers and defenders, are best mirrored in his rendition of the Platonic diagnosis. The crucial part of Plato's analysis is identified as 'the transition from the democratic to the despotic soul', no doubt central to the experiences of both thinkers. The analysis focuses on the confusion between day and night, dreams and wakefulness, thus having much to do with a misapprehension of liminality. Given that, during the night in dreams the unconscious forces are let loose, in order to have a well-ordered soul it is necessary to take precaution before sleep, and also to take proper care of the passions during the day, having them 'neither starved nor surfeited'. The opposite is done, however, by the despotic person, who would let 'the lust of his dreams enter his waking life'. Thus, '[t]he decomposition of the well-ordered soul leads, not to disorder or confusion, but to a perverted order'.

This 'deepest lust which casts a glow of evil over the life of passions' Plato calls '*Eros tyrannos*', a 'satanic double of the Socratic Eros' (*ibid.*). Voegelin gives here a full analysis of the duality of this fundamental spiritual moving force. Plato recognised that the two spiritual forces 'are intimately related', as he was 'acutely aware of the spirituality of evil and of the fascination emanating from a tyrannical order', with its 'qualities of luciferic splendor'. Both forces are characterised as *mania*, and are represented with wings. But the differences are also fundamental. The '*Eros tyrannos*' is not a positive and productive force, but is rather parasitical, having the character of a sting that 'insatiably drives to waste'. Their opposition represents a 'cosmic dualism'; furthermore, Voegelin even risks the conjecture that 'in the dualism of Eros the dualism of Good and Evil is reduced to its experiential basis'.

The task of reconstruction: the 'order of the soul'

Such a diagnosis of utter social corruption and cultural disintegration leads one either to despair and to resignation to fate, or to an attempt to counter the decay. Plato chose the second path, though realising that it would involve an 'effort of an almost miraculous kind' (*ibid.*: 4–5). As the roots of corruption involved the key impulses of the individual soul, the effort of regeneration must also reach to the core. An analysis of the true order of the soul, however, must start with the proper analysis of one's own experiences; must be in one way or another autobiographical. The problem of transmitting this knowledge, of having an impact on others, on the surrounding society, only comes afterwards, as a problem of communication. Correspondingly, Voegelin starts his presentation with the autobiographical 'Seventh Letter'.

The text, Plato's own *Apology*, is one of the first autobiographies. It is also a test case for Plato's theoretical considerations, which could be, and were, read from a number of different angles – as an attempt to impose a 'totalitarian' blueprint on another country; as the test case of the exaggerated idea of the philosopher king; or as revealing Plato the Sophist, the philosopher who, after failing at home, goes to another city to vindicate his ideas. Not so, according to the convincing analysis of Voegelin (*ibid.*: 3–6, 14–20).

First of all, the letter details, recalling *The Suppliants* of Aeschylus (*ibid.*: 11), the 'hesitations of the soul' related both to the leaving of the home city and to the conditions under which advice can be given elsewhere. The trial and death of Socrates and the succession of ever more corrupt regimes in Athens, tyrannical or democratic, convinced Plato that the situation is hopeless, and it is pointless to take part in political life. By 390 BC, as shown by the *Gorgias*, composed around that time, the situation had become so intolerable that it provoked something like a 'crisis' in Plato's life (*ibid.*: 5, 14). Using the Hirschmanian typology of options, loyalty was out of the question, voice became impossible in the sense of public speech and, as Plato was adamant that '[u]nder no circumstances [should one] ferment violence and revolution in [one's] fatherland' (*ibid.*: 17), the only remaining option was exit. Thus Plato went to Sicily.

Participating in the political life of Sicily, however, was a different matter. In the 'Letter', Plato carefully ponders on the conditions under which it is ethical to participate in the political life of another city. The Sophists of all ages come without invitation and assert their intellectual superiority over the indigenous citizens whom they denigrate as uneducated, mere objects of their civilising mission. Plato, however, was invited by his friends. This indicates an audience willing to listen, and the presence of *philia*, the very foundation on which the polis is built, thus an existential community between the host and the guest. Even further, Voegelin argues that the bond between Plato and Dion was particularly strong, involving the 'intimacy of the erotic relationship' (*ibid.*: 18).

Given the links of *philia* and *eros*, Plato could proceed with his advice. This advice, however, does not have the form of a blueprint. Quite on the contrary, the hopelessness of the undertaking becomes visible when the king, instead of following the advice of Plato in being concerned with the true order of his soul, or with the care of his self (as Foucault would put it), simply writes a philosophical treatise. 'The attempt to formulate the intimacy of erotic community as a doctrine is worse than futile: it is the desecration of a mystery' (*ibid.*: 19). At this stage, with less care than Foucault, Voegelin seems to espouse the idea that the central part of a philosophy cannot be written down; that 'no serious man will write of the really serious things for the many' (*ibid.*: 20). One should note here that Voegelin refers approvingly to 'Letter Two', widely regarded as inauthentic, even quoting the paradoxical instruction to burn the letter after reading it. Following Foucault, one could argue that – far from taking Plato at face value – one could rather diagnose here the experiential basis of a mistrust of writing, and in general of public communication, that would become the core of neo-Platonic esotericism and mysticism. Though there are things which cannot be put into words, a philosophy concerned with the regeneration of political life cannot start with such a claim. At best, such a statement is a 'performative paradox'; at worst, it is an expression of the hubris of the mystic, which can easily turn into the direction of a Nietzschean ressentiment.

The first step towards the order of the soul is the 'spiritualisation' of the personal exit from the polis. One must start by leaving behind the corrupt society. But, as one is inside, being part of this society, this means that one must be able to look at this world with a novel eye; one must 'wonder' at the world (*thaumazein*) with new eyes.[35]

But the overcoming of the reality of a corrupt society requires more than intellectual effort. It is not enough simply to reach a higher level of understanding, to 'contemplate' the world from above; one must be able to tear oneself away from this world and turn around (*ibid.*: 68). It is this sudden transformative experience that is captured by the Platonic term *periagoge*, the leaving of the cave, one of the central terms in Voegelin's thought as well. This is a conceptualisation of conversion, and would gain a religious meaning in Christianity, but Voegelin emphasises that, in Plato, the 'experience remains essentially within the boundaries of the Dionysiac soul' (*ibid.*: 115).

The sudden turning-around is a necessary starting point towards the true order of the soul, but nothing more than a starting point. It must be followed by a long and arduous quest, research, or *zetesis*. The parallels, but also the differences, with Foucault are again remarkable. The term would be central for Foucault's interpretation of Socrates and Plato as well, but for Foucault the emphasis was on the transformation of the entire life into a philosophical way of life. Voegelin, however, is interested in the order of the soul, and *zetesis* for him proceeds, following Heraclitus, through the analysis of experiences (*ibid.*: 83), towards the discovery of the order of the psyche, leading to the 'augmentation of the Logos in his soul. There is no knowledge of order in soul except through the *zetema* in which the soul discovers it by growing into it' (*ibid.*: 95).

In the *Ecumenic Age*, with the help of the concept of metaxy, the conceptualisation of the search for order gains a further dimension. The human side of the research, characterised as a search for the 'ground', is complemented by the 'pull' from the side of the divine.

The problem of social corruption and the struggle of the philosopher to disengage himself from a corrupt society are familiar themes even for modern thought. The 'pull' from the divine is less so. However, according to Voegelin, it is an integral part of Plato's thought. This point reaches its full significance in the next and last step in the ascent to the order of the soul, in the recognition of God as the unseen measure.

Before analysing further this claim, we first need to identify the exact problem to which this claim is the response, and its significance. The breakdown of order, a 'time of trouble', in itself is not a new experience (Assmann 2001). In the ancient empires, such events led to the historiogenetic constructions, modelling the socio-political order on the order of the cosmos. In less complex societies, the breakdown of order was solved through the sacrificial mechanism and scapegoating. In the axial age, the threat of annihilation through imperial conquests was countered by the eruption of transcendental experiences. In the case of Plato, however, the divine measure is not given as a direct revelation, but is the result of a philosophical conversion, reflexion and search.

The comparison with Foucault is again most instructive, here illuminating the limits of the Foucaldian position. Any situation of dissolving order, any problematisation of the conduct of life, poses the question of the standard of education or restoration. For Foucault, this standard was given by the identity of speech and conduct in Socrates. This, however, does not yield a proper solution, as the nihilist pursuing pure self-interest also acts according to his words. Implicit in the Socratic stance is the claim that his behaviour follows ethical standards. And the question to be posed now concerns the nature and source of such standards.

The issue goes to the heart of the conflict between Socrates/Plato and the Sophists. According to the Sophists, as contained in the extant opening claim of the book of Protagoras: '"Of all things the measure is man"' (OHII: 294). According to Plato, however, '"God is for us the measure of all things, of a truth; more truly so than, as they say, man"' (OHIII: 254, as quoted from *Laws*, 716c). Both sides of the contrast require further clarification. The claim of the Sophists is not to be taken lightly. It is pronounced by Protagoras, the representative figure of the classical generation of Sophists, respected by Plato. The claim itself was experientially based, expressing the experience of both Ionian exiles and the Athenians. It is not accidental that the *Antigone* of Sophocles, presented just a year after the arrival of Protagoras in Athens, contained the famous sentence about man being the most wonderful of all things. The statement of Protagoras can be considered as indeed the confession of faith of all humanists, whether in the Renaissance, in the Enlightenment, in nineteenth-century liberalism or in the twentieth century.

Plato therefore does not denigrate the claim, but finds it wanting. And, according to Voegelin, he does so emphatically, as the sentence quoted above is not an isolated claim but can be considered the quintessence of Plato's position. This is a point to which Voegelin would repeatedly return, up to his last piece, completed (or almost) on his death-bed.

The problem with the argument of Protagoras is that the measure must be beyond decay and corruption, while human beings are mortal and subject to corruption. Athens in the 'Golden Age' provides a prime example of this fact, as its very achievements fuelled the over-confidence, pride and hubris that soon corrupted the entire social order. Protagoras and the Sophists serve as another example. Protagoras is a respectful person and a good professional teacher but, as he can only teach speculation and rhetoric, he cannot transmit virtue, and his students became arrogant nihilists. In order to survive the corroding influence of time, human measures must be put into the form of laws and institutions. But such techniques of 'social engineering' can only prevent bad things from happening, they cannot create a mobilising 'spirit'.

At the height of his thought, Plato asserts that the only proper standard is God. Here, however, we reach not only the height but also the limit of Platonic thought. The problem is very similar to the paradox of Socrates, whose *daimon* only told him what *not* to do. By a systematic research of his own experiences, Plato came to the realisation that the measure is unseen and divine. But in the absence of a transcendental experience, he could not put this measure into a form that would be not only convincing, but also resounding in its effects. Plato might have founded a philosophical school or an Academy, but he did not found a new society. Such a feat, evidently, can only be accomplished by prophets, and not by philosophers. The ultimate irony of the Platonic position is that he, perhaps alone of all philosophers, demonstrated the ultimate futility of all such undertakings.

These limits are illuminated by the other aspect of his vision of the divine as the 'player of the human puppet' (*ibid.*: 231), recalling the Heraclitean vision of Zeus as a playing child. The image is presented by the Athenian Stranger in *Laws* (644d–e): 'Let us suppose that each of us living creatures is an ingenious puppet of the gods, whether contrived by way of a toy of theirs or for some serious purpose – for as to that we know nothing; but this we know, that these inward affections of ours, like sinews or cords, drag us along and, being opposed to each other, pull one against the other to opposite actions; and herein lies the dividing line between goodness and badness.' Bringing together the two places in which Voegelin comments on this image, the central aspects of the interpretation are the following. The field of the play is the human soul (OHIII: 259). The 'cords' are the various internal 'drives' or 'logismoi', the spiritual forces inside the soul that move human beings (*ibid.*: 232). One of these forces is golden, the 'way of truth', the others are of smaller quality. The 'gods' play on us by pulling, at different times, the various type of cords; and humans can take part in the game as well by yielding to this or that impulse. The truly serious play, however, is to learn to use the golden cord only, or the way to reach God. However, due to the corruption of times, 'men have forgotten that they are the playthings of God and that this quality is the best in them' (*ibid.*). The point is then made even more emphatically by Voegelin: Plato argues that the only proper self-identity of human beings is given as the 'playthings of God'. The claim is certainly the opposite of the Sophists' claim, and is the opposite of human pride and hubris; but it seems excessive on its own count. It also leads Plato to a single possible conclusion: he is the only one ' "who has the knowledge of these things" ' (*ibid.*: 234), he alone can 'understand', and he therefore has to withdraw from the community, becoming, indeed, the Athenian 'Stranger'.

The abyss became unbridgeable; and from his lonely stand Plato gains a further, even more terrifying vision of the divine, the creator-god (demiurge) who is playing at a chessboard, shifting the pieces. Here we leave the field of the soul, and witness a silent and terrifying game. According to Voegelin, '[t]he Mover of the Pieces is the last and most awesomely intimate revelation of the Platonic God...drawn from the cosmic depth in the soul of Plato' (*ibid.*: 236). One could argue that, in this imagery, beyond Heraclitus, Plato seems to have returned outright to Anaximander.

There is, however, a less tragic and terrifying aspect of the Platonic imagery, which returns the argument to society and at the same time helps to introduce the second basic theme, the question of the communication of the experience and the teaching of the measure. This is the recurrent concern with play and playfulness. Voegelin refers here to the work of Johan Huizinga (1955), who made use of the common root, in Greek, of 'play' (*paidia*) and 'culture' (*paideia*).[36] Huizinga emphasises the importance and seriousness of play. It is not only central to humans, but it is the sign of the 'spirit'; it had even entered the animal world. This demonstrates that animals are more than mechanical things, and humans are more than reasonable beings. Play is an 'influx' of the spirit, an 'overflow' beyond the 'normal', ordinary level of existence; it is an aspect of transcendence. Beyond this description, it is not difficult to recognise the affinities with the concept of 'liminality'.[37]

Voegelin takes the argument further by recalling the etymological affinities between play and culture (*paidia*) and child (*pais*) (OHIII: 259–60). In this way the imagery of humans as the playthings of gods gains a different connotation, and comes closer to the Christian view – though the forbidden word 'innocence', the central aspect of childhood, does not appear in Voegelin's account. It also moves the interest to the other aspect associated with children, the question of education, as Plato defines culture (formation) in the following way: ' "By paideia I mean virtue in the form in which it is acquired by a child" ' (*ibid.*: 260, from *Laws*, 653b).

How to teach the 'order of the soul'?

The philosopher, by turning around and leaving the cave, managed to come to the light of truth. But how can he communicate his experience and turn others around as well? The previous section, in which Plato becomes the 'Stranger', indicates not only the difficulty of the undertaking, but also the fact that it is unlikely that Plato discovered the answer.

The problem is already posed in the first great diagnosis, the *Gorgias*, and in a most significant way. The problem 'at stake is that of communication and intelligibility in a decadent society' (*ibid.*: 29); in a society where words lost their transparency and meaning, and where public discourse was appropriated by the Sophists. The problem is the old question of waking up the sleepwalkers, to shake them out of their slumber and turn them around, towards a search for order and truth.[38] However, the linguistic symbols, used by the Sophists to 'enlighten' the 'masses', have become useless, and the radical strategy of an existential shake-up has been similarly abused by the Cynics. The philosopher can only address those who are willing to listen; but, in the final count, these are already the philosophers.

Faced with this problem, Plato starts by relying on the common element of human existence, immediate personal experience (*pathos*). This is a strategy that, indeed, would become central for the history of philosophy, including the call of Descartes to return to experience (as opposed to the books of the scholastics), and the similar call of Husserl. Pathos identifies a 'passive experience'; it is 'what happens to man, what he suffers, what befalls him fatefully and what touches him in his existential core – as for instance the experiences of Eros' (*ibid.*).[39] The task of the philosopher is to touch his interlocutors by evoking this level of common human experience: '[i]f one can penetrate to this core and reawaken in a man the awareness of his *conditio humana*, communication in the existential sense becomes possible' (*ibid.*: 30).

On the basis of this conviction, and after the failure of his first trip to Sicily, Plato attempted in the *Republic* to communicate his ideas and exert an effect on his native city by drawing the outlines of a polis based on the true order of the soul. The work, however, failed to exert the desired effect, and this had a major impact on Plato's thought. The first revision is contained in *Phaedrus*, a 'manifesto which announces the emigration of the spirit from the polis', where Plato 'is resigned to the fact that the polis has rejected his appeal' (*ibid.*: 139). In the case of such exits, just as in the case of transformative experiences, the danger of derailment is particularly great, and in the case of Plato three such parallel slidings can be identified. Importantly, Voegelin fails to strike a critical tone here, which not only would result in problems in his interpretation of Plato, but is a sign of a certain ('Gnostic') derailment of his own undertaking.[40]

First of all, given the lack of societal response, Plato embarked on the building of a community of his own, by founding the Academy. This created a precedent for the long-term tradition in which philosophical and spiritual reformers would set up a school or a sect on their own. Second, the lack of success in drawing upon the common experiential basis of all human beings made him incline to drive a gap between two basic human types, 'a lower type of human beings, close to animals, and a higher type of semi-divine rank' (*ibid.*: 141). Such ideas may also have been influenced by the Eleatic tradition, especially the figure of Empedocles. Voegelin notes that such self-divinisation 'seems absurd in the realm of Christian experience' (*ibid.*), but does not draw many further consequences. Finally, Plato moved beyond the orbit of the polis and established direct parallels between the cosmic order, nature and the soul (psyche), tracing the rejuvenation of the order of the polis (*ibid.*: 169) to the very creation of the cosmos. Taken together, these elements clearly move towards the direction of the phenomenon of Gnosticism.

The clearest example of such dangers is the next step in Plato's attempt to exert an effect, the return to myth in the form of the 'philosopher's myth'. This is the point at which Voegelin's argument clearly goes astray and cannot be accepted, though one has to be very careful in distinguishing such critical remarks from a mere reassertion of the Enlightenment position that Voegelin rightly questioned. The crucial issue at stake is identified by Voegelin as 'the embodiment of the idea in historical reality' (*ibid.*: 184), or even the problem of 'incarnation' (*ibid.*: 198–9). Given that the Socratic strategy of having an effect through reasoning failed, rendering Socrates almost indistinguishable from the Sophists in common opinion, Plato moved to the level of the unconscious forces. The unconscious is also experientially based. It is the collection or 'distillation' of past experiences: fears, sentiments, dreams, sufferings, joys; and not only at the personal but also at the collective level. The myth is the symbolic expression of these forces and experiences, and therefore cannot simply be dismissed with the help of rational arguments. Quite on the contrary, a purely rational approach to the myths is corruptive, cynical, nihilistic.

In characterising this 'new' field of the unconscious and myths, Plato refers to the complex playfulness and childhood, even alluding to an age of innocence (*ibid.*: 185–6). The ' "stories heard…in earliest infancy" ' have a fundamental and ineradicable appeal, and Plato feels only ' "resentment and disgust" ' against those who question these stories through abstract speculation (*ibid.*: 190). These stories authenticate themselves, belonging to the deepest, indeed the foundational level of the unconscious, and it is only in 'times of transition' (*ibid.*: 191) that their truth can be questioned and lost.

This is exactly what has happened in the previous decades in Athens, undermining the very foundations of the sense of communality (*philia*) among the citizens of the polis, and this is what the philosopher has to counteract by the creation of new myths. This is based on Plato's conviction that the field of the unconscious forces – that, we could argue, were opened up by the 'liminal' period of transition – can only be affected with the help of myths, not by rational argument. The analysis of this field is advanced through an analogy between the cosmos and the psyche. The unconscious is not only the field of rival spiritual forces, 'good' or 'evil', but these forces can also be classified according to their direction. Apart from the ascending forces of *eros*, there is also the descending force of *peitho* (persuasion). In the account of the creation of the cosmos, this is the force that 'induces the Ananke of the chaos to submit to the Nous' (*ibid.*: 203); and, by analogy, this is the force through which the Idea can become incarnate, through the soul, in reality.

As the unconscious is the field of spiritual forces and movements, and such forces are deeply ambivalent, the new player of the myths must not lose the 'sense that dangerous forces are playing through him' (*ibid.*: 192). This ambivalence is further elaborated in the discussion of the links between power and spirit. While 'desperately' trying to put his Idea into effect, Plato did not lose sight of the fact that the real problem is not the separation between (real and objective) power and (mere ideal) spirit, but that 'bad' spirituality can also be evoked, and even more easily, than 'good' spirituality. Tyranny also uses 'spiritual powers', but of different kinds. On the other hand, Plato seems to imply that the 'spirit' also needs political means of compulsion. Voegelin calls attention here to the 'ambiguousness' of Plato's position (*ibid.*: 226), and also states that here the 'limits of the Platonic conception of order' are reached (*ibid.*: 227). He also seems to indicate that this impasse would only be solved by the Church (*ibid.*: 226, 228). The point, however, is left to the further volumes of *Order and History*, which would never be published, as then promised.

The last step of the argument is contained in the final pages devoted to Plato, often referring to the concluding section of the *Laws*. Here we return to the argument left in suspense at the end of the previous section, the idea that the education of the measure can best be compared to the teaching of children through play. Even more importantly, this conclusive argument, at the end of the *Laws*, returns to the theme of *Protagoras*, the teaching of virtue, and the result that it is only feasible as an art of teaching the measure.

The relevance is all the more evident as Voegelin starts the argument from the diagnosis of Athens. A central aspect of social disorganisation is cultural decay due to the propagation of 'bad taste' in public places. Education should thus focus on the acquisition of good taste, a sense of distinction and discrimination.[41] The aim of education, therefore, is to attain a 'state of attunement' (*ibid.*: 266) to the right order.

The arguments of both Plato and Voegelin, however, remain strangely inconclusive here. Plato calls for coercive measures, leading even to the setting-up of a
'spiritual court' (*ibid.*: 265). Voegelin plays his usual role of defending Plato
against totalitarian implications, without recommending the solution of Plato.
Strangely missing is the evocation of the fundamental issue to which the arguments of both the *Protagoras* and the *Laws*, and of Voegelin's commentary, lead
to: if the central problem of Plato's thought is the 'incarnation of the idea', the
central issue of education is the art of teaching the measure and of staying
attuned, in a good taste, to the measure, then is not the solution to this problem
the incarnation of the measure? This problem will be revisited in the Conclusion
to this book.

Part III

Michel Foucault

Parrhesia and the care of the self

7 Foucault's historical method

Four striking images: recurrence and forgetting

Readers of Foucault are well accustomed to the striking scenes with which he repeatedly started his books, or their major parts: the 'ship of fools' and the enclosing of the mad, the curing of hysteria by Pomme, the execution of Damiens, the scenes of plague or the image of the Panopticon. This device, perhaps to mark a break, is completely absent from the published second and third volumes of the *History of Sexuality*. Similar theatrical scenes, however, were employed in Foucault's lectures. Indeed, it is possible to identify a few crucial, spectacular images or scenes, central not simply as illustrations but also as capturing the very 'essence' of the argument, in Foucault's last period as well.

The four most important of these are the following:

- the figure of Septimus Severus, Roman emperor, and the scene of the sky painted on the ceiling of his auditing chamber, representing the very order of the world;
- the figure of Dr Leuret, a French psychiatrist of the mid-nineteenth century, and the scene of his special treatment developed to cure the mentally sick;
- the figure of Oedipus the king, and the quest for his identity;
- the scene of baptism.

Each of these four scenes was presented at particularly significant places in lectures from Foucault's last period. The first was the surprising opening scene of the first lecture of the 1980 Collège de France course, the public demonstration of the fact that Foucault was completely elsewhere than where his audience thought him to be. The second, on the other hand, was the scene with which Foucault started his lectures during his major 1980 US tour, and also the important 1981 Louvain seminars, where he tried to connect his storyline back to contemporary concerns. The third figure was discussed in both the second and the third Collège de France lectures of 1980 as a further elaboration and partial re-specification of the first 1980 lecture, and also in the second of the six

Louvain seminars. The fourth scene, finally, was discussed in the fourth, fifth, sixth and seventh courses of 1980 as the first phase of the discussion of Christian techniques of self, the main theme of the 1980 course.

Furthermore, two of these four figures were recurrent concerns for Foucault, associated with particularly significant periods of his life-work. Thus, the Leuret scene had been referred to in a 1963 publication, signalling the shift of Foucault's interest from illness and mental illness and their institutional treatment, to language, literature and the autonomy of discourses, and then again in 1977, the year of Foucault's 'crisis'. The figure of Oedipus, on the other hand, was evidently used at the beginning of his first, 1971 course at the Collège de France, illustrating then the newly introduced concept of power/knowledge.[1]

Given the pronounced importance and the repetitive recurrence of these scenes, one might wonder why they have so far received hardly any attention in the secondary literature. There is, however, a very simple reason: Foucault did not publish these scenes. He not only failed to include them in the published volumes of the *History of Sexuality*, but he also edited them out, with perplexing consistency, from his written publications. Thus, the figures of Septimus Severus and Oedipus did not appear in the published course outline of the 1980 course; even more importantly, and almost inexplicably, though a significant part of the course was devoted to baptism, one of the three Christian practices of the self discussed in the course, the published course outline only makes reference to the other two. One could only speculate on the reasons for the omissions. A possible argument is that these were eventually omitted as part of a strategy to focus on the final results of analysis, and to underplay the actual path taken, as if to eliminate the 'traces' by which Foucault arrived at this position – which, however, is problematic on its own. It might also be related to a change in style, the avoidance of the rhetorical modality characteristic of the earlier books.

Emperor Septimus Severus and his cosmology

Septimus Severus was Roman Emperor between AD 193–212, at the start of the turbulent third century. Before him, there was the splendour of the second century so appraised by Edward Gibbon, the rule of Trajan and Hadrian, a period of stability and prosperity, and then of the Stoic Emperors, Marcus Aurelius and his son Commodus. Soon after the reign of Septimus Severus the main period of the persecution of Christianity would begin, ending with the conversion of Constantine in AD 313. Thus, his rule could be situated in between the Stoic and the Christian emperors, at a time when Oriental influences were already felt. Finally, the concrete context was provided by a major period of crisis, the civil war of 192–3 in which, after the murder of Commodus, several elected Emperors were fighting for power, and it was this anarchy that was ended by the rise to power of Septimus Severus.

Foucault's account is based on a single image. In the main room of the Emperor's palace – the room that was used for wielding justice and passing sentence – the constellation of planets at the exact moment of the Emperor's birth was painted upon the ceiling. Foucault lists three reasons for this arrangement. The first point is related to justice. The image of the sky above showed that the judgements passed there were not ephemeral and contingent, but rather they fitted into the very order of the world, as if dictated by *logos* itself. The second point is linked to power. The Emperor, as everyone knew, had won his position by force, by defeating his enemies in a bloody civil war. The imagery of the main room, however, intimated again that this was not accidental, but rather was founded on the stars, or the order of the cosmos. Finally, the representation of the sky also showed the true fate of the Emperor in advance, the certainty of his power and the impossibility that this could be defeated. Thus, the painted ceiling established a connection between the present, the past and the future, and between justice, power and truth. In sum, the image connected the exercise of power to the manifestation of truth – the open, public manifestation of truth, exactly where the most public activity of the Emperor, the wielding of justice, was undertaken. However, adds Foucault, in contrast to this account, a part of the sky was missing, was painted only in the private room of the Emperor, visible only to himself and the closest members of his family, and this was the constellation of the hour of his death.

The rest of the lecture presents a contrast and then an interpretation. The contrast is given by the figure of Oedipus. Foucault claims that the image of the starred sky is the exact inverse of the story of Oedipus; later Foucault would even add that this is the real 'anti-Oedipus'. The fate of Oedipus is not written in the sky, but rather is the consequence of his actions, of his wanderings; it was a hidden and unknown fate, and not a happy one; even further, at the start of the play Oedipus springs his own trap by announcing that the source of the plague must be chased out of the city. The stable, visible, manifest order of things, the confluence of truth, justice and power, is contrasted with fatality and ignorance, until the only persons capable of revealing the truth, the humble shepherds, enter the scene.

The contrast between Septimus Severus and Oedipus in temporal terms is most puzzling. Foucault usually presents contrasting images of two practices that were close in time, and in sequential order, so as to mark a clear break. In this case, however, the second figure originates many centuries before and not after the first. Foucault resolves the puzzle by turning the figure of Septimus Severus into a concept, that of the court.[2] The court is not simply a source and locus of power, but also contains an extraordinary concentration of culture, including highly elaborate rituals that focus on the manifestation of truth. These rituals were just as central for the exercise of power in the courts of the sixteenth and seventeenth centuries as they were in the times of Septimus Severus.

With this period, the period of Reformation and Counter-Reformation, Foucault returns to a clear temporal storyline, and also to more recent times. The contrast is between government by the manifestation of truth, and government based on the principle of rationality – first, reason of state, and then four other different types of rationality. This line of investigation, however, would not be taken up later in the course. Instead, the second lecture would start with a clarification, and then return to the figure of Oedipus.

The story of *Oedipus Tyrannos* told and re-told

When introducing the discussion of Oedipus at the start of his 1980 lectures, Foucault contrasted his account with the version of the story he presented nine years previously. As the 1971 Collège de France lectures were not available on tape at the Foucault Archives, it is not possible to pursue this claim. However, a version of this account was presented as the second of his five lectures given in between 21 and 25 May 1973 in Rio de Janeiro. Given Foucault's practice of presenting in his external lectures a condensed version of his Collège de France courses, it is very likely that the substance of this lecture closely approximates the 1971 Collège de France lecture. Thus, even in 1971, at the moment of his sudden change from an archaeologist of knowledge to a genealogist of power, the story of Oedipus played a major role for Foucault, as it was taken to introduce and illustrate the guiding concept of Foucault's research at that time, power/knowledge (*pouvoir–savoir*) (DEII: 555).

Foucault's account of the story of Oedipus is fitted into a triple context. The first is contemporary social theory, or more exactly, the kind of approach Foucault considers to be compatible with, or similar to, his own. This is marked by the names of Deleuze, Guattari and Lyotard. More specifically, Foucault claims that his work fits into the line of the *Anti-Oedipus*,[3] by emphasising power relations in the study of desire and not the unconscious. However, Foucault's perspective is also different from the line taken up by Deleuze and Guattari, as it is not trying to 'liberate' desire from the Freudian approach – a difference that would soon permanently distance Foucault from Deleuze.[4]

The second element of context, closely related to the previous, is the diagnostic intent. In proposing the 'Oedipus complex', Freud presented a diagnosis in the classical medical sense, even though this diagnosis was, for better or worse, highly unorthodox. Deleuze and Guattari, on the other hand, diagnosed Freud's diagnosis, arguing that it was only an attempt to repress desire on its own, to limit it within the circumscribed context of the nuclear family. The diagnosis of Foucault, however, is a diagnosis of modernity, in the classical Nietzschean – Weberian sense, even though presented – arguably – in a rhetorically excessive manner. Thus, he is defining his aim as being 'to bring to light what remained up till now in the history of our culture the most hidden, the most occulted, and the most deeply invested: the relations of power' (*ibid.*: 554); or claims that it is to analyse not the economic relations, but 'the political relations that invest the entire frame of our existence' (*ibid.*).

The third aspect of context is the concrete theme and the historical background in which Foucault fits the story of Oedipus. This is the history of legal procedures, or judicial techniques – a reference that would be repeated in the second cycle of his analyses of the play, about a decade later. In fact, the analysis that follows will be organised alongside the identities and differences between the two presentations, starting with their common core.

The common core of Foucault's account of Oedipus

Foucault uses as the background against which the novelty introduced becomes visible an episode from the *Iliad*, the chariot race organised to celebrate the death of Patroclos. The race itself is a typical agonistic contest of a warrior aristocracy, and in order to assure adherence to the rules, Achilles – the organiser of the race – dispatched an 'observer' or 'witness' (*histor*).[5] At the end of the race, a conflict breaks out in which Menelaus is accusing the winner, Antilochos, of cheating. But in order to assess the charge, he does not turn to the witness, but rather he asks Antilochos to provide an oath that he did not cheat – which he fails to do. Foucault interprets this episode as the old, agonistic procedure of the establishment of truth, where truth is authenticated by the (noble) character of the person speaking, while eventual punishment is left to the gods. The procedure followed is 'trial' (*épreuve*) and not 'inquiry' (*enquête*).[6]

The play of Sophocles shows, by its very structure and dynamics, a different mechanism, manifesting the new legal procedure. Foucault defines the play as the 'first evidence [*témoignage*] we have of the Greek judicial procedures' (*ibid.*: 555), while in 1981 he would call it a 'foundational representation [*représentation fondatrice*]' of the new type of jurisprudence, where the emphasis shifts to inquiry, procedure and the calling of witnesses.[7]

In order to indicate the difference, Foucault starts his account by noting that elements of the old procedure are present in the play, most notably in the conflict between Oedipus and Creon, where Creon offers to settle the conflict by giving an oath. This, however, is not accepted by Oedipus, in spite of the insistence of the Chorus (composed of the elders), in opposition to the definite result obtained in the *Iliad*. Oedipus persists in calling for a proper procedure in order to establish the truth.

The idea that the play closely follows the structure of a trial is, of course, not new, and has been pursued and debated abundantly in the literature on the play. The question concerns the manner in which Foucault argues for the relevance of this judicial aspect.

It is customary to interpret the play as an investigative murder trial, the search for the murderer of Laius. This investigation is, of course, embedded into a broader, or at least a different, framework, as the play begins not with the events of the murder, but with a typical, highly representative crisis situation: a plague that is threatening Thebes; and eventually the murder trial would turn into a quite different investigation, an inquiry into the origins, or the 'identity', of Oedipus.

The basic model of Foucault's interpretation, however, both in the 1971–73 and the 1980–81 versions, is different. It identifies the 'law of halves' as the fundamental underlying structure of the play. By this, Foucault means that in the play the discovery of truth progresses through a series of half-truths that various 'agents' possess or proclaim, and the final truth, revealed at the end of the play, will be the result of all these half-truths put together.

The play, or the successive realisation of the truth, unfolds at three levels: the first is the level of the gods, represented by the Delphic oracle and the seer, Tiresias;[8] the second is the level of the aristocracy, represented by Oedipus and Jocasta, his wife; while the third is the level of the slaves, the concrete agents being the two shepherds. These three levels closely correspond to the three main social classes, the three estates, or even the three functions of Indo-European mythology, a reference Foucault is explicitly making in both 1973 and 1980 (*ibid.*: 569); they also correspond to the three main modalities of time: the future, where only the gods and their designated 'agents' can see; the present, belonging to the aristocracy, the authoritative agents of rightful action; and the past, preserved in the memory of the slaves who have undergone, 'lived through' or 'suffered' events and thus can provide a 'testimony' of what they have 'experienced' or 'endured'.

At the first level, the Delphic oracle – asked about the source of the plague – utters a half-truth: the reason is a 'pollution', caused by a murder, the murder of Laius, and the fact that the murderer still lives within the city, unpunished. The oracle fails to identify the murderer, and can't be forced to do so. Tiresias, the seer, when pressed, identifies Oedipus as the murderer;[9] this is the other half-truth. This, however, is not accepted by Oedipus, which then leads to an escalation of conflict. The old method of oracular pronouncement is not accepted at face value in the 'new world' of democratic Athens.

Thus the play moves to the second level, an exchange between Oedipus and Jocasta, his wife. Here two further half-truths are put together: the person Oedipus killed before he came to Thebes seems indeed to be Laius, according to the version of the events told to Jocasta, but there is still a minor discrepancy, so there is need to listen to the testimony of the sole surviving slave. At the same time, further disturbing but still inconclusive details come to the surface, both from Oedipus and Jocasta, about the background of both royal houses. As the second level thus also fails to yield a satisfactory result, the play moves to the third and last level, the testimony of the slaves.

This is the crucial level of analysis for Foucault, both in the early 1970s and 1980s. Here Oedipus as a 'tyrannos' is investigating the two slaves, using all the weaponry of the legal process and his privileged position. However, due to a sudden, and unasked for, revelation by the first 'slave' (who had arrived as a messenger from Corinth to announce the death of king Polybios) that Polybios was not the father, only the foster-father, of Oedipus, the target of the trial shifts from murder to the identity of Oedipus. Putting together the two half-truths possessed by the two slaves, the riddle of this identity is solved, together with the murder, revealing finally the accuracy of all the oracular truths of the gods that were challenged in various places of the play. Between the announced truth of the gods and the lived, witnessed truth of the slaves, the correspondence is perfect. What is significant is that the out-of-ordinary truth proclaimed by the gods that has the character of 'lightning' (*la lumière de la vérité de l'éclat*) needed an 'empirical' and 'everyday' validation from the slaves; or the announcing (*énonciation*) of the truth was displaced from a future-oriented, prognostic and prescriptive truth to a past-oriented, retrospective truth focusing on testimony (*témoignage*) (*ibid.*: 561).

Foucault would repeat this reconstruction of the play's structure in 1980–81, with minor alterations. The difference would reside in the interpretation given. Even there, we should start with the common elements.

First of all, Foucault reveals the source of his interpretive technique, or rather the constructive mechanism of the play. The 'law of two halves' corresponds to the 'famous Greek technique of the symbolon' (*ibid.*: 560). This was a piece of pottery which was broken in two halves, thus allowing the person possessing one of the pieces to authenticate himself when the two pieces were fitted together. Thus, the 'history of Oedipus is the fragmentation of this piece whose integral, unified possession authenticates the detention of power and the orders given by it' (*ibid.*). This is the ancient, magical–religious concept of power, a type of power one possesses by divine right or delegation, characteristic of the story of Septimus Severus (thus the qualification as 'anti-Oedipus'), or the type that is opposite to the characteristic of modern power that, according to Foucault, is not something possessed, but is rather exercised. By organising the play in this way Sophocles can be said to 'imitate' the gods, or 'side with' the gods, as in this case the 'agent' who broke the 'piece' in halves, requiring human beings to put them together again, could only be Apollo.[10] However, in the Foucauldian reading the play also documents the point at which this traditional account of the gods becomes untenable, or at least weak, by itself. The putting together of the pieces requires human agency: the search of Oedipus first, that becomes the dynamics, or the 'motor' of the entire play, and then the testimony of the slaves.

This point will be repeated, with some important variations yet to be discussed, in the 1980–81 version. The fundamental difference lies in the presentation of the figure of Oedipus at the conclusion of the analysis.

1971–73: Oedipus as a figure of power/knowledge

In 1971 and 1973 Foucault used the figure of Oedipus in order to introduce the concept of power/knowledge. In fact, the figure was presented as the very embodiment of the concept. Foucault argued there that, while Oedipus was usually conceived of as a man of ignorance and blindness, he was in fact a man of knowledge and of vision. This is even woven into the fabric of his name, since the Greek 'oida' or 'eido' (the same word as the Latin 'video') means both to see and to know.[11] But his knowledge is a new kind of knowledge: not a knowledge possessed, a knowledge characteristic of the ancient wise men and priests, but rather active, technical intelligence, or *gnomé*;[12] a type of knowledge that is to be deployed in inquiry, investigation or search (*zetema*);[13] and that yields a discovery or the finding (*heuréka*) of the truth.[14]

Even more important for Foucault than the knowledge of Oedipus is his power. But it is exactly here that the interpretation went astray, and where the account would be corrected in 1980–81. Foucault started by reading the title of the piece, *Oedipus Tyrannos*, as an indication that the entire piece is about Oedipus as a king, or about his power. This, however, is a slip, as Sophocles used the simple title 'Oedipus' (Jebb 1887: 4), the current title being a post-Aristotelian invention. The slip becomes magnified in the interpretation. In the entire play, continues Foucault, it is 'essentially the power of Oedipus that is in question' (DEII: 562).[15] The chief interest of Oedipus is never his innocence, only the defence of his power, from the start of the play which defines his deep involvement in the crisis situation, through the conflict with Creon, up to the very last word (*ibid.*: 562–3). In these pages Foucault is giving a biased, one-sided, untenable interpretation of Oedipus, not going much beyond the level of the radical Marxism of the period, transforming the character into a puppet figure infatuated with power, clinging to it at any cost, a figure that would have never become one of the greatest tragic characters of world literature, and that is refuted by numerous instances in the play.[16]

After this first round of misguided discussion of the meaning of the word 'tyrannos' in the 'title', however, Foucault engages in a second round of much more fruitful and less rhetorical analysis of the exact meaning of the word 'tyrannos'. He argues first that Oedipus in the play was a tyrant in the technical, historical sense of the word – a person who gained power through a series of adventures, and who consequently encountered an alteration of fortune or destiny, involving ups and downs. He was also a person who provided service to the city, by 'redressing' or 'curing' it, giving justice in the economic or legal sense.

Oedipus as a *tyrannos*, however, also has negative characteristics (*ibid.*: 565–6). He acts as if the city belonged to him, as if he possessed it, which is a misunderstanding of his own position and the nature of his power. He does not assign importance to laws, but rather governs by his own orders and will. He is, in short, 'a man of excess' (*ibid.*: 568), and the dynamics of the entire play would first bring out these characteristics and then deliver the final judgement.

The last and decisive point concerns the main source of the power of Oedipus, or of 'tyrannical' power in general: technical knowledge based on solitary intelligence (gnome) (*ibid.*: 567). It was this intelligence that helped him to gain power by solving the puzzle of the sphinx, and it was this knowledge that he now deployed to solve the mystery of the plague. In this case, however, his own intelligence leads him to a trap, transforming the 'subject' of the investigation into an 'object': a trap that he set up exactly for himself by the – typically tyrannical – proclamation of the punishment for the polluter right at the start of the investigation. These characteristics, taken together, render the figure of Oedipus as seen in the play of Sophocles a representative figure of power/ knowledge (*ibid.*).

Given the way that Knox in his analysis identified the Oedipus of Sophocles not with the historical figure of the tyrant, but rather with the average Athenian citizen of the fifth century BC (Knox 1957: 67), it would be most interesting to see whether Foucault saw possible parallels with the more contemporary representatives of power/knowledge. However, this theme was not pursued by Foucault, at least not in the 1973 version. Instead, two final comments were made at the end of the lecture. First, Foucault interpreted the end of the play as Oedipus becoming 'superfluous'. His excess of knowledge and power at the end only led to the undermining of his own position, as it only helped to reveal the truth possessed, not by him, but by the gods and the slaves. This interpretation of Oedipus as a figure of transition *par excellence* is extremely promising, but is left suspended, inconclusive. This might be a consequence of the fact that this neutral, non-moral interpretation of the conclusion of the play corresponds closely to the claim that the play is all about power, not guilt, innocence or morals, and is similarly untenable.

The concluding remarks, instead, are devoted to a comparison with Plato and the Sophists.[17] Similarly to Sophocles, argues Foucault, Plato criticised and devalorised the excess knowledge of Sophists, and this led to the great Western myth that political power is blind, and that power can only be exercised in the absence of knowledge. It was this myth, he claims, that Nietzsche started to liquidate. 'Behind all knowledge [*connaissance*]...there is a power struggle. Political power is not outside knowledge [*savoir*], it is interwoven with knowledge [*savoir*]' (DEII: 570).

However, of course, Plato's charge against the Sophists was not their excess of knowledge, but rather their complacency, self-conceit, arrogance and hubris (typical traits of tyrants, by the way),[18] combined with their lack of care about the truth, and the subsequent Western tradition problematised the link between power and truth, and not power and knowledge. This will be precisely the line along which Foucault would radically modify his analysis in 1980.

1980–81: Oedipus and the manifestation of truth

The contrast starts with the strongest possible sense, and at the conceptual level. If Foucault used the figure of Oedipus to introduce the concept 'power/knowledge' in 1971, in the first lecture of 1980 he claims to have gone beyond this concept, replacing it with government by (the manifestation of) truth, and introduces Oedipus as the representative figure of the procedure for rendering the truth manifest – in opposition to the timeless order represented by the figure of Septimus Severus.

The contrast is just as explicit at the concrete level. The second and third lectures of 1980 would be devoted to the play, and Foucault starts by reminding his audience that the play was already analysed nine years previously, but now the analysis will be different. However, one must be careful here in what can be taken at face value in this and similar 'attempts at self-criticism'. Foucault does not simply repudiate his previous analysis, in fact his entire work of the 1970s; but he does not have the time and energy to draw the line between what can and what cannot be still maintained from the earlier work (a proper task for criticism and commentary). At any rate, the presentation of his previous self is far from being fully accurate.

Thus, in 1980 he starts by arguing that this time the presentation will not focus on desire and the unconscious, when even the first presentation was given in opposition to these themes. The difference, however, can be read out of the content of the two accounts. In 1971–73, Foucault started by opposing the standard account, according to which the play was about forgetting and ignorance. In 1980–81, however, he puts the reasons for forgetfulness and the nature of Oedipus's ignorance at the heart of his version of the story. Similarly, in the first version, the play allegedly was all about power; now, says Foucault, without using the same 'essentialist' language, the crucial issue is truth. Finally, as an explicit contrast, he claims in the later version that the central point is not how Oedipus became entrapped by his own decree, but rather it concerns the techniques and rituals of truth.

Now that the contrast between the two versions, centring on the shift from the unveiling of a purportedly omnipresent power to the concern with the truth, is established, we can move on to reconstruct the new version. This starts with a new interpretive framework, taken from the *Poetics* of Aristotle, identifying as the two central elements of tragedy the reversal of fortune of the main characters (*peripeteia*), and the ensuing act of recognition. According to Foucault, who is again emphatically analysing the play and not the myth, these two elements are central for this play as well, except in a reverse order: it is the recognition, at the end, of the true identity of Oedipus that leads to the radical reversal of fortune of the hero. It is this reference to Aristotelian theory that allows Foucault to pose the two central questions of his analysis. First, how is it that, so far, Oedipus was ignorant of the truth, that he failed to see, and what was the role in this that he was a king? Second, what exactly made possible the discovery of the truth, or the realisation of divine prophecy? The second lecture of 1980 would deal with the latter question, while the third lecture, a week later, is devoted to the former.[19]

The second lecture discusses the first and third levels of the previous account, or the 'liturgy of truth' as related to the gods and their seers, and the slaves, closely following the previous version. The emphasis is now on the contrast between two modalities to approach the truth: the gods see everything, always telling the truth; their words have the force of the truth, but they can't be forced to reveal the truth. The slaves, on the other hand, witnessed only because they became parts of a spectacle that was imposed upon them from the outside, and can be forced to reveal the truth; but they can tell the truth because they were there and saw things with their own eyes, because they 'live' in the truth, because they were *present* and thus became *witnesses*. The key verb used by the gods and their seers is therefore 'I affirm', or 'I proclaim', that this will happen; the key word of the slave-witnesses, however, is 'I recognise', or 'I admit', that this is what has happened.

The central conclusion is the same at this stage as in 1973: at the end the truth proclaimed by the gods and recognised by the slaves will coincide exactly.

However, now Foucault draws the conclusion, responding to his first question, in much clearer terms. Two things were necessary so that the forecast of the gods became true. First, it required the disobedience of the servants – that instead of killing the son of Laius himself, as he was instructed, the shepherd passed the task to another shepherd in secret.[20] And second, the 'uncertain truth of the gods' became only visible, accepted, via the truth-telling of the servants. The message now is that the gods indeed tell the truth, but this truth can only become accepted, evidently visible, through the contribution of humble human witnesses. The word of the official servants of the gods, the seers, is no longer sufficient.

The third lecture returns to the second of the three levels, to discuss the question of Oedipus's ignorance. His ignorance is rooted at the same place as his surfeit of knowledge was identified in the earlier account: in *excess*, the main characteristic of the tyrant. The more Oedipus knew – and he could not escape wanting to know more, as he wanted to know everything – the more he had to recognise his ignorance. Thus, instead of the cryptic argument about becoming 'superfluous', Foucault returned to the classical concern with the ignorance of Oedipus.

This, however, does not mean that he now would simply reassert the common platitudes, nor that the previous analysis could not be used. In fact, the central argument and most of the details closely repeat the earlier account. The difference is mostly at the level of the perspective and the concluding remarks. The central problem, of which Oedipus becomes a representative figure, is certainly not power/knowledge – a concern restricted to Foucault's work of the 1970s – but the problem of the links between the individual self and truth, the central problem of Foucault's entire work. More specifically, the issue at stake concerns the possibility, and the necessity, of the individual to discover and authenticate his own truth.

Foucault perceives here a deep-seated resistance to uttering true statements in the first person singular. The seer speaks the truth – but it is not his own truth, only the word of the gods, transmitted through him. The slaves also speak the truth, but they are merely forced to tell what they have witnessed, the true significance of their speech escaping them anyway, becoming visible only when put together in the context of an inquiry of which they are not the subjects. In an aside, Foucault even alludes to dreams as a possible subject matter to investigate in the framework of 'aleaturgy',[21] in the sense that the interest in the truth-content of dreams is instigated by the fact that the person who tells a dream does not possess the truth as a subject of knowledge. This leads Foucault to formulate the problem of the entire 1980 course as the question of identifying the moment in Western history when 'the telling of truth can authenticate itself', or when 'the person who speaks can say that this is me who detains the truth'.

The figure of Sophocles's Oedipus is thus situated in this history, and at a significant point. Oedipus wants to know it all, certainly knows a lot, and is most skilful and intelligent. But he does not know himself, his own identity, especially his true origins, and the moment this truth is revealed he becomes utterly devastated. This indeed carries a lesson concerning the relationship between political (especially tyrannical) power and truth. According to Foucault, this can be formulated in two ways.

First, the technique of tyrannical power, which is quick, astute and inquisitive intelligence, cannot be deployed towards itself. The moment when Oedipus applies his technique not to the solution of a problem, but towards the discovery of his own identity, he is lost. In fact, this moment can be exactly identified: it happens when the play moves from the second to the third level. At the end of the second level, after the exchange between Oedipus and Jocasta, there remains the slight discrepancy between the accounts, the difference between one killer or several robbers. The discrepancy is slight, but Jocasta claims that the account was given publicly and it would be difficult to recant. The lie of the slave surviving the killing is easy to explain in psychological terms: it is much easier to tell the story of several robbers killing the king and the three other members of his escort than to tell the truth of a single killer. But this would only have been a further reason why it had been easy to reinforce the slave in his account, had Oedipus been really and truly only interested in power, as a historical tyrant was in fact supposed to be. But Oedipus failed to grasp this possibility, being more interested in his true origins than in clinging to power at the price of a lie. The story, however, is even more complex here, as – reflected in a few lines of the Chorus – Oedipus's excess, and also his forgetfulness and ignorance at this very moment, reach even higher pitches. When learning from the messenger that Polybios was not really his father, instead of realising the truth that Laius was his father – as Jocasta does, and immediately leaves the scene and kills herself – he suddenly entertains foolish hopes about divine origins. In conclusion, the change of fortune, the *peripeteia* of Oedipus, is not simply due to the revenge or the trap of gods, but to the active deployment of the central technique of tyranny, against his own self.

Second, and at the deeper interpretive level, at the start of the fourth lecture, Foucault returns to the Platonic point, dismissed in 1971–73: the king should ignore his origins, or true identity, as power can only be exerted if truth is not made manifest.

In the April 1981 Louvain seminars Foucault repeats the account, with only three, closely related, differences. First, after the reference to the *Iliad*, Foucault now adds a second historical background point. In the *Works and Days* of Hesiod he identifies a major moment of change in Greek judicial procedures, when alongside the previous two litigants and their agonistic game, focusing around winning and cheating, there appears a third person, who will become the judge, and whose main concern would become what is just (*dikaion*), a word that was not even present in Homer. Second, a more pronounced role is played here than in his Collège de France lectures by the famous line of the Chorus, 'violence and excess engenders the tyrant' (line 873). Finally, the conclusion will be related not only to truth but also to justice: Oedipus wanted to use his intelligence, his shrewd technical knowledge, to escape the will of the gods, but a proper judicial process, which is based on the same inquisitive spirit, can only reinforce the gods.

Concluding remarks

Though Foucault failed to make a single reference to this analysis of Oedipus in his printed work, it played a crucial role at two significant instances in his career, marking the two main swift turns in his work: the move from the archaeology of knowledge to power/knowledge, and the eventual replacement of this latter with the concern with the links between the subject and truth. Though the second version was much more convincing than the first, it was still marred with enigmas and puzzles, only reinforced by the lack of a full, published version. In what way was the figure reminiscent of aspects of the modern self? How about the baffling similarities with the central concerns of Christianity (especially the links between truth, presence, witnessing, confession and subjectivity)? And what can be made of Foucault's somewhat ambivalent attitude to excess?

These questions of course cannot be answered without an interpretive effort, and this can only be undertaken with some degree of seriousness later in the chapter. At this point, however, it is worthwhile to insert another digression on the work of one of the main reflexive anthropological sociologists, René Girard, and his interpretation of the Oedipus story.

Girard on Oedipus

The analysis of Oedipus is situated at just as prominent a place in Girard's work as it is in Foucault's, but in this case it is spelled out explicitly. It is contained in the third chapter of *Violence and the Sacred*, following the introduction of the two key concepts of the book, 'sacrifice' and the 'sacrificial crisis', in the opening chapters. This is not accidental as Girard, in common with Foucault, also takes Oedipus to be a representative figure. It represents, however, something different, even the diametrical opposite to Foucault's case: for Girard, Oedipus will be a paradigmatic illustration of the scapegoating mechanism.

In assigning such a central role to the figure of Oedipus, Girard, just like Foucault (or even Deleuze and Guattari), follows in the footsteps of Freud. However, in the modality of his analysis, Girard boldly proclaims to go beyond these master thinkers. While Freud is focusing exclusively on the myth, and Foucault is only interested in the play, Girard explicitly attempts to give a single and unified interpretation to both myth and play, claiming that in doing so he cannot rely upon his predecessors (Girard 1972: 113–14). The question whether he actually succeeds in presenting such an integrated approach will be a central question for the analysis of the section.

Girard's analysis starts at the level of the play, with an aspect that was widely held to be one of its central achievements: the strongly individualised character of Oedipus. It begins with the traditional view that Oedipus was impulsive, having a 'propensity' to anger (*ibid.*: 105–6). Analysing the scenes describing mimetic violence, he traces this characteristic to an illusion of superiority, or hubris, the characteristic usually identified with tyrants in general and Oedipus in particular. Girard, however, notices this characteristic in all the three main agents involved in these conflicts, including Tiresias and Creon. Merely at the level of psychology and character, therefore, Oedipus cannot be identified. What would eventually single him out are the mythical charges of parricide and incest. These charges, however, argues Girard, are indeed mythical and only mythical, thus false. They are uttered solely in the context of struggles between rival factions. Instead of being concerned with the truth-content of these charges, the innocence or guilt of Oedipus, one should rather reconstruct the underlying mechanism at stake (*ibid.*: 112).

It is at this point in the chapter that Girard calls for the integration of the mythic and tragic perspectives; but, in fact, it is also here that his analysis shifts definitely to the level of myth. It starts with the very first and last scenes of the two related plays: the image of the plague at the beginning of *Oedipus Tyrannos*, and the rivalry for the tomb of Oedipus at the end of *Oedipus at Colonus*. Both scenes are interpreted as elements of a myth and not of plays. The presence of the plague is the situation that sparks off an entire play, and Girard reads it as *the* typical representation of the escalating conflict and non-differentiation characteristic of a sacrificial crisis (*ibid.*: 117).[22] The competition among cities for the place where Oedipus would die, however, once a new oracle declared that it would have the value of a talisman, is read as the standard mythical transformation of the sacrificial victim into the figure of the sacred, the *homo sacer* (*ibid.*: 130–1). It is in between these two end-points that the plays unfold, and their central concern, according to Girard, is the enactment of the classical themes of myths and rituals: the transformation of Oedipus into a sacrificial victim through the mechanism of scapegoating.

The central thrust of Girard's analysis focuses on the complementarity of the two main levels of the myth: the collective level of crisis, indicated in the plague, and the level of the individual hero, Oedipus, ending with the assignment of guilt and responsibility (*ibid.*: 116–20). The two levels strictly complement each other, each containing one 'half' of the story.[23] The plague motive puts the emphasis on the collective level, on universal contagion, but violence and non-difference are eliminated. The motives of parricide and incest work exactly in the opposite manner: they contain the themes of violence and non-difference in a manner exaggerated out of all proportion, but the collective level, or the aspect of contagion, is absent. The two motives each disguise the sacrificial crisis, but differently. The fusion of the two themes, taken together, defines the crisis itself (*ibid.*: 118).

This fusion is visible in the ways that the crisis ends in the myth and in the play. The dynamics of the play, according to Girard, is to transfer all responsibility to Oedipus. The saving of the city requires that all violence be transferred to a single individual, and thus unanimity would end the escalation of mimetic rivalry and violence. This indeed happens at the end when Oedipus reassures the Thebans by assuming full responsibility for the crisis. Girard concludes in no uncertain terms: 'The inquiry concerning Laius, as we saw, is an inquiry concerning the sacrificial crisis itself....The entire inquiry is a chase after the scapegoat which returns, at the end, against the person who started it' (*ibid.*: 119–20).

At this stage, the analysis moves to the level of comparative mythology, introducing the coming chapters of the book. The story of Oedipus according to Girard is only one example of how myths contain, in a veiled form, collective violence and the reaching of unanimity through scapegoating. Even further, it assumes firm and widespread belief in the mechanism of scapegoating and sacrifice.[24] With this, Girard's analysis becomes safely anchored at the level of myth, and not tragedy, though containing a few crucial asides about this other level as well. Girard wonders about the extent to which Sophocles himself suspected the truth (*ibid.*: 122), and argues (alluding to Derrida and Foucault) that the play attempted an at least partial 'deconstruction' of the myth, and was in this sense not the survival of an archaic ritual, but rather an 'archaeology' (*ibid.*: 129). But these remarks remain cryptic, enigmatic, and Girard's relative lack of interest in the play aspect of the Oedipus story is made evident in a remark made at the end of a major article in which he plainly stated that 'all drama is a mimetic re-enactment of a scapegoat process' (Girard 1978: 153).[25]

In Foucault's account, Oedipus is presented as a figure of transition, of crisis, suspended between the eternal order of things, of truth and justice as written in the stars, and the truth of the self to be deciphered by the – Christian and post-Christian – hermeneutics of the subject. This aspect of crisis and transitoriness, however, was not rendered explicit in Foucault's account – magnified by a most amazing omission of any reference to the plague at the start of the play. Girard, on the other hand, puts the concern with crisis at the centre of his analysis, thus complementing Foucault's account. However, his analysis has a major shortcoming of its own. He is considering the story as an almost archetypical representation of the classical, archaic sacrificial crisis, neglecting any concern with the actual context of the play. Significantly, the historical figure of the tyrant, and the city of Athens, play no role in his account. Focusing on the foundational crisis of all culture, Girard pays no attention to the way in which the play, in opposition to the myth, attempted to capture exactly the novel modality of the then-contemporary crisis. Thus, instead of simply correcting Foucault's account with Girard's, the two interpretations should be contrasted with each other – not in the sense of a staged mimetic rivalry (which version is correct; and which of the two master thinkers holds the truth?), but rather through the mutual illumination the two interpretations give to each other.

The first striking thing that becomes evident when looking at Girard through Foucault concerns the lack of any reference to the legal connotations of the play. While Foucault's interpretation through power/knowledge and Girard's reading of mimetic violence share evident similarities (for example, each of them focuses on the scenes in which Oedipus and Creon appear together), their basic reading of the play as a representation of the new legal procedures (Foucault) versus the scapegoating mechanism (Girard) could not be more opposed. This is not just a rhetorical formula, but should be understood in the strictest possible sense. The claim can be substantiated if we put three pieces together. First, they both claim a foundational role for their version of the story: a 'foundational representation' of the new legal procedures for Foucault, and a representation of the foundational violence of all human culture for Girard. Second, Girard repeatedly stated in the first chapter of his book that it is the absence of a judicial system that explains in 'primitive' societies the existence of the sacrificial mechanism (Girard 1972: 30, 34, 49). Third, it seems that the play cannot be at the same time the repetition of the same sacrificial mechanism *and* the representation of its opposite, the new judicial mechanism.

We seemed to have reached a dead end here, as a single piece of work clearly cannot possibly be taken to be not simply a member of two different classes, but the *foundational* representation of two mechanisms that are polar opposites.

The contradiction can be resolved in two steps. First, in spite of all appearances and claims to the contrary, Foucault and Girard are talking about different things. Foucault explicitly states that he is only analysing the play, and not the myth. Girard claims to do both – but the main thrust of his argument in fact stays at the level of myth. The two versions therefore can and should be put together. Second, however, these two halves in fact *are* together, being present jointly in the play of Sophocles. This is because the play was written during an extremely rare type of time period: at an inflexion point, a *Sattelzeit* or a liminal moment in which the old has not yet disappeared fully, while the new is already present. This, in fact, is the exact opposite of the classical van Gennep–Turner version of liminality. In that account, liminality is a gap, a vacuum created by the fact that the old has already collapsed while the new has not yet appeared. The liminal moment captured in the play, however, is a liminality of plenitude, not of vacuum. The joining of the mythical and the legal aspects in the play is therefore not a work of interpretive effort, but rather the very fabric of the artistic genius that created the play. In this sense it is the transitional character of the play that made it timeless – just as it is true for the only other play to which it could be fully compared, Shakespeare's *Hamlet*.

The contrast between the approaches of Girard and Foucault therefore shows that we must talk about two different kinds of crises. There are the pre-historical 'foundational' crises of small-scale tribal village societies, which do not yet possess a legal system; and there are the transitory situations of 'advanced' civilisations, in which such 'liminal' crises represent a temporary suspension of the legal order.

It is in this context of a historical period of transition that we can return to the figure of Oedipus, and his representational value for a 'genesis of modernity'. Oedipus is a king both at the start of the play and as a mythical, even more or less historical, figure. Kings are widely identified as sacrificial victims – in fact, at both the start and the end of the play, Oedipus makes it clearly evident that he fully assumes this position. But the play was conceived in a moment of accelerated change, crisis and transition, at a period when belief in myths, in the entire traditional, established and ritualised system of religion, was widely shaken. In order to render the sacrificial mechanism acceptable, the scapegoat had to assume a disproportional, excessive character, taking upon himself all the various traits usually associated with sacrificial victims; and the mechanism had to be complemented with a legal procedure, as the traditional designation by an augur became unacceptable.

Such an accumulation and magnification of character traits in itself could have turned the character of Oedipus into an unconvincing, unbelievable figure, belonging more to a farce than a tragedy. After all, exaggeration, or magnification out of all proportion, is a major trick-of-the-trade of comic and not tragic genres. In the case of Oedipus as a figure, and *Oedipus Tyrannos* as a play, however, it worked, because the central distinguishing feature of the new type of person was exactly *excess* – first, in the historical form of the self-made tyrant, but then, as we have seen, in the embodiment of the average Athenian citizen. Excess, therefore, becomes twice over the characteristic of Oedipus. First, due to the old, mythical aspect, or rather to its weakening: the sacrificial mechanism was only credible if the victim, the scapegoat, was charged with a bunch of exceptionally repulsive, monstrous crimes. And second, because – in the temporary, transitory, liminal situation created by the collapse of the old order – the new figures who came to dominate the scene, first in politics and then in everyday life, were bound to be driven to excess.

The various spiritual 'ideologies' and 'movements' emerging in this period, from philosophy to prophecy, from Christianity to Gnosticism, all attempt to put an end to this crisis in one way or another. The follow-through of these attempts will be the central interest of Foucault throughout the rest of his work.

Dr Leuret's strange therapy of self-identification

At several important moments of his intellectual trajectory, Foucault discussed in print and in public lectures the strange therapeutic practice employed by a French psychiatrist, Dr Leuret, at about the middle of the nineteenth century. The topic first emerges in a short piece entitled 'Water and Madness', published in October 1963 (DE16).[26] The date is significant, as it was at this time that Foucault accomplished one of the most important reorganisations of both his professional and his private life, among other things abandoning the planned continuation of his genealogy of madness, and turning to literary criticism and the analysis of discourses that eventually culminated in *The Order of Things*.[27] The publication can be read as an attempt to leave at least a trace of the problem that kept bothering him and that he was not able to solve.

Foucault returned to this theme in late 1977 when he published, with a short preface entitled 'The Scaffold of Truth', Leuret's 1840 book 'On the Moral Treatment of Madness' (DE208). One of Foucault's most hidden publications, it appeared at another crucial juncture of his career, widely asserted to be the moment of his 'crisis'. The theme popped up again, and with a vengeance, at the start of the 1980s. Though missing from the 1980 Collège de France course, it became the scene with which Foucault started his lecture during the major 1980 US tour,[28] and then also served to introduce the important 1981 Louvain seminars, the last time that Foucault would connect – though in a rather inconclusive manner – in a series of lectures the themes Antiquity, Christianity and modernity.[29]

The full significance of the recurrence of this theme can be realised if it is joined to the recurrence analysed in the previous section, the figure of Oedipus. Taken together the two scenes cover and identify the major break-points in Foucault's career: the literary turn of October 1963, the turn to the analysis of power/knowledge in January 1971, the outbreak of the 'crisis' in 1977, the partial repudiation of power/knowledge in January 1980, the recognition that the central problem underlying his work concerned the link between subjectivity and truth that happened in the second half of 1980, and finally the joining of the two scenes in the 1981 Louvain seminars. The significance of the bringing-together of these recurrent themes is shown not only in the content of this short course, but also in the first explicit discussion of the concept of 'problematisa-tion', contained in a May 1981 interview given to André Berten, who invited Foucault to Louvain; and also in the fact that it was at this moment that, after a break lasting for about two years, Foucault granted a public interview and started to publish pieces of his most recent research.[30]

The persistent recurrence of the theme and its significance was explicitly recognised by Foucault in these last occasions. In an American lecture he claimed that '[s]ince I first read this passage of Leuret, about twenty years ago, I kept in mind the project of analysing the form and the history of such a bizarre practice' (Foucault 1981: 3), while in 1981 he stated, even more emphatically, that this practice 'struck' him,[31] a statement reinforced by the claim made at the conclusion of his introductory comments that his starting point was an 'astonishment' over the multiplication and proliferation of truth-telling in our societies.[32] Beyond the fact of recurrence, this admission is clearly a sign of the evident puzzle the practice caused for him, a puzzle that for long he was not able to solve.

While the play of Oedipus is complex but well-known, the cure of Dr Leuret is very simple but unfamiliar. Leuret put patients who were behaving 'madly' under a sudden and strong cold shower. After a while, he asked them whether they were mad. In the case of a negative response, he continued the 'therapy' until they finally agreed 'yes, I am mad'. At that point Leuret considered the patient to be cured.

The four different interpretations Foucault gave of this scene in 1963, 1977, 1980 and 1981 circle the theme from various angles, until at the end of the 1981 version the crucial point is finally identified. The 1963 reading (DEI: 270–1), in the elliptic, baroque style characteristic of Foucault's work at that period, puts the emphasis on the perspective of the patient, on the experience undergone and suffered, in line with the interest manifested in *Histoire de folie* about the 'experi-ences of madness'.[33] In contrast to the positive curative powers widely associated with water in various cultures and also prominent in Western history, both in a spiritual and a medical sense, the therapeutic effect of Leuret's method is purely negative: it is painful, humiliating, reduces to silence, and chastises, under the supervision of the doctor (*ibid.*: 270). Furthermore, magnifying all this there are elements of surprise, of aggression and of violence. The aim of the technique is to force individuals to confess their madness, to make them recognise their illusions, that they had been behaving in a delirious way, in sum to make them recognise *themselves* as mad and thus to re-conduct them to health.

The purpose of the water cure is thus to bring forth the 'naked truth'. It is, argues Foucault, baptism and confession at the same time, having the joint functions of a religious ablution and a tragedy; it is an effort to move back to before the 'Fall', and thus a recognition of oneself in oneself (*ibid.*). While the style is clearly sententious, exaggerated, one will easily recognise in a nutshell almost all the central themes of Foucault's last years, discussed in this and the following chapters: the concern with baptism and confession, central for Foucault's 1980 Collège de France course; the concern with truth-telling and the identity of the self gained through speech, the main theme of the 1983 and 1984 Collège de France courses; and the similarity between such scenes and tragedy, reflected in the recurrent interest in *Oedipus Tyrannos*.

The 1977 version shifts the focus onto the doctor as a figure of power, and onto some matters of context (DEIII: 331–2). The latter in this piece means the physical and interpretive setting in which the cure is deployed, incorporating three elements. First, madness is perceived not simply as committing error, but rather as a profound incapability of truth, of being in error, even of living in error (*ibid.*: 331). Second, this mode of being is conceived to be an insurrection, a revolt, a resistance. The final element of context is institutional: it is the emergence of the hospital as a machine for cure.[34]

While these elements of context are general, according to Foucault Leuret's technique reveals unique features that are resumed in five points (*ibid.*: 331–2). The first three define the new modality of action, or power, exercised by Leuret. Using this technique the doctor can fabricate truth at his will; obedience to the doctor has the character of submission to the very truth of reality; and the starting point is the trick that the very reality of the illness is refused, interpreted as a refuge to escape authority. Taken together, these three elements make out the doctor to be a figure of pure power, not simply a person caring about the curing of the sick. It takes little interpretive violence to point out that this figure corresponds to the modality of power exercised by the absolutist ruler, or the historical tyrant that is the first model for Oedipus.

The fourth point returns to the perspective of the patient, resuming the analysis done fourteen years earlier: the suffering endured by the patient is not justified in terms of the remedy, but rather remains an arbitrary exercise of power, applied without justification, with the sole aim of redress.

The final point resumes the previous analysis, close to the conclusion of the previous piece, but moving to a higher interpretive level. The aim of the 'submission-suffering' game identified above is to force a confession of truth. The logic, however, is not inquisitorial. It requires more from the subject than a mere admission, an active performance as indicated by the word *recognition*. Foucault argues that the technique focuses on recognition in four different senses of the word: apart from the sense of involved admission described above, it also means knowing something (sanity, in opposition to madness) 'anew'; it refers to the formal sense of the word, or the explicit formulation of the statement in a clear, loud voice; and finally, the declaration means that the patient was mad, but is mad no longer.[35]

In 1980, further elements of context were added. The curing of madness through self-recognition was an ancient therapeutic procedure, applied in the seventeenth and eighteenth centuries (Foucault 1981: 3). The novelty was that, instead of trying to persuade the patient of the unreasonable and erroneous character of his/her ideas, the cure aimed at obtaining an act, the explicit affirmation of 'I am mad'. The procedure – the opposite of a performative speech act – is efficient, as madness as a reality disappears when the patient asserts the truth. At this point, however, instead of providing an explanation of the effectiveness of the procedure, Foucault rather defines the problem this practice poses and then goes into a presentation of his own intellectual trajectory. The first is summarised in the following question: 'What conception of truth of discourse and of subjectivity is taken for granted in this strange and yet widespread practice?' (*ibid.*). Concerning the second, the only thing interesting for our purposes is that Foucault traces the technique back to Christianity, to the obligation of the exploration of the self and of the telling of this to others, or a duty to become a witness against oneself.

It is only in 1981 that Foucault finally solves the riddle, the reason underlying the efficiency of this 'bizarre' procedure. He starts by adding further elements of context, now focusing on recent (1838) legal changes and the shift of emphasis to the symptoms of the body in medicine.[36] More importantly, he spells out that the key modality of the cure is the link established between truth-telling and purification. At the level of interpretation, compared to the previous accounts, there are three novelties. First, the technique brings out the risks and costs associated with truth-telling. This is the first time Foucault identifies this theme that would be central for the last Collège de France courses. Second, more than before, Foucault emphasises the fact that – in spite of the violence applied – admission requires active engagement, the admission of the truth in full liberty, and the special form of a self-affirmation. The final point is the most important, and – as Foucault argues – the most difficult to notice: this is that the mere fact of telling (the truth) modifies the relationship to the self; or, that the patient declares an identity, but changes this identity by its very declaration.[37] Thus, the issue that preoccupied Foucault for over two decades, but that he was not able to formulate with sufficient clarity up to this moment, was the transformation of the mode of being of the subject through true discourse, the telling of the truth, especially if this truth refers to the subject itself. It is not accidental that this issue would be central to the first Collège de France lecture of 1982, in which Foucault would define this concern as the central question of spirituality.

The scene of baptism

The fourth major scene defines the last period of Foucault's work, and – with the benefit of hindsight – its entire trajectory. It is not related to a singular figure, whether unknown as was Leuret, famous as was Oedipus, or striking in its context as was Septimus Severus. It is, however, clearly a scene, well known by everybody: the ritual of baptism, which is also a rite of passage, an initiation ritual, or rather *the* initiation ritual characteristic of Christianity. Never in his published writings or in his public lectures (as far as I am able to ascertain) did Foucault make any reference to his analysis of baptism. Yet it was clearly present in his 1980 lectures, and with some emphasis. Baptism was, apart from penitence (*exomologesis*) and the techniques used in the direction of conscience (*exagoreusis*), one of the three areas covered in this course. It took up four of the twelve lectures, and came immediately after the two lectures devoted to the Oedipus story, while the remaining two themes – the only ones mentioned in the published course outline – took up about two lectures each.

Even further, the discussion of baptism is intertwined with repeated, almost dogged efforts by Foucault to give a better definition of the central theme of the course of this year, and of his entire life-work. Such attempts were made in the first lecture and at the start of the second, then dominated the fourth and the fifth, but would not return in the last five lectures. The persistent efforts made in these lectures can be read, without much exaggeration, as an indication of the central importance of this theme for Foucault's work. If this is the course of Foucault that is the most exploratory, experimental, then this is the part where this characteristic became most visible. One can follow from week to week the way in which Foucault returns to the theme, from a slightly different angle, modifying the previous account, providing a better angle, accompanying all this with a new, slightly different specification of the underlying guiding question. Didier Eribon argued that *La volonté de savoir* was the book in which Foucault's thought moved the most (Eribon 1991: 275), and he is no doubt right. But that was the book where Foucault's 'crisis' started, and it is most appropriate that among the Collège de France courses his thought 'moved' the most at the last course of the 'crisis' years. In fact, the 'movements of thought', or the 'cogitatio' of one's ideas will be a central theme of one of the last two courses of 1980. Finally, Foucault explicitly acknowledged, and in a most striking manner, the tentative, 'mobile' quality of his thinking during the course. Towards the end of the fourth course, he stated that 'the only type of theoretical work I'm capable of doing is to leave, in as intelligible a manner as possible, the traces of movements by which I am no longer there where I have just been'. As a consequence, his work can't be read as a permanent edifice, only as 'a trail of permanent displacements'. In the analogy of negative theology, he could be called 'a negative theorist'.

Baptism, the first of the three concrete themes studied in the course, is introduced through the term 'acts of truth', and in contrast with 'acts of faith'. The former means the manner in which the subject is inserted into manifestations of truth. Foucault lists three main types: the priestly sacrifice of animals, witnessing, and confession (*aveu*). The first case involves the subject solely as an operator, the second solely as a spectator, while the third implies the joining of both through self-reflexivity. Foucault adds here that, in the rest, 'acts of truth' will always means reflexive truth acts. The specificity of Christianity is defined, then, as the coexistence of 'acts of truth' and 'acts of faith'. The course, states Foucault, will only deal with the former, denying any interest in the study of 'acts of faith'. The problem, however, is that this very separation only emerged, within the institution of baptism, with Tertullian, as Foucault would point out later. Thus, by trying to separate *a priori* the two interlinked themes, Foucault does serious injustice to the question he undertook to study, and this would mark not only the entire course, but seriously limit his understanding of Christianity in the sense of the problem he defined as his own. In this sense the contrasts with Weber and Voegelin will provide particularly striking and helpful complements.

In light of the preceding, when reconstructing Foucault's ideas we cannot simply follow through his line of presentation, but need to make three corrections. We must incorporate results which were presented, because evidently reached, only later in the course; we must systematically analyse baptism with the help of the concept 'rite of passage', a term Foucault was using only in passing and late in the course; and it is necessary to refer to some elements of context or background.

Starting with the last point, baptism could be a particularly suitable subject for a genealogical analysis, as the Christian practice can be clearly traced to two different sources. One is the traditional Jewish initiation rite, circumcision, which in the most classical sense leaves a 'mark' on the body for life. This practice, of course, was not restricted to Judaism, but it certainly served as a visible mark of the Covenant with Yahweh. By the first century BC, however, with the emergence of pagan (Greek or Roman) converts to Judaism, circumcision was replaced by immersion in water. This practice also served to mark repentance, a return to the proper ways, preached by new prophets like St John the Baptist, or by the new Qumran sects.

The other thread can be traced to the initiation rituals practised by various Greek philosophical schools. Here a pioneering role was played by the Pythagoreans, and the technique can be traced to Eastern, especially Hindu sources. Central in this rite is the gaining of illumination through knowledge, based on a belief in the saving power of knowledge, a preoccupation shared by Brahmins, Platonists and neo-Platonists, and by Gnostics.

Didache

Foucault starts his analysis with a text from the beginning of the second century AD, the Didache, which is the oldest book of Church rules that has survived. This start, however, is still late, as Foucault passes over the important developments in the New Testament, which span the era of St John the Baptist with the Didache. This includes the crucial act of recognition by John, with which the story of the Gospel, or the teaching mission of Jesus, starts;[38] the conclusion of the Gospels;[39] and the start of Acts.[40] These elements are significant not simply as they round up the historical context, but because they represent a condensed set of issues central to both the Weberian and the Foucauldian problematic. Baptism for Christianity means neither the reception of a mark or sign, nor even a purification ritual or the gaining of an illumination through secret rituals and esoteric knowledge, but rather the gaining of a special kind of power, the Holy Ghost as a gift, for which the word 'charisma' in the original theological sense was used; a gift that foremost becomes manifest in speech – a power of speech enabling the apostles to fulfil their mission to convert; a conversion that is highlighted by the ritual of baptism. The problem of the codification of this ritual, which is the central theme of the first Church codebook, emerged when all the apostles, or the living witnesses, had died, sparking an outbreak of struggles for recognition and power in the early Church (Pagels 1982).

Returning to Foucault's account, the Didache made no distinction between acts of truth and acts of faith, but rather it described a very straightforward initiation rite. The phase of preparation involved the learning of the basic Christian principles, which – in the absence of a well-defined dogma – focused on the distinction between the 'way of life' and the 'way of death', and on ritual purification (fasting). The rite itself was the application of water, preferably fresh water; while the effects of the rite are not specified, as being taken for granted – this is the arrival of the Holy Ghost and the ensuing possession of charisma.

Justin Martyr

In the next phase the apologists elaborate further the meaning of the act, and especially its effect. Foucault discusses the First Apology of St Justin, the most important of the apologists, written around AD 155/56. Strangely enough, Foucault fails to mention the point, significant especially from the perspective of his later work, that Justin was considered as a major figure of transition, being the first Christian father who was sympathetic to classical (especially Platonic) philosophy, using the distinguishing robe of the philosophers, the *pallium*, even after becoming a Christian, and thus all later Church fathers could be thought of as his disciples. Concerning the act itself, Justin emphasised the point that it was not enough to know the difference between the two ways, but one had to demonstrate the recognition of this truth, or there was a need for an act of faith. Acts of truth and acts of faith still coincide, but the two aspects are now conceptually separated. The central part of his work, however, concerns the explicit elaboration of the third phase of the rite, its consumption or effects. Three such effects are singled out: baptism leaves a mark or stamp (*sphragis*), not visibly, but in the relationship with God; it indicates a re-birth, or a second birth, the start of a new life in opposition to the first, material birth and the following blind and ignorant life; and finally it leads to an illumination, a recognition of oneself through the light of God. In this way baptism became a 'cycle of truth', with an act of faith at the centre of the rite.

The transitional role played by Justin can be demonstrated through the place of this text in the 'genealogy' of baptism. One might capture here the instance when Christianity and Platonic philosophy became joined. In this way the complex and powerful intellectual apparatus of Platonic philosophy was added to the simple Christian affirmation of the truth of faith and the unreflexive work of the Holy Ghost. The combination was intellectually extremely powerful, but the insertion of the Platonic conception of 'illumination' would soon cause serious troubles and eventually instigate a major reorganisation.

At this point Foucault turns to a discussion of the works of Tertullian, one of the most important theologians before Augustine, on baptism and penitence. According to Foucault, the central role of Tertullian was to separate decisively acts of faith and acts of truth, by breaking up the previous unity of the conversion experience (*metanoia*) into the different rituals of baptism and penitence. The discussion is again highly tentative, the successive lectures (especially the sixth and the seventh) going through the same material in a slightly different fashion, making the summary particularly difficult. One of the reasons for the difficulties Foucault had in identifying the exact difference made by the contribution of Tertullian might have been that a key element of the context in which Tertullian worked, the debate concerning the possibility of repeat baptism, started at least a century earlier, and Foucault only analysed this debate later in the course, in the seventh and the ninth lectures. At this point, therefore, it seems advisable to reverse the order of the presentation and turn to this discussion before the analysis of Tertullian.

Foucault focuses on two pieces: in the second part of the seventh lecture a text by Hippolytus, a contemporary of Tertullian, a student of Irenaeus and thus a protagonist in the Gnostic controversy; and then in the eighth lecture a writing of Hermas from the early years of the second century AD. It is not clear why Foucault systematically reversed the chronological order here – at any rate the following presentation will follow the genealogical sequence, integrating the 'genealogy of penitence' into the 'genealogy of baptism'.

Hermas

Hermas's *Shepherd* belongs to the start of the second century, thus coming before Justin and the encounter with classical philosophy. Though written in the form of an apocalyptic vision, its content is rather empirical, staying at the level of practical wisdom. Its discussion of baptism and penitence forms part of a debate that lasted well into the third century. The problem was the following. In the classical texts that were codified into the New Testament at this very period, baptism, or the arrival of the grace of the Holy Ghost, was a once-for-all-time event, a singular occasion to transform the individual and repent all sins. Whoever committed sins after baptism was considered hopeless for salvation, in light of a well-known passage of the Epistle to the Hebrews (5:4–8). Due to the increasing persecution of Christians, however, many were forced to give up their faith, only to repent later and try to re-join the Church. While in the classical framework this was considered impossible, Hermas came up with the claim that such a *second* repentance was possible, but only once.

Hermas's argument was a practical, empirical concession to the pressures of daily difficulties, supported by his vision of a Church whose building is a continuous process, where attempts should be made to fit back the stones that had fallen off. At the theoretical level, however, for Hermas as for Justin, the repentance of sins in baptism was received as a lasting seal or stamp (*sphragis*), and was solely the working of the Holy Ghost and the charismas that came through its possession, not even making a distinction between the possession of the Holy Ghost and the charismas. A systematic elaboration of the theological or theoretical problem that such a 'second baptism' posed, however, was not attempted by Hermas.

Hippolytus

The problems posed by relapse eventually called for the systematisation of the preparation for baptism, which around the years AD 170–80 led to the emergence of the institution of 'catechumenate', or the proper manner of administering baptism. The work of Hippolytus addressed this question, becoming one of the first Church codebooks to regulate the proper way of conduct towards the assumption of baptism. The full title of the work of which Foucault only mentions the first half is 'The Apostolic Tradition, or the Charismas' (gifts of the spirit), showing that the work still adhered to the classical interpretation of baptism. It is also worth mentioning that Hippolytus took up a position strongly opposed to the integration of philosophy with Christianity.

In order to reduce the possibility of relapse, the preparation for baptism became a long process. It started with a formal application, supported by two members of the community as witnesses. It progressed through years of learning and a series of exams, where matters of knowing the main doctrines of the faith were combined with an auditing of the conduct of life of the candidate. It was only once the candidate came through this series of tests and trials, emerging as an 'athlete' of the Christian faith, that the ritual of baptism could take place.

It is by analysing baptism as described by Hippolytus, that Foucault explicitly used the concept 'rite of passage'. The text shows that the ritual increasingly took up the shape of an exorcism. In order to assure a full success of the 'second birth', a rite of dispossession, a quasi-juridical transfer of sovereignty from Satan to God had to take place. Through a process of mortification, one was required to 'die' before being born anew – thus, comments Foucault, the previous paths of the Didache were duplicated, the 'way of life' itself becoming accessible only through a previous death. Baptism was therefore an effective trial of truth, where a frequently used image was the tempering of metal by fire.

The text, therefore, makes two main processes visible: the codification of truth on the one hand, the origins of the later catechisms, and the complementary technique of shaping the self, or the conduct of life, towards a permanent struggle on the other. The full conclusions were drawn by Origen, for whom any baptism on Earth would only be provisional, the real baptism only taking place in Heaven, with baptism on Earth becoming no longer a short transition period but rather a permanent model of life. There can be hardly a clearer illustration of the emergence of the explicit programme of permanent liminality.

We can now return to Foucault's discussion of Tertullian, presented in the earlier lectures.

Tertullian

Tertullian's chief contribution to the emergence of baptism as we know it was the bringing together in a novel synthesis of the contributions of Hermas and Justin. Tertullian was the son of an officer of the Roman army, trained as a lawyer, well-educated in classical philosophy. His work was situated at the intersection of the two major controversies of his time: the handling of the consequences of the persecutions, and the debate with the Gnostics. His best-known idea is the invention of the doctrine of 'original sin' that, according to Foucault, replaced the 'two ways' of the Didache. No doubt related to this fact, he was a major target for both Nietzsche and Weber. Nietzsche concluded the first essay of the *Genealogy of Morals*, as a particularly horrifying example of ressentiment, with a page-long Latin quote from Tertullian, while the 'sacrifice of the intellect', a recurrent concern of Weber, can be traced back to the famous 'credo quia absurdum' of Tertullian: 'I believe because it is absurd'. Foucault follows his main predecessors in assigning major importance to Tertullian, claiming that his ideas represented a 'mutation' in the order of thought.

How did the concept of 'original sin' provide a solution to the problem created by the gap opened between baptism and penitence? This can be understood by considering the stake of the fusion between New Testament ideas and the philosophical tradition, as pioneered by the second-century Apologist. Baptism as a rite of passage showed evident similarities with the initiation rituals that were used in philosophical schools with the various concepts of conversion.[41] It is this similarity that was elaborated, for example, in Justin's identification of the main effect of baptism as being illumination or enlightenment. However, from this perspective, it was not possible to regress from a state of enlightenment once attained. This was because in Platonic philosophy illumination was to be gained solely through knowledge. Thus, Platonic (and later neo-Platonic) philosophy would always remain potentially close to various versions of Gnosticism. The novelty of Christianity in this regard, as Foucault would emphatically point out, was not the Nietzschean idea of the introduction of sin into an innocent world, but rather the completely novel idea of committing a sin once the light was seen.

The relapse after baptism, however, posed serious difficulties for Christian thought, irrespective of the philosophical influence. Baptism meant the assumption of the Holy Ghost and the resulting charismatic gifts by every single Christian, and the Holy Ghost could not fail. The solution of Hermas may have been based on gentle forgiveness and prudent wisdom, but he was not armed with a proper intellectual argument to support his position and had to rely upon the authority of an apocalyptic vision, a method of argument that, with the spread of Christianity, at the time of the daily debates between Christian and pagan philosophers was no longer acceptable. Furthermore, the proper solving of this dilemma was of utmost practical importance, as the Platonic interpretation of baptism as illumination and the classical Christian idea of the impossibility of a failure of the Holy Ghost went hand-in-hand in their emphasis on *perfection* and the resulting hubris, thus feeding Gnostic pneumatism.

The solution of Tertullian turned out to be so powerful because it worked on three levels. The first was theological, and this was an aspect that Foucault failed to cover in sufficient depth. In the logic of Christianity, baptism implied the descent of the Holy Ghost and its becoming an internal force within the individual person in the form of the charismatic gifts of the spirit. Relapse after baptism implied that there had to be a force inside the self that opposed this force. Tertullian identified this force as the 'other inside the self', or the Devil, and he connected this presence to the 'original sin', or the fall of Adam transmitted physically, through semen, to every single human being. Though sounding today an obscure piece of outdated demonology, when translated in the language of Girard, and especially as pursued by one of his closest associates, Jean-Marie Oughourlian, this can be read as a crude version of the theory of the triangular mimetics of desire, the Devil inside being nothing else than the imitated desire of the other (see Oughourlian 1982).

The second level was philosophical. Once Tertullian shifted the focus from illumination and perfection to the struggle within the individual between the Holy Ghost (that is, behaving according to the Christian ways, or the 'imitation of the life of Christ') and the Devil (that is, imitating the desire of the other), then the individual had to be provided with proper arms in this struggle. Tertullian's preference for Stoic philosophy was well known,[42] and in this respect his contribution was to shift the philosophical underpinning of Christianity from Platonism to Stoicism. The part of Foucault's 1982 Collège de France course that is devoted to Stoicism could be read as an elaboration of the background of the Tertullinian 'psychomachia', or struggle within the soul.

At the third level, from the perspective of rites of passage, Tertullian shifted the focus from the last phase, or the effects of baptism, to the first phase of preparation. This is closely related to the previous points. In spite of all their differences otherwise, first-century Christians, Platonic philosophers and Gnostics shared a belief in the saving power of illumination, or the 'light' gained at the moment of a conversion experience. For them, the effect of initiation was an indelible stamp, and thus the central concern was the effect of the act. Once, however, the possibility of a relapse was seriously considered, the preparation for the ritual, and for the struggle in general, became all-important. This could not mean solely the preparation for the 'first' baptism, but it implied the second baptism, or penitence, as well. Eventually the preparation and fortification of the individual self against the sinister influences of the 'enemy inside' were transformed into a permanent ritual, an entire way of life.

With the help of this three-fold thematisation, we can now turn to the way Foucault identified the exact break or 'mutation' that happened with Tertullian. This point was fundamental for Foucault's 1980 course, but was made in a series of approximate steps. Central to this discussion, reflected in the last, comprehensive definition of the central interest of his work, was the concern with the transformation of the self, through the work done by the self on oneself, and not simply through a moment of illumination. The difference between these two different interpretations of spirituality would return in the 1982 course as well.

The break introduced by Tertullian can be captured first of all in the modification of the relationship between purification and truth. The soul is no longer only the subject but also the object of purification, which must precede the rite itself, involving a long process of struggle. This struggle is the subject matter of penitential discipline, leading eventually to the transformation of the entire life into a life of penitence.

Approaching from a slightly different angle, Tertullian solved the problem of the relapse after baptism, or the paradox of the 'second baptism'. A second baptism, properly speaking, is indeed a contradiction in terms. But it was possible to 'repent' again, or to have a second penitence. Simple as this idea sounds to us, it required a profound modification of the conceptualisation of the conversion experience, breaking up the unity of the Platonic *epistrophe*. For Plato, the access to truth and illumination belonged to one and the same moment. As the soul was of divine substance, there was a unity between knowledge (*connaissance*) and recognition (*reconnaissance*), and the central way to knowledge lay in the recollection of memory (*anamnesis*), the discovery of the divine nature of the soul. With Tertullian, this unity was broken into two pieces. The access to truth in matters of faith was settled with the progressive codification of dogma, while ascetic exercises were developed in order to help the struggle against the alien inside. This created a division between faith and confession.

This broken unity can also be seen in terms of attitudes with respect to doubt, and lies precisely along the faith/truth/confession lines. In many languages, doubt can be traced to duplication, or splitting in two.[43] Doubting is incompatible with the Platonic unity of the conversion experience. It is, of course, also strictly forbidden concerning items of faith. However, instead of a philosophical impossibility, this is now due to a prohibition of a canonical kind. Concerning the self, however, doubt is not only allowed, but is strictly recommended.

Foucault's position concerning these developments is profoundly puzzling. It is clear that at this period he was able to formulate his central concern in a way he had not been able to before, connecting the questions of government, truth and self not simply through the 'manifestation' of truth, as he planned at the start of the course, and as he would never do again, but rather through the transformation of the self, by the self, through a relationship to truth. On the other hand, he had considerable reticence concerning the discovery. The theme of baptism and his analysis of Tertullian would never make it to print, and no allusion would even be made to the links between Tertullian and the Stoics in the 1982 Collège de France course. Furthermore, from various lectures up to the published volumes of the *History of Sexuality*, Foucault recurrently made one major, summary reference to Christianity: that its overriding concern was the renunciation of the self. Yet, his own analysis in these lectures showed that the case was not so simple. Central to early Christianity was not the renouncing of the self, but the conceptualisation of the self (or the soul) as a battlefield of two forces: the divine forces, or the assumption of the Holy Spirit in the form of charismatic graces; and the evil forces, which in the periods of persecution centred on apostasy, then increasingly became associated with the sins of the flesh. At stake was not the 'renouncing of the self', but the proper 'arming' of the self in this 'spiritual battle' against the 'evil forces'.

Foucault's lapse in this regard was helped by the fact that in his analysis he systematically omitted references to one of the sides, whether in the form of the descent of the 'Holy Ghost' (which was from the beginning opposed to the Platonic 'ascending' motion of the soul in conversion), or the granting of 'charismatic' grace. The problem was not that Foucault did not take a position in matters of faith, but rather that he failed to include the very argument. In this way, crucial elements from the early Christian conceptualisation of 'truth' and 'self' went missing, restricting the full potential of the work, and leading to the untenable claim about the purely self-renouncing character of Christianity.

Conclusion

Thus, the methodological/rhetorical technique of striking contrasting images, associated with Foucault's earlier works, can be found even in the last period, and they are arguably just as important as the earlier ones. The difference is that these remained unpublished, and one is left to guess both the reasons for the lack of publication and also their exact significance.

Concerning the former, the most important point is that all of these images appeared (or reappeared) at a singular moment in Foucault's intellectual trajectory: in 1980, or the year when Foucault got close to resolving the problems in his work that precipitated the crisis of the late 1970s and when his work turned definitely towards the more remote past. They therefore were marks of a moment of transition in Foucault's work, that on the one hand only underlines their importance, but on the other could explain the lack of published references.

Concerning the latter, the four scenes taken together define the stakes of Foucault's last period. Given the complexity of the images, the absence of a clear temporal sequence and the lack of explicit guidelines, the interpretive effort must necessarily be tentative.

The four scenes taken together define two major, and fundamentally different, modes in which the relationship between individual human beings and the world in which they lived was organised. In one limit case, as depicted in the scene around the figure of Septimus Severus, the order of human affairs was modelled on the very order of the world. In the other limit case, represented by the cure of Leuret, the source of order became relocated in the inside of the self, as the very truth of this self. In between, the transition is represented by scenes and figures from classical Athens and Christianity.

8 The Socratic Moment as philosophical parrhesia

The last period of Foucault's work presents special difficulties. It was not only interrupted suddenly, but it is divided between two major areas which, though they overlap, pursue quite different concerns, none of which is yet published fully. One is the *History of Sexuality* project, of which two volumes appeared in print just at the moment of Foucault's death, and a third volume, the planned book four of the series, exists in draft manuscript form.[1] The other is the series of lectures Foucault delivered at the Collège de France between 1980 and 1984.[2] Of these five courses, only the 1981 course deals at all with the theme of sexuality.

For reasons that have been discussed in detail elsewhere (see Szakolczai 1998), it seems to me that the central thrust of Foucault's last research is contained in the Collège de France courses, and not the published (or still in manuscript) *History of Sexuality* volumes. As a consequence, the following three chapters will mostly deal with these lectures.

The discussion will follow two basic principles. First, the guiding thread will be Foucault's analysis of parrhesia, discussed in his 1983 and 1984 lectures, and the study of philosophical asceticism and the care of the self will be fitted into this line of analysis. In this respect the 1983 Berkeley seminars (see DV) will be followed as a model. Second, the division into three main time periods (classical Greece, fifth–fourth centuries BC; the early Roman Empire, first–second centuries AD; and early Christianity) will be based on both the 1982 Collège de France course and the planned *History of Sexuality* series.

As we saw in Chapter 7, Foucault used a key methodological device of selecting a particular scene, figure or image to present his argument. For the care of the self in 1982, the figure was Socrates and the text a Socratic dialogue with a somewhat problematic status, *Alcibiades*. For parrhesia in 1983 he used a play of Euripides, *Ion*; while in 1984 it was once again the figure of Socrates and a relatively little known Socratic dialogue, *Laches*. There was, however, a crucial text that recurred – and in significant ways and contexts – in each of the three years. The figure is again Socrates; the image is his death, and the scene is his defence in front of his accusers. This text is the *Apology*, no doubt the most famous of all Socratic dialogues; one of the most widely read texts of all philosophy. The text furthermore illustrates the tight links between philosophical parrhesia and the care of the self, documenting the shift from political to philosophical parrhesia through the effect the scene exerted on Plato.

The *Apology*

In Foucault's 1982 course

In his 1982 course on the care of the self, Foucault discussed the *Apology* at the very beginning.[3] The discussion was short and centered on a single issue: the Delphic maxim of 'know yourself' was not simply introduced into philosophy in the context of the 'care of the self', but was subordinated to it. This is documented in the *Apology*.

In just a few words Foucault makes two series of important points. The first series clarifies the meaning of the 'care of the self'. Socrates is presented in the dialogue as the 'master' of the care of the self. This, however, does not mean that he teaches others how to behave. The relationship between the care of the self and the care of others is tight and more complex. The role of Socrates is restricted to warning the citizens of Athens that they should care about themselves. Even more narrowly, his task is related to the first instance: to the moment of awakening. It is in this sense that he compares himself to the gadfly.

The second series is concerned with self-justification. Though standing in front of a tribunal, an experience Socrates never had before, he does not feel ashamed, and for three reasons: because his mission was ordered by the gods; because it was disinterested, as he received no material reward for his activities; and because it was useful for the city, because by taking better care of themselves, citizens would also care more for their city.

In the 1983 course

In the 1983 course on parrhesia Foucault returned to the *Apology* – the sole text common to the two courses. The points discussed were different, but the place and context similarly highly significant.

This time the text was analysed towards the end of the course, in the penultimate, ninth lecture given on 2 March 1983, together with *Phaedrus*. The latter dialogue would feature prominently in the published second volume of the *History of Sexuality*, in its concluding chapter on 'true love'. The context is the difference between parrhesia and rhetoric, or the separation between philosophy as modified by Socrates and Plato and the concerns of the professional teachers of rhetoric, the Sophists.

In his analysis Foucault makes three points, referring to three passages. The first point is concerned with truth (*Apology* 17a–18a). Socrates claims that his accusers are telling lies, while he is always telling the truth, using words that are his *own*, that are *sincere* (he says what he means), and that are *just* (he says exactly what he says). However, Socrates also refers to a more 'objective' criterion in assessing the truthfulness of his own talk. According to Foucault's interpretation, here Socrates used the concept of 'etymological' or 'authentic' logos. According to this view, words are to be linked to reality through their etymology. Falsity comes by adding, in order to produce an effect, something to the original meaning of words. A language remaining close to the sources of reality is truthful, is adequate to what it refers to, while rhetoric constructs speech according to *techné*.

The second point refers to politics (*ibid.*: 31c–32a). Socrates defended himself against the charge of not taking part in politics with three arguments. He did so by following the advice of his *daimon*, which never gave him positive orders but warned him against participating in political life to avoid premature death; this was not an act of cowardice, as earlier in his life he had behaved bravely in actual combat; and finally, he did so because his task was not direct participation in politics, but rather it concerned the subjects who participated in politics.

The third point basically repeated the central argument of the 1982 course (*ibid.*: 30a–b). The role Socrates effectively played in the city was to speak to all of those who were willing to listen, and to incite them to take care of themselves. The target of his activities was therefore not politics but everyday life itself.

In the 1984 course

In 1984, most unusually, Foucault returned to the *Apology* for the third time in a row. The place and context of the discussion only underlies the significance of this repetition, and at the same time assigns it a clear meaning. The analysis is again at the very start of the course,[4] and the text is again analysed jointly with another Platonic dialogue, this time *Phaedo*.[5]

While the previous two discussions of the *Apology* were short and focused only on a few selected points, this one is comprehensive, concerning both text and context. Foucault starts with a general claim about the genre of the text, and then comments upon its first sentences. The *Apology* is a juridical discourse, giving an account of a tribunal, and the first words of Socrates in front of his judges are concerned with truth. These two points become significant, especially when taken together. The *Apology* is foundational, the founding text of philosophy as we know it, and in more ways than one. This is the last public speech of Socrates; it is arguably the most significant Socratic dialogue; and it gives an account of the central experiential basis of Plato's entire work. This foundation, however, is tightly connected to law. At this point one should recall Foucault's analysis of *Oedipus Tyrannos*, and for several reasons. This is a text to which Foucault returned several times; it is also a text of exceptional significance, concerning both its place in ancient Greek mythology and theatre, and its modern interpretations; and finally, it was also read by Foucault as a foundational representation of 'modern', procedural jurisprudence.

The *Apology* is also about truth. Just as in 1983, Foucault refers to the claim of Socrates that he is speaking the truth while his opponents are telling lies, but gives a slightly different interpretation. His opponents use rhetoric so skilfully that Socrates himself almost believes them, forgetting himself, losing his memory. It is against this loss of self, fighting the seduction of rhetoric, that he is proposing a different kind of discourse, the inverse of rhetoric. This is the courageous telling of the plain truth, or the use of parrhesia. If this were not enough, and striking in itself, Foucault underlines the message by two interpretive comments: first by claiming that Socratic parrhesia will lead to the truth about ourselves; and then by calling attention to the tight connections that exist in this Socratic way of thinking between the truth of the self and the forgetting of oneself. These sentences were not pronounced with a diagnostic intent. They represent a clear revaluation of the related comments of 1982 on memory, self and reminiscence, and the first and perhaps only instance in which Foucault was talking about this link between truth and self in a non-diagnostic way. At this stage, however, all this remains highly cryptic, and would need further interpretation that can only be given at the end of this entire part.

A suggestion, however, can be offered even here, especially given the concrete context of the links between the 'foundation' of philosophy and the judicial process. In terms of key words, the law is about justice, while philosophy is about truth. Foucault's analyses of *Oedipus* and of the *Apology* call attention, individually and taken together, to the tight links between justice and truth. The links are indeed so close that in many cultures and languages no distinction is made between them.[6]

In fact, this is exactly how the 'foundation' of 'modern' law and philosophy, as represented in these texts, should be interpreted – a *differentiation* between previously undifferentiated, or compact, entities. And in this process of differentiation, the central issue is the same as was identified in Chapter 6: the differentiation and contrast created between the 'self' and the 'world'. In the undifferentiated world of 'ma'at' or 'asha', individuals exist only as parts of the cosmos; their existence does not carry an inherent justice, truth or value; they have no axis on their own.

Foucault's interpretation follows Socrates through a series of negative and positive self-definitions of his task and brings out the elusive characteristics of the text and the person. Socrates specified that his task was *not* political. Given that the word 'parrhesia' emerged, and with a distinct political meaning, at just around the time when the public activities of Socrates started, this reinterpretation was particularly significant, and was to be clarified first. In justifying his neglect of the business of participation in politics, Socrates referred as the highest possible authority to the voice of his *daimon*. The voice of this 'spirit', however, never told him what to do, it only gave negative advice concerning what *not* to do.

The next question, then, is the positive definition of the task. Here again the highest authorities are evoked, now in the shape of the Delphic oracle. In response to a question posed by one of Socrates' disciples, the oracle said that Socrates was the most knowledgeable of men. This then set the task of verifying this claim, which made Socrates embark on a search (*zetesis*). The results of this search, however, were again negative, or at least paradoxical. Socrates confirmed his own belief that he was not particularly wise. The gods, however, did not lie; the specific way in which Socrates was more knowledgeable than all the other citizens of Athens was that he lacked their *ignorance* of their ignorance. He knew that he did not know, thus he was wiser. In this way, Socrates, or his soul, became a model, a touchstone (*basanos*), not by giving concrete guidance or an example of what to do, but by warning that whatever one does should be based on a proper care of the self.

At this point Foucault resumes and interprets the positive task of Socrates. It is a four-fold process. It starts at the moment of awakening (*éveille*); the incitement for care. Significantly, in his own case Socrates assigns this to the gods, the Delphic oracle. The second phase is the research (*zetesis*), or the search for a new mode of living. This is central, according to Foucault, for the new type of parrhesia, philosophical as opposed to political, as politics does not start with a search. The third phase is the moment of testing (*épreuve*), when the results of the search are put to the test, in order to assess their validity. Finally, the last stage is concerned with the permanent care of others, in the form of a vigil (*veille*), whose substance is assuring that the others keep taking care of themselves.

Foucault makes three major interpretative claims with this analysis. Central is the claim that this text is 'foundational' in the sense of introducing a new type of parrhesia, philosophical as opposed to political, centring on the activity of research, or on the transformation of life into a search (*zetesis*). Second, this separation between political and philosophical parrhesia is the central accomplishment of the voice of the *daimon*. Thus, the two points in which 'divine' forces intervene are not simply rhetorical devices, deployed to refute the accusations, but they perform a very specific function. They give the two main initial impulses, they play the role of rearranging the entire field: first, by convincing Socrates *not* to play the game of politics that is played by everybody else, the game that defined *the* specificity and identity of Athens; and then, to 'awaken' Socrates, to start his search. Socrates could only play the role of awakening others as he himself was 'awakened'; and the impulse for this was not of his own making.

The final claim not only summarises the analysis, it establishes the link between the courses of the past three years. The central concern of the *Apology*, and indeed a theme that traverses all of Socrates, is to establish the proper discourse of the care of the self. This discourse is now found in philosophical (as opposed to political) parrhesia.

The origins of parrhesia

The word 'parrhesia' was invented in historical times. The conditions of this emergence, though not emphasised by Foucault, are central for understanding its historical trajectory.

The term was created by simply putting together two words: pan, or everything, and rhésis, or speaking. The literal meaning of the term, therefore, is to 'speak everything' or 'tell everything'. Apart from being a noun, it also had a verbal version ('parrhesiasthai'), and a term to denote the person employing parrhesia, which was not used in classical texts (DV: 3).

The term was invented in the mid-to-last decades of the fifth century BC, its first evidence in writing being in the plays of Euripides (*Hippolytus*, 428 BC). Since the beginning, the term was associated with Athenian democracy, and was used later by Polybios to identify the exact nature of this political system. However, as there were other terms available to denote the right to free speech, it is necessary to investigate the exact reasons why the need was felt, right at the zenith of the democratic experience, to invent a new term to capture this experience.

The reconstruction of the conditions of emergence of this term has two different aspects. The first is to identify the specificity of the historical practice in the context of which parrhesia emerged, or the specifically Greek, even Athenian, innovation of conducting communal decision-making on the basis of deliberation in a public assembly. The second is to analyse the reasons why, within this practice, the need was felt to come up with a new name, just at the zenith of the success of this practice. The first is the institutional aspect, or, in Foucault's terminology, 'le politique'; while the second is 'politics as game and as experience', or 'la politique'.[7] The first question has been exhaustively discussed in a classic article by Arnaldo Momigliano (1973), while for the second issue, following a suggestion of Fredrickson (1996: 165, fn. 16), I use the work of Giuseppe Scarpat (2001 [1964]).

Public assembly and the institutional right of free speech

Momigliano's article traces the background practice of political assemblies, especially the use of deliberation and the expression of dissent, in the context of historical civilisations, paying little attention to anthropological evidence. Though emphasising the very limited character of the available information, he finds little evidence for the use of this practice. Given the domination of kingship in the civilisations on historical record (see Frankfort 1948), this is not even surprising. The few indications of such a practice can be traced either to remote origins, as in the case of Mesopotamia,[8] or to cultures that for a long time were at the edge of historical civilisations, like the Hittites (Momigliano 1973: 253) or the Macedonians (*ibid.*: 257). From this, Momigliano draws the Weberian conclusion that the presence of political assemblies can be associated with some kind of military democracy.

Momigliano finds two exceptions to this general pattern: ancient Israel and classical Athens. The exceptionality of the first is traced to two characteristics, the Covenant and prophecy (*ibid.*: 255–6). The first implied that the relationship with divine authority had a contractual character, making space for unusual informality and outspokenness of behaviour in front of superiors. But the real specificity of the Hebrew case is due to prophecy. Momigliano defines the prophet as an 'unpredictable messenger' of Yahweh, who not only speaks in the name of Yahweh, thus commanding authority, challenging even the king's

power, but even claims to stand in Yahweh's council. Though using a legal terminology, rooted in the Covenant, in this way prophecy 'introduces into Hebrew
life an element of freedom of speech which breaks all the conventions' (*ibid.*:
256). This claim is especially important, as Momigliano identifies here the same
distinction between institutional politics and politics as experience that Foucault
introduced for Athens in his analysis of parrhesia.

The classic case of freedom of speech, however, is traced to ancient Greece,
especially to Athens. Momigliano cautions us that the Athenian political
assembly (*ekklesia*) is the only assembly about whose activities we know in some
detail, and even there only from the fifth century BC onwards. Very little is
known about the origins of this practice. Negatively, it was helped by the fact
that, after the collapse of the Mycenean civilisation, kingship disappeared for a
long time from the Greek landscape. Some positive indications can be found in
the Homeric works, but these allude only to a rudimentary 'military democracy'.

After a short discussion of Sparta, Momigliano turns to Athens. Though the
exact origins of Athenian democracy are unknown, it is certain that one of the
two terms associated with freedom of speech, parrhesia (the other being
isegoria) emerged in Athens. *Isegoria*, denoting the equal right of speech in the
assembly, is associated with the legal and institutional aspects of citizens'
rights, and was closely related to another central value of Athenian democracy,
the equality before the law (*isonomia*), while parrhesia was more associated with
freedom (*eleutheria*), especially freedom from the limitations imposed by tyranny.
Momigliano even identifies here a conflict between democracy as freedom, as
represented by parrhesia, and democracy as equality, as represented by
isegoria.

There are two further points of importance in Momigliano's account of
parrhesia: the claim that in the late fifth and early fourth centuries the word
'parrhesia', being more recent, was used more frequently than was 'isegoria'
(*ibid.*: 260); and that already at about the same time the use of both words
became problematic. The best example for this is Thucydides, the historian of
the Peloponnesian War and thus of the demise of Athens, who preferred not to
use either of the two words, as he perceived that the basis of democracy was
neither the equal nor the free right to speech, but good faith in both the speaker
and the listener. If this is attacked or absent, even the most democratic proceed-
ings will be poisoned.

Politics as experience

There are three expressions in Greek relevant to freedom of speech: isonomia,
isegoria and parrhesia (Scarpat 2001: [1964] 15–46). While the term 'parrhesia'
emerged at the zenith of Athens, Scarpat calls attention to the fact that Athens
identified itself at its highest moment with the other two terms.

The first of the three concepts is introduced by a text of Herodotus,
recounting a conversation between three Persians concerning the advantages
and disadvantages of the three main forms of political government. The eulogy

of democracy is based on a combination of negative and positive elements. Negatively, democracy is praised by the demonstration of the shortcomings of its opposite, tyranny. The Persian king, Cambyses, illustrates the main vice of tyranny, hubris (excess), in his own personality. But Herodotus does not stop here, and argues that tyranny even transforms the everyday man as, while it engenders hubris on the one hand among the rulers, it also engenders envy on the other. Even further, tyranny combines both vices, as the tyrant becomes not only hubristic, but also invidious of others, not accepting even a praise that is only moderate (*metrios*, that is, with measure, without excess). In opposition to the excess and envy engendered by tyranny, the isonomia of democracy, used both by Herodotus and Thucydides to characterise democracy, means three things: government according to the laws, equality before the law, and the equality of effective powers.

Isonomia is the general institutional context of democracy, while isegoria defines a specific right related to speech: the right to intervene with one's own words in the assembly (*ekklesia*), or the right not just to the equal application of laws, but even to take part in legislation. Taken together, isonomia and isegoria cover basically what we understand as the concept of citizenship rights.

The two words, however, were evidently not enough to cover the way democracy was experienced, and this led to the invention of the third word, parrhesia, that soon became the most popular term to indicate the specificity of Athenian democracy. In trying to describe this concern, Scarpat claims that, with this word, the emphasis shifted beyond formal rights to the effective use of this right, the actual act of saying, the full enjoyment of citizens' rights. It is at this point that Foucault's interpretation of the experiential component of parrhesia fits into the work of Scarpat.

Political parrhesia: Pericles

In introducing the term parrhesia, beyond describing its meaning, Foucault made use of three texts: *Ion*, a play of Euripides; the funeral oration of Pericles, as told by Thucydides; and the description of the specificity of the Achaean political system by Polybios.

Polybios

In order to justify the significance of his key word, Foucault refers to the same authority as Voegelin, and in the same sense: the importance of the term parrhesia, just as that of the *oikumene*, was recognised by Polybios. Polybios was not simply a historian of the Hellenistic period, but the first comparative historian. He personally experienced the Roman conquest of Greece, which gave him the opportunity to reflect, on the spot, on both the similarities and the differences between these two cultures, and the deep-seated reasons for the Roman victory. His central problem was to assess whether mankind would benefit from Roman rule or not (Fritz 1954: 34–5).

Foucault mentions Polybios at two places in the 1983 course. At the end of the second lecture, in introducing the term parrhesia, he notes that Polybios identified Athenian democracy by two terms, isegoria and parrhesia. The first was related to the equality of rights to speech (in the assembly), and the second to the freedom to take up speech. At the start of the fifth lecture, after the long discussion of *Ion*, he returned to this passage, and gave a more detailed interpretation. Isegoria refers to the statutory right every free citizen of Athens was granted by the constitution (*politeia*) to speak. Parrhesia, however, was something different; it was what permitted an individual to take the initiative and thus the 'ascendance' over others, by telling in the assembly what they really thought about the way the city should be governed, with full belief in the truth of their proposal.

Ion

Ion is analysed by Foucault in considerable detail. In the 1983 Collège de France course the discussion extends from the second part of the second lecture up to the first part of the fifth lecture, and so lasts for a good five to six hours, which is the longest time Foucault devoted to any single text in his courses. The main lines of the analysis were repeated in the second of the six 1983 Berkeley seminars. The play was used to introduce the theme of parrhesia in a similar way that he used *Oedipus Tyrannos* to introduce the 1980 course; in fact, the analogies with the play of Sophocles were explicitly drawn in the first part of the third Collège de France lecture of 1983.

The play is based on the mythological foundation of Athens. Just as in the case of *Oedipus*, Foucault's analysis is based entirely on the play, and not on the myth. This reiterates a profound concern of Foucault with questions of foundations in the Collège de France courses of the 1980s, whether it is the foundation of law (*Oedipus*), of philosophy (the *Apology*), or of democracy (*Ion*).

This story, though well-known by contemporaries, is much less known today than the other two foundational discourses analysed by Foucault, so we must start by summarising the content. This is helped by the fact that, as usual for the plays of Euripides, the action is summarised at the beginning of the play. Furthermore, it is of some importance that, among all the plays of Euripides, this summary is given by Hermes, the great Greek trickster 'god'. The figure of the trickster, in many mythologies, is closely associated with foundations. Hermes also played an important role in *Prometheus Bound* by Aeschylus, where Prometheus, another Greek trickster figure, was engaged in another founding act, the separation between man and the gods. Given the topic of this play, such allusions could not pass unnoticed by contemporaries.

Ion is the son of Apollo and Creusa, but – in some sense alluding to Oedipus – he does not know his parents. The reasons, however, are different. Apollo raped Creusa,[9] and once Ion was born, out of shame he even forced Creusa to abandon the child to its fate. Driven by a sense of remorse, however, he then saved the child and took him to his own temple at Delphi, where Ion was brought up as a temple servant. Creusa was married to Xuthus, but the marriage failed to produce any issue. They decided to go to Delphi and ask the advice of the god (as Creusa well knew, it was the very same god who had earlier raped her), concerning any hope for a child of the marriage. The play starts at the moment when Creusa, entering the sanctuary at Delphi, meets Ion. The two, of course, fail to recognise each other.

The play is the story of how, trying to make sense of the statements of the oracle, the protagonists start a search, a *zetesis*, and eventually discover their respective identities as son and mother. Foucault uses the same technique of fitting together the half-truths as he did with *Oedipus Tyrannos*. The technique deployed in the play is the same, but the character of the agents is quite different. In the play of Sophocles there was a clear separation of status between the gods (and their agents, such as the oracles and seers), the royals and the servants. In *Ion*, this hierarchical structure is erased. The gods behave as human beings, commit crimes and feel a sense of guilt, while the royals mingle with the servants. Finally, the main protagonist of the play, whose search for the truth and whose struggle for the courage to tell it becomes the central engine of the play, is a woman, Creusa. If the central concern of *Oedipus Tyrannos* was the finding of the true identity of the hero, the central concern of *Ion* is the finding by Creusa of the strength to tell the truth.

Foucault emphasises here that parrhesia was therefore rooted, not in an institutional right, but in the courageous talk of the weak of the injustices of the strong. This means, on the one hand, that truth and justice are intimately connected even here, as in the *Apology*; and on the other, that parrhesia is closely connected to the 'powers of the weak', identified as one of the main characteristics of liminality by Turner (see especially Turner 1969: 108–13), and also singled out for attention by Pizzorno (1987: 39–41).

Foucault takes the significance of this point to the limit. The play is widely recognised as one of the first and most important sources for the meaning and significance of the word parrhesia. Foucault is presenting and analysing the standard passages, like the claim that the use of parrhesia is the most cherished among the rights of Athenian citizens; or that not being able to use free speech is among the hardest deprivations of exile. However, he argues that by the very logic of its action, the play makes even more fundamental claims about parrhesia. Athens could only have been founded by Ion as a result of a series of courageous acts of truth-telling by his mother, Creusa. Without these acts, Ion would have remained a temple slave. Thus, parrhesia as an activity and not as a legal right was the very foundation of the polis; Athens was founded on truth-telling.

This claim, of course, is historically untenable, even logically incoherent. Parrhesia originated in Athens, yet the play argues that it existed even before the foundation of Athens. The play therefore is often considered to be purely fictitious, even ideological. Yet, by tracing an institutional right to acts, practices and experiences, one might argue that it is 'more true' than simple historical narrative.

The second main concluding comment of Foucault is related to the modality of this foundation. In the play, truth-telling is not simply identified as the foundation of Athens, but it actually shifts the cultural centre from Delphi to Athens. In a nutshell, a genuine secularisation thesis is presented here: Athens is founded on the secularisation of parrhesia. Oracular truth-telling, based on the cult of Apollo at Delphi, was central for Greek culture. The ability to say what one thought was also a privilege associated with the gods, especially Zeus. In this particular case, however, Apollo does not, because he cannot, tell the truth – that by raping Creusa he committed a crime. The very fact that this action has become problematic indicates a major shift. Greek mythology is full of violence committed by gods against humans. So far, such acts were accepted without difficulty; in this play, however, this has become problematic.

This is recognised by Apollo himself. Like humans under similar circumstances, he feels shame, has a sense of guilt, and cannot tell the truth. The consequence is that he has to use further force and constraint against Creusa and Ion, the victims of his caprices, has to use deceit, tricks and lies, tools that in classical mythology belong to the arsenal of semi-god trickster figures, not the gods themselves. Ultimately, at the end of the play, when according to the classical tradition he is supposed to appear and wield justice, he fails to appear, falling silent. Democracy is positively based on parrhesia, negatively on the silence of the gods.[10]

While the first uses of parrhesia in the plays of Euripides were positive, even eulogical, in his later plays the meaning of the term changes, gaining an ambivalent connotation. Soon after the experience of democracy led to the coining of this word, problems emerged right at the core of this experience.

Pericles and the good exercise of freedom of speech

The Golden Age of Athenian democracy is inseparably linked with the person of Pericles, even identified in textbooks as the period in which Pericles exerted a decisive influence over Athenian politics (462–429 BC). The coining of the term parrhesia, and its comet-like career, is closely identified with this experience. Returning to Euripides, by the time of *Orestes* (dated 428 BC), the meaning of the word has already become ambivalent. This seems to indicate that the word was coined in order to express the experience of the 'Golden Age' once it was all but over, even helping to explain its collapse.

The close association between Pericles, democracy and parrhesia, however, brings out a paradox. If parrhesia expressed the quintessence of the democratic experience, and the word was created in order to characterise the Athens of Pericles, then it is particularly puzzling that in his praise of Pericles Thucydides stated that in this period 'Athens, though in name a democracy, gradually became in fact a government ruled by its foremost citizen' (Thucydides: II, 65). This also makes it clear that the person of Pericles holds a key for understanding the functioning of political parrhesia. Here Foucault's analysis adds a distinct contribution to the standard literature, and helps to solve the puzzle.

Of the three main speeches of Pericles, on face value the most relevant is the second, the famous funeral oration, in which Pericles eulogises, in an idealised form, Athenian democracy (*ibid.*: II, 35–46). Though not using the word parrhesia, among the virtues of democracy ample space is given to the right of political participation and free speech. According to Foucault, however, this is the least important of the three speeches for the study of parrhesia. More relevant is the third speech, delivered after the plague that broke out in Athens in the first year of the Peloponnesian War (*ibid.*: II, 47–54). In this speech Pericles, who is accused of misleading Athens into the war, and thus indirectly even of causing the plague, defends and justifies himself, thus delivering his own 'apology'. Foucault argues that the speech is a perfect illustration of the actual exercise of parrhesia, and for two reasons. In meeting the accusations, Pericles does not use rhetorical tricks to flatter his adversaries, looking for their favours, but rather he directly attacks them. He demonstrates by example the central character trait of the parrhesiast, the courage to tell the truth in the face of risks. The second point is related to the content of his reproaches. Recalling his past advice, he demonstrates that his accusers have lost their memories, forgetting that in the past they gained glory exactly by following his advice. Even further, they not only forgot his advice, but also their own courage.

The most important of the three speeches, however, according to Foucault, is the first (*ibid.*: I, 140–4). This is the speech in which Pericles decisively influenced the Athenian *ekklesia* in deciding about the war. His behaviour on this occasion shows a paradigmatic example of the good use of political parrhesia.

In this speech, all four poles of political parrhesia are present. The first is the constitutional right of free speech, the condition of possibility of parrhesia, guaranteed for every Athenian citizen. Pericles does not make use of any other status or privilege. However, second, he does exercise power through his speech, capturing the initiative and thus gaining ascendancy over the others. Political parrhesia is not just about equal rights, but also about effective action. Third, this ascendancy is gained as much by the rationality of the argument put forward by Pericles as by its personal character. More than presenting convincing arguments, Pericles tells what he personally thinks is true. This is in fact how he starts his speech, making the same basic argument that he has always put before. He does not select a view to fit the moment, but gives a personal, true and identical position. Finally, in making his speech, he also takes up personal risks, accepting the consequence of the course of action he suggests.

Thus, far from being paradoxical, the link between the experience of democracy, as expressed in the word 'parrhesia', and the person of Pericles was almost 'necessary'. Parrhesia can only be personal. Democracy is based on equal rights; but the right adjustment between parrhesia and democracy does not mean that everybody could effectively speak – this would only result in chaos – but that such an institutional arrangement renders it possible that the most suitable person rises to power, in the sense of influencing decisions about the right policy, and not somebody selected on the basis of blood rights or status. In Weberian language, we could say that, through parrhesia, Athenian democracy established the possibility of charismatic power in politics, beyond the two previously existing forms of charisma, military and religious.[11]

Isocrates and the bad exercise of freedom of speech

If democracy is the system that can assure that politics is guided by truly charismatic persons, then the quick collapse of Athenian democracy provides valuable insights into the problems faced by the first emergence of such a political form. Foucault demonstrates the wrong adjustment between democracy and parrhesia through two discourses of Isocrates (436–338 BC).

At the start of his 'Discourse on the Peace', Isocrates reproaches the citizens of Athens that they have a tendency to expel all those public speakers who strike a critical tone. They only accept criticism in the theatre, in the form of a comedy, but not direct critique in the *ekklesia*. The dream of *Ion* therefore was not realised. Instead of listening to the genuine parrhesiasts, they rather follow the demagogues and the flatterers.

The next text clarifies the exact characteristic of this new personality type. The flatterer is not saying what is useful for the community. His concern is his own pleasure, and for this reason he tries to please the others. In this way bad parrhesia, like bad money, chases away the good. Bad parrhesia can be characterised by three features, opposed term-by-term to the three specific characteristics of good parrhesia, using and abusing the same constitutionally guaranteed rights. If those who take up the floor do not try to further the solution of problems, then ascendancy will be perverted: the worst and not the best will rise to the top. Furthermore, speakers under such conditions will not express their personal opinion, but rather whatever conforms to the current majority opinion – what everybody else thinks and says. Finally, such a way of speaking does not require courage and is not risky, but is rather done in the pursuit of individual security and success.

Conclusion: the paradoxes of parrhesia

The texts of Isocrates were not isolated instances, but parts of a general problematisation of democracy. Already at the end of his discussion of *Ion*, Foucault made some general comments on the functioning of political parrhesia.[12] He returned conclusively to this theme after the discussion of the two examples of good and bad parrhesia.[13]

In assessing the exact links between parrhesia and democracy Foucault made three sets of tightly connected comments, representing a successive elaboration of the problematic. He started by asserting that the circularity of *Ion*, that parrhesia is assumed there as a cherished right even before the foundation of Athens, should not be taken as an authorial lapse, due to ideological purposes, but that it alludes to the fundamentally circular relations that exist between democracy and parrhesia. The next two sets of comments will attempt to resolve this circularity.

The first set is analysing the exact link between Athenian institutional practice, or the constitution (*politeia*), and the actual exercise of power, ascendancy (*dynasteia*). In the terminology introduced by Foucault, this is the difference between 'le politique' (the legal framework), and 'la politique' (politics as a game and experience). In this way Foucault returns to a more precise definition of his long-standing concern, the definition of a type of power that is not legal, or the question of 'governmentality', giving a clear meaning to what exactly we are to understand by 'non-legal power'. This does not, or does not necessarily, mean a type of power that is beyond or against the law. The problem, rather, is that the formal, legal requirements in themselves do not, and cannot ever, specify how power actually will be exerted; what will happen in the decision-making process, or who will gain ascendancy.

It is exactly here that the role of parrhesia can be identified. Parrhesia establishes the actual link between legal-institutional arrangements and the effective game of politics. The institutional framework, the right of participation and the equal right of speech, assured the possibility of parrhesia; and the actual exercise of parrhesia, on the other hand, assured the smooth functioning of the political game, that effective decisions would be reached in an assembly where thousands of people could have made lengthy interventions.

This is the 'theory' of parrhesia. The effective functioning of parrhesia in Athens, however, in the cases of both good and bad adjustments between parrhesia and democracy, brought out two paradoxes. The paradox of good parrhesia is the following. Political parrhesia assumes a democratic form of government and the equality of rights (*isonomia*). However, the ability to use parrhesia is not equally distributed. Democracy, through parrhesia, only works if in fact only the few will actually speak. Thus, the proper exercise of parrhesia leads to the ascendance of the few, ultimately perhaps of only one, thus threatening the very constitution of democracy.

The 'bad' adjustment is the consequence of the other, almost perfectly symmetrical paradox. Democracy can only exist and survive if there is a possibility of speaking the truth openly and frankly. However, under the same conditions of democracy, true discourse is threatened by flattery, or the use of rhetorical, untrue speech, and the more so the more such democratic right will actually be exercised.

Calling attention to the significance of these twin paradoxes, in a rare aside Foucault warns that modern democracies cannot neglect them, just as they rightly pay attention to institutional and legal issues.

The two paradoxes form a logical system. Historically, however, they constitute a series. The first paradox, due to the 'good' adjustment between democracy and parrhesia, was succeeded by the second. While parrhesia as a term was coined to express the everyday experience of political democracy, now the citizens of Athens experienced the self-elimination of democracy by the uncontrolled use of parrhesia. This led to a joint problematisation of democracy and parrhesia.[14]

Of the various modes in which the link between democracy and parrhesia was problematised, Foucault singled out one for attention. It became evident that neither institutional rights, nor simple frankness, were sufficient to ensure a proper functioning of democracy. This led to the question of who exactly is capable of speaking the truth; or, the problematisation of political parrhesia led to the issue of the problematisation of the *subject* in politics. This way of posing the question, however, brought together the political question of speaking in the assembly with the philosophical question of access to truth. In other words, parrhesia shifted from politics into the field of philosophy. This, according to Foucault, was the fundamental significance of the Socratic–Platonic moment. In Weberian terms, this can be characterised as a shift from 'natural' charisma (as in the case of Pericles) to the problem of artificially produced charisma and its various kinds of 'ascetic' techniques.

The origins of the care of the self

Foucault says very little about the origins of the care of the self. His related remarks were dispersed in the course, and at one point he explicitly stated that a genealogy of ascetic techniques was not his problem (CF82: 400). Nevertheless, the short asides contain issues of significant interest, and the repeated return to the theme also indicates that Foucault also considered this point as not trivial. After all, he argued that the care of the self was the very starting point of the entire philosophical tradition.

Remote sources

Foucault provides glimpses into the historical background of the care of the self at four different places in the course. First, in the second hour of the first lecture, just at the beginning of his discussion of *Alcibiades* and in the context of the problem of education, he makes a passing reference to Sparta and the traditional privilege of having time to be concerned with oneself (*ibid.*: 32–3).

At the beginning of the second lecture, and still within the general problem of education posed in Athens, he returns to the theme in greater detail, now focusing on philosophy (*ibid.*: 44–8). The remarks, though short, can be situated at three different levels. On the most basic level, he acknowledges that the presence of some related techniques can be observed in virtually every culture. Second, he singles out four such techniques as being influential in Greece well before Plato or Socrates: rites of purification, the concentration of the soul, the retreat or withdrawal, and finally the practice of trials of endurance. Third, he adds that such techniques were even brought together in a coherent way and within the context of an influential spiritual movement in the various Pythagorean schools.

The third occasion is at the start of the second hour, where Foucault complements the account given earlier by referring to a book by Henry Joly and the shamanistic origins of such techniques (*ibid.*: 64). Finally, he starts the eleventh lecture by adding a few points he failed to mention in the previous week, and these would again focus on the Pythagoreans and on the shamanistic background of Greek philosophy (*ibid.*: 395–400). Though here, referring to a critique voiced by Pierre Hadot, he places question marks behind the idea, he would repeat the suggestion later.[15]

These cryptic and dispersed remarks require some commentary, all the more so as Foucault would not return to this theme in 1983 or 1984, except for small points: one on the etymological origin of the term '*melete*' (at the start of the fourth lecture), the other on the Eastern origins of the care of the self.

The first thing to notice is that Foucault practically never refers to the pre-Socratics, outside the Pythagoreans. This is all the more surprising given the importance attributed to them by Nietzsche and Heidegger, his two main sources. The almost complete absence of the name of Heraclitus in Foucault's oeuvre in this respect is particularly striking. In fact, even the references to the Pythagoreans refer only to their contribution to philosophical education, and even in the context of the asides on shamanism he fails to mention the names of Parmenides, Empedocles or even Pythagoras. Here we can only indicate this problem, and cannot even try to offer a solution.

The second problem concerns the persistence of the references to the alleged shamanistic origins of the techniques of philosophical asceticism. Here it is necessary to take up and complement Foucault's references. This will start with the work of Jean-Pierre Vernant (1990 [1965]: 371–92), who attempted to re-pose the question of the origins of philosophy.

Vernant emphasised that the manner in which philosophy was born out of mythical and religious thought is not at all as clear-cut as the customary text-books make it out to be. Up to the Socratic turn, the earlier philosophers take up an in-between position between these various realms of thought, often being quite strange personalities – quasi-mythical figures, divine men or even demi-gods, being completely out of line with normal everyday life and ordinary human beings.[16] Instead of focusing on doctrine alone, Vernant emphasises the novelty of the philosopher as a human type, and argues that a central aspect of this novelty was the idea of the soul leaving the body, or a novel concept of personal immortality. It is in this context that Vernant mentions the ideas concerning the shamanistic origins of Greek philosophy, though acknowledging that the more probable origins are in techniques of yoga (*ibid.*: 388, fn. 44).

In his recent book Pierre Hadot took up a strongly critical position against this suggestion (Hadot 1995b: 276–89). However, Hadot's arguments are not fully convincing here, reminiscent of the traditional reticence of philosophers and historians to use anthropological material, while the allusion of Vernant to yoga seems to open up a path worthwhile investigating. In this respect the work of Mircea Eliade on yoga contains further clues.

Eliade argues that the techniques of yoga, central for the destruction of '"normality"' (Eliade 1969 [1954]: 294) which rendered possible the rejection of the world characteristic of the religions of India (*ibid.*: 9–10), have remote origins, going way back before the Aryan conquest. While he acknowledges that the origins of ascetic techniques are lost in remote times and contain universal elements, he argues that they also show some specific affinities with shamanistic initiation rites. Three of these are singled out for attention. The first is the myth of immortality (*ibid.*: 314). The second is related to the ordeals of the shamanistic initiation, which involves an experience of dismemberment of the body and a personal descent into 'hell' (*ibid.*: 314–15). It was this descent that enabled the shaman to perform his main curing activity: fetching the souls of sick persons stolen by the demon of death by leaving his body at will and descending into hell to collect them (*ibid.*: 320).[17] Finally, the third specific point of shamanism consisted in the emphasis on ecstasy. This shamanistic complex is very old, according to Eliade, to be found among both Australian aborigines and the archaic people of North and South America, especially those close to the polar regions. It developed in two different directions: it degenerated into trances and possession by spirits, later associated with shamanism; and it was spiritualised into the techniques of yoga.[18]

Philosophy as a way of life

In the recognition that ancient philosophy should not be considered as a systematic exposition of ideas, but rather as an attempt to formulate and propagate a way of life, a crucial role can be attributed to the work of Pierre Hadot (1993, 1995a, 1995b, 2001).[19] It was, however, due to Michel Foucault that the discovery, striking in itself, became more than just an internal affair of the historians of ancient philosophy. The works of Hadot on conversion and spiritual exercises served for Foucault as crucial guides in his studies from the late 1970s onwards. As a result, in the autumn of 1980 Foucault contacted Hadot in order to suggest him as a candidate for the Collège de France (Hadot 1993: 229; 2001: 214). In 1983 Hadot came to be elected, and within about a decade he became one of the most influential figures in French intellectual life.

If Hadot was a pioneer, he was not alone. As he discovered in the 1970s, similar concerns were formulated, independently, by the Swiss philosopher André-Jean Voelke and the Polish philosopher Juliusz Domanski (in Voelke 1993: viii, and in Domanski 1996: viii). And Foucault could have championed the case because the parallels between the existential problems as expressed by the ancient thinkers and the situation of modernity was indeed striking (Davidson 1995: 5).[20]

Such a proposed reinterpretation of the entire history of philosophy, thus of one of the main sources of modern Western thought, is of course extremely weighty, significant, and must be supported by a careful (re)assessment of the sources and origins of philosophy. The protagonists of the new interpretation perform this task in two steps: the first concerns the very emergence of philosophy, while the second examines the role played by Socrates and Plato.

The references by Hadot to the pre-Socratics are unfortunately meagre in quantity and substance. His key point is that there is no genuine record of the use of the term 'philosophy' before Plato, the alleged uses by Pythagoras and Heraclitus being later additions (Hadot 1995b: 35). As he considers that the etymology of the term 'philosophy' provides its very programme, referring to the *Symposium* (*ibid.*: 81), his disinterest in the pre-Socratics is understandable.[21] Still, the exact nature of the Socratic break can be put into a better perspective by summarising here the account of Patocka, who similarly traced the central concern of philosophy to the Platonic 'care of the soul' (see Szakolczai 1994).[22]

Starting upon the beaten track, Patocka argues that philosophy grew out of the world of myth. As a background, he singles out for attention three well-known myths: the tree of knowledge and the expulsion from Paradise, found in the Old Testament, the Mesopotamian myth of Gilgamesh, and the Oedipus myth.[23] The world of these myths shares two fundamental dualities, one intellectual, the other diagnostic. The first is the profound opposition between 'being at home' (*chez soi*) and 'being a stranger', or the experience of the alien, the uncanny (Patocka uses the German word *unheimlich*, which literally means 'homeless'), culminating in the 'danger [*péril*]' which is the 'nocturnal element of the world' (Patocka 1983: 64). The other is a perception that something is not in order in the world, in the world of humans; that we are beings who are 'not in a good order' (*ibid.*: 56). The question then becomes the origin of this uneasy experience.

Evoking the work of Kerenyi, Patocka discusses the question of the extent to which myths are centrally concerned with foundations (*ibid.*: 66–8). This is inserted into a broader discussion on clarity and manifestation.[24] In the world of myths, 'clarity' or 'manifestness' is the 'domain of the gods' (*ibid.*: 66, 68). Human beings don't see clearly; they wander around, they are blind, they err.

It is against this background that philosophy irrupts into the world, and in two different ways. On the one hand, related to the diagnostic side, the task of philosophy is to cause humans to 'wake up [*réveiller*] out of their somnolence', and in this sense even Socrates is only a continuator of this tradition (*ibid.*: 59). On the other hand – and it is here that Patocka traces the main originality of philosophy – the problem of philosophy is the 'manifestness' of the world, the sudden amazement that the clear and manifest world is available for human knowledge, or aims at revealing (*dévoiler*) things in the very structure of reality (*ibid.*: 69–70). This dual perspective allows Patocka to identify the emergence of this philosophical vision with the pre-Socratics, focusing on Anaximander and Heraclitus (*ibid.*: 70–4), and then he continues, within this tradition, with the care of the soul (*souci de l'âme*) as exposed by Socrates and Plato. Patocka can perceive a continuity where others only saw a breakthrough in the work of Democritus, the 'last' pre-Socratic phusiologist who 'invented', according to Patocka, within the traditional field of phusiologia, the care of the soul (*ibid.*: 76–91). The philosophy of Socrates and Plato therefore only represented a displacement of emphasis within the care of the self, and not its invention.[25]

Domanski's account of the rise of philosophy reinforces the storyline of Patocka and connects it to Hadot's analysis of Socrates. Domanski starts from the pseudo-Platonian definition of philosophy, composed just around the time of Plato's death. According to this, philosophy pursues three main goals: a desire for knowledge, an entire ' "theoretical *habitus* concerning what is true" ', and a ' "care of the soul related to the right reason [*epimeleia psuches meta logos*]" ' (Domanski 1996: 5). The first two correspond to the classical (Aristotelian) concerns, establishing a continuity with the Ionian phusiologist, while Domanski put the emphasis on the third, identifying the difference made by Socrates.

The basic difference of the philosopher *as* a philosopher, in the etymological sense of the term, thus lies not just in a way of thinking, but in a distinct way of living (*ibid.*: 19–20). It is this distinctness that was embodied in the personality of Socrates, characterised by the significant terms 'philosopher par excellence' or 'philosophical hero' (*ibid.*: 20). At this point, Domanski refers to the heart of the path-breaking work of Hadot,[26] which we will take up from here.

Let us start with the title of the essay. Hadot is writing about the *figure* of Socrates, not simply his ideas, as it was this figure as such that exerted a decisive impact on Western thought (Hadot 1993: 29).[27] The role of this figure is then defined as a mediator, between the norms and transcendental ideals and human reality (*ibid.*: 77). But it is exactly here that the fundamental paradox of the figure of Socrates appears. One would expect a harmonious figure as a mediator of divine laws and commands, but the appearance of Socrates is exactly the opposite: he is ugly, 'disconcerting, ambiguous, troubling' (*ibid.*: 79). He resembles outright the Silenes, those strange, half-animal, half-human creatures, close to the Satyrs, and also the figure of Hermes.[28] For Kierkegaard, Socrates was simply a 'kobold' (*ibid.*: 80).

These characteristics render Socrates unique, making him stand apart from the crowd. This is captured by the designation *atopos* or *atopotatos*, frequently used to characterise Socrates in Plato's dialogues. Etymologically, the word 'means "out of place", hence strange, extravagant, absurd, unclassifiable, and disconcerting' (Hadot 1993: 96; 1995b: 158). In a particularly significant line (*Thaeatetos*, 149a; see Hadot 1993: 96), Socrates even utters this designation: 'They say that I am a most eccentric person [*atopotatos*] and drive men to distraction [*aporia*]', linking it up with the root word of liminality.

Hadot interprets this *atopia* in two different ways, not contrasted explicitly. Following Kierkegaard, he declares Socrates to be the epitome of the individual, the first individual in history: ' "he was the Individual" ' (Hadot 1993: 96; see also 93). But these characteristics of Socrates were also simply masks, on the basis of which he could deploy his famous irony. His external appearance, marked not only by his ugliness but by the use of the same coat, his always walking barefooted, unshaven and unwashed (*ibid.*: 100–1), served the purpose of embarrassing people, putting them off guard, thus performed a 'methodological' role in his investigations (*ibid.*: 80–2).

The first individual who is merely wearing masks seems contradictory in itself, and also to be going against the Socratic concern with truth, as noticed by both Kierkegaard and Nietzsche (*ibid.*: 83–5). This paradox also closely resembles the paradox noticed in the term 'person' by Mauss (1986), which – in French – at the same time means nobody and the heart of the individual, the 'person', while also being closely related to the actor, the person who is on stage (*personnage*). The etymology provided by Mauss also takes us close to the answer: the etymological root of the term is the Etruscan word for the mask, used in rituals. If the first philosopher and the first individual are the same 'persons', this has to do with the experience of 'liminality'.

At this point Hadot indeed turns to the *Symposium*. If the figure of Socrates wears a mask, or even *is* a mask, then one must ask whose mask it is. This is identified in the *Symposium* as Eros.

According to Hadot, the entire play is organised so that the reader would have to intuit (*deviner*) that the figures of Eros and Socrates are identical. At the banquet, every participant was asked to do a eulogy for Eros; Socrates declined, telling instead a story told by Diotima; at this point Alcibiades entered the room, half-drunk, and did a eulogy for Socrates. But beyond this structural equivalence, there are also a number of common points in the respective descriptions of Eros by Socrates and of Socrates by Alcibiades. This starts with the genealogy of Eros, his father being inventive and resourceful (*euporia*), while his mother was poor, even mendicant (*aporia*). These two words, while derived from the same root *poros*, were also used to characterise Socrates. Furthermore, Eros is not a god, only a daimon, an intermediary between the humans and the gods; and in his appearance as the bizarre hunter, the characteristic traits of Socrates are also visible. Hadot here (Hadot 1993: 100) refers to the passage already quoted in Chapter 4 on page 75 (*Symposium* 203b–c), and compares it in detail with the characterisation of Socrates in the speech of Alcibiades.

At this point Hadot gives his own interpretation. Starting from the previous characterisation of Eros/Socrates as a daimon (a mediator) and an atopos, Hadot adds that the etymology of 'poros' is passage. This means that Socrates is only a Silenos in the sense of opening towards something which is behind him. For Hadot, this means that philosophy is an appeal to existence. This includes, and at a privileged place, the forces opened up by Eros: '[o]ne of Plato's greatest merits will always be that he was able, via the myth of Socrates/Eros, to introduce into the philosophical life the dimension of love – that is, of desire and the irrational' (Hadot 1993: 104, 1995b: 163). An aspect of this concern is the erotic dimension of pedagogy, to be taken up by some early Church fathers, and later by Nietzsche (Hadot 1993: 104–5); and also by Foucault. But it also poses the problem of the demonic dimension of love.

Hadot recognises the need to describe at this point this 'demonic dimension', and takes as his guide Goethe. Goethe characterises this as an in-between force that is neither divine nor human; neither diabolical nor angelical; both separating and uniting the beings, which nevertheless exerts an 'incredible power' over beings and things (*ibid.*: 106). Hadot continues by referring to passages from Goethe's *Urworte: Orphisch*, the same ones that played a central role for Weber (WB: 474). Hadot concludes that this force is beyond good and evil, inseparable from existence: '[t]he encounter with the demonic, and the dangerous game with Eros, cannot be avoided' (Hadot 1993: 108; 1995a: 165).

After the comparison with Eros, in the next section of his article Hadot turns to the parallels with Dionysus. If in the previous section he used mostly Kierkegaard, here his interpretation is guided by Nietzsche; and if there the parallels were strong with Voegelin's work, especially the metaxy in the *Symposium*, here it is the parallels with Foucault that stand out, as the section mostly deals with the *Apology*. Central for the section is Nietzsche's interpretation of the last words of Socrates. However, as here Hadot reveals more about Nietzsche than about Socrates, we cannot pursue the discussion further.

Hadot and Domanski, just as did Voegelin, Foucault or Patocka, emphasise that if the central theme of classical philosophy is the care of the self or the soul, it grew out of the reflection on the experience of the death of Socrates by Plato. This is the experiential basis of the 'meditation on death [*melete thanatos*]', identified as the central technique of the care of the self by Domanski (1996: 14–18) just as by Foucault (CF82: 457–60). But, added to the peculiar, 'atypical' character of Socrates, and separated from the original experiential context, becoming an aim in itself, and incorporating various 'Eastern' influences (Jonas 1958; Hadot 1993: 201), it contributed to the world-rejecting 'Gnostic' turn of philosophy. Already in Plato, the meditation on death became more than a spiritual exercise, an attempt not only to live another life (Domanski 1996: 2), but not to live at all (*ibid.*: 14). In this sense the philosophical way of life became synonymous with withdrawal, escape or flight (*ibid.*: 9), with virtue serving as a place of refuge (*ibid.*: 16).

It is with these two major points at hand, the philosophical way of life as a hard and unique road to virtue and as a philosophical rejection of the world, that Hadot and Domanski arrive at the problem of Christianity. Hadot here puts the emphasis on the survival of philosophical techniques in the context of monasticism (1993: 59–74). The account of Domanski contained in a section entitled 'The questioning [*mise en doute*] of the ancient conception by the church fathers' (Domanski 1996: 23–9) is, however, as Hadot himself admits (*ibid.*: viii–ix), much more nuanced and interesting.

Domanski confronted directly the problem which not only Nietzsche, Weber and Foucault, but even Voegelin, failed to tackle: the actual encounter between philosophy and Christianity. Even further, he posed the question of the way philosophy was perceived, and criticised, by the early Christian fathers. On the basis of the reassessment of the practice of ancient philosophy, he managed to accomplish a breakthrough concerning the precise links between these two forms of thought and spirituality.

Domanski started from two well-known facts: that the affinities between philosophy and Christianity were numerous and recognised by early Church fathers, to the point that they often referred to Christianity as philosophy (Domanski 1996: 23), having a particularly high appreciation of Socrates and Heraclitus (*ibid.*: 26–7); but that the hostility of the first Christians towards philosophy was also particularly strong, rooted in the attitude of St Paul. Thus, it only happened in the second half of the second century AD, with St Justin, that a Christian presented himself as a philosopher (*ibid.*: 26), and the spiritual techniques and exercises used by philosophers were only integrated with the spread of monasticism.

This opposition did not centre around ideas, theories or ideological conflicts, as the traditional view of philosophy as a system of ideas would suppose, but rather the practice of philosophy, the very possibility of philosophers puting their ideas into practice. Here we should recall that the central concern of Socratic/Platonic philosophy was exactly the effective power of ideas. It was here that the strong ties of politics and ethics, the salvation of the polis and of the individual citizen were tied, and this was also the basis of the Socratic reorientation of parrhesia from politics to ethics. The Christian critique continued this line, by arguing that philosophers not only fail to become an effective guiding force in the city, but fail even in transforming their ethical ideals into practice.

This attitude was no doubt rooted in a diagnosis of contemporary philosophers, but it developed into a general point by attacking philosophical practice at its roots, singling out exactly its world-hostile character, its *atopia*. Domanski refers to the position of St John Chrysostom, all the more authoritative as he was one of the main legislators of the monastic way of life, influential in transferring philosophical techniques into Christian life. According to Chrysostom, *atopia* is a sign of 'pride and search for appreciation, applause and glory' (*ibid.*: 28); or of inauthenticity. Philosophers must call attention to themselves, need the signs of recognition, as otherwise they would not able to put their ideas into practice. At this moment the criticism of philosophy reaches its final stage and aim. Such a failure is not even surprising, and is certainly not due to bad faith on the part of philosophers. It is simply because, 'left to its own forces the human being, even if he manages to recognise this ideal, is nevertheless unable to realise it' (*ibid.*). This is only possible with the help of the 'grace of god', or charisma, conceptualised in early Christianity through the interlinked ideas of the descent of the Holy Ghost and parrhesia. The force necessary to put the ideas into practice comes from the imitation of Christ.

The conclusion, rendering intelligible the oblivion of the very idea of a philosophical way of life, was that for Christianity philosophical ideas, especially the philosophy of Aristotle, could be useful, but philosophical practice, outside the borrowing of the concrete techniques, was without value.

Philosophical parrhesia: Socrates

In his 1982 course, Foucault devoted special attention to the Socratic dialogue *Alcibiades*, selected as the paradigmatic text to introduce the course, defined as the 'very theory' of the care of the self (CF82: 32). However, in the 1984 course the dialogue would become as if 'subordinated' in importance to the *Laches*, as a further indication that the analysis should be revised in light of the later lectures on parrhesia, and inserted there.

The Alcibiades

If Pericles served as the model type for the proper use of parrhesia, then one could not find a better example than Alcibiades for illustrating the need for political education. The parallels between Pericles and Alcibiades are manifold. Pericles was the leader of Athens in its Golden Age; Alcibiades was its most talented, but fatally flawed, leader in the time of the collapse of Athenian power. Pericles was balanced in his judgements and persistent in his advice; Alcibiades, however, wasted his talent as a result of hesitation and incoherence. Pericles symbolised the greatest period of Athens; Alcibiades its demise.

The dialogue is considered as one of the earliest, in the neo-Platonic tradition as *the* earliest, of Socratic dialogues. Alcibiades, the young and promising but highly conceited Athenian aristocrat, becomes part of the circle around Socrates. He is destined for a political career, based on his credentials and talent. Socrates, however, tries to convince him that all this is not enough to become a proper statesman; he also needs to learn how to take proper care of himself.

Pericles and Alcibiades were both born politicians, in the sense of possessing a 'genius' (born talent) or 'charisma' (innate, 'gift-like' capacities). In the case of Pericles, this was enough for him to become a balanced and successful leader. In the case of Alcibiades, however, such inborn abilities were no longer sufficient. He needed a proper education. The contrast between these two leaders gives a textbook illustration of the difference between natural and artificial charisma. It also makes possible a sociological explanation of the difference. In Pericles' case, a normal process of growing up, of being inserted into the everyday world of human activities, could still be taken for granted, and there was no need for special care and education to guide the full flowering of these talents. In the case of Alcibiades, however, such a 'natural' education could no longer be taken for granted.

Foucault's analysis of the basic storyline is summarised in four points. The conclusions are drawn at a general level. However, it can be shown that this analysis is specific to, or tailor-made for, the case of Alcibiades; and furthermore, that it is exactly at *that* level that the general significance of this story lies.

According to Foucault, the emergence of the care of the self in philosophy is first of all connected to the exercise of power. Socrates argues that Alcibiades needs to take care of himself, as this is a precondition for the effective government of others. Foucault here contrasts this preoccupation with a politics based on status, and argues that the dialogue marks a passage from politics based on privilege to politics based on effective government. The proper reference point, however, is provided not by the 'traditional' politics of statutory rights and privileges, but by democratic Athens led by the parrhesia of Pericles. The aim of Socrates is to form Alcibiades so that he should become just as effective a politician as Pericles was.

Here we reach the second general point: the necessity of the care of the self is linked to deficient education. The critique of education in classical Athens was a commonplace in the period, especially in contrast to Sparta and later Persia. However, it applies again with particular significance for the case of Alcibiades. As Alcibiades was the adopted son of Pericles, he was perfectly positioned to receive the best introduction into charismatic parrhesiastic politics. Unfortunately, Pericles did not care enough about Alcibiades' education, entrusting it to a slave. There is no reason to worry, however, as – and this is the third point – there is still time to correct the defect. The care of the self must be done at a proper age, and this is exactly the moment of entry into politics, the change from youth into adulthood, or exactly the current age of Alcibiades.

By identifying the exact historical moment, it is possible to recognise the general significance of the individual case. Alcibiades died in 404 BC, aged 46, so the time when he entered politics was at about the crucial period 431–428 BC, singled out already for attention. It was also the exact moment at which Socrates started his search (*zetesis*), as he still took an active part in the battle of Megara in 432/431. We can now also identify the exact stakes of this first stage of the activity of Socrates. This was not the introduction of the care of the self into philosophy; rather, it was the other way around, the introduction of the care of the self into the new sphere of politics, in order to produce, artificially, the charismatic parrhesia that alone could make democracy work. The first congenial idea of Socrates was to become the teacher of Alcibiades.

In order to be effectively educated, one must first of all recognise one's own ignorance. This is the fourth point of Foucault; and here we must recall the particularly tricky mode in which Socrates gained the attention and confidence of Alcibiades, as told in the *Symposium*.

The attempt to compensate for the defective education of Alcibiades, however, failed, and this led to a turning point both in the career of Socrates and the logic of this text. Concerning his career, Socrates moved to a more general political level: the problematisation of everyday conduct, with the aim of producing the proper, democratic citizen. Concerning the text, Plato moved to a broader theoretical level, and posed the question about the exact nature of the care of the self, and of the 'moving forces' of conduct, or the soul.

What is the 'self'?

Starting with the question of the meaning of the 'self' (*heautou*, the reflexive pronoun), Plato quickly arrives at the 'soul', and even identifies the 'soul' with 'man'. Far from labelling this as Platonic metaphysics, Foucault insists here on identifying the precise mode of thinking pursued by Plato. First of all, Foucault argues that Plato's analysis is highly conscious about its own reflexive character. The soul which is the object of care is one's own soul, and the central element of self-reflexivity implied in this identification of the soul is defined as a movement of thought. This movement, furthermore, uses as its instrument language, and is driven by a special characteristic of thought which is questioning. This instrumental relationship between the soul and the tools of language is then transposed to the field of daily activities, in which the soul is defined in its relationship to three main spheres and activities: relationship to the body, or dietetics; social relations, including the leading of the household, or economics; and 'sexual' relations, or erotics (CF82: 58–9). The soul is what takes up a transcendental position with respect to what surrounds it. In this way Plato introduces the soul as a subject-soul, and not as a substance-soul. This subject-soul is defined exactly in relation to the three main areas of everyday activities. This three-fold thematisation, in fact, will take up a central role in the published volumes of the *History of Sexuality*, where it will be the basic organising principle of the substantive chapters of Volumes 2 and 3. This can be taken as a particularly clear illustration of the way in which at the centre of the Socratic questioning (identified by Foucault as the first main step in identifying the character of the soul) is the problematisation of the entire realm of the everyday conduct of life. The 'soul', therefore, is identical with 'man' in this sense of being both the reference point and the moving force of the entire realm of everyday activities.

What is the meaning of 'care'?

The 'care' of the 'soul', therefore, refers to the way in which this 'control centre' is to be handled in order to assure its proper functioning and thus the proper everyday conduct of life of every individual. According to Foucault, it is here, and not in the definition of the soul, that metaphysics is introduced in the thought of Plato. This is because this activity of 'care' is indexed to the knowledge of the self, implying a third reference in the text to the Delphic principle of 'know yourself', and in this case is a final and definite victory of this principle over the care of the self (CF82: 66).

This knowledge of the self, however, is very different from the Christian hermeneutics of the self. It is focusing on the eye, on its movements, especially in the way the pupil reflects the image of the other (*ibid.*: 68).[29] When applied, by analogy, to the soul, this movement results in the recognition of the soul as the divine element inside human beings, or the access to truth.

A proper analysis of the Platonic view on this access to truth would require the analysis of conversion (*epistrophe*). Though already in his 1980 course Foucault gave elements of this analysis, he fails to enter this topic here. The question of transforming the mode of being of the subject by truth-telling, however, would be taken up in the analysis of Epicurean parrhesia, in the tenth lecture.

In the 1984 course, Foucault would repeatedly contrast the *Alcibiades* as the 'theory' of the care of the self with the *Laches*, the paradigmatic dialogue on parrhesia. We need to continue by summarising Foucault's main ideas concerning this second piece.

The Laches

The theme of *Laches*, another early Socratic dialogue, is the provision of the best education for the sons of Athenian aristocracy. Something was evidently not working in the city, as even the sons of people with a proper descent failed to achieve anything distinct. In the piece, the problem is posed in the form of a search for the best possible teacher.

The dialogue is discussed in great detail in the fourth of the 1983 Berkeley seminars (14 November 1983) and in the fourth of the 1984 Collège de France lectures (22 February 1984). The central ideas of the two versions are closely related, but the mode of presentation was different. For Foucault, the centrality of the dialogue lies in the close ties it establishes between parrhesia and the care of the self.

The start of the dialogue explicitly introduces the term parrhesia, and it immediately gives the reason why the protagonists decide to turn to Socrates, and not to the professional teachers, the Sophists. In opposition to them, Socrates does not only talk, but he also provides a test of what he is saying by his conduct. The main thrust of Foucault's commentary is devoted to the way the protagonists describe this 'parrhesiastic game' of Socrates.

The new game Socrates introduced into Athens is the examination of one's conduct, by giving an account of one's life and providing reasons concerning the way in which one is behaving. The distinctiveness of this game is given in both negative and positive terms. Negatively, it is neither political nor technical. It is not restricted to the agora, and it does not imply the acquisition of concrete skills. In positive terms, Foucault starts by emphasising the personal character of Socratic parrhesia; that it requires close contact, proximity, the actual touch. This is necessary because the target of Socratic education is to acquire a certain modality of living, a conduct of life that links up the way in which one is talking with the way in which one is living. It is this modality that can only be acquired through personal example and direct contact.

But what is exactly the character of this connection between life and thought; between *bios* and *logos*? Foucault uses two words, 'harmony' and 'courage', whose relationship is defined in slightly different terms in 1983 and 1984. On the one hand, in line with the classical Greek emphasis on harmony, moderation and measure, this link must be harmonious. Socrates is characterised as a *mousikos aner*, or as somebody devoted to the Muses (DV: 65). The emphasis is not on the artistic, formal aspect of harmony, but on courage. In 1984, slightly inverting the argument, Foucault starts by emphasising courage, and it is in this context that he qualifies the message, saying that mere physical courage, the taking up of a critical position, is not enough, it also requires a certain manner of discourse, a harmony between what is said and the mode of conduct of the person who is talking. The hesitation of Foucault's exposition reinforces the ambivalence of the dialogue on courage. The dialogue is supposed to clarify the meaning of the term. However, it turns out that the definition of courage is an impossible undertaking.

This does not mean that the dialogue is inconclusive. Though unable to define courage, all participants are able to *recognise* who is courageous, and also to agree that Socrates manifests the proper, harmonious and courageous link between *bios* and *logos*. Socrates is more than a professional teacher: he is a touchstone (*basanos*), or somebody who does not simply tell people what to do but also demonstrate this in his acts, in the proper links between his speech and behaviour. *This* is the link between parrhesia and the care of the self.

Socrates is thus invited to act as a teacher. However, he still has to accept the invitation; and this depends upon whether his would-be hosts truly understood the character of the parrhesiastic game. The crucial issue is that, just as this game is not restricted to the field of politics, it should also go beyond the short period of adolescence. But his interlocutors understood this point, and are willing to pursue the Socratic game for their entire life. Thus, Socrates accepts the invitation.

Phaedo: *the testament of Socrates*

Foucault devoted the second half of the third lecture of 1984 (15 February) to the last words of Socrates. It is entirely based on the interpretation given by Georges Dumézil in a book that was literally just off the press,[30] and in which, according to Foucault, Dumézil finally offered a convincing solution to the enigmatic last words of Socrates. The presentation, also due to shortage of time, starts *in medias res*, and it is only at the beginning of the next lecture that Foucault gave a short contextualisation. The very fact that Dumézil talked about Plato sounded perplexing, but the actual way in which he did so was even more so. The book had a strange title and consisted of two parts, the first devoted to Nostradamus, the second to the last words of Socrates, both parts starting with an elaborate, baroque story tracing Dumézil's interest back to his youth.[31] This way of proceeding was first of all an 'ironic juxtaposition' of two texts that could not have been more different. One was as alien from the system of modern rationality as one could imagine, while the other was centred around the death of Socrates, and thus the foundations of philosophical rationality. Yet, using his structural and philological method, Dumézil was able successfully to analyse both texts together. And there was something more, undermining the irony of presentation. After all, there was something intriguing in the fact that, after 2500 years of philosophy, nobody had managed to understand the meaning of these last words; that the efforts devoted to this task were scarce, and most of them failed to show a proper care even with elementary questions of syntax.

Faithful to his method, Dumézil starts by looking at things as if under a microscope, taking the most minute fact about the words scrupulously seriously. The last words are the following: ' "Crito, we owe a cock to Aesculapius. Pay it and do not neglect it" ' (Dumézil 1984: 140). Thus, it was indeed an illness; and serious enough to preoccupy Socrates in his last minutes.

The next point to investigate is the reason why the statement was addressed to Crito. Crito was a rich disciple of Socrates, who tried to bribe the guards so that they would let Socrates escape his prison, and also tried to convince Socrates to escape, by arguing that letting himself die would be condemned in the eyes of the 'others' because he had not used all possible means to stay alive. This is the theme of the third dialogue around the death of Socrates, *Crito*.

In his answer, Socrates focuses on a need to make distinctions. What really matters is not the opinion of the others, but the truth. A worry about the general opinion formed of us by the others is indeed an illness – not an illness of the body, but of the soul, of the logos. This was the illness from which Crito has been cured. Reviewing the terminology of Sophocles and Euripides, Dumézil shows that the expression 'illness of the spirit' was indeed in use at the time (*ibid.*: 152–8), and was even used in the *Phaedo* (89a, 90e). But there still remains a problem: why did Socrates say that 'we' owe a cock, and not just Crito? The reasons are partly the existing links of sympathy and friendship, partly the possibility of a relapse, a return to this illness, that exists until the last moment. Most important, however, is the general character of Socratic dialogue – that everybody takes part in the discussion, that there is a 'solidarity with truth', or a 'principle of homologia'.

At this point Foucault takes Dumézil's analysis further, focusing on the exact type of curing activity performed by Socrates, through logos, with the help of the gods. This was not a specific medical or psychiatric practice, but rather the general activity of 'epimelesthai', or taking care of somebody, to prevent the possibility that a badly formed opinion deteriorated the soul.[32] The term is also present in *Phaedo* (115b), and a similar reference is made in the structurally analogous place of the *Apology* (41a). The last words of Socrates thus mean the same thing as he always said: do not stop taking care of yourselves. In fact, 'do not neglect' in Greek is *me amelesete*; so the word 'neglect' also refers to an illness, the illness of forgetfulness, that also needs to be cured, and by care.[33] The circle is closed around the care of the self, the gods, surveillance and parrhesia.

The concluding words of this lecture were particularly powerful, both intellectually and emotionally.[34] The last words of Socrates link tightly together the gods and human beings: the concern of the gods, transmitted through Socrates, is that men should take care of themselves. If the death of Socrates founded classical philosophy, then this took place in the special form of truth-telling (veridiction), a type of courage, a testing of the soul (*épreuve d'âme*) that does not belong to politics.

The break-up of the Socratic unity

Socrates was a paradigmatic figure of transition, standing with one foot in each of two different worlds. One could apply to him the same words that Elias used to characterise Erasmus: his work 'came at a time of social restructuring' and was 'the expression of [a] fruitful transition period' (Elias 2000:[1939] 63), as 'he occupied a unique position among all those who wrote on the subject', due to a particularly fortuitous combination of his 'personal character' and of living in 'this relatively brief phase of relaxation between two great epochs' (*ibid.*: 66). With his death, the threads he kept together became dislocated, fragmented, and taken up by a number of different schools.

The unity of bios and logos became separated into the opposite but interdependent excesses of the Sophists and the Cynics. The former emphasised discourse (rhetoric) without being concerned with truth (especially truthful conduct), while the Cynics downplayed discourse, placing the emphasis on excessively 'truthful' behaviour. Plato, considered as the most faithful student of Socrates, in important respects turned away not just from politics but also from the public sphere, influenced by the Pythagoreans. The Sceptic, Stoic and Epicurean schools all branched off, in one way or another, from these developments.

In his courses, focusing on parrhesia, Foucault only discussed two of these developments: Plato in 1983, and the Cynics in 1984.[35] Both these discussions were extremely important and deeply problematic. Their importance can be seen in the amount of space devoted to them in the respective Collège de France courses. Plato is discussed from the sixth to the eighth lectures of 1983, and again in the second part of the tenth and final course. Given that in this course a huge amount of time was devoted to the general discussion of the theme and the paradigmatic analysis of *Ion*, it is no exaggeration to claim that, just as the 1982 course was mainly devoted to the Stoics, the main subject matter of the 1983 course was Plato. Similarly, in 1984, after the four introductory and parabolic lectures, Foucault turns to the Cynics, and leaves them only in the first hour of the ninth and final lecture.

The problem concerns the modality of the discussion of Plato. It is not situated on the horizon of a 'genealogy of modern subjectivity'; the tone is occasionally quite involving. This presents three problems. First, given that it clearly goes against the general style and approach of Foucault, the question is what can be read out of this change. Second, complicating matters even further, Plato and the Cynics present opposite extremes. For Plato, according to Diogenes Laertius, the Cynics were a 'Socrates gone mad'.[36] They just cannot be offered as exemplary at the same time, and to imply a complete reversal of position between 1983 and 1984 would be too much to propose. Finally, such an interpretation would also go against some of the explicitly critical claims of these same lectures.

Plato

Foucault introduces his discussion of Plato with three comments. The first is about the general importance of philosophical parrhesia, arguing that the problematic of parrhesia had a decisive impact on the thought of the ensuing seven centuries (thus, up to the rise of monasticism). Second, Plato took further the shift of meaning from politics to everyday conduct by theorising the soul of the individual as the proper target of parrhesia, and thus connecting parrhesia to the guiding of the soul, or psychagogy. Finally, Foucault connects the appearance of a new type of personality, the philosopher, exactly to this activity, locating here the contrast between the philosophers and the Sophists. Each of these points will be taken up later.

Foucault's discussion of Plato is limited to the passages in which the word parrhesia occurs. The first passage, in the *Republic* (V, 557a–b), distinguishes between good and bad parrhesia. According to Plato, the problem with the democratic right of free speech is that it might lead to the selection of proper leaders, but it can also promote licence, where everybody does what he pleases. In an almost Girardian language, Foucault argues that the Platonian distinction between good and bad parrhesia is a distinction between differentiation and undifferentiation.[37] In the latter situation the 'democratic man' will be captivated by his desires and pleasures, and become the prisoner of the worst kind of passions: the longing for the superfluous and an envy towards everybody else. Shifting to Voegelinian language, the problem of political parrhesia poses the question of the order of the soul.

Foucault continues with two passages of *Laws* (III, 694a and VIII, 835ff) and one of *Gorgias*.[38] Political parrhesia is transferred here from democracy to monarchy. The analysis can be resumed in two central points. On the one hand the founding values of democracy, the sense of community and friendship (*koinonia* and *philia*) are now used to legitimate unequal rule. Distinction is necessary, and the Prince must work to maintain it, but – attenuated by philia and parrhesia – the koinonia can be maintained. On the other, this requires somebody who is able to use parrhesia and act, through the monarch, on the souls of the citizens. This is the philosopher.

The most important part of Foucault's discussion of Plato, however, is devoted to Letter Seven. This autobiographical letter contains the story of Plato's three trips to Sicily where – on the invitation of his friend Dion – Plato attempted to advise Dionysius, the tyrant of Sicily, including the reasons for this political activity and the most important presentation of the theory of ideas.[39] The special significance of this discussion is underlined by Foucault's introductory comments. He expressed a wish for a more private reading of the letter, due to its character and importance, and elaborated on the special significance of the genre: letters can be important due to their philosophical content, but at the same time they also serve as techniques of self. One should note here that the discussion is much longer than the previous one, containing the bulk of Foucault's discussion of Plato, and that here, and only here, the discussion is not restricted to the few passages in Plato's work where the term parrhesia appears, but Foucault gives a general interpretation of the entire letter. He justifies this by arguing that this text is just as important for the genealogy of political thought as counsel as are *Republic* or *Laws* for the other line of political theory, dealing with the foundations of political order.

A short discussion of (the probably not authentic) Letter Five serves to sketch the general context. Plato is not even interested in giving counsel to the Athenians, as democracy is already lost there. This is because no 'friendship' (*philia*) exists that would make a political community possible. Thus, he tries to think ahead and develop a proper way to give rational political counsel to monarchs.[40] The proper 'occasion' (*kairos*), so central to parrhesia, has shifted from democracy to monarchy.

Though presenting the details of the three trips, Foucault's emphasis is on the exact modality of Plato's intervention. Though the text does not call Plato a parrhesiast, Plato acts as one, just like Pericles did before. He took personal risks by addressing a more powerful person and by telling, plainly and frankly, the truth. Furthermore, just as Socrates, and in opposition to the Sophists, Plato is interested in the links between thought and reality. The modality, however, is different from the previous bios–logos link. The central concern of Plato is that his discourse should not remain pure words. He is looking for effective influence; his concern is the link between *logos* and *ergos*.

Foucault's discussion focuses on two questions: under what conditions can the philosopher be certain that his words would work effectively (*ergos* and not just *logos*); and if granted this real function, what can he actually say?

Effective advice

According to Foucault, the letter defines an interrelated set of three conditions the philosophical advice must fulfil in order to be effective. First of all, the potential audience must be limited: the advice must be addressed only to those who are willing to listen. Though seemingly banal, the comments added by Plato make a series of important points. They indicate that the main analogy of the philosopher's activity is not the lawgiver but the physician, who only intervenes when an illness appears, but who suggests, beyond a quick cure, an entire diet, or a regime of living. This counsel, however, must be addressed to the 'political will', and if this will is not good, it is simply superfluous, as if one would talk to the wind; or would even risk death. This passage, while explicitly rejecting all forms of violent social criticism, even merely verbal violence, also contains an implicit critique of Socrates. The philosopher who tries to 'wake up' people only wastes his time – perhaps even his life.

But how can one recognise such a 'willingness' to listen? The problem is complementary to the Socratic problem of the recognition of a real parrhesiast. Here, however, Plato specifies a method. This method is not conceived as a tool of knowledge, but rather it lies in the way members of the potential audience conduct themselves. It is this conduct of life that has to be methodical, and cover three main aspects. It must start by a definite choice of a certain way of life, which then is never to be abandoned. This way or path (*cheminement*) implies a series of activities and exercises. Finally, such exercising must be performed continuously and without an end, extended to everyday life and connecting these daily activities to reasoning. In opposition to other texts, Plato emphasises here that this methodical conduct of life does not imply a conversion in the sense of the redirection of the gaze, rather a continuous practice, a work on the self by the self. Though the expression is not used by Foucault here, the 'method' implies a philosophical way of life.

This point, however, leads to a deeply problematic circle. The circle is similar to the two paradoxes analysed by Foucault concerning the relationship between (political) parrhesia and democracy, and could be called the circular paradox of the link between (monarchic) politics and (philosophical) parrhesia. In order to be politically effective, the philosopher needs a willing audience. Such an audience, however, practically must be composed of philosophers themselves. Under such conditions the advice is all but superfluous. If the audience is unwilling, however, if it is not composed of philosophers, then there is no point even to bother, as the advice would be ineffective, or superfluous in another sense. Thus, if the dual paradox of political parrhesia and democracy leads to the elimination of both, the paradox of philosophical politics leads to an impossibility of action.

The third point of Foucault is that this method, or this way of life, must be put to the test. Here Plato first shows that Dionysius failed this test, and then presents a positive theory of knowledge, the famous five-step theory of ideas. Dionysius failed both by what he did not do and what he claimed to have done. He refused to follow the continuous practice of philosophy, but he claimed to have written a philosophical treatise. This is problematic, not from the perspective of an esoteric refusal of writing, but because the central aspect of philosophy is not about the content of knowledge, but rather it lies in a certain type of 'cohabitation' (*synisia*). This is close to the point made in the *Laches* about intimate closeness, but Plato here provides a detailed theoretical support. He starts by the analogy of a 'light appearing in the soul', explicitly opposed to the metaphor of enlightening. The latter activity, the sudden intrusion of light, can even be dangerous, blinding. It is in order to further illustrate the point that he exposes an entire theory of knowledge. The gaining of knowledge advances in five successive steps. The three lower ranks are naming, definition and image. The fourth level is science (*episteme*), the right opinion (*ortho doxa*) formulated concerning the quality of things, with the help of the mind (*nous*). The fifth and final level, however, is the knowledge of being itself. This is the level of philosophy, and it requires not just any mind or soul, but a soul of good quality that is continuously trained by the activity of thinking.[41]

This theory defines the reality and the possible effect of philosophy. The task of philosophy is not to give laws and adjudicate the different spheres of life and professions; it offers no substitute to the other four levels. Quite on the contrary, it is based upon them. Its distinctiveness lies in the opposition to the once-and-for-all acquisition of a definite knowledge, in perpetual practice and work on the self.

The content of counsel

At first sight, the counsel again looks trivial, banal, the kind of moral exhortation that is exactly bound to be ineffective. But Foucault begs to differ. Plato does not give a prescription, does not try to define politics or reduce it to morality and moralisation, but rather he offers a different kind of advice. This is supported by three passages, two from Letter Seven and one, the most important, from Letter Eight.

In the first passage of Letter Seven (331d–332c), instead of deliberating on the best possible form of government, as asked, Plato provides a diagnosis of the ills of Syracuse. In his positive counsel the focus is on the analogy between the city and the citizens, in the form of self-mastery and 'work on self' (*travail sur soi*) that is necessary to attain a proper 'state of health'. In the second text he again refuses to provide positive advice about the running of the city, offering instead just a suggestion concerning how those who should define the laws are to be selected, and arguing that the leaders of the city should demonstrate respect for the laws.

The most important, however, is the third passage. With the civil war already broken out and the constitution suspended, Plato now agrees to enter the discussion about the best way to govern the city, or the best *politeia*. The concrete advice is not something particularly new or exciting. Plato proposes a monarchy in the manner of Sparta, following the principle of separation between military and religious power, and argues for the need of an institution to assure the existence and maintenance of the laws, the guardians. The important thing, rather, is that this counsel is introduced in a passage where Plato explicitly states that he will use parrhesia (354a).

Foucault lists a number of reasons to support Plato's claim: Plato gives a personal opinion; there is a tension between the concrete situation and the stable identity of his opinion, as was the case with Pericles; his views address both the common good and each and every citizen; and his opinion involves a challenge, and thus risks. The most important and last point, however, returns to the previous line of argument: in order to have a real effect, the people must already be awake.

It is not clear whether Foucault actually concluded the lecture at this point.[42] At any rate, the content of this discussion did not dissipate the puzzles raised earlier. It is simply unclear what is the main point Foucault wanted to make in this analysis of the specific type of 'political parrhesia' by Plato, not repeated in 1983 in Berkeley and not even alluded to in the 1984 Collège de France lectures. The previous discussion of Socrates, repeated in both cases, indicated a shift to political from philosophical parrhesia, with parrhesia becoming a central tool in guiding the soul (*psychagogy*). The best-known part of Plato's theory is exactly an elaboration of the theory of the soul. Foucault, however, explicitly rejected following this line, and instead focused on Plato's political activities and the political uses of the word parrhesia, carefully stopping the instant he got close to a discussion of the soul.

This leads to the ultimate tension between the 'myth' of the philosopher-king on the one hand and the 'reality' of the philosopher as the challenger of political power. The real meaning of the philosopher-king, argues Foucault (dismissing the 'fantasmagorias' [sic] of Popper), is not to bring legislation to everybody, but to call attention to the practice of philosophy for those who are willing to listen. If anything, this does not mean that the philosophers must be kings, but rather that kings must be philosophers, which might be considered as paradoxical, but is not an imperialistic claim. On the other hand, however, this does not solve the problem of the 'reality' of the philosopher. It seems to push Foucault to the proposition that the only possible real effect the philosopher can expect may be achieved by adopting a courageous polemical position against the actual holders of power.

Whatever the 'correct' interpretation, in the 1984 course Foucault gave a detailed account of the Cynics, and this discussion centred exactly on their agonistic position versus political authority.

The Cynics

Both the content and the place of Foucault's discussion of the Cynics poses a series of problems. It is not surprising that, if the secondary literature so far had only scarce knowledge of his studies of parrhesia, the lectures on the Cynics went almost completely unnoticed.[43] They, however, must have been of considerable importance for Foucault, as he devoted to these lectures the better part of two months of his life (February–March 1984) when he already knew that his end was very near, and when, due to recurrent illness, he could have easily escaped this obligation.

If Foucault's last courses, especially from 1982, are tentative, then this discussion of the Cynics is the most tentative of all. Foucault repeatedly states that the analysis he proposes is only a first approximation; that he is not yet up to the task. He often goes through the same material from several angles, repeats points made earlier in a slightly different or more systematic way. Research on which the lectures were based was conducted just before and even during the course. In the Berkeley seminars delivered just a few months previously, in November 1983 (see DV), the reference to the Cynics was still minor and insignificant.

The place of this discussion is also perplexing. One gains the impression that it represents a deviation from the announced theme of the course; that Foucault only decided about an extensive discussion of the Cynics at the last minute, perhaps already in mid-course. At the start of the third lecture (15 February), Foucault claimed that the course would be about ethical as opposed to political parrhesia; this is the theme introduced by the *Apology*. Now, in the long discussion of the Cynics, the words 'ethics' and 'parrhesia' are rarely mentioned. The latter certainly does not take up a central place. The theme of the lectures, instead of truth-telling, became the problem of 'true life', and in a rather peculiar way. Halfway through the first hour of the fifth lecture (29 February 1984), just before the start of the discussion of the Cynics, Foucault mentioned the problem of 'true life' as a theme he wanted to study, but claimed that he is not yet ready for such a course, and made a – not fully convincing – allusion that perhaps he will return to it next year. The first discussion of the ancient Cynics was introduced as an example of the problem of the link between truth-telling and the care of the self. The discussion was quite general, and indeed focused on parrhesia. However, he began the seventh lecture (14 March) by announcing as though it was the title of the lecture, 'Bios Cynikos as true life'.

The links are also problematic to the previous, 1982 and 1983, courses and the first lectures of 1984. There is reference to the *Laches* and the *Alcibiades*, but no reference to the earlier discussion of the *Apology* and *Phaedo*, nor the long discussion of Plato. The pulling-together of the threads, therefore, requires an interpretive effort.

This will be based on the interpretive principle used before, the argument that post-Socratic philosophies can be understood as a fragmentation of the unity which Socrates, a figure of transition, still kept together. The Cynics, the Sophists and Plato represent opposite extremes, along three main axes. First of all, the central message of not simply Socratic philosophy, but the figure of Socrates himself, was the attempt to harmonise life and thought, bios and logos. In opposition to this, the Sophists placed exclusive emphasis on persuasive discourse, neglecting exemplary life, with the consequence of denigrating the concern with philosophy as a way of life. The Cynics, on the other hand, emphasised solely bios and not logos, so much so that they hardly had a doctrine or a theory. Cynicism rather consisted of a series of stories and anecdotes.

Similarly, the Socratic concern focused not simply on discourse, but on truth. It is the personal truth of one's words that must shine through one's conduct. The Sophists and the Cynics again took up the opposite sides of this unity. The former had no interest in the truth of logos, only in its convincing presentation; while the latter pursued the concern with truth, but only in conduct, not in words. Finally, with respect to Plato this time, the Cynics also took up opposite positions concerning the place of human beings among the gods and the animals. Plato emphasised the divine nature of the soul, and thus the divine element within humans; while the Cynics made manifest their latent animality.

Though not using the same words, Foucault's introduction shows several similarities to the analysis proposed above. His theme is defined as the foundation of ethical as opposed to political parrhesia, and the discussion of the *Laches* in lecture four is resumed at the start of lecture five in contrast to the *Alcibiades*. Starting from the same care of the self, the two dialogues go in opposite directions. The *Alcibiades* poses the question of the nature of this 'self' that is to be cared for, and moved, through the knowledge of oneself and the discovery of one's soul, to the recognition of its divine nature; while the *Laches* puts the emphasis on life (*bios*) and not the soul (*psyche*), on the manner of conduct, the giving of form to existence. Foucault traces here the division between 'two great traditions' in Western thought: the metaphysics of soul and the aesthetics of existence.[44] It is this second thread that he will take up now, by using the Cynics as an example of the true life.

The first sketches

Foucault starts tentatively by posing two questions: why are the Cynics interesting as a subject matter; and what relevance do they have for his general project, a history of the links between the subject and truth? The first question is addressed by a series of general characterisations that bring out the inherently puzzling and paradoxical character of Cynicism. Though being a philosophical school, few of their writings have survived. Instead of a body of doctrine, one encounters a series of stories, scenes, figures and anecdotes. This would seem to indicate that the Cynics were at the margins of philosophy. This, however, is only a partial truth. The Cynics were very widely spread in time, place and number. They were at both the margins and the heart of philosophy, an at once universal and banal form. In the terminology of Turner, the Cynics can be identified as the liminal form of philosophy *par excellence*.

Cynicism, thus, is more philosophy as a way of life than as a set of doctrines. But the exact form of Cynic conduct posed a series of further puzzles and paradoxes. It was at the opposite extreme of the form of conduct usually associated with philosophers and sages; a calm, serene, balanced search for wisdom, justice and truth. The Cynics were liminal in their way of living as well: wandering erratically, being – assertively – without home, and rejecting all forms of social engagements in the sense of spouses or children, performing even their bodily functions in public and without a sense of shame.[45] This was a shocking and aggressive public manifestation of a certain kind of truth: the truth of the animal bases of human conduct, in opposition to the conventions and rules of human society. Their aim was to get rid of any aspect of conduct that could not be driven back to nature or reason, and to make appear, in their nakedness, only the most indispensable things.[46] Thus, 'cynicism made out of life, of existence, of *bios*, an *aleaturgy*, a manifestation of truth';[47] one could add, in the most extreme possible way.

We can now address the central issue: what is the reason Foucault undertook this study at this extremely significant moment? An answer can be attempted by studying carefully the allusions to the present. The key, arguably, is contained in the second hour of the fifth lecture (29 February); a discussion introduced by the elusive words that Foucault would now take a 'promenade, excursion, errance'. After a short review of the secondary literature, Foucault sketches the three main practices that transmitted Cynic life to modernity, or the three great 'vehicles' of Cynicism: the figure of the Christian ascetic (especially representatives of Christian anti-institutionalism like the Dominicans, the 'dogs of the Lord'), the political revolutionary (in the various forms of secret societies, militantism, leftism, etc.), and the modern artist (mentioning the scandals, from Manet up to Francis Bacon and Samuel Beckett). The broad significance of these three practices would itself merit attention. But at the particular moment, a few months before his death, the deeply autobiographical elements of all three practices might take precedence for Foucault: the Catholic background and the Jesuit education of the early years; the turn towards art criticism in the 1960s, in the footsteps of Nietzsche; and finally the experiments with extreme forms of leftist political activity in the 1970s, in the shadow of Marx. It is not stretching the evidence to argue that the 'promenade' or 'errance' mentioned at the start of the lecture not only indicates the rather erratic mode of presentation, but is a direct reference to his own existential itinerary. This, however, is by no means a personal matter. What Foucault tried do in the last analysis was indeed a 'genealogy of the critical attitude' (DV: 112), or an attempt to trace modern forms of social criticism to their Cynic roots.[48]

Systematic presentation

The more systematic presentation begins in the second hour of the sixth lecture (7 March). Foucault starts by defining Cynicism as a form of parrhesia in life itself. He refers to two crucial characterisations of the Cynics by their contemporaries, that they were the 'prophets of parrhesia' and the 'martyrs of truth'. This poses the question of why life itself became a privileged place for parrhesia; what is the meaning of a 'true life'? Foucault's answer can be reconstructed through the following steps. It starts by a four-fold characterisation of the word 'truth'. Second, Foucault showed that all four were used to characterise philosophy as a way of life, even though philosophy was not defined as a 'true life'. Third, he argued that four of the five main principles of Cynic conduct were very similar to the basic ideas of philosophy as a way of life. The radical difference only came with the fifth principle: the idea of altering (or revaluating) the value of the currency. At this stage he showed how Cynic life represented a systematic re-evaluation of all the major values of Ancient culture, along with the four meanings of truth. The interpretation is finished by elaborating the meaning of the metaphor of the 'money-changer'.

The Greek word for truth (*aletheia*) has four meanings; or, in Foucault's terminology, truth has four axes. First of all, negatively, something is true that is not hidden, not dissimulated, not curved. Second, it should not receive any supplementary additions; it should not be mixed or altered, but should be self-contained. Third, it should be direct, straight, without detours and leanings, without mixture and multiplicity. In this sense, truth also implies justice as conformity to customs, rules and laws. Finally, truth is what is beyond change, what is incorruptible and maintains itself, what cannot be defeated. Truth is identity.

In the next step Foucault shows, first on the example of 'true love',[49] and then directly of the philosopher, using texts by Plato, that this four-fold thematisation can indeed be applied to philosophy as a way of life, as specified by the classical texts.

However, the life of the philosopher was never characterised as a true life. Thus, the next step is to show the relationship between Cynic conduct and the central principles of philosophy as a way of life. This is indeed how, after another series of introductory remarks, he starts the crucial seventh lecture. Philosophy is a preparation for life; it implies a care of the self; it only studies what is useful in and for existence; and a philosopher should make his life conform to these principles. The Cynics followed, though in their own particular way, all these principles. But they added a fifth, which radically altered the set-up: and this was the principle of changing the value of the money, a principle which the Cynics attributed outright to the Delphic oracle.[50]

At this point, Foucault illustrates the three main challenges thrown by the Cynics to the central values of ancient society: self-debasement to the point of slavery, as opposed to being a free citizen of the polis; poverty to the level of mendacity, as opposed to being a proud head of the household; and gaining a bad reputation through shameful conduct. The discussion is summarised in two words: animality and humility. On the one hand, Foucault argues that all three challenges promote, in opposition to the social customs, a life according to nature, interpreted as a return to the simplicity of animal-like existence.[51] At the interpretive level, the claim is made that this was a game of self-humiliation, that could be compared to Christian humility. The difference, according to Foucault, lies in the fact that, for the Cynics, this represented a reassertion of sovereignty (and this is in fact the way the last of the four meanings of truth is revalorised), while for the Christians, it implied a renunciation of life.

This was, however, just a first analysis, and in the second hour of the lecture Foucault returned to a more detailed study of the Cynic revalorisation of the currency alongside the four traditional axes of truth. The first three points do not add anything fundamental to the points already made about the attacks on the main values of Antiquity, or the public standards of decency in the name of nature and truth. Arguably, the analysis is also a bit tenuous. Just as the three different meanings of truth, not surprisingly, are closely related, the Cynic alterations of meaning also relate to each other, by transforming the principles and exercises of a truthful, straight and coherent philosophical life into a public scandal by regressing into animality. Foucault's analysis will be picked up from the fourth point, made at the start of the eighth lecture (21 March). The most important, and most paradoxical, reversal of the Cynics is the assertion that their way of the 'true life' is the sovereign life; or that the Cynics are the real kings. Foucault starts by analysing the famous anecdote concerning the encounter between Diogenes of Sinope and Alexander the Great.[52] The anecdote is summarised in three points: the Cynic is the real king; however, he is 'misunderstood' or 'not recognised' (*roi méconnu*); and, most important of all, he is a money-changer.

This is the third time Foucault starts to analyse this central characteristic of the Cynics, and now he goes to the root. In this summary, elements of all three discussions are investigated.

First of all, Foucault argues that the idea that the Cynic is fundamentally a money-changer is not only the most important, but also the most general characterisation. A series of accounts claim that a related episode stood at the start of the philosophical vocation of Diogenes: that he was exiled because his father counterfeited money; or because he did it himself. Still other accounts claim that this was a mission conferred upon him by the Delphic oracle.

From matters of context Foucault shifts the emphasis to the meaning of the two terms. The etymology of the term 'money' (*numismos*) is a derivative of the word for laws (*nomos*). The alteration of the currency is thus directly alluding to the changing of the laws. On the other hand, the term used for the activity of changing is *kataskopos*. This word has both positive and negative meanings, allowing both the crime of counterfeiting or debasing the currency, and the reestablishment of its real value. At the conclusion of this discussion Foucault goes back to the parallel with the Delphic maxim 'know yourself'. Beyond matters of asserted ceremonial genealogies, the question to be posed is the exact relationship between the two principles attributed to the Delphic oracle, or their primacy. One such connection is given by Julian in his 'Discourse against the Ignorant Cynics'. According to him, one must assign primacy to self-knowledge. It is only by recognising the truth about ourselves that we can change the false currency, the opinions others have about us, with the truth. The Cynics, of course, opted for the primacy of the second. The Cynics attempted to alter the currency not by pursuing the path of self-knowledge, or the knowledge of one's soul, but by a certain practice, a way of life. This has two main elements: it is a hard life (but a 'short road' to virtue); and it is a mission.

The very word 'Cynic' means dog-like, and it alludes to the difficult, taxing character of the way of life the Cynics assumed as their own. This is a life of indifference, a life without shame, but not a life without purpose. According to Aristotle's characterisation, the Cynics are critiques, living a life of discernment (*diakritikos*). Dogs are also guardians, and the aim of the Cynics is to act as watch-dogs, to save the others. Only instead of searching for the logos or showing positive examples, they demonstrate, through their own lives, that the lives that others live are false. Thus, their animality is only the manifestation of an 'other life'. Here Foucault makes another highly hypothetical conjecture about a possible future topic, for himself or for others, the distinction between 'another world' (*autre monde*) and 'another life' (*vie autre*). These are central concepts in two great lines of development in Western philosophy, to be traced back to the same Socratic heritage and the same key dialogues, the *Alcibiades* and the *Laches*. Starting from the question of the nature of the 'self' that has to be cared for, the first arrives at the soul and its immortality, or the 'other world'. The other line, however, poses the question of the life that would be a life truly devoted to the care of the self, and thus arrives at 'other' forms of life. These two lines were not completely divergent. Christianity and the Gnostics both considered a certain way of life as a precondition to the other world, or to salvation. The question, however, was posed with full radicality only in the Protestant ethic, which asserted that 'access to the other world can be defined through a form of life that absolutely conforms to the very existence of this world'.[53] Thus, life according to the requirements of this world and access to the other became identical. In Foucault's reading of Weber, this is the way in which Christianity became modern.[54]

The second crucial aspect is that the Cynics' way of life was a life of mission. This incorporates three elements. First, it means that it is not a matter of choice, but a service, and also a fight to exclude from this way of life anything that does not belong there. This opposes the Cynic modality from the more 'permissive', less militant Socratic mission. In the next two points, the analogy is directly with the analysis of Plato's Seventh Letter, though no reference is made to this here. The recognition of the Cynic is not done through signs or marks, nor indeed through the help of others at all. The only way for recognition is through being approved by oneself (*de s'être éprouvé soi-même*). Thus, the Cynics are self-recognised, self-approved, self-appointed. But beyond a simple act of naming, this involves hard practice, tests of endurance and deprivation, devel-oping the ability to defeat the challenges. Finally, the substance of the Cynic way of life is defined as 'philosophical warfare'.[55] The Cynic not only fights with himself to endure deprivations, but is aggressive and even violent, commit-ting unjust acts, waging an outright war against his society. This is possible because his entire life is in the service of mankind. The Cynic is a barking watchdog, an enlightener (*kataskopos*) and 'supervisor' (*surveillant, episkopos*); a universal 'vigilant' (*veilleur*). Thus, he cannot get married and cannot have chil-dren, and must be detached from all concrete, private duties. He is a (let us reiterate: self-appointed) 'functionary of the whole mankind', thus responsible only to mankind, but at the same time also being the 'true functionary' of the *politeia*, as charged not simply with concrete duties like the collection of taxes, but rather with the problems of good and bad, servitude and freedom, happi-ness and unhappiness.[56]

The conclusion of this discussion, contained in the first part of last lecture, is very provisional and adds little that is new. The Cynics proclaimed themselves as 'true kings', though through an aggressive polemics they reversed all the key features of political sovereignty. This vigilant and militant lifestyle has three main consequences. The Cynics indeed became happy, self-contented and indefeasible – but this was because they managed to define their own field and game. Second, Foucault thematises the justification the Cynics gave of their own aggressive vigilance as an exact coincidence between the care of the self and the care of others. With a less sympathetic reading, one could argue that in this way the self-appointed guardians of mankind, by abusing themselves, claimed the right to abuse others. Finally, the aim of the Cynics was to instigate a change. But as the world cannot be led to its truth, this is only possible in the sphere of relations to oneself.

9 Hellenistic–Roman parrhesia

Introduction

Foucault considered the philosophy of the first centuries AD, especially the late Stoics, as a crucial moment of transition between classical philosophy and Christianity, and discussed it in his 1982 course. As was outlined in the Introduction to Chapter 8, the material covered in this course should ideally be revised in light of Foucault's last two main discoveries, parrhesia and problematisation. Concerning the former, this chapter will follow the indications of the 1983 Berkeley seminars by inserting the material about care of the self into the general line of discussion of parrhesia. Concerning the latter, however, the pursuit of a properly genealogical design has proved to be impossible within the limits of this book.

Still, even though the chapter refrains from the task of connecting Foucault's analysis of Hellenistic and Roman authors to classical Greek thought, a short allusion concerning the possible way of proceeding will be given here. This is all the more possible as the links between Plato, the Sophists and the Cynics, analysed in Chapter 8, and the Stoic and Epicurean thought to be analysed in the present chapter, are historically tight.

Though Foucault only discusses the first centuries AD, Stoic and Epicurean philosophy emerged centuries earlier. Their conditions of emergence are of particular importance, as these were just as tightly rooted in politics as had been the case in the previous periods. If the break-up of the Socratic unity of bios and logos, of parrhesia and the care of the self was connected to the collapse of democracy, best marked by the thought of Plato, then the new developments are related to the thought of Plato and the rise of the Macedonian empire, best marked by the thought of Aristotle. In fact, Stoic and Epicurean thought can be defined as philosophical schools, or forms of thought, in which the experience of living under an emerging empire has been reflected upon, and problematised.[1]

Just a quick glance at a few dates indicates the plausibility of such an interpretation. Aristotle lived between 384 and 322 BC; and the key dates in the rise of the Macedonian Empire were the rise to power of Philip II (382–36) in 359 BC, and of Alexander the Great (356–23) in 332 BC. If Aristotle was the private teacher of Alexander the Great, much following the guidelines of Plato, the rise of Epicurean and Stoic thought coincides with the liminal experience of living through, at a particularly sensitive age, the emergence of the new type of ecumenic empire, and the resulting interpenetration of various forms of European and Asian thought. This can be shown by the birth and death dates of the founding figures: Epicurus (347–270 BC) and Zeno of Citium (366–280 BC); see also Cleanthes of Assium (331–232 BC) and Chrysippus of Soli (280–204 BC).

Foucault's discussion of Hellenistic and Roman parrhesia is organised according to two main opponents of parrhesia. In the professional sense, parrhesia was opposed to rhetoric, while in the moral sense, it was opposed to flattery. The first dividing line was covered in Epicurean texts on philosophical education, while the second preoccupied Stoic authors.

The Epicureans

Socratic–Platonic philosophy, based on the joining of parrhesia and the care of the self, posed the following dilemma. The solution to the crisis of the polis lay in the artificial production of charisma, or the shaping of individuals capable of parrhesia. However, a purely technical education carried out by professional rhetoricians could not accomplish this task. Even further, this shaping of individuals was supposed to produce some kind of community feeling. The problem was thus to develop a 'non-technical technique' of parrhesia that would at the same time produce a community. The Epicurean practice of parrhesia, as presented in the text of Philodemus, responded to this dual exigency (see DV: 72–4; CF82: 370–3; Glad 1996).

In opposition to rhetoric, parrhesia was not a technique to be appropriated. Yet, as the aim of philosophical parrhesia was to effect a transformation at the mode of being of the subject, it had to have criteria of efficiency. This was true to such an extent that spiritual guidance would soon be considered outright the 'techne of technes' (by Gregory of Nazianzus; see DV: 74). Three aspects of parrhesia accommodated this paradoxical exigency. First of all, a central element in parrhesia was selecting the right moment, the grasping of occasion, or *kairos*. Parrhesia as a technique was not about the validity of truth content, but the acquisition of the proper modalities of decision-making (*ibid.*: 72; CF82: 367). Second, and in a similar vain, education as parrhesia was not concerned with the transmission of true knowledge, but rather the proper modality of correcting error. Much of the discourse of Philodemus is concerned with finding the right way between a criticism that is too severe and one that is too mild, as both of these extremes fail to exert a proper impact. A criticism that is too mild does not reach the threshold of being noticed; while extreme harshness only provokes an opposite effect. Finally, as if to underline the paradoxical character of parrhesia as a non-technical technique, the Epicureans also emphasised the personal qualities of the teacher.

The central innovation of the Epicureans, however, according to Foucault, lay in the other aspect of their doctrine, linked to the community side. In order to reinforce the mutual ties of friendship within the group, inciting the benevolence of all members towards each other, the Epicureans invented, alongside the traditional vertical parrhesia that was passed from master to students, the practice of horizontal parrhesia. This meant that students had an obligation to tell in group meetings what they thought, what they had in their hearts, admitting the errors they committed or recognising their weaknesses (CF82: 373). According to Foucault, this represented the emergence, within the context of Antiquity, of the practice of confession. However, it seems that Foucault's interpretation here was unnecessarily anachronistic and non-genealogical. Seen from the present, one could indeed detect the roots of Christian confession here; but seen from the past, one should rather recognise here a certain nostalgic feeling towards classical Athenian democratic parrhesia. This would allude to affinities between classical Athens, the Epicureans and Judeo–Hellenistic thought that have a fundamental importance for the rise of Christianity.[2]

The central importance of parrhesia among the Epicureans was a return, in the context of philosophical communities, to the question of community-shaping force. Though this practice had no 'revolutionizing consequences', the fact that such an 'impractical ideal' had been 'voiced' at all has its importance (Glad 1996: 58–9). This new ideal linking friendship, community and authority, openness, truth-telling and confession had two aspects. On the one hand, authority within the group depended not on personal qualities or status, but ultimately on the sole authority of Epicurus. On the other hand, this meant that the transformative potential of such a group depended solely on Epicurus as a healer and purifier, given the maxim that ' "[t]he basic and most important [principle of the group] is that we will obey Epicurus, according to whom we have chosen to live" ' (Philodemus, as quoted in *ibid.*: 59, fn. 171). But outside their own sect, the Epicurean principle failed to create a new community.

The Stoics

Following the indications of the 1983 Berkeley seminars (see DV), the first of the two ensuing sections will discuss parrhesia and personal relationship in Stoicism, while the 1982 discussion of Stoic techniques of self will be inserted into the second section.[3]

Parrhesia and personal relationships in Stoicism

As opposed to the Epicureans who were organised into schools and communities, the Stoics offered their advice in the context of interpersonal relationships. In this context the distinction between a true friend and a flatterer, the subject of a piece by Plutarch, becomes of prime importance (see DV: 89–92; Engberg-Pedersen 1996).

Plutarch problematises this distinction as a question of *recognition*. In the line of thought that started with Plato and extended to the neo-Platonists, the Cynics and the Gnostics, recognition is traced to self-knowledge and thus is to be performed by the subject itself. This position, however, was not accepted by the Stoics, who in this respect would constitute an important step toward Christianity, especially the thought of Tertullian. For the Stoics the self cannot separate the flatterer from a true friend, as it is blinded by the illusion produced by self-love. The solution of Plutarch is to rely on true, trusted, steady friends.

Another Stoic thinker, the famous physician Galen, suggests a different solution (DV: 92–4; CF82: 378–82). Galen further generalises the principle of mistrust, arguing that neither a foe nor a friend can be accepted in this case, as both are liable for bias. Instead, one should rely on somebody who takes up a neutral position, a complete stranger – a person, however, who has passed some other, crucial tests, by being of good reputation, and also of a certain age and wealth. According to Foucault, Galen formulates the principle of a need for direction that later would be repeated by the early Church fathers (CF82: 381). In Galen, friendship is replaced by a trial or examination.

The third Stoic thinker discussed is Seneca, especially his Letter 75 to Lucillus that – without being defined so – is a 'complete exposition' of parrhesia (translated as *libertas*) (*ibid.*: 384–5). The letter is a kind of personal apology, as Seneca here addresses the charge by Lucillus concerning the character of his letters, especially the character of criticism contained in them. According to Seneca, his letters contain nothing artificial or researched (thus opposed both to rhetoric and to flattery). They are fully transparent and manifest an identity of speech and conduct, as it is only in this way that they can exert a proper effect not on the intellect but on the soul of the recipient, stamping their message on memory. The message is effective, therefore, not to the extent that it is true or conforms to law, but because of its personal character; because the letter shows that these thoughts are really his own. Seneca supports this by a particularly striking metaphor. The personal character of such parrhesiastic words is like a kiss – not the kisses of a lover, but the kisses one gives to a child. These kisses are pure, simple and transparent, and do not refer to anything else but the tenderness of the act itself; and furthermore such a kiss implies a fundamental *presence* of the self. Foucault resumes the discussion by claiming that at the centre of parrhesia lies an adequation of speaking and behaving, or a certain self-authentification of truth (*ibid.*: 389). However, in the context of this highly significant metaphor, one can evoke a word otherwise not much used by Foucault, the word 'innocence'. A statement is parrhesiastic in so far as it contains the authentic and innocent presence of the personality of the individual uttering these words.

The 1982 discussion of parrhesia is concluded with a contrast between pedagogy and psychagogy. A pedagogue is concerned with the transmission of true knowledge, while the aim of the psychagogue is to change the mode of being of the subjects. It is this psychagogic concern that would be taken up in Christianity, by diverting truth-telling towards the disclosure of the truth about oneself.

The transformative impact of true discourse, defined also as the question of 'spirituality', and the direction of consciousness or the soul were themes that regularly came up, and at central places, in Foucault's last courses, without full elaboration. Here a short discussion will be inserted on the term 'psychagogy', using the work of the noted mythologist Karl Kerenyi,[4] as it helps to pull together a number of threads discussed previously while pointing out particularly clearly the ambivalent nature of such concerns.

Kerenyi on psychagogy

Kerenyi introduces his book entitled *Hermes, the Guide of Souls* by contrasting his undertaking with the classical work of Walter Otto. In spite of all his erudition and perspicuity, Otto took for granted the classical image of Hermes, thus failing to notice in this personality perhaps its essential, certainly its most archaic aspect, which today looks 'revoltingly repulsive' (Kerenyi 1984 [1942]: 9). The book aims to restore the full ambivalence of this figure.

In the fashion of a true genealogist,[5] Kerenyi starts by the assessing the difference in the presentation of Hermes between the *Iliad* and the *Odyssey*. The first epic is not the genuine realm of the figure. Hermes never appears there as a psychagogue, he does not try to deceive, and is only a master thief (*ibid.*: 10–13). This is not because the god is a recent invention, rather he is alien from all heroic deeds (*ibid.*: 12). In the *Odyssey*, however, all his major characteristics (the psychagogue, the messenger (*angelos*), the mediator between life and death, and between the gods and men) are present, revealing him to be at home in the homelessness (*ibid.*: 18–21).

The figure is similarly illuminated by the contrasts with two gods, the two main protagonists of the *Birth of Tragedy*, Apollo and Dionysus. The contrasts between the deceiving, tricking, insolent and rude Hermes and the serenity of Apollo are evident. Furthermore, it is exactly in contrast with Apollo that, in a Homeric hymn, Hermes receives his task. While divination in the classical, oracular sense was assigned to Apollo, Hermes also became a diviner of a kind: not an Olympian god, only a daimon; a 'spirit' who – according to his mood – could lead but also mislead with his advice, and who always performs his function very quickly, literally with 'deadly speed'; a daimon who furthermore receives his function through a special initiation. The affinities between Hermes and Dionysus are much more evident; still, they are far from being identical (*ibid.*: 88–92). In some representations, Hermes appears as a bearded man; in others, as a clean-shaven youngster (*ibid.*: 96). Further adding to the confusion, while the cult of Hermes is closely associated with phallic statues, Hermes is also represented as an androgyne, well indicated in the expression 'Hermaphrodite'.[6]

These differences lead to the heart of the underlying personality. Beyond the ambivalence of the Hermesian character, we find a dual conceptualisation of origins, recalling Dumézil's analysis of Janus. On the one hand, the phallic figure of Hermes captures the connection made by the Greeks between origins and powers (*arkhe*) and male virility. On the other, origin in a second sense is connected to mediation and transition: between night and day, life and death, animal and human life, and the realm of gods and of human. It is in this sense that Hermes is the inventor of language ('hermeneutics'), the patron of eloquence and commerce (see the common etymological roots of 'interpreter' and 'entrepreneur'), the god of science (recalling the figure of Hermes Trismegistos and of Hermetic forms of knowledge), of comfort and the arts of life, and the guide of the souls to the Underworld.[7] This is his main role as a 'psychagogue': a mere servant, accompanying the soul of the dead to Hades, but also a dangerous trickster who 'steals' the souls on his own account, thus uniting the diverse Homeric functions of the master thief, the messenger and the trickster.

The various aspects of the character could suggest that, behind the identity of name, there are several different gods (*ibid.*: 54). Kerenyi, however, not only argues for the unity of the figure, but that it creates a world on its own. The word is taken seriously, as Kerenyi analyses its Hungarian meanings that express an 'archaic, long forgotten wisdom of language' (*ibid.*: 56). *Világ* in Hungarian means not only the 'world' but also 'light' (*világosság*), while the adjective *világos* stands for 'clear', but could also mean 'world-like'. The 'idea' of Hermes is at the same time clear, transparent and world-like – that is why it could become so convincing.

The world of Hermes is the world of liminality. His phallic statue was placed near the doors, at the threshold.[8] As such statues were found in every house, Hermes had few temples, as a 'point devoted to him was found everywhere there were human beings lived and died' (*ibid.*: 100). His celebrations evoked the clearest aspects of liminality: in some, the servants and slaves were raised to high positions and their masters served them; in others, stealing and robbing were permitted (*ibid.*).

The liminal world of Hermes even had an Archimedean point: '[t]he reality of the Hermesian world proves that at least there is one point from which the world opens up for us; even more, beyond a panoramic view it indicates an activity which suddenly starts to work again, instigating the world for the realisation of further Hermesian masterpieces and master conneries' (*ibid.*: 64). In order to capture this point, Kerenyi turns to a familiar story: the story of the birth of Eros, as told by Plato in the *Symposium*. In his account Kerenyi translates 'Poros' as 'way', and highlights all the terms used in the text that are etymologically connected to it, emphasising the affinities of both Poros and Eros with Hermes (*ibid.*: 67). Though the story is invented by Plato, the figures behind it are certainly real. Nobody would question the reality of Eros, while Poros contains the positive characteristics of Eros, and '[j]ust as in the Hesiodian genealogy of gods a figure is more substantial, cosmic-encompassing, world-carrying, in our earlier expression *világosabb* that is, both world-like and clear [A.Sz.], the closer he is to the origins, the same holds true for Poros' (*ibid.*). Kerenyi here refers to a seventh-century BC poet, Alcman, who mentions Poros as one of the two oldest gods, identified in the standard commentary with the Chaos of Hesiod, while Kerenyi adds that the other god mentioned there was the female Aisa (*ibid.*: 67–8). Kerenyi concludes his account by mentioning that, according to a non-classical, rather hidden, underground tradition, collected together by Cicero, Eros was considered to be the son of Hermes (*ibid.*: 70).

But if Hermes can thus safely be considered as the Greek god of liminality, this should be understood in the full meaning of the term, beyond romanticism. The 'betwixt and between' moment is not just the celebration of the collapse of institutional and structural rigidities, or the replacement of the old year, month or day with the new, but also the opening up of the well of the unconscious, the liberation of potentially disruptive, even destructive forces. This is best shown in a section of Kerenyi's long analysis of the Homeric hymn devoted to Hermes, substantiating the initial claim about 'revolting repulsion'.

This is shown first of all in the fact that the true realm of Hermes, his world (*világ*) is not the world of the clear (*világos*) day and light (*világosság*), but the night. Kerenyi here returns to Otto's account on the experience of the night. The description can be considered as a condensed rendition of aspects of liminality, replete with expressions like standing vigil, wandering, loss of distance and prox- imity with the space losing its dimensions. At night, even the sensations become ' "strangely uncertain" ', where the ' "kindest idyll will be mixed with something alarming, while the terrifying attracts and seduces" ' (*ibid.*: 58). The night is also a state of undifferentiation: ' "There is no difference between living and dead, everything is at the same time soulful and soulless, alert and sleepy" '. Every single thing plays a strange game with the wanderer, with horrible movements turning out to be harmless, and vice versa. Most importantly, the night is a place where ' "danger looms everywhere" ' (*ibid.*: 59). Still, it is exactly this experience of the night that is the very substance of Hermes, giving it *világ-osság* (world-ness, or light). The night is the place of the engendering of life and death, in indissol- uble unity. Resuming the analysis, Kerenyi argues that while most of the characterisations of Hermes show him as if from the outside, it is from the aspect of the night that the inner, or experiential, aspects of the figure become visible. In spite of all his deceiving, theft and robbery, he can also be 'charac- terised by divine innocence. Hermes has nothing to do with sin or guilt. What he brings forth from the fountain of life is exactly this: the ' "innocence of birth" ' (*ibid.*: 61–2).

If, however, from the inside the acts of Hermes are innocent, their effects are repulsive and devastating. This is illustrated by a story from the Homeric hymn where Hermes sees a turtle, imagines it in an instant as the stuff for a lyre, and then immediately cuts off its head and legs, prepares the instrument and even plays on it (*ibid.*: 32–4). The god acts with amazing quickness, including both imagination and execution, and also with merciless cruelty that becomes 'titani- cally horrible' when he laughs at his victim, adding irony to the cruel deed: 'all this is done not naively, but by playful mercilessness' (*ibid.*: 33). Still, at the end, the 'divine trickster' carries the day, as the result of his act is the sound of music, luring out of the death of his victim the only phenomenon that sweetens the hard life of mortals.

The book ends on a Nietzschean note. The figure of Hermes contains a 'great secret', a glimpse into the 'deep night' of the 'arch-beginnings' (*ibid.*: 104), which is the 'deepest and never fully conceptualised knowledge of the Greeks about the friendly coexistence of the Hermesian–spiritual aspect of the world with its animal–divine aspect' (*ibid.*: 105), where Hermes stands for the 'luring of the radiating life out of the dark arche-depth' (*ibid.*: 108), showing affinity with Silenos. Silenos was the tutor of Dionysus, while, as we have seen, the Silenes were phallic, half-human, half-animal beings, similar to the Satyrs (*ibid.*: 105).

Parrhesia and techniques of examination in Stoicism

In the 1983 Berkeley seminars the discussion of parrhesia in the three Hellenistic philosophical schools is followed by a section on 'parrhesia and techniques of examination' in Stoicism (DV: 94). This discussion draws on Seneca's *De Irae*, a text that played a central role in Foucault's analyses of the care of the self, not only in the 1982 Collège de France course, but also before and after.[9] Foucault also discussed in brief another text by Seneca, a piece by Epictetos also used in the 1982 course, and planned to cover two texts by Marcus Aurelius. This could safely be taken as an indication that this is the way Foucault would have re-inserted the 1982 discussion of Stoic techniques of self into a general framework defined by parrhesia.

Since the Socratic reorientation towards the problematisation of the conduct of life, a central question of philosophy was the proper way of orienting human beings about their daily conduct. The traditional methods of education could not provide an answer to the Socratic question without undergoing a funda-mental re-shaping, as imitation assumed a taken-for-granted background home as the standard for everyday life, while initiation was directed towards the out-of-ordinary. The professional education championed by the Sophists and Socratic philosophy addressed the same question, and even shared certain similarities in their answers, as their perceived identity clearly indicates.

The differences between the two methods can be best thematised if both are considered as taking up and developing for their own purposes the main avail-able 'model' of education, initiation rites. The ideal–typical model of professional education closely follows a rite of passage. It starts with a period of preparation, culminates in examinations, and ends with a reintegration into society, at a higher level on the social ladder.

The classical model of a rite of passage does not represent a problem for professional education, as there the point of entrance is not problematic. It is defined either by rights, by certain individual–demographic characteristics, or the aim of acquiring certain skills. At the moment of entrance the only 'problem' is the scarcity of places or resources, usually solved by applying the method of examination at that very moment. In the case of a philosophical life, however, the starting point is problematic. Philosophy in the ancient sense does not involve the teaching of particular skills, but rather the realisation that the taken-for-granted ways of daily conduct are thoroughly problematic, thus one must change one's entire way of life. Thus, the question starts with helping to recognise this very need for education.

As a result, the stages of this type of 'philosophical education' will be consider-ably different from the rites of passage, even though sharing common elements.

The first step, to be invented practically from scratch, is the starting of the path, or the 'recruitment' of candidates.[10] The solution to this problem is analogous to restricting entry in case of scarcity. There, the central part of the ritual, the moment of 'testing', is advanced before the stage of preparation; here, the need for a philosophical education is realised through a 'conversion'. The stage of preparation becomes the second step, followed by trial or examination. The huge difference is the absence of the last stage, the rite of reaggregation. The reason is rather obvious: if the entire process started with the realisation that the course of normal everyday life is unacceptable, then the 'education' process cannot be concluded by a reintegration into 'society'. The model of the rite of passage helps to realise how genial a solution the Socratic idea of a philosophical life was: as it is not possible to return to things to the norm, the entire life should be transformed into a testing ground.

Conversion

The initial moment of a philosophical education presented a major, and basically unresolved, problem for classical philosophy. In opposition to various forms of esoteric and mystic ways of thinking, philosophers wanted to be effective, to transmit their ideals into reality, to transform reality. For these purposes they had to find some way to their audience. Socrates tried to awaken his audience, first of all through Alcibiades, by convincing them of their ignorance, almost driving them to desperation in this way. This method, however, proved to be a rather unhappy combination of two shortcomings, being excessively intellectual on the one hand, while only relying on negative emotions, almost a loss of identity, on the other. Plato and the Cynics, here again, took up the exact opposite poles. The Cynics transformed the Socratic wake-up call into outright, loud barking;[11] while Plato put the emphasis on the internal process of awakening, the wondering at the world (*thaumazein*), not so far from mysticism, and practically restricting appeal to the born philosopher.

According to Foucault, the philosophers of the Hellenistic–Roman period posed the problem of the starting point of a philosophical education in different terms. Instead of the Socratic game of ignorance, recollection and memory, the Stoics identified the problem as malformation (CF82: 125–6). This left no room for a return, but rather posed the question of the formation of the subject as a subject.

The concern with malformation, however, rendered the problem of a starting point even more acute. Somebody who is not simply uneducated and ignorant but is also badly formed is unable to identify his own situation, thus cannot be the agent of his own transformation. Foucault illustrates this situation through the writings of Seneca who offers here a diagnosis and an analysis of this thorough entrapment (*ibid.*: 126–30).

Seneca identifies the pathological state in which the subject finds him/herself as a result of this malformation as *stultitia*.[12] This is a state of mind in which one is continuously agitated, but is unable to make up one's mind, to come to decisions.

Persons who are in this state have three main characteristics. First, unable to resist the influences that come from the external world, they are dispersed in space. Being open to all winds, they cannot discriminate. Second, they are also dispersed in time. They live in a state of perpetual change. They don't remember anything, let their life flow through their hands, living without memory. Finally, and most importantly, stultitia is fundamentally a weakness of the will. It is a will-power that is inert and lazy, 'limited, relative, fragmentary and changing' (*ibid.*: 128).

Central to all aspects of *stultitia* is an absence of will-power that would give the subject the strength and focus to be oneself and break the circle of abandonment to the impulses coming from outside. After the diagnosis, here we reach the identification of the trap. The door of the cage is open; one should only gather oneself together and walk out. However, the nature of the 'spiritual disease' is such that exactly this will be missing.[13] In order to escape, the subject needs somebody who pulls him out, by giving a hand, but also exerting a discreet but firm pressure. This person is the philosopher.

The next question is how to perform this operation. It is here that the significance of parrhesia lies in this literature. The problem is again formulated in the form of a paradox, referring to the balance between the two aspects of this 'friendly force'. Some pressure is necessary to overcome *stultitia*, as otherwise one would fall back to the previous state. But it must be gentle, as excessive force does not convince but frightens away.

Two problems, however, are still left over. They concern the exact aim, or the finalisation, of this turn towards philosophy, and the reason why this is to be called a conversion. Starting with the second issue, the use of the term is not an interpretive effort by Foucault. Epictetus, for example, used the expression *epistrophé eis heauton* (HS3: 81). Foucault here also relies closely on the work of Hadot, developing it further. Hadot argued that even though the term 'conversion' (metanoia) in our culture gained an almost exclusively religious meaning, it had an ancient, philosophical meaning (Hadot 1993: 175–82). As an example, Hadot gives the term 'epistrophe', used by Plato and the neo-Platonists. Foucault, however, claims that in between these two usages, there was also a third meaning of the term, and this was exactly the conceptualisation of the turn towards the self by the Stoics of the Roman Empire.

This third modality of conversion is opposed term-by-term to the other two. Platonic *epistrophe* focuses on the idea of perfection. It establishes an opposition between this world and the other, has as its central theme the liberation of the soul from the body, and assigns a privileged role to knowledge. Christian *metanoia* similarly opposes another world to this world, but does this in the manner of a sudden transformation, a unique event, a passage from death to life, from darkness to light, and connects it to a rupture in the self, the renunciation of the self. Finally, Foucault argues that in Christianity the link between politics and salvation, already weakened in Platonic philosophy, is broken (CF82: 185).

Philosophical conversion characteristic of Stoicism also turns away from a taken-for-granted involvement in the world, but does so not by displacing the gaze from the outside world towards the self. The Stoic remains inside the world, refusing to escape it; but instead of getting dispersed in the affairs of the world focuses attention on his own business, systematically fighting the temptations of curiosity (*ibid.*: 213–14).

The second major issue concerns the finality of this activity. Here again Foucault uses a term with a predominantly religious meaning, but interpreted in a broader sense (*ibid.*: 174–8). Salvation (*soteria*) in Plato did not mean a sudden and dramatic event, but rather a permanent link between the care of the self and the care for others. Its purpose was to escape the slavery of passions through a mastery of the self. The Stoics further accentuated this element. In the empire, where the link between the care of the self and of others, characteristic of the polis, was hardly possible, the proper formation of the self, in the sense of inner-worldly conduct, became a principal goal. It is in this sense that Foucault talks about the 'auto-finalisation' of the self (*ibid.*: 172–3, 198, 246, 304–5), or of 'auto-subjectivation', instead of 'trans-subjecti-vation' (*ibid.*: 206), with central consequences for the formation of the self in Western culture.

At this moment of his life, Foucault closely identified himself with this 'culti-vation' and 'auto-finalisation' of the self. But it is also clear that, from the perspective of the work on parrhesia, the limits of this perspective become visible. A recognition of affinities between Stoic and modern concerns, instead of sketching the outline of possible answers, rather should help to sharpen diag-nosis. The reappearance of Stoicism would always happen in a specific type of historical period: periods of transition or dissolution of order (Szakolczai 1999). It is always a symptom of crisis, never able, in itself, to come up with answers. The problem is not simply that the Stoic turn towards the self might, against itself, become a vehicle of egotism; but that this sober rejection of mundane concerns, proposing as an ultimate value the stability and identity of the self, did never and could never become a force of renewal, not to mention community-building spirit. Nietzsche was here again close to the truth by intimating Stoicism as the form of thought *par excellence* of the elite of the 'last men'. The Stoics manage to recognise the futility of the lives people live around them, totally absorbed in the 'world' or in 'society', and purport to resist such influences, but are entrapped in another form of escapism. Stoicism only became a historical force with neo-Stoicism – but this happened in the context of the rise of Protestantism and the modern state.

Preparation

The path towards a philosophical way of life starts with a 'conversion', in the sense of a redirection of one's attention, away from the distractions of the world, towards oneself. But this moment is only the starting point of a long period of practice and preparation. This preparation involves the same activities as any 'rite of separation': the acquisition of knowledge (*mathesis*), and the performance of certain practices of hardship (*askesis*).

MATHESIS

The link between knowledge and self-formation is both a constitutive issue of Western thought, and – posed in the form of the link between veridiction and practices of the self – a central issue for Foucault's own work (CF82: 220–1). Foucault reviews the manner in which the question of the priority between the knowledge of man and the knowledge of things was discussed in Cynic, Epicurean and Stoic thought.

For the Roman Cynic Demetrius, preferences are clear: mere knowledge of things is worthless; one should aim at gaining knowledge which is useful for one's life. This position does not imply a rejection of the outside world, only the prioritisation of a 'relational mode of knowledge' (CF82: 226). This means that only those aspects of the external world are useful that can have as their effect the transformation of the mode of being of the subject. It is for this aspect of knowledge that Plutarch would develop the concept of *ethopoiesis* (*ibid.*: 227; see also HS2: 19). The Epicureans even had a concept for ethopoeic knowledge, *phusiologia*. This word did not refer to a particular area of knowledge, separate from other areas, rather 'the modality of the knowledge of nature to the extent in which it is pertinent for the practice of self' (CF82: 228–9). The significance of *phusiologia* is visible in the fact that it was opposed to the Greek term of culture, *paideia*. For Epicurus, *paideia* as general culture is a pointless undertaking, a form of sophistry, a fabrication of devices in order to become admired by the crowds. *Phusiologia*, however, prepares for life, for resisting the influences of the external world.

At this point Foucault briefly refers to two concepts of Epicurean thought relevant in the context: *paraskeue* and parrhesia. Both terms would be discussed in considerable detail later, in the eighth and tenth lectures.[14] The term *paraskeue* is used not only by Epicurus, but by Cynics and Stoics as well. Its meaning, often translated into Latin by the word *instructio*, is preparation against future events, or the equipping of individuals with means to resist such eventualities. *Paraskeue* has four major aspects. First, far from the simple acquisition of useful skills, it is compared to the training of athletes for combat. Second, this training, however, has a verbal aspect: it implies the acquisition of a set of persuasive and effective verbal statements. Third, though these statements are founded on reason, what matters is not their sophistication but their permanent presence as tools for help. Finally, they have to be immediately available, always close at hand. It is the task of the ascetic exercises to ensure the acquisition and proper functioning of this equipment.

Foucault again reserves special space and attention for the Stoics. In the seventh lecture he discusses the idea of Seneca to gain knowledge of the world in order to ascend to a position from where it is possible to look down at ourselves from perspective, recognising our smallness. In this way, the contemplation of the world becomes tightly linked to a *contemplatio sui*: it is by realising that we are only points in the world, driven by necessity, that we can become rational (*ibid.*: 268). The first hour of the eighth lecture, discussing Marcus Aurelius, yields the same result, though starting from the opposite pole. The path suggested by philosopher-emperor is to be immersed inside, in the smallest details (*ibid.*: 278), penetrating to the heart of things (*ibid.*: 293). Doing so, however, one must always have the essential in front of one's eye. Thus, the representations must be filtered with the help of spiritual exercises (*ibid.*: 280–1).

Though starting from opposite directions, Seneca and Marcus Aurelius valorise the same kind of knowledge: a type of knowledge that neither objectivises human beings nor is searching for the obscure secrets of the inside of the soul, but aims at having an effect on the subject. They are interested in 'spiritual knowledge'.[15] They want to use this knowledge, however, for different purposes: Seneca to ground the identity of the subject, and Marcus Aurelius to dissolve individuality.

ASKESIS

Foucault's central interest in the course concerns the exact techniques that were available for individuals in their practice of self-formation and transformation. The techniques themselves were not novel, and can be traced back at least as far as the Pythagoreans. The novelty was that in the first two centuries AD, an entire 'culture of self' developed around them (*ibid.*: 302).[16]

After these short introductory comments, however, instead of discussing the techniques of *askesis*, and without even calling attention to this fact, Foucault returns to the themes of *paraskeue* and parrhesia. The discussion of the ascetic techniques would be interspersed with this analysis, in the ninth, eleventh and twelfth lectures. This hesitation indicates beyond doubt both how central the links between the care of the self and parrhesia became for Foucault at this stage, and exactly focusing on the links between (or ascendancy of) speech and practice, parrhesia and askesis, also how undecided he still was at that stage.

The discussion is divided into two parts. One is devoted to the techniques of philosophical teaching, using mostly Epicurean texts. This is covered in the ninth lecture, inserted between the discussion of paraskeue and parrhesia, two other concepts whose significance Foucault first recognised among the Epicureans. The second part, on techniques of self properly speaking, fills the last two lectures.

Philosophical education involved the acquisition of three main skills: listening, writing and speaking. Foucault's discussion is intriguing for two reasons. On the one hand, it gives a glimpse into the formation of those basic skills of the acquisition of knowledge that are simply taken for granted today, so much so that they are no longer treated specifically.[17] On the other, the discussion is organised around the concept of parrhesia, introduced in the next lecture in the course. Students must start their education by observing silence, while the teacher – in order to be effective – was supposed to speak using parrhesia. The right of speech was only granted to more advanced students, when all participants had to use parrhesia.

Much more important is the discussion of the two main techniques of askesis developed by the Stoics, covered in the last two lectures of the course. One cannot emphasise strongly enough the significance of these two lectures for Foucault's work: this is the culminating point of the course, its *'raison d'être'*, the assessment of the Nietzschean 'ascetic ideal' in an entire course devoted to the history of the techniques of self, beyond the limited focus of sexual asceticism.

The specific character of 'Stoic–Cynic asceticism' (*ibid.*: 401) is defined again through contrasts with Platonism and neo-Platonism. Negatively, it involved the rejection of the idea of the divine nature of the soul; while positively, the philosophers of the empire manifested a profound suspicion of the self and formulated as their main task the fight against its weaknesses. More than ever before, this enables Foucault to consider the philosophical asceticism of the first centuries AD as a moment of transition between Platonic philosophy and Christianity, as both these aspects would be taken up in Christian thought: the former in the second and third centuries, in the fight against the Gnostics; the latter in monastic thought, helping to develop a spiritual arsenal to combat temptation (*ibid.*: 403–4).

But Foucault goes further here. These same techniques would not just survive in the monastic context of Christianity but would re-emerge, with a novel intensity, in the fifteenth and sixteenth centuries, and then in the Reformation and the Counter-Reformation. By the late sixteenth and early seventeenth centuries, everyday life had been invaded by these techniques, as the life of every 'pious' Christian came to be 'literally covered with and doubled by exercises that one had to follow and practise from day to day, from hour to hour', following the manuals, though with a difference between Catholic and Protestant modalities (*ibid.*: 404).

Foucault divides these exercises into two groups: techniques of meditation (*meletan*), and practical exercises (*gumnazein*). The latter include the standard stock of exercises of endurance and abstinence, while in the former category the practical, preparatory ascetic techniques involve the various ways in which the truth of representations is assessed.[18] The greatest part of these lectures, and thus the culmination of the course, however, is devoted not to ascetic exercises as preparation, but to testing (*épreuve*).

Testing

The distinction between preparation and testing is not easy to make, argues Foucault, as the two are highly interdependent (CF82: 411). This statement, however, is problematic, as it fails to realise how specific such an interpenetration is. In the classical setting of a rite of passage, there is no way in which the preliminary rites of preparation and the actual ritual performance can be confused. The prolongation of the preparatory stage was already a special feature of the classical conception of philosophy as a way of life. In imperial Stoic thought there occurs a further inflexion, a highly consequential novelty: the stage of testing is generalised and extended to the entire life.

This first of all implied an inversion of the relationship between the two terms 'philosophy' and 'life'. Philosophy in the classical sense assumed a characteristic mode of living, with its ascetic techniques and external signs. In the new, Stoic modality, all events and experiences of life, its trials and tribulations became the testing grounds for the philosopher. His distinctness lay not in a specific mode of living, but in the manner in which he related to the life events and daily experiences that occurred to everyone.

Beyond this shift from techniques of preparation to testing there lay a reorientation of the conceptualisation of experience, from its active to its passive aspects. Ascetic preparation traditionally meant a training for fight, in the active, agonistic sense of liminality, experience and performance. Life as a whole conceived of as testing implies a shift of focus to experiences passively undergone or suffered, in the sense of *pathos*. Indeed, Foucault identifies the positive evaluation of suffering as an important novelty of Stoic thought.

This can be seen by contrasting Seneca and Epictetus. For Seneca, in line with traditional Stoic thought, suffering is valuable to the extent that it activates thought to eliminate the feeling of suffering. For Epictetus, however, suffering is good in itself, as it presents an occasion for testing. Foucault admits that the value of suffering was already a central element of classical tragedy, referring to the figures of Prometheus, Heracles and Oedipus. But there, the tribulations meted out by the gods belonged to an agonistic setting, a tug of war between gods and man, related to some specific and significant events. If, however, life becomes a testing ground through experiences of suffering, then this assumes a fundamentally different thematisation of the links between humans and gods. The thought of Epictetus demonstrates exactly this novelty, while at the same time also a certain uneasiness concerning this idea.

In Epictetus, still in pagan context, there appears the idea that behind all the experiences and sufferings of human life there is a benevolent and paternal god who distributes the trials, reserving the harshest treatment for his favourite sons (*ibid.*: 422). This rudimentary theodicy created theoretical difficulties that the Stoics failed to solve. Most importantly, it posed two questions: what is the finality of this testing, and what is the basis of discrimination between two kinds of people, those selected and those not selected for undergoing the test? In Stoic thought, argues Foucault, 'there is no precise problematisation of these two themes' (*ibid.*: 427–8). This would only come with Christianity, where even a most important theological answer will be given to both questions, in the form of salvation and of predestination.

In the next and last lecture Foucault analyses the way in which this interpretation of the sufferings of life was developed into a series of techniques of meditation. The discussion is introduced by a series of general comments on the manner in which such reflexive exercises or meditations should be considered as constitutive of the subject (*ibid.*: 441), suggesting an 'analytics of the forms of reflexivity' instead of a general and universal theory of the subject (*ibid.*: 444). This testing of the self as a subject of truth was practised in three forms of exercises. The first is a prior reflection on the various possible kinds of future calamity (*praemeditatio malorum*). This exercise was based on a fundamental, both diagnostic and symptomatic, suspicion concerning the future. Foucault refers here to Plutarch, who considered that a main reason for *stultitia* is an excessive preoccupation with the future (*ibid.*: 446–7). The aim of the Stoics was to effect a radical cure of this disease. They argued that the future is nothingness, it does not exist, and therefore there is no reason to worry about it (*ibid.*: 446). The meditative exercises systematically eliminated the future, by 'presentifying' it (*ibid.*: 452). The next step involved a certain elimination of reality itself: if Stoic thought 'presentifies the entire future in this way, this is not done in order to render it more real. On the contrary, it is to render it the least real possible, or at least to eliminate the reality of whatever, in the future, can be envisioned or considered as bad' (*ibid.*).

In this way the diagnosis turns into a symptom. The Stoics noticed in their contemporaries a fundamental uncertainty and imbalance, a loss of confidence in themselves and of trust in the stability of their life-world, translated into an anxiety about the future. But their positive advice is even more chimerical: it is to cancel the future, to deny reality, to remedy despair by asserting the very meaninglessness of hope.

The second technique, the meditation on death, fulfils a similar purpose, the main idea being to live every single day as if this were the last. The third and final technique is the examination of conscience, a theme already discussed by Foucault, and at a central place, in the 1980 Collège de France course. The fact that Foucault reached this point in the concluding part of the 1982 course is most significant, and alludes to the need to integrate the two types of analysis. The discussion, however, was cut short to make way for the concluding comments, which were indeed of exceptional significance (*ibid.*: 464–7). They are devoted to a single concern: the assessment of the significance of the idea of human life as a life of testing; an interpretation perfectly compatible with the concept of 'permanent liminality'.[19]

Allusions that in late Stoic thought the entire life was transformed into a testing were frequently made in the course (*ibid.*: 412, 420, 426–7). Here, however, Foucault elaborates the full significance of this idea. Concluding the short section on examination of conscience, he establishes close links, if not identity, between ascetic techniques, the task of preparation and life as testing: 'if philosophising means to prepare oneself, then [it means] to put oneself in a disposition where one would consider the entire life as a testing. And asceticism, or the set of exercises available to us, is what permits us to prepare permanently for this life which will be nothing else than a life of tests, up till the end' (*ibid.*: 464). Thus, here the importance of the specifically philosophical exercises is reasserted, but in the context already defined by the transformation of the entire field of everyday life as the realm of the philosopher. It is the idea of life as a testing ground that enables us to draw the links between life and asceticism ever tighter.

Foucault next reasserts the difference between philosophical and Christian asceticism. While the aim of the latter is to renounce the self, the aim of philosophical asceticism is 'a certain manner of constituting the subject of true knowledge as a subject of right action'. In this way, one has as the 'correlative of oneself' a world that is a world perceived, recognised and practiced as a test' (*ibid.*: 465).

At this point Foucault steps back, admitting that the analysis is perhaps a little too systematic. But he does not retract. A degree of abstractness was unavoidable, as his aim was to present 'the movement by which, in ancient thought, from the Hellenistic and imperial period, the real was thought as the place of the experience of the self and the occasion for the testing of the self' (*ibid.*). It is to this movement that Foucault traces the various forms in which objectivity and subjectivity were treated in Western thought, focusing on the shift of techniques of testing from the subject to nature.

The lecture closes with two concluding comments of considerable methodological relevance. The first clarifies the central concept of experience, related to the types of testing: '[t]hat *bios*, that life – I want to say: the manner in which the world presents itself immediately to us in the course of our existence – is a testing, this should be interpreted in two senses. Testing in the sense of experience, or that the world is recognised as that through which we are experiencing ourselves'; and also 'testing in this sense that this world, this *bios*, is also an exercise [through which] we will be formed, transformed and directed towards a goal', be it salvation or perfection (*ibid.*: 466). Second, it is to this vision of life, world and reality that Foucault connects two processes, corresponding to the two main forms of Western thought: the philosophy of the subject and scientific–objective thought.[20]

Following Foucault, one can retrace the idea of permanent liminality to the late Stoic conceptualisation of life as a testing ground. The appearance of this peculiar idea, however, presents a series of problems. Foucault has already identified two, the questions of finalisation and discrimination, properly problematised only in Christianity. Further difficulties concern the inner strength of maintaining such a pressure, and the possibility of a mass appeal of such a solution. In the 1982 course, Foucault seems to opt for the feasibility of a purely philosophical option. The problem is that here, just as in the case of classical Greek philosophy, the 'brute facts' of history do not seem to do justice to this position: Antiquity was succeeded by a Christian and not by a Stoic civilisation. Beyond this sociological point, there is a further issue concerning the possible sources on the basis of which 'inner strength' could be developed. The Stoics tried to develop a form of thought that would resist the corrupting influences of the external world, liberating individuals from their *stultitia*. Such a way of posing the problem has two shortcomings. First, it fails to address the question of the 'nature' of the 'world' that can only be rejected and resisted. The Stoic is condemned to live his life in a world whose basic organising principles seem to him thoroughly contemptible. Second, even the limited success of maintaining an integral existence within this world requires efforts, and ancient philosophy seemed to be on the losing side in this battle against the corrupting external world.

The literature on parrhesia offers a most striking example in this regard.

An epilogue: Themistius on friendship and hypocrisy

Since the efforts of Socrates, the central concern of ancient philosophy, in its various forms, was to empower human beings by generating an internal force that would give individuals both the conviction and the power to conduct themselves in a way that is at the same time truthful and encompassingly stimulating, able to act as a community-forming principle. The Stoics and the Epicureans, in both Greek and Roman times, represented the two different, even opposed poles. The former took up the idea of the philosopher-king, or the philosopher as the advisor of the emperor; while the latter directly organised philosophical communities. However, the two not only shared a common problematisation, but were also similarly insufficient in their efforts. The empire under Stoic emperors was not significantly different from earlier or later times; and the various philosophcal schools or communities never managed to be more than obscure sects of the leisure elite.

Concerning the narrow theme of parrhesia and friendship, the shortcomings of the purely philosophical approaches, and of the entire world of which they were a part, can be best illustrated by a late example. Themistius (c.317–388 AD) was neither Stoic nor Epicurean, but simply a teacher of philosophy in the late Roman Empire. His twenty-second oration, 'On Friendship', gives a glimpse into the last stage of the literature on parrhesia and friendship in late Antiquity with remarkable parallels to current developments in modernity.[21]

Themistius starts with the classical theme, the opposition between the true friend and the flatterer who is only pursuing his own interests in human relationships, the search for money or power. However, according to Themistius, the biggest danger to friendship is no longer represented by simple flattery, but by a more basic, because deeper, vice towards which flattery only represents a step: hypocrisy. This discussion is contained, in the form of an allegory, in the last pages of the Oration (Penella 2000: 104–7).

In opposition to the self-interested deception characteristic of flattery and adulation, hypocrisy is 'a kind of inauthenticity that displays itself as friendship but does not have friendship's unfeignedness' (Konstan 1996: 17). The hypocrite tries to appear desirable simply because she is desperate for attention and human contact due to an acute degree of lack of inner harmony and certainty: '[i]n order to appear desirable, she pretended to feel desire for those who came to her' (Penella 2000: 107). The hypocrite, though engaged in 'self-prostitution', is not a deceiver but a fake; she is not betraying or exploiting an intimate relationship, but rather demonstrates 'a failure of sincerity…Hypocrisy in this sense is almost devoid of practical content: it is revealed not in action or motive so much as in a fundamental bad faith with oneself' (Konstan 1996: 17–18).

At this point, the work of Themistius turns from a diagnosis of its times into a symptom itself, indicating that 'the classical priority of virtue as the basis of friendship has begun to give way, albeit partially, to a conception of friendship founded on personal attraction' (*ibid.*: 18). In listing the qualities of friendship, Themistius again starts by following the classical literature, but 'then introduces a point that is perhaps of his own invention': instead of following the path of virtue that is too difficult, perhaps friends should rather possess complementary vices; and, reversing completely the classical perspective, he argues that the purpose of appearing virtuous is only to become more attractive to others. Here Themistius turns to a discussion of the techniques to conquer friends, not so different from the techniques of erotic conquests: '[w]hat one is tracking is simply the object of desire' (*ibid.*). This language of conquest and chase is not an interpretive exaggeration: Themistius 'sustains the hunting metaphor throughout his discussion' (Penella 2000: 16). Thus, argues Konstan, the search for friends came to 'involve just the skills that are emblematic of Friendship's antitype, Hypocrisy, and her entourage of Deception, Plotting and Trickery' (*ibid.*).

At this point Konstan evokes a few contemporary discussions of friendship, referring to the close links between intimacy, self-disclosure and friendship, in order to emphasise the analogy with modernity. Strangely enough, no allusion is made to the important links with the practice of confession. The parallels of the previous discussion with modernity could also be deepened in at least two further directions: the problems concerning the arguably frightening increase in the insincerity and inauthenticity of human relationships in contemporary life, manifested in phenomena like the 'banal', *alexithymia* and 'total *Zerrissenheit*';[22] and the ever growing short-circuiting of friendship and sexuality. It is of considerable significance, and a good indication of the progress of nihilism, that after decades of – not very effective – analysis and criticism, fashionable forms of contemporary thought actually promote both processes.

On the other hand, even in ancient times, there emerged a critical discourse addressing this very issue. Konstan himself alludes that the 'opposite term of hypocrisy…parrhesia may have undergone a new inflection, from frankness to a kind of personal sincerity' (*ibid.*). This has indeed happened to the word in the early Christian literature. At this point we should return to Foucault's last-ever lecture, devoted to the theme of Christian parrhesia.

10 Christian parrhesia

Introduction

After the long discussion of the Cynics, in the second hour of his last-ever lecture on 28 March, 1984, Foucault showed a glimpse of his reading of Christian parrhesia. The short discussion was broken up into three parts: the use of parrhesia in Judeo–Hellenistic texts, in the New Testament and in the patristic literature, thus going into areas where Foucault had never ventured publicly before. Given the shortness of the discussion and the exceptional importance of the material, it will be necessary to supplement Foucault here with a more extensive discussion of the sources.[1]

Parrhesia in Judeo–Hellenistic texts

According to Foucault, the use of parrhesia in the Greek translation of the Old Testament (the Septuagint) and related Judeo–Hellenistic texts can be summarised using three shades of meaning. The first is the traditional sense of boldness and frankness of speech, the only special element being its link to the integrity of the heart. The second implies a more serious displacement. While parrhesia in the Greek texts emphatically referred to relations between humans, here it became a mode of relationship to God. It is the opening up and ascendant movement of the heart towards God (Foucault here refers to Job 22:21–8; see Schlier 1954: 873), implying immediacy and intimacy with the divine. Though linked to prayer, the emphasis is not on verbal utterance, but on the movement of opening up (the reference here is to Philo).

The third sense again refers to a man–God interaction, but in the opposite direction. Here parrhesia is a 'gift of God',[2] or the very being of God when it manifests itself, most important of these manifestations being his wisdom and anger. Here it is the sudden presence, or eruption, of the otherwise hidden god that is expressed with the word parrhesia.[3]

Foucault's conclusion is that it was through this mutual relationship between man and God, one implying a movement up towards and the other down from God, that parrhesia was displaced.

Foucault's analysis must be complemented here by a few additional points.[4] First of all, Foucault fails to mention the most significant use of the term, its only occurrence in the Pentateuch, a reference to the Exodus as a standing-up to and deliverance from the Egyptian yoke (Lev. 26:13).[5] The passage is significant due to both its context and the impact it exerted on the entire Judeo–Hellenistic literature. It evokes the events of the Exodus, but at the same time warns against excessive pride, emphasising that the basis of this liberation is faithfulness to the Covenant.[6] It is this theme of the Exodus that would be further taken up and spiritualised in the Judeo–Hellenistic literature 'in these two, indissolubly linked senses: the rising up (*relèvement*) of the soul and free taking up of speech (*libre assurance de parole*)' (Jaeger 1957: 224). Thus, since the first occurrence of the term, there is a tight connection between a judicial and a spiritual basis of parrhesia, which would be taken up in the New Testament (*ibid.*: 224–5).

The same legal connotation can be seen in the connection made between parrhesia and the Day of Judgement in texts originally written in Greek (Scarpat 2001 [1964]: 89). There are also connections with other aspects of the Greco–Roman meanings. Thus, parrhesia is granted to the 'friends of god' such as Abraham and Moses (*ibid.*); while Klassen, referring to the passages in the Book of Job, argues that '[i]t seems that the Greek democratic right or privilege is transferred to the heavenly court, especially into the context of judgement' (Klassen 1996: 235).[7] Finally, moving towards the meanings of the New Testament, in the account on the Maccabean revolt parrhesia is used to characterise the martyrs (*ibid.*: 237).[8]

Parrhesia in the New Testament

In this next short discussion Foucault identifies two important shifts compared to both Greco–Roman and Judeo–Hellenistic meanings, and a simple typology of the contexts in which the term was used. The changes reside in the fact that parrhesia no longer characterises the manifestation of the divine, and that, though boldness remains important, the central element of parrhesia, instead of speech, becomes the quality of the heart. Underlying the first point, the term is used only once in the Synoptic Gospels (Mark 8:32). At the same time the image of God earlier identified with parrhesia, the sudden outbreak of the 'wrath' of the 'hidden god', disappears. The second point, however, is a hasty generalisation, immediately qualified by Foucault's own typological sketch.

In the New Testament, parrhesia is applied to two kinds of people: to the Christians in general, and to the apostles. In the former context, parrhesia means a confidence that God will listen if one prays to him, or – says Foucault – if we demand from him what he wants of us. It establishes circularity between obedience and belief. The apostles, however, use courageous truth-telling in their missionary activities, which is closer to the Greek tradition.

Given the significance of the discussion of parrhesia in the New Testament, it is necessary to complement here Foucault's sketch with more details.

The occurrences

The significance acquired by the term parrhesia in the New Testament can be supported by both the frequency and the places of its occurrences. The term, with its verbal version parrhesiadzomai, appears altogether forty times in the New Testament (Klassen 1996: 239; Scarpat 2001 [1964]: 93–4), mostly in a very pronounced context. In Acts it appears 'both first and most often in the account of Pentecost and the first believers (Acts 2–4)' (Winter 1996: 187), thus at the very start of the piece, and it also closes the narrative, being its concluding word (*ibid.*: 186–7).

The very first appearance of the word (in Acts 2:29) is exceptionally significant, even foundational, in about half a dozen ways. It is used for a speech by Peter, the 'first' apostle. Immediately preceding the speech there is the arrival of the Holy Ghost at Pentecost and the ensuing charismatic gift of speech (*glossolia*). This is significant, not only because it underlies, *pace* Foucault, the close ties between speech and parrhesia in the New Testament, but also because of the foundational contrast it establishes with the story of the Tower of Babel (Gen. 11:6). There, the tie between man and God was severed by the building of the Tower.[9] Here, the restoration of this link is announced, as a literary motive, by an opposite divine act, the sudden granting of the ability to use and understand any and every human language.

The context in which the word parrhesia appears in Peter's speech is also extremely dense and charged. Peter asks whether he can speak freely, or use parrhesia, about David, evoking the nearby tomb of the Patriarch – who is defined not as a king but as a prophet – and recalls the promise of the Messiah. It is in this context that he delivers an oration of Christ, which combines a funeral oration with a eulogy of the resurrection.[10] Finally, it is shortly after this scene that the mission of preaching the Gospel by the Apostles starts, through the charismatic gift of free speech granted by the descent of the Holy Ghost at Pentecost.

Before this, however, and immediately after delivering his oration, Peter is arrested and charged to appear in front of a tribunal. Thus, at the level of literary metaphors, after the funeral oration of Pericles, there is an allusion to the other great public document on parrhesia, the trial of Socrates – a parallel explicitly drawn by Winter (1996: 190). In this trial Peter is charged to name the authority on whose basis he was performing miracle cures. The response of Peter 'was filled with the Holy Ghost' (Acts 4:8), and after his speech the tribunal duly recognised the 'parrhesia' of Peter (Acts 4:13), in spite of the fact of his being uneducated. Winter emphasises that this external recognition plays the role of confirming the parrhesia of Peter, a literary device that will be used later as well.

At this point Winter concludes this analysis, claiming that the language of Acts 2–4, with such 'allusions to classical writings', indeed 'evokes a description of Jerusalem that is a conflation of ancient Israel and classical Athens' (Winter 1996: 191). But this new parrhesia is not spoken in the polis (*ibid.*: 192). Here the links between Jerusalem and Athens receive a further tightening. In the very next event the community of believers is called an *ekklesia*, using the word applied earlier to the democratic assembly.

The new community to which the term *ekklesia* would be applied, just as the main protagonist of this community, is indicated by the next set of occurrences of the term parrhesia, now in the context of the conversion of Saul on the road to Damascus. From this point, the use of the word parrhesia is transposed from Peter and the 'original' apostles to Paul.

It is not possible to follow here further Winter's insightful analysis, which convincingly shows that all pairs of uses of parrhesia in Acts (as the word is always used in pairs, at the start and the end of important segments of the narrative) perform a crucial function in the narrative. We must summarise, shortly but systematically, the central characteristics of the use of parrhesia in the New Testament.

Parrhesia in the Gospels

As a start we need to qualify Foucault's claim about the merely human uses of parrhesia in the New Testament. The problem concerns the exact manner in which parrhesia is directly applied there to Jesus. Without pretending to enter theological dilemmas, the question is to make sense of the fact that the term parrhesia is all but absent from the Synoptic Gospels (though it is present once, further complicating matters), while being quite abundant in the fourth Gospel (where there are nine occurrences). How can both this absence and presence be jointly explained, and in a coherent framework? It is somewhat perplexing that the standard literature on Christian parrhesia did not seem to have posed this problem explicitly.

A starting clue might be taken from the contrast between Luke and Acts. Though both books were written by the same person, while the concept of parrhesia is used quite generously in the latter (having altogether fourteen occurrences), it is fully absent from the former. This seems to indicate that parrhesia belongs to the story of Christianity, and not the life of Jesus.

Such a hypothesis renders the problem of the presence of the word in Mark (8:32) even more acute. This enigma, however, according to Klassen, was resolved by Lohmeyer.[11] Lohmeyer argues that the passage is ' "hardly intelligible" ', and can only be understood through the African version of the text, where this proclamation is placed *after* the resurrection. This suggestion, negatively, eliminates the word from the life of Jesus, as far as the Synoptic Gospels are concerned, while it positively establishes a link between Christian parrhesia and the resurrection.

We now have to turn to the Gospel of John, where the term is used quite frequently and always as a noun, and not as a verb, in opposition to the relative usage in the body of the Acts. The first tentative remark is that the discussion of these occurrences in the existing literature is much less insightful or convincing than the discussion of the Pauline work. The reason may be due to the fact that most discussions treat the fourth Gospel together with the first letter of John (where the word parrhesia is used four times), as the 'Johannine' texts. In this way the specificity of the fourth Gospel usage, and the problem posed by the very existence of this usage, is ignored.

The article by Klassen makes several major steps forward. It analyses separately the two major Johannine occurrences, situates the discussion in the framework of the Cynic–Stoic usage of parrhesia, and offers a short typology summarising the analysis of the fourth Gospel (Klassen 1996: 243). Beyond the boldness–openness dichotomy, he identifies a public vs private dimension, claiming that this latter usage was unknown in Hellenistic Greek, and arguing that this could have been taken over from the Cynics. This would support the relation between Jesus and the Cynics, argued in some recent publications (*ibid.*: 231, 244). The problem, however, is that this typology ignores the question of who is actually using parrhesia in the nine passages, or its meaning in the various contexts. In order to arrive at the exact meaning of parrhesia in the fourth Gospel as applied to Jesus there, and only there, we need to conduct a more detailed and specific analysis of the nine occurrences. This will be done by taking the analysis of the Acts by Winter as a model.

First of all, the passages can be arranged with the same geometrical or musical precision, though not in doubles but triplets, with John (7:4,13,26), (10:24; 11:14,54), and (16:25,29; 18:20) composing the three trios. The game of dualisms between life and death, acts (actual or in speech) and recognition, activity and justification is replaced by a set of triads.[12] Each triad has a similar structure, while at the same time they respond to each other, creating an ascending motion. The first starts with a charge of Jesus's relatives: 'why are you not showing yourself publicly [this is expressed by the word parrhesia], to the "world" [implying Jerusalem]?' This charge mirrors the charge against Socrates about not taking part in politics. The answer of Jesus is also similar: by doing so he would be killed; and his 'time' had not yet come. The next use of parrhesia, a few sentences down, is doubly negative: it does not refer to Jesus, but generally to the multitude; and it states that nobody dared to speak openly about him, nobody was using parrhesia. The third passage is a response to the two previous ones. It applies to Jesus, and in the conventional meaning of bold speech, to an open justification of his previous activity, the use of the Sabbath for curing.

The second triad again starts with a reproach, but by different people and in a different manner, implying a different meaning of parrhesia. This time the Pharisees charge Jesus to speak openly, but the charge only parallels similar questions posed earlier by the disciples themselves, who several times wondered why Jesus was not speaking plainly, and were struggling to understand the message (see, for example, Matt. 15:15). Of special importance is a verse in Matthew stating that Jesus always spoke in parables (Matt. 13:34), followed directly by a reference to the revelation of 'things hidden since the foundations of the world' (Matt. 13:35), used by Girard as the title of one of his books. The answer to this charge again comes immediately, and both in deeds and words. Most directly, the term is used again in John. 11:14, where Jesus 'openly' and plainly stated that Lazarus was dead. This, however, is only the prelude to one of the most striking miracles in the Gospels, the resurrection of Lazarus. The third occurrence (John. 11:54) repeats the refusal of parrhesia. Jesus again stopped public activity and left Jerusalem, as the Pharisees were plotting to kill him.

The second triad underlines the message of the previous one: Jesus in the Bible is decidedly *not* a parrhesiast: he does not speak publicly, in the sense of directly addressing the centre, the Temple of Jerusalem, but in the provinces; and he does not speak plainly, but in 'obscure' parables. The reason is partly to avoid being killed 'before his time', just like in the case of Socrates; but partly, especially concerning the use of parables, it is simply not given, at least not as yet.

It is the third triad that gives the response to the questions raised in the previous two. The context is the Last Supper. In the first element of the triad (John 16:25), Jesus uses the word parrhesia for his own mode of speaking, in the sense of 'plain' speech, though announced for the near future, and in contrast to speaking in parables as in the past. The disciples immediately recognise this: now he was indeed speaking plainly (John 16:29). In the final occurrence, Jesus uses the word in front of the high priests, as applied to his past activities, and positively: in the past he was always teaching publicly, and not in secret (John 18:20). This may seem to be in contradiction with previous occurrences (John 7:5 and 11:54), alluding to a reticence for public activity. The meaning of 'public', however, has a different shade between the one and the other. Teaching was always done in the open – though not in Jerusalem – before 'due time'.

The central question to be answered after all of this is the following: was Jesus a parrhesiast or not? In terms of Foucault's four-fold classification, given at the end of the second lecture of 1984, the answer is a clear and emphatic 'no'. Jesus was aware of the parrhesiastic game, but he consciously decided not to play it. He was not speaking plainly, and this was precisely because of an event that was to happen in the future. Just as the game of Socrates was not political, the game of Jesus was not parrhesiastic; at least, not up to a point in time. In fact, the time horizon is central here: the related passages indicate an ever-shortening time horizon,[13] leading to a moment when Jesus would accept a full parrhesiastic game; where he would speak in both senses of the word 'open': plainly and with full publicness; which will be the moment when the message would be revealed.[14] The passages also are constructed to allude to two further aspects: that the message will be not simply about words but about acts and events, and the most important of them, matters of life and death; even further, about death and resurrection. It is this simple and plain message that would be carried by the Christian parrhesiasts; the apostles first of all, and then all Christians.

Parrhesia in Acts and Letters: a typology

In order to better illuminate the use of parrhesia in Christianity, a simple typological schema was developed. This is based on the fact that, in the New Testament, parrhesia is used by two different human agents (the Apostles, especially Peter and then Paul; and all Christians in general); towards three different audiences (persecution, singling out scenes of trials; other Christians; and God); and in three meanings: as bold speech, as inner confidence, and as intimacy.

The combination of three agents, three addressees and three modalities gives altogether twenty-seven different categories. Many of these, however, turned out to be empty. Bold speech was only addressed in the New Testament to hostile audiences, which were almost always Jewish;[15] the source of parrhesia was exclusively God; while intimacy was felt both towards God and in the Christian community. Concerning bold speech however – a special case – the standing of a formal trial was thought to deserve special attention. The resulting combinations and cases are contained in Table 10.1.

For a better understanding and interpretation of the table it is helpful to refer to the Latin translations of the term. This first of all clearly separates all those instances in which parrhesia is applied to Jesus. Parrhesia in the Gospels is translated by the word *palam* (plainly),[16] just as is the only similar occurrence in the Letters, in the 'outlier', Colossians (2:15). The correspondence is mutual, as these ten cases include most of the altogether fourteen occurrences of *palam* in the New Testament.[17] Concerning the other thirty occurrences, *fiducia* (trust, confidence) is by far the most frequent translation, with twenty-two cases plus a single case of *confidentia*. Even here the correspondence is mutual, as fiducia, though frequently used in the Latin version of the Old Testament (though never as a translation of parrhesia), hardly ever occurs in the Vulgate apart from translating parrhesia. The third group includes a few highly significant cases in which parrhesia is translated by boldness (*audere*, to dare; and *audenter*, boldly), and perseverance (*constantia* or *constanter*).

Type 1: Bold speech (audere and fiducia)

A quick glance at the table reveals that the largest number of occurrences refer to the use of bold speech by the Apostles, especially Paul, during their missionary activities, when facing adversity, especially from the Jews in the Temple (Type 1). The most significant, highly charged, first and thus truly archetypical of these scenes, however, recalling the funeral oration of Pericles, is the first public speech by Peter in the Temple in Jerusalem. This will be taken as the representative scene of the first type.

Type 2: Addressing a trial (constantia)

A subsection of this group contains the two occasions in which parrhesia is used in the context of a trial (Type 2). In both these cases, and almost only in these

Table 10.1 Types of meanings of parrhesia in Acts and Letters

		Bold speech vs Persecution	Bold speech in Trial	Inner Source God	Intimacy with Christians	Intimacy with God
Apostles	Peter	Type 1 (1)	Type 2 (1)	Type 3 (1)	Type 4 (1)	
	Paul	Type 1 (9)	Type 2 (1)	Type 3 (5)	Type 4 (2)	
Christians				Type 5 (5)		Type 6 (3)

two cases, parrhesia is rendered by 'perseverance'. In the context of a trial, therefore, 'parrhesia' means a resistance to yield to pressure and change one's beliefs. The representative scene of this type is the penultimate occurrence in the Acts, towards the end of the last and most important of the five public apologies of Paul in front of his judges, the model of which can be taken as the *apology* of Socrates.[18]

Type 3: Trust in God (fiducia)

The next type (Type 3) identifies the source of this boldness in faithful trust in God. In these cases, parrhesia is exclusively translated by *fiducia*. The fact that in the Greek original the act of bold speech and its source, its 'psychological' or spiritual support, is expressed by the same word is highly significant, as it alludes to exactly the kind of unity of experience that, according to Foucault's 1980 Collège de France lectures, would be broken in the practice of Christian confessional. However, Foucault there contrasted fourth-century BC Greece with third-century AD Christianity, and did not yet recognise the significance of parrhesia. Here, however, in the first century AD, the same unity of experience can be identified within Christianity, using exactly the word whose general significance was discovered by Foucault.

Of these occurrences the most important, on both qualitative and quantitative grounds, is the Letter to the Ephesians. Two of the five occurrences of Type 3 contained in this letter make a very strong and clear connection between boldness and trust in God. Furthermore, a third occurrence of parrhesia in this letter[Eph. 6:20], right after the second, reasserts bold speech as the central mission of the apostle, being the second and last case, after the very first occurrence of parrhesia in Acts (2:29), in which parrhesia is rendered by the word *audere*. Even further, two of the three occurrences in this letter take place in the last two verses, just before the concluding 'coda'. The fact that this happens in this particular letter is also of considerable significance. Though for a long time the authenticity of this letter was questioned, recent research not only tends to accept the authorship of Paul, but argues outright that '[i]t deserves to be called his testament' (Barth 1993: 188). Thus, parrhesia – at the same time as the manifestation (as bold speech) and the source (as trust in God) of the apostle's mission – is the ultimate word of Paul's testament, reinforcing the fact that it was the last word of the Acts as well.[19]

Type 4: Intimacy among Christians (fiducia)

The next series of occurrences (Type 4) imply a further displacement. Parrhesia as confident, self-assured behaviour not only alludes to God as the source of boldness, but also implies intimacy among the Christians. It is in this sense that the word occurs twice in the Second Letter to the Corinthians. It was this sense of intimacy that led to the – untenable – suggestion that this letter belongs to the Hellenistic 'friendship letter' genre (Fredrickson 1996). Finally, this letter belongs indeed to a special genre, as it is Paul's personal apology, written in order to justify the modality of his missionary activities, especially a perceived incompatibility between his personal kindness and the harshness of his written words. Thus, after the two great archetypical scenes of the funeral oration (of Pericles) and the public apology (of Socrates) in front of the judges, we have here two basic literary genres as representative of the second meaning of parrhesia: the testament and the personal apology.

Connected together, these four types constitute a series. This series starts with missionary activity, through its testing in trials and the character of the force that gives strength, to the community-building power of this force. The series represents the Christian equivalent of the exact same dynamics noticed in the Greek and Hellenistic literature. Starting from bold public speech (*Ion* and Pericles), there was a movement towards the building-up and testing of the internal force of the individual, with Socrates and Plato, up to the circles of friendship in the Stoic and Epicurean schools. Furthermore, this entire series is contained, as if in a nutshell, in the first four occurrences of parrhesia in Acts. This starts with the first public preaching of Peter (Acts 2:29), continues with his trial (4:13), moves to the assertion that the source of strength is God (4:29), and is concluded with an intimate prayer by the entire community (4:31).

This analysis can be complemented and concluded through the remaining two types. They seem to double up the last steps of the previous series, providing further confirmation and at the same time a clear differentiation from the Greek–Hellenistic schema. There are five occurrences in which parrhesia refers to confidence in God, and three in which it expresses intimacy with God. These two types rhyme with both previous pairs. With respect to Types 3 and 4, they duplicate the move from the inner self to intimacy. However, as if to prevent any close association with Hellenistic friendship, the reference point is always God, and there is also a clear shift from friendship (*philos*) to Christian love (*agape*) as the central value. As compared to Types 1 and 2, the new types are also linked to each other as problem and solution. Even the problems are quite similar: in Type 1, this is persecution, while in Type 5, it is apostasy due to a weakening of faith.

The last two types are represented by two series of four occurrences in two texts: the Letter to the Hebrews and the First Letter of John. The similarity of meaning is indicated by the fact that seven of the eight cases are translated by *fiducia*, and the remaining one by *confidentia*; and there is a close (but not perfect) correspondence between Type 5 and Hebrews and Type 6 and 1 John. The deviations from the rule, however, are highly significant, as they summarise, introduce and connect the two types, performing a crucial transitional role.

Type 5: Openness towards God

There are four occurrences of parrhesia in Hebrews, calling for a confidence in and openness towards God. They form two pairs.[20] The first pair (Heb. 3:6 and 4:16) plays a major role in the first Christological argument, contrasting the superiority of confidence in Christ with Moses (Heb. 3:1–6), and concluding the first paraenetic section (Heb. 4:14–16). The second pair performs an even more important role in the climax (Heb. 10:19–12:19) to the central argument of the letter (Heb. 7:1–10:18; see Mitchell 1996: 219). The third occurrence is situated in the very first sentence of this climax (Heb. 10:19), which started with the second paraenetic section (Heb. 10:19–35), while the fourth (Heb. 10:35) represents the end of this paraenesis and the highest pitch of this letter. A few verses later comes the sentence 'For faith is the substance of things hoped for, and the evidence of things not seen' (Heb. 12:1), singled out for special attention by Voegelin (NSP: 122; also SPG, AN). The fourth and last occurrence is in the negative, containing a call for not rejecting confidence in God, and is translated, in this single case, by *confidentia* instead of *fiducia*.

The general interpretation of the letter, given by Mitchell, is also of considerable importance. Relying on the work of Lindars, he argues that the context is not simply apostasy, but the wavering faith of the recently converted, pointing out the strong parallels with the discussion of conversion in Philo (Mitchell 1996: 221–3).[21] This establishes parallels between the issue of conversion to Judaism by Greeks and the conversion to Christianity, and also creates a line of meaning of parrhesia running from the democratic *ekklesia* of Athens, through the Hellenistic Synagogue, up to Christian *ecclesia*.

Type 6: Intimacy with God

In 1 John, emphasis shifts from confidence in God to the warm intimacy of the Christian community with God. The two letters closely relate to each other, as if the questions posed in the former (as an exhortation) would be answered by the latter. The fourth and last use of parrhesia in Hebrews, calling for not losing confidence in God, rhymes with the first use in 1 John (2:28), the only one in this letter where the meaning is confidence in God and not intimacy in the community with God, and also carries a clear eschatological connotation. The next three meanings, spread evenly through the remaining three chapters, explore this experience of intimacy, replacing the Hellenistic terminology of friendship with the Christian terminology of heart (1 John 3:21) and love (*agape*, 1 John 4:17), concluding with the striking definition of parrhesia as 'if we ask anything according to his will, he hears us and provides us with what we ask' (1 John 5:14), that was considered by Klassen as a clear denial of the possibility of a close connection with the Cynics (Klassen 1996: 251).

Thus, after the two great scenes (representing Types 1 and 2) and the two main literary genres (representing Types 3 and 4), the last two types, Types 5 and 6, can be represented by two crucial experiences: the experience of conversion (in so far as it is linked to intimacy and evoked by parrhesia), and the experience of Christian love (*agape*). The two are furthermore closely related, establishing a narrow parallel and even a tight direct affiliation between Athenian democracy based on philia, Hebrew Synagogue based on the Covenant (through the experience of Greek converts) and Christian community based on love.

Furthermore, these two types are also closely integrated with the previous four; a series that becomes especially marked if we link together the six representatives: the scenes, literary genres and experiences. The problem of missionary activity and persecution, contained in the first two types, rhymes with the problem of conversion and apostasy in Type 5; the strength to preach, derived from God in Type 3, is linked to the love of God expressed in Type 6. This latter connection is further reinforced by the Ephesus link: the representative text of Type 3 was the Letter of Paul to the Ephesians, while it was exactly the Johannine community of Ephesus that was the circle in which 1 John was written.[22] Finally, one should mention that the sequential order of our discussion, based solely on the internal logic of the occurrences of the word parrhesia, almost exactly followed the order of publication of the texts in the New Testament.

Parrhesia in patristic and monastic texts

The third and last part of the second hour of Foucault's last lecture was devoted to the patristic and monastic literature on parrhesia, where 'things became more complicated and interesting'. Not so much a depreciation of apostolic Christianity, this should be read rather as another allusion to Nietzsche (1967, I/6). This is all the more likely as Foucault immediately refers to the rise of Christian asceticism, and the simultaneous appearance of ambivalence in the meaning of parrhesia. This will become the central issue of the short discussion: what is the exact reason why, just as in classical Athens there was a correlation between the rise of the care of the self and the pejorative meaning gained by parrhesia, the same happened in the Christian context?

Though Foucault talks about ambivalence, there was rather a clear displacement of emphasis. If in the Christian context the parrhesiast *par excellence* was the martyr, and the problems of 'excessive' free speech were generated in the monastic context, then the sequential order is fairly straightforward. The rise of monasticism is associated with the end of prosecutions and the vacuum created by the disappearance of the figure of the martyr. While parrhesia became too tightly associated with resistance to persecution, the rise of monasticism required a new structure of authority, with emphasis shifting from immediacy with God and fellow Christians to respect of and obedience to established authority. Here confidence and intimacy of the faithful Christian with God became replaced by a trembling of the sinner before God, where the rule was silence and speech was considered a sign of arrogance and presumption. The individual needs intermediaries; left alone, he can only find the devil, and not God. In this new context of asceticism and obedience, parrhesia became associated with three great errors: the forgetfulness of the fear of God; the forgetting of the need of ascetic exercises, or the care of the self; and excessive familiarity with God as opposed to the need to consider him as living in a strange, alien place, showing the affinities between monasticism and Gnosticism.

Foucault summarises the discussion by arguing that the positive and negative meanings of parrhesia discriminate between two great kernels of the Christian experience: the mystic experience, emphasising confidence in God and face-to-face interaction with God as the source of truth; and the ascetic experience based on fear of God and obedience. According to Foucault, while the first was increasingly marginalised, the second became the basis of Christian pastoral.

This comment, read in itself, could be considered to be either insignificant, or a rather cryptic preference for mysticism.[23] But it does have a definite context, and a rather significant one. This is the Nietzschean concern with the 'ascetic ideal' and the 'ascetic planet'; or the exact stakes of the fateful encounter between Christianity and asceticism. In the *Genealogy of Morals*, Nietzsche defined Christianity as a religion of ressentiment, produced and propagated by ascetic priests. It is only a slight exaggeration to claim that the entire works of Weber and Foucault were devoted to testing this hypothesis. Their results were concordant and fundamentally negative: Christianity was originally the religion of charismatic prophets and parrhesiasts. The problem thus becomes to identify the exact moment in which asceticism became inserted into and took over Christianity. In a genealogical language, the question is about the conditions of emergence of the 'ascetic ideal' within Christianity and its lasting effects. In the language of Weberian sociology, it concerns the 'routinisation' (*Veralltäglichung*) of charisma in Christianity, or the replacement of natural charisma with the artificial production of charisma.

In the last words of the course, Foucault connects the emergence of the concern with the decoding of the truth of the self to this Christian turn of monastic asceticism. This was discussed in great detail in the 1980 Collège de France course. It is, however, beyond the scope of this book.

Conclusion

Modernity, by its meaning and even its name, is associated with what is recent, new, up-to-date. Its most recent impersonation, 'globalisation', however, does not carry such a temporal limitation in its name. As the previous chapters demonstrated, the phenomenon is very old indeed. As is increasingly recognised in social and political thought, the modern 'global age' has its antecedent in another period of 'globalisation' that started about two-and-a-half millennia ago, in the 'axial age', and ended with the collapse of the Roman Empire, about a thousand years later. This was not simply an age of empires, but of empires that strove for world domination, trying to conquer the entire inhabited planet, and thus they had 'ecumenic' ambitions.

Globalisation, then and now, has as its main objective the elimination of all border lines and limits, whether through military empires or multinational enterprises. The breaking of boundaries, however, implies the suspension of all stable structures as well, the destruction of the taken-for-granted background practices that give meaning to human existence. The lifting of limits opens up the realm of the unlimited or the liminal. The world of globalisation is the world of permanent liminality.[1]

Globalisation, though looking as inexorable then as it does now, encountered resistance. Two regions, at the margins of the first birth pangs of the global empire, gained particular notoriety with their modes of resistance: Greece and Israel, with Israel having a head start due to the 'Abraham tradition', developed against earlier types of empires. Greece was a land of small city states, lacking even the classical form of large-scale social organisation, yet – for a series of reasons and accidents – successfully defeated, against all the odds, the Persian Empire, launching the democratic experiment of Athens with unbounded world-historical significance, delaying globalisation by 150 years, even though the experiment soon failed. The political resistance of Israel was much less successful, but in the realm of thought and spirituality it came up with ideas that at least matched the performance of the Greek mind and soul.

At this level, resistance focused on two things: the diagnosis of the causes of the rise of the empires, the impulses that lay behind the limitless and meaningless expansion of power; and the development of an alternative way of living with the strength to resist, at the level of the human heart, mind and soul, the impulses that drive the expansion of military power.

The two concerns are easy to separate analytically, but in fact they address the same thing: the very moving forces of human conduct. They entered a realm that, evidently, no form of human thought managed, dared or cared to open up for reflexive thought before, especially not at a 'mass' level: the internal dynamics of human motivation. This immediately led to a major puzzle: the sources of 'good' and 'bad' conduct turned out to be very difficult to separate. Human beings are driven by certain internal 'daimons', 'spirits' or 'spiritual' forces, that pull them and instigate their desires, but such forces include at the same time love and hate, benevolence and envy, magnanimity and greed. Even further, these various 'spiritual' moving forces could easily transform themselves into each other.

The unreliability and flimsiness of these impulses is particularly great during uncertain, in-between situations and periods, but the age of the rising empires and conquests was exactly a period of widespread turbulence and uncertainty. Liminal periods, as Arnold van Gennep (1960 [1909]: 189)noted in his survey, are especially conducive to two types of impulses and dividing lines in human life: religion and spirituality on the one hand, and gender and sexuality on the other. The axial age and crucial junctures in the ecumenic age were the contexts for the rise of the main world religions; and the power of love, whether in the form of Eros or otherwise, was central for most religious and spiritual movements.

Furthermore, at the limit-point of the related reflections, a gender-related difference becomes visible. It looks as if liminality itself had a gender, and it was male. Combining the story of the Socratic Eros with the figure of Yahweh, the emergency god of the Patriarchs, the myths of Hermes and Janus and a fragment of Heraclitus quoted at a central place by Voegelin (OHIV: 187), and also the Gnostic figure of Sophia and the Egyptian *ma'at*, a definite pattern starts to emerge. In this pattern, the liminal activities that are out-of-ordinary and in-between, requiring heroic performance but also marked by incompleteness and strife, are carried by masculine words and male figures. The starting and ending points of liminality, however – whether in the sense of poverty or of plenty, according to Plato or Heraclitus, or in the evident sense of the 'home' – are female.

A short sociological analysis of an etymological dictionary supports this insight from a different angle. According to the Larousse dictionary of the roots of European languages' the two roots that gave rise to by far the largest number of words are 'per' and 'ker' (d'Hauterive 1948: 85–9, 153–6). 'Per' is the root of liminality, as has already been analysed, using Victor Turner, and the most elementary experience it conveys is that of going across. The basic idea behind 'ker', however, is to 'curve', leading to the 'circle'. The circle as a metaphor is particularly telling, as it is both empty (as indicated in the sign zero), but also represents fullness (as the circle is closed).

From this perspective it looks as if permanent liminality, the world of permanent striving and proving, the world of warfare and conquest, and in general of unrest and recklessness, is a male world *par excellence.*

In the 'axial' and 'ecumenic' ages, these periods of imbalance and instability, the thought of the great thinkers, whether philosophers or prophets, champions of the mind, soul and spirit, was oriented towards finding a balance and restoring a modicum of order and meaning to human existence. These efforts centred around two main concerns, visible with especial clarity in the work of Plato, but just as present in many others: the questions of measure and of inner force. The problem of measure is the following: given the extremely tricky character of human motivation, or of the 'spiritual forces' that, for better of worse, keep hold over human beings, how is it possible to separate the 'good' from the 'bad', to give some guidance for the conduct of life? The second problem concerns the inner strength to comply with the measure. How do we convince others to follow the proper, just, truthful life, and to persist on this road, in spite of the various temptations and distractions?

In both Greece and Israel, the tentative answer centred on the links between speech and conduct. In other words, the resistance to globalisation, in that period, was both logocentric and moralising. There were some 'models' revealed by prophets or discovered by philosophers, who tried to convince their audience of the correctness of their suggestions, and central to this was that they proposed to live according to these suggestions. But the rate of success of prophets and philosophers was extremely meagre, even within their – small – home orbit. The prophets were caught up in a permanent tug of war with the kings and the people, trying to change their hearts and minds; while philosophers waged a similarly hopeless struggle to awaken their audience from their active slumber.

Central to the relative success of prophets and philosophers was the possession of charisma, a certain kind of convincing speech. In the form of parrhesia, this was also explicitly reflected upon as central to the Greek experience of democracy. But the gift of charisma was accidental and unreliable, while the artificial production of charisma required such difficult and sustained efforts that any mass effect was simply out of the question.

The embodiment of the right measure and the provision of inner strength to live accordingly were the two major modes in which the problem of the rise of globalisation, as an age of empires, conquests and violence, was posed in Antiquity. It is to this form of problematisation that Christianity gave an answer that proved to be, sociologically speaking, effective. Weber's key term, charisma, Foucault's glimpses into Christian parrhesia, and Voegelin's chapter on the vision and experience of Paul (in OHIV), each represent attempts to come to terms with this central problematic. However, none of them ever came to pose the problem in this form directly.

For this reason, this is the point at which this book must draw to a close.

Notes

Introduction

1 The first two volumes were also published in this series; see Szakolczai (1998, 2000).
2 See Eisenstadt (1986, 1999, 2000), and the special issue of *Daedalus* (Winter 2000) devoted to the theme of 'multiple modernity'. Among earlier efforts, see especially the works of Benjamin Nelson.

1 Weber's historical method

1 This passage was inserted into the text in 1920.
2 Significantly, this idea is mentioned in the context of distinguishing between the external, objective or scientific perspective on a type of behaviour, which emphasises the difference between the 'correct' and the 'fallacious', and the perspective of the persons performing the action, 'who will instead distinguish between the greater or lesser ordinariness of the phenomenon' (ES: 400). It is quite a pity that Weber does not elaborate here or elsewhere on the difference between working with a dichotomy between ordinary and out-of-ordinary, or a gradation of ordinariness.
3 Significantly, Weber is using here the Diltheyian term '*Erlebnis*'.
4 See FMW: 271; see also Nietzsche (1967: 31–4).
5 In fact, this is the central theme of the last section of the manuscript chapter on religion in ES.
6 Charisma is the Weberian equivalent of the Nietzschean 'will to power'. The closest equivalent to charisma in Foucault's work is parrhesia, which has evident affinities with Weber's interest in the prophet as prototypical charismatic figure.
7 See PE: 80 and the *Zwischenbetrachtung*.
8 See especially the passages on the 'effective work of thought' in the 'Nietzsche, Genealogy, History' essay (DE: 84).
9 Throughout the book the terms 'permanentisation' or 'routinisation' will be used interchangeably. The English translation of *Economy and Society* introduced the term 'routinisation' as the translation of *Veralltäglichung*. This term, however, is unfortunate, as it evokes the connotation of a normal, ordinary course of action becoming repeated and eventually turning into a habit, a routine. It fails to convey the Weberian point of an emergency action becoming permanent in its modality and consequences.
10 See especially the works of Frankfort and Mumford.
11 See here the discussion on 'hydraulic civilisations' that took off from the work of Karl Wittfogel.
12 Being born in 1898, Dumézil belongs to the great World War One generation. Though this is little recognised, the impact of his work on Foucault can only be compared to that of Canguilhem.

13 Weber makes it clear that conquest is only one of the possible ways of permanentisation, as similar social differentiation can also develop inside any tribe continuously threatened by war (ES: 1134–5).

14 This idea can be linked up with Mauss's etymology of the 'person', traced back to the Etruscan word for the 'mask' worn during rituals.

15 See AJ: 96–105. For more details, see Chapter 2.

16 See the passage on the 'theatre of calling' referred to on p.16, and a passage in the 'Protestant Sects' (FMW: 320) quoted in Szakolczai (2000: 121).

17 The various terms for 'sacred', 'sacrifice', 'king/sovereign' and 'gift', in various languages, move in a tight circle. See the Latin *'homo sacer'*, the German *Opfer* (offering) for sacrifice, the Italian *regale* (royal) and *regalo* (gift), or the Hungarian *áldozat*, meaning both sacrifice and victim, and having as its root the verb *áld* (to bless).

18 At this point the work of Mauss, who put the terms 'gift', 'sacrifice' and 'prayer' at the centre of his scholarly interest, complements that of Weber. See also the work of Tristan Riley (1999) who connects, through Robert Hertz, Nietzsche and Mauss.

19 Indicating the absence of this problematic in the Weber literature, the term 'sacrifice' (*Opfer*) is absent from the index of the German edition.

20 This is the basic idea of the famous essay by Hubert and Mauss, and is still accepted in a matter-of-fact way in most writings on anthropology and mythology.

21 The term 'charisma' is only mentioned at the start of p. 422.

22 This is also the starting point, *pace* Hobbes, for Nietzsche and Elias.

23 Here Girard follows Gabriel Tarde's unjustly forgotten 'classic' of sociology.

24 The word *émissaire* has some importance here, as Weber named 'ethical prophecy' as 'emissary prophecy *"Sendungs"–Prophetie*' in the *Einleitung* (FMW: 285; MWG I/19: 107); and given the importance Girard (and also Weber) attributes to prophecy in the fight against the sacrificial mechanism.

25 For a complementary account, see Giorgio Agamben's *Homo Sacer* (Agamben 1998). Agamben took as the point of departure of his analysis of the sources of the concept 'sovereignty' Foucault's work on bio-power, especially the last chapter of the first volume of the *History of Sexuality*. Central to his work is the idea that the Greeks distinguished between two words for life: *zoe*, or mere life; and *bios*, or 'meaningful' life. This distinction also appears, with some emphasis, in Foucault's first lecture of the 1981 Collège de France course. To close the circle, the affinities and direct links between Girard and Foucault would also deserve a study. Foucault never refers to Girard in his written work, while Girard does make reference to the *Order of Things* (Girard 1978: 598). Jean-Michel Oughourlian, co-author of *Things Hidden*, further elaborates this point in his book *Un même nommé désir*. Even more importantly, in his autobiographical interview, apart from highly praising references to the work, Girard implied regular personal contact (Girard 1994: 112–13). This should not be surprising, as Foucault visited the French Department at the University of New York, Buffalo, twice in the early 1970s, exactly when Girard was there on a Guggenheim fellowship, and they acknowledge the same members of the Department as their closest contacts (Eugenio Donati and Josué Harari; see Girard 1972: 6, and DEI: 35, 41).

26 Girard could have referred to Nietzsche as well here (see, e.g., Preface to *Human, All Too Human*, Nos 6 and 7).

27 For a particularly incisive elaboration of this point, see Mittendorfer (2000).

28 The index of the English edition even fails to list the term among its entries.

29 See also ES: 245, and editorial footnote 7.

30 One can refer here to the classic work of Ruth Benedict (1934).

31 This is the title of the first section of the chapter in ES.

32 It is important to remark at this point that the dual-faceted world image characteristic of the religion dominated by magic is entirely the work of reconstruction, and is not the product of 'indigenous' thought. The first explicitly dualistic world image was

formulated by Zoroaster, or the 'first prophet'. The distance of prophecy was necessary to perceive, as if from the outside, the two sides of this dualistic world – those
living inside evidently did not gain this distance. One should note already here,
however, that this dualism was characteristic of settled, agricultural, village popula-
tions, and not of hunter-gatherers, whose world-view was quite different, much more
prone to incorporate ambivalence (see Turnball (1968 [1961]) and Guenther 1999).

33 Though Weber never explicitly theorised this process, as he was more interested in
the specific line of development that led directly to the rise of Western modernity,
related ideas can be found in several, and significant, places in Weber's work, especially in *Economy and Society* (in Chapter IX, on 'Political Communities'); in sections of
his 'economic sociology' (especially Chapter III, pp. 356–69); and in the theoretical
distillation in the 'Conceptual Exposition' (pp. 31–6, 40–3).

34 In this context Foucault's discussion in the last pages of his 1982 Collège de France
lectures (discussed in Chapter 9 of this book) is of particular interest.

35 The social life of small-scale societies is of course elaborate and highly differentiated,
mostly along kinship ties. It is only their experience of the 'world' that is unified.

36 This is discussed in detail in Chapter 2.

37 This is the way Weber characterised the order of India and, more especially, China
(RC: 28, 100). See also the Egyptian concept of *ma'at* (discussed in Chapter 5 of this
book).

38 Similar times of trouble occurred in Egypt as well, but these never led to a revolt
against the order of things, against *ma'at*.

2 Ethical prophecy

1 Significantly, in the chapters on classical prophecy in *Ancient Judaism* he will alter this
way of proceeding, arguing that the classical prophets do not form a type, each being
'attuned' differently.

2 This is reviewed in Chapter 5.

3 This makes it evident that the real source of the 'secularisation' thesis, criticised by
Blumenberg and attributed to Lowith (Blumenberg 1983), is indeed Weber. Karl
Lowith (1897–1973) became one of Weber's most faithful disciples, after having
attended the 'Science as a Vocation' lecture as a soldier returning from the front (see
Lowith 1988: 37–9). Becoming a student of Husserl and Heidegger, he might have
communicated some of Weber's ideas to his professors.

4 The passage is not about prophets; however, it comes just before the aphorism on
world-negation, quoted on p. 33.

5 Contemporary theories of recognition (like Honneth's or Taylor's) depart from Hegel
and not from Weber. For a theoretisation of recognition that, while not ignoring
Hegel, pays central attention to the Weberian perspective, see the work of Alessandro
Pizzorno (1987, 1991, 2000).

6 Weber emphatically makes the point that ethical prophecy only emerged in a well-
defined area, the Eastern Mediterranean and the Near East. From a strictly
'evolutionary' perspective, it is worthwhile noting that this same area was previously
the birthplace of large-scale entities (empires); of the city; and even of agriculture
(Diamond 1998).

7 The closeness to the last period of Foucault's work is particularly striking here. Given
that Foucault's interest on 'pastoral power', discussed in 1978 in the Collège de
France course and resumed in the October 1979 Stanford lectures, coincides with his
systematic study of Weber, this passage in Weber might have played the role of a
catalyst, in the sense of an *'opérateur'* (HS2: 18–19) in Foucault's last work.

8 See ES: 464,WuG: 283. Cf. the 'cultivation of the self' by Foucault in the third
volume of *The History of Sexuality*.

9 Foucault also traced the 'care of the self', through Socrates, back to the Delphi oracle.

10 In his 1975 lectures Foucault also adds the specific role of German penal practices (CF75: 159–60) – an aspect strangely ignored by Weber here.

11 Henri Frankfort (1897–1954) also emphasises the peculiar characteristic of the Hebrews as a people; that their 'coherence was derived from a shared nomadic past rather than from what they had achieved as a settled community' (Frankfort 1948: 337). On Frankfort, a major source for two important reflexive historical sociologists, Mumford and Voegelin, and member of the same World War One generation, see Wengrow (1999). In this interpretation it is particularly important to underline that Wengrow considers Frankfort not simply a classic of archaeology (who has become somewhat neglected in contrast with V. Gordon Childe who drew extensively on Herbert Spencer and Karl Marx), but as a thinker with a philosophical bent who made a major contribution to the social sciences.

12 As is shown in Chapter 3, Weber would discuss the rise of the Occidental city in very similar terms.

13 Though, as a sign of ambivalence, he was also near, often even too near (AJ: 127). Though at least since the Zoroastrian revolution and its dualism such ambivalent features in the gods seem to be unthinkable, this was common among nomadic people, where the creator god also had another face as a trickster (see Guenther 1999).

14 This development closely mirrors Foucault's discussion of the transformation of parrhesia from a political virtue, associated with the agora, first into a philosophical technique, associated with the care of the self, and then into a technique of monastic asceticism (see 1983 and 1984 Collège de France courses, and also DV).

15 The expression 'court society', of course, has been rendered famous by Norbert Elias, and in explicit opposition to Max Weber's emphasis on the Protestant ethic and the city bourgeoisie. However, the term is used by Weber himself, and in a meaning not far from Elias's (see for example AJ: 101, 107). Given the importance Elias attributes to the term in his reading of the emergence of modernity, the issue is not trivial. In my view both are right, in the sense of capturing different aspects of the process. Weber is emphasising the *difference* of modernity, and locates it in prophecy and the city, and their eventual combination in 'modern sober bourgeois capitalism', based on inner-worldly asceticism. Elias, however, just as do Mumford (in the 'Baroque City') or Foucault (in his emphasis of *'raison d'état'*), recognises that another crucial factor in the emergence of modernity is the revitalisation, in the form of absolutism or divine-right kingship, of the ancient 'court society', or is a combination of a *return* of the 'world' (i.e. the 'court society'), with the reasserted *rejection* of this world. This point is elaborated in more detail in the Conclusion. However, let it be mentioned here that, apart from the 'court society', a number of other Eliasian concepts can be traced back to Weber's essays, like group charisma (used both in AJ and RI), or the established and the outsiders (see Weber on in-group and out-group morality; AJ: 343). It is also not surprising that most of these references are to be traced back to Weber's *Ancient Judaism*. What could have been more self-evident for Elias, a former intellectual leader of the *Blau–Weiss* Zionist youth movement, than to study in detail this book, once he moved from Breslau to Heidelberg and started to study sociology under Alfred Weber?

16 This event is theorised in the *Einleitung* as the central element of a religious ethic, its 'annunciation' and 'promise' (FMW: 270).

17 Strangely enough, in the concluding pages of the chapter in ES Weber would consider Judaism as a 'world-accommodating' and not a 'world-rejecting' religion.

18 As was pointed out earlier in the chapter, the interpretation of the Abraham tradition and the work of Henri Frankfort lead to a somewhat different result. The crucial issue concerns the various meanings of the word 'world'. Weber's restrictive interpretation

of 'world rejection' as a flight from the entire universe into a 'second world' of super-natural reality points again to the overly Nietzschean inspiration for this idea.

19 Weber's model case here is China again; see the frequent references to the lack of revolution in China (RC: 14, 62), and its attribution to the absence of prophecy: 'The Chinese "soul" has never been revolutionised by a prophet' (*ibid.*: 142; see also *ibid.*: 224–5, 229–30).

20 The lack of remuneration is another novelty of classical Hebrew prophecy. In fact, the acceptance of money was considered as a major dividing line between 'true' and 'false' prophecy (Zeitlin 1984: 234).

21 For Weber's identification with the figure of Jeremiah, see WB: 594, discussed in Szakolczai (1998: 179). It is well worth recalling here that in Weber's discussion of prophecy in ES, Jeremiah does not even make a passing appearance; the only reference to him is in the context of the sociology of law. This is because Jeremiah is not just atypical of the type of prophet Weber eschewed there, but in most cases he is exactly the contrary. Mentioning only one example, Weber focuses on the *disciples* attracted by the prophets – but Jeremiah has none, apart from his servant and scribe; he speaks alone, feared and hated by the 'people', and even after his doomful predictions have turned out to be true, he fails to build up a congregation, disappears evidently without a trace, somewhere in Egypt.

22 For a few examples, see Jer 1:16 on those who, instead of praising God, 'worshipped the works of their own hands' (thus establishing a direct link between hubris and idolatry); and Jer 9:26 on those who 'are uncircumcised in the heart'; or the repeated passages about those who have 'hardened their neck' (e.g. Jer 7:26).

3 The city

1 Orihara (1994) also supports this claim on a philological basis.

2 The passage 'Each sees what is in his heart', contained in the 'Ethical Neutrality' essay, was selected by Wilhelm Hennis as the motto of his major reconstructive essay, 'Max Weber's Central Question' (see Hennis 1988: 21).

3 For example, on the last page of the 'real' conceptual part Weber defines the Occidental city; then he devotes an entire chapter to the same theme; and finally much of this discussion is repeated in the long historical chapters.

4 The Occidental city will thus emerge in 'striking contrast to the Asian conditions' (ES: 1236, the first sentence of the section on 'The Occidental City'). The previous pages contained an extensive survey of the Asian and Near-Eastern city, including references not only to China, Japan and India but also to Egypt, Mesopotamia, Phoenicia and Russia, ending with a short discussion of Mecca.

5 Weber mentions that the etymological root of the Chinese character of the city is 'fortress' (RC: 13). Greek etymology (*akropolis*) yields a similar result, just as does Hungarian (*vár* – *város*), while the German and Russian words for city are derived from the word for mountain (see *berg* – *burg* and *gor* – *gorod*).

6 Even the otherwise omnipresent word 'charisma' is missing from these 150 pages, except for a short section on family charisma in a less-pronounced part of the manuscript.

7 For a reconstruction of the arguments for the 'peaceful' character of commerce in the early modern period, see Hirschman (1977).

8 These two words came to play an all-important role in the entire work of Marx, as 'Communism' and 'bourgeoisie'. The parallels may not have been fully unintended.

9 See also the frequent use of the term 'usurpation', associated with various parts of Europe, e.g. as 'usurpatory innovations' (ES: 1251); as 'revolutionary usurpation' in Italy (*ibid.*: 1253); as 'usurpatory *coniuratio*' related to the cities of Flanders (*ibid.*: 1255); or as 'revolutionary usurpation' again, related to France (*ibid.*: 1256).

10 Here the account is somewhat confusing and repetitive, as Weber first discusses the socio-economic bases of the rise of sworn confraternities, and then repeats the same for military confraternities (ES.: 1242–31, 260). At this point in the text I simply summarise these two discussions together.

11 Weber also touched upon the case of the 'Germanic North', especially the role played by the mutual protection guilds, but argues that – especially due to the 'lack of urban knighthood' – the Northern cases showed more 'archaic traits' (ES: 1256).

12 The omission of any discussion of the monastic contribution to the rise of the Occidental city is striking here, especially given the importance Weber attributes to monasticism elsewhere in his work. There is only one reference to monastic orders in the entire manuscript, but it is negative, identifying the monastic orders as a hindrance to the rise of cities (ES: 1333). Monastic orders, however, played a particularly important role in the rise of the Occidental city, especially in the foundation of inland cities. The affinities between monasteries as 'brotherhoods' with the German and Italian military 'fraternities' also seem to warrant further investigation.

13 Weber says 'up to' this time, but this must be a lapse. It makes no sense, and the next sentence refers to the example of the Frankish king Clovis, living after the collapse of the Roman Empire.

14 This passage, together with the previous ten pages, was only added to the text in 1920 (see MWG I/19: 213–26).

15 This difference has ramifications up to the present day. Effects include the roots of 'totalitarianism' in continental city communes in opposition to the special Anglo-Saxon development, of which the different inflexions of the Greek 'politeia' vs 'police' and 'Polizei' in the continent vs 'policy' England are a telling sign (for more details, see Knemeyer 1980; Horvath and Szakolczai 1992); but there is also the different experience of contemporary city life in England or the continent. The privatisation craze of neo-liberalism, with its lack of understanding and respect for the conditions of city life, can be safely rooted in the Anglo-Saxon landscape.

16 In the long and unfinished – even untitled – final section of the manuscript, Weber directly contrasts Ancient and Medieval city democracy. However, he curiously fails to allude to the fact that precisely the character of Italian city development, the 'circular path of the Italian cities' that was unique in Europe (ES: 1322), has striking similarities to the circular development of political forms described in Plato's *Republic*.

17 For a few examples, see Eisenstadt (1963), Voegelin (1962, OHIV), and Wallerstein (1979).

4 Voegelin's historical method

1 See also Foucault's analysis of the Cynics (Chapter 8), and also the similarity with the mentality of Communist Party apparatus members (Horvath and Szakolczai 1992).

2 The lack of reference to Dilthey in Voegelin's work is somewhat perplexing.

3 An important aspect is the downplaying of the Nietzsche–Weberian inspiration of his work, still acknowledged as central in 1942–3.

4 The inspiration of *The Protestant Ethic* is particularly visible here.

5 Concerning the use of gendered adjectives and pronouns, I have to warn the reader that the mother tongue of the author is Hungarian, and Hungarian syntax simply does not recognise gender differences.

6 This intellectual encounter between Turner and Dilthey, or between (British) social anthropology and (German) philosophical anthropology, was a most significant event for social thought. The lack of recognition of its significance is probably due to Turner's death shortly after the discovery he made, and the posthumous character of his main related publication (Turner 1985).

7 See also the common English practice of having 'ford' in the name of localities.

8 See also Foucault's analysis of Nietzsche's terminology of origins as descent and as emergence in his famous 'Nietzsche, Genealogy, History' essay (DEII: 80–6).

9 Portunus was originally the god of doors (porta), but once that function was taken over by Janus, he became the god of harbours (port). Janus was also the god of bridges.

10 There are also crucial modern allusions to this theme, all mediated by the figure of St Januarius, a medieval saint whose blood starts flowing on special occasions. See the beginning chapters of Freud's *Psychopathology of Everyday Life*, a crucial page devoted to the etymology of 'experience' by Victor Turner (Turner 1985: 226), and the title of Book Four of Nietzsche's *Gay Science*, a book published just after *Daybreak*.

11 It is rather perplexing that Voegelin fails to allude to the narrow similarities between the 'truth of the process of history' as discovered by Anaximander and the idea of eternal recurrence, given that he often refers to Eliade's *Eternal Return*; that he was familiar with Nietzsche's work; and that Nietzsche traced his own idea to Heraclitus. One can't escape the conjecture that Voegelin *had* to cling here to the idea that Anaximander made 'the' discovery of 'the' truth, blinding him to the parallels with earlier similar ideas and their significance.

12 Voegelin only alludes here to their ideas (e.g. OHIV: 174), discussed in detail in OHII.

13 From the perspective of Eliade, such references gain further significance. In so far as philosophers reasserted the eternal recurrence or shied away from direct reflection on the epochality of history, it was the task of the historians to reassert the significance of the events.

14 If Prometheus stole the fire, Hermes was the thief of the souls.

5 *Israel and Revelation*

1 For details, see Szakolczai (1998).

2 A number of other thinkers came to this realisation at about the same time; see Mumford (1956), and Hamvas (1995). Johannes Kühn, the professor of Reinhart Koselleck, also gave his 1947 Leipzig inaugural lecture on a similar theme (Reinhart Koselleck, personal communication).

3 This volume is again of importance. For Jaspers, this was the first publication after his promotion to the philosophy chair, breaking a silence lasting for a decade which gave ample opportunity to his opponents to question the wisdom of the decision. This silence basically lasted from his 1920 talk on Weber to his Weber essay published in 1932, and was followed by his major three-volume book. The 1931 volume was also the inaugural book for the Suhrkamp series that proved to be one of the most successful book series of the century, with well over a thousand volumes now published. In fact, the publication of the one-thousandth volume of the series gave an opportunity to publish a book, edited by Jürgen Habermas, to reflect on the work and the question of Jaspers, while the leading Hungarian sociologist Elemér Hankiss organised a conference in 1995 at Georgetown University in the United States taking up the title and the concern of Jaspers.

4 His account could be directly contrasted with the more recent work of Wallerstein (1979), which argues, along materialist and Marxist lines, that the two crucial periods of history were the Neolithic age with the agricultural revolution, and the rise of the modern world system.

5 Voegelin's references to Toynbee's work also support this hypothesis. Toynbee discussed the work of Jaspers in his Preface to Volume Seven of his *History*, published in 1954. In OHI, however, Voegelin only refers to volumes 1–6 (see OHI: 15, fn. 1, 120, fn. 3). This indicates that Voegelin only fully recognised the significance of this work of Jaspers in 1956–57, and through Toynbee.

6 On the methodological level, Voegelin would comment later on the 'Introduction' as being 'the form which a philosophy of history has to assume in the present historical situation' (OHIV: 57).

7 Voegelin repeatedly pointed out that a period of spiritual outbursts that excluded Moses, Jesus, Mani and Mohammed from history cannot possibly claim to be 'the' axis time of history, especially from a 'spiritual' perspective.

8 The word, in fact, was used already in OHIII; but there is a difference between the mere use of a word and its distillation as a crucial symbol.

9 This term would also become the title of a later piece, and is identical to Elias's 'figuration'.

10 A paper should be written on the 'traps' into which Weber, Voegelin and Foucault got themselves through similar promises.

11 One must note here that Jaspers did not ignore the rise of empires in his work; it was only absent in Voegelin's earlier account of Jaspers. This absence would indeed weigh on the second and third volumes of OH.

12 The first paragraph of this account, in a chapter on Mesopotamia, summarised the first pages of Voegelin's original introduction to the *History of Political Ideas* (see HPI: 225).

13 See also Assmann (2001). On the concept of trauma, see Giesen (2002).

14 It is worthwhile noting here that, in the index of the book, Voegelin gives three references to the term 'metastatic faith' for p. 195. The word, however, does not appear here at all. Evidently Voegelin only developed the concept later (see also Rossbech 2001), and did not reintegrate it into the text; however, at the stage of indexing, he thought it relevant to indicate that the roots of metastatic faith lie in the original, compact experience of Abraham.

15 Thus, Abraham is discussed on pp. 189–95, Moses on pp. 380–427, Elijah on pp. 334–51, while the discussions of Isaiah and Jeremiah are basically intertwined. Now, of course, a problem-oriented discussion might take some liberties with chronological order. However, the experiential methodology requires much chronological faithfulness, and due to the peculiar organisation Voegelin evidently loses track of important problems – like the 'eschatological problem', singled out as central in the Elijah chapter, reinterpreted in the language of metastatic faith in the discussion of Isaiah, but omitted from the chapter on Deutero Isaiah, which is most perplexing given that he is widely assigned a major role in the history of eschatology.

16 The concluding pages of the classic work of Henri Frankfort illuminate this point with particular incisiveness. The centre of the prophets' attack against the kings was the key value of the ancient Near East, 'the harmonious integration of man's life with the life of nature'. Due to its transcendentalism in Hebrew thought this possibility was denied, as 'nature appeared void of divinity'. Thus, '[i]n Hebrew religion – and in Hebrew religion alone – the ancient bond between man and nature was destroyed', and every Hebrew 'stood under the judgement of God in an alien world' (Frankfort 1948: 342–4).

17 As a good indication of ambivalence, at one point Elijah is said to have killed the other prophets (18:40), while at another he complains of being charged so (19:14). The story about rainmaking also alludes to the affinities between the charisma of prophets and of magicians. According to Weber, 'King Ahab called Elijah a mischief maker', or trickster (AJ: 109).

18 Such a dividing line is equivalent with the contrast between the parrhesiast and the flatterer.

19 See especially the metaphors of the 'stiffened neck' (Jer. 7:26) and the 'uncircumcised heart' (9:26).

20 In this context, however, it is particularly intriguing that, apart from a single reference (and there it is only used to mark the context), Voegelin simply fails to discuss the Book of Job. The possible links with Weber are again intriguing here, as one of Weber's explicit plans was to supplement his analysis in AJ with a study of this book.
21 See OHI: 507, fn. 17, which shows that the analysis made use of the Hebrew original, as well as of the extant scholarly literature.
22 It is not clear why Voegelin thought that this affair had a 'comic touch' (OHI: 165).

6 Plato and the order of the soul

1 Tyre is a Phoenician city a short distance from Jerusalem. The symbolic links thus established between Crete, Europe, Greece and Palestine are highly significant.
2 The concept of trauma is taken from the recent work of Bernd Giesen (2002).
3 On the taming of the warrior aristocracy, see Elias (2000 [1939]).
4 See Foucault's analysis of *Oedipus Tyrannos* in Chapter 7.
5 This would be taken over by Weber as the last word of his *Economic History*.
6 This parallel was also central for the 'axis time' interpretation of Hamvas (1995).
7 This would explain why the names of Midas (the 'Midas touch'), Gordius (the 'Gordian knot) or Croesus ('as rich as Croesus') are still household names for us, even though the peoples of which they were rulers have been long forgotten by now, and why Cyrus (Ciro), Darius (Dario) and Xerxes (Serse) are still used as first names in Italy.
8 See the *Persians* of Aeschylus, telling the tale of the Persian Wars from the perspective of the enemy who lost; a most amazing innovation.
9 Another good example for historiogenesis is the history of philosophy, going back to the school of Aristotle. Such a history assumed a singular point of origin in Thales; then progressed through an unbroken line of continuity, up to Socrates, Plato, the founding of the Academy and Aristotle. This history was further systematised by Hegel, in his *History of Philosophy*. This fact is of considerable significance, as Hegel always considered his *History of Philosophy* and *Philosophy of History* to be highly interrelated enterprises. It is not necessary therefore to look to the obscure Gnostic literature for the sources of Hegel's philosophy of history: the model is provided by cosmological historiogenesis, as carried over into Greek thought by Hesiod, Herodotus and Aristotle. Significantly, Diogenes Laertius lists Thales among the seven sages, the title 'first philosopher' being reserved for Anaximander. The biographical method is an important path to overcome historiogenesis. Unfortunately, Hegel beat Schleiermacher at the academic race, just as Rickert beat Dilthey.
10 On hubris, see the classic work of Louis Gernet (2001 [1917]), a main source of inspiration for Jean-Pierre Vernant, especially pp. 17–48, 189–216, 389–422.
11 The absence of a sustained discussion of Sophocles in Nietzsche and Voegelin identifies a crucial lacuna in the work of both thinkers. The contrast between the pristine order of Aeschylus and the decadence captured by Euripides is too easy, and – as Voegelin does not fail to mention – relies too closely on the contemporary evaluation of Aristophanes (OHII: 244–5). The plays of Sophocles, however, are so significant precisely because they present figures who struggle to keep the balance. Voegelin's charge that Sophocles only presents exceptional characters (*ibid*.: 252) is therefore not tenable, and is refuted in detail by the classic work of Knox (1957), published in the same year as OHII.
12 This would be singled out for attention in Voegelin's 1958 inaugural lecture (SPG). A year after its American publication, David Landes would publish a classic work on the history of Western technology under the title *Prometheus Bound* (Landes 1969).
13 Foucault would define freedom in a similar way.
14 It does not help, though, that Voegelin fails to mention this fact here, drawing the analogy between Aeschylus and Plato excessively close.

15 The fate of the Sophists, and later the Cynics, also indicates the manner in which the heroic victim of one persecution can become the persecutor or the corruptor in the next case, as the social and intellectual history of the twentieth century provides ample evidence.

16 These lines would become the proudly announced credo of Karl Marx at the end of his Preface to his doctoral thesis (see SPG).

17 Euripides first won first prize for his plays in 442 BC, the supposed year of the arrival of the Sophists in Athens.

18 The affinities between 'empirical' and 'imperial' would be well worth a study.

19 As a caricature of the idea of 'man as the measure', Plato presents Hippias and self-sufficiency.

20 The first year of the Peloponnesian War witnessed the first outbreak of plague in the ancient world. The disease is not fully identified (Herlihy 1997), but was certainly extremely traumatic. Arguably this disease was developed by Thucydides into a general theory of wars. On the crucial importance of plague for social and literary theory, see Girard (1978).

21 Exile is a liminal position. It is also not accidental that Voegelin draws the parallel with Machiavelli, who similarly wrote his chief works in exile.

22 Anaximander drew the first known map of the Greek world, with 'the outline of land and sea' (Diogenes Laertius: II, 1), which was only improved upon some fifty years later. In doing so, he relied on the relevant efforts of Thales in astronomy (Thrower 1996 [1972]: 19).

23 The point of Pierre Hadot that ancient philosophy was first of all a way of life is further illustrated by the fact that most philosophers have lived long lives, with at least six of the best known (apart from Xenophanes, Pythagoras, Gorgias, Democritus, Isocrates and Cleanthes) living for about 100 years.

24 Tradition assigns special significance to the date and place of birth of each. Aeschylus was supposed to be born in Eleusis, the place of the traditional mystery plays; Sophocles in Colonus, the legendary burial place of Oedipus, his main hero; while tradition claims that Euripides was born on 23 September 480 in Salamis, the exact date and place of the famous naval victory of Athens over the Persians.

25 The great Sophists did not come directly from Ionia, but from the Ionian diaspora of colonies: Protagoras from Abdera, in Thracia, and Gorgias from Lentini, in Sicily.

26 The respective birthdates are: Popper, Adorno and Parsons (1902), Sartre (1905), Bourdieu, Boudrillard and Habermas (1929), Derrida (1930).

27 Patocka, however, considers Democritus as a main philosopher of the care of the soul, together with Plato, and specifically warns against denigrating Democritus as a mere 'atomist' (Patocka 1983). See also his appendix entitled 'Democritus and Plato, founders of metaphysics'.

28 As a particularly striking parallel, Voegelin emphasises the manner in which the three key terms of Parmenides, way, truth and being, become incorporated into the Christian orbit in the famous passage of the fourth Gospel: 'I am the way, the truth, and the life' (John 14:6; see OHIII: 204).

29 This is the title of a classic work by Mircea Eliade (1954 [1949]). This work was often cited by Voegelin, while he showed no sign of having read Eliade's book on yoga.

30 This sheds further light on the implications of the hubris of Oedipus.

31 Voegelin alludes here to the strong affinity with Plato's later definition of philosophy in *Phaedrus* (278d) as a way towards wisdom and not its possession.

32 The difference is important, as the Christian-monastic hermeneutics of the self, diagnosed by Foucault, does not appear in Greek thought.

33 Voegelin frequently states that, in classical Greek, the isolated individual, living alone and thus deprived of the experience of participation, was called *idiotes*.

34 See also Patocka (1983: 100).

35 See OHIV: 191. Peculiarly, in OHIII Voegelin connects the term only to Aristotle.

36 As an entertaining piece of cultural history, in the Preface to the book Huizinga tells that the typesetters repeatedly 'corrected' the subtitle, so that even the published book has 'The Play Element *in* Culture'.

37 The comparison between liminality and play was a recurrent theme of Victor Turner, up to the subtitle of his last published book, 'The Human Seriousness of Play'.

38 'Anthropological sleep' was also a prominent theme in Foucault's work.

39 Etymological considerations provide further insights. Many of the terms used in the definitions of Voegelin, like 'passive', 'suffering' (as Latin *passio*), and further relevant terms like passion, but also pathetic and pathology, can all be traced back to the Greek 'pathos'. It also illuminates another aspect of liminality. This can be seen in the related Greek word 'patos', meaning a path, a trodden or beaten way, which is at the root of such English words as passage or path. The difference between *peira* and *patos* is that one is discovered, while the other is 'suffered', as rendered so plastically by the expression 'beaten path' or the term 'blazing of the trail', also central for Victor Turner.

40 A particularly revealing example of this occurs in his short reference to Schelling (OHIII: 193). In his discussion of the myth of creation by the Demiurge, Voegelin cannot avoid evoking the problem of Gnosticism. However, he does so by 'exteriorising' the charge for Schelling, ranked second only to Plato as a theorist of myth, but found guilty of Gnosticism. In my view, this entire argument should be considered as pinning down Voegelin's reading of Schelling at the point in which his own undertaking became side-tracked into an excessive interest in myth.

41 This evokes parallels with the work of Bourdieu on distinction.

7 Foucalt's historical method

1 Foucault's 1971 lectures were not available on tape in the Foucault Archives at the time of research. However, a condensed version of this analysis was repeated in the 1973 Rio lectures (DE139).

2 Here Foucault's reliance on the work of Elias is particularly evident.

3 The English version of Deleuze and Guattari's 1972 book appeared in 1977 with a Preface by Foucault.

4 The contrast between Foucault and Freud, in fact, starts from interpretive strategy. While Freud would emphasise the mythical element of the play, and was not concerned with the dramatic staging, Foucault, quite on the contrary, would express no interest in the myth, and would pursue solely the dynamics of the play (DEII: 554).

5 *Iliad* XXIII: 359.

6 In the English language is preserved up to the present day this aristocratic character of the legal procedure in the dual meaning of the word 'trial', while in German, at the opposite end, a legal trial is called *Prozess*.

7 Of the various interpretation of *Oedipus*, the excellent work of Bernard Knox (1957) pursues this line of interpretation, while emphasising also how this fitted into the victorious march of the 'scientific spirit' of the time and place, fifth-century BC Athens. At several points Foucault's interpretation follows Knox so closely that it is likely that Knox's book was a main source for Foucault. It is therefore all the more surprising that in his interpretation Foucault fails to bring out other points of correspondence between Knox's argument and his own work. Apart from the link between legal and scientific reasoning, that could have come close to Foucault's interest in 'power/knowledge', Knox also emphasises the way in which Oedipus consistently, along a series of dimensions, changed from the 'subject' of the inquiry into its 'object', a concern that is at the heart of *The Order of Things*.

8 While Foucault, following an entire line of interpreters, identifies Tiresias as a prophet, this has problems in a Weberian terminology. Tiresias was obviously neither an ethical, nor an exemplary, prophet, but rather an old-fashioned diviner.

9 Even the incest; see lines 366–7.

10 In fact, this is – at least up to a point – the interpretation of Knox, who is reading Oedipus as a character dominated by hubris, and representing in this sense not the usurper or the tyrant, which at that time was already a character of the past, but rather the average citizen of contemporary Athens, more specifically the Sophists who wanted to make 'man the measure of things' (Knox 1957: 109, 184), against which Knox refers to the Platonic maxim of God being the measure of things (*ibid.*: 184), which is also the message of Sophocles. In his milestone work *Tragedy and Civilization*, Charles Segal also refers to this same passage of *Protagoras*, adding that at the same time man 'became more exposed to the violent, irrational urges of his own nature. As creatures of men, the institutions of civilization, the *nomoi*, lost their privileged sanctity as the work of gods,' and became more perishable (Segal 1981: 5–6). As we saw in Chapter 6, this passage also had a particular significance for Voegelin.

11 See DEII: 562, 567; see also Knox 1957: 127. Foucault is even making use of the composite name as 'one who is knowing with his feet', i.e. as somebody who gained knowledge through travels and wandering. Segal argues that the name Oedipus translated as 'know-foot' recalls the answer given to the Sphinx (Segal 1981: 207).

12 See DEII: 566, and also Knox 1957: 124–5.

13 Knox 1957: 117–20. The word inquiry (*enquête*) is central for Foucault's entire 1971 course, and *zetema* would also be widely used in the Collège de France lectures of the 1980s.

14 See DEII: 566–7; see also Knox 1957: 129–31.

15 One might wonder whether Foucault was influenced by Girard's reading of the play as being all about violence. It might be relevant in this regard that Foucault would distinguish between power and violence in his 1979 Stanford lecture. At that time Girard (and also Voegelin) was in Stanford.

16 To mention only one counter-factual: in what way did Oedipus promote his claim to power by blinding himself?

17 This point is repeatedly pursued by Knox (1957: 110, 162), and was central to Voegelin.

18 Knox's analysis of the arrogance and hubris of the tyrant is one of the central, and recurrent, themes in his interpretation. The famous passage of the chorus, 'Violence and pride engenders the tyrant' (line 873) is quoted repeatedly throughout the book (see, e.g., Knox 1957: 53, 102), and at one point he states that just in the first part of the play, line end fourteen and line fifteen begin with the pronouns 'I', 'mine', or one of their derivatives (*ibid.*: 21).

19 Foucault Archives, C62 2 and 3 (for details of the Archives, see Chapter 8 Note 2 on page 256 below).

20 This disobedience in a way only mirrored the attempt of the royals to escape the divine commandment, which in the older version, told for example by Aeschylus, implied outright disobedience, as there the oracle warned Laius not to have any offspring.

21 Foucault took this term, in the sense of a 'liturgy of truth', linked to the exercise of power, from Heraclides, a philosopher living in the fourth and third centuries BC (referred to in the lecture of 9 January 1980).

22 Given the importance the plague plays in *Discipline and Punish*, it is quite astonishing that Foucault made no use of this image in his analysis.

23 In spite of similarities, the two levels of Girard's analysis are different from the three levels identified by Foucault, and Girard is not using the *symbolon* motive either for the fitting of the two halves.

24 About this, see also Burkert (1983).

25 Girard also explicitly states that he has no interest in the drama aspect.

26 Leuret's name is absent from the original (1954) edition of *Maladie Mentale et Psychologie*, and is not in the bibliography of *Histoire de folie* (1972 [1961]), but a short reference is contained in the second edition of *Maladie Mentale et Personnalité*, pp. 85–6.

27 For a detailed analysis of this moment, see Szakolczai (1998: 213–16).

28 See the James lectures (DE295; for the English original, see Foucault 1981), the Dartmouth lectures (Foucault 1993), and the Howison lectures (Foucault Archives, D2 (1–2)). These lectures were based on the same notes (see Blasius 1993: 198).

29 See Foucault Archives, D201.

30 That the publication of the 'Sexuality and Solitude' piece, based on his James lectures, was not supervised by Foucault is shown by the fact that Leuret's name is consistently misspelled there as 'Louren' (Foucault 1981: 3).

31 '[C]e passage de Leuret m'a frappé' (Foucault Archives, D201, p. 3).

32 See Foucault Archives, D201.

33 See Foucault 1972 [1961], Chapter 4.

34 It was at the same period that Foucault published his seminal essay on 'The Politics of Health in the Eighteenth Century' (DE168), his contribution to the collective volume 'Les machines à guérir'.

35 On the question of the links between recognition and identity, see Pizzorno (1987, 1991, 2000), and also Della Porta, Greco and Szakolczai (2000).

36 Foucault Archives, D201, p.3.

37 Foucault Archives, D201, p.9.

38 'I baptise you with water: but there standeth one among you, whom ye know not;...he which baptiseth with the Holy Ghost' (John 2:26, 33; see also Matt. 3:11–16, Mark 1:7–11, Luke 3:16–22).

39 Matt. 28:18–19, and John 20:22–3.

40 Acts 1:2,5,8; 2:4.

41 Foucault discusses 'metanoia' and its Latin translation 'penitentia', and also 'epistrophe' and 'conversion'.

42 For example it is reputed of the remark made about Seneca that he often talked as if he were a Christian.

43 See English 'doubt', Italian 'dubbio', German 'Zweifel' or Hungarian 'kétség'.

8 The Socratic Moment as philosophical parrhesia

1 A typescript of this volume is deposited at the Foucault Archives, but is not available for consultation. However, in the late 1980s and early 1990s a few researchers were allowed to take a look. This copy seems to be a rough draft, with a large number of major orthographical errors, evidently never read by Foucault. There also seems to exist a more polished copy, with Foucault's last corrections, but this is in the possession of Foucault's family and is not available for research.

2 These courses, with some gaps, were available on tape in the Foucault Archives from the late 1980s onwards. In the Archives, they can be found under the following catalogue numbers: 1980 course – C62; 1981 – C63; 1982 – C65; 1983 – C68; 1984 – C69. In the book, the individual lectures will be identified by their date of delivery. Written publication is underway; so far the 1975, 1976 and 1982 courses have been published. A final remark: as Foucault only taught between January and Easter, I will only identify the courses by their actual year of delivery. Thus, the (formally) 1981–82 course, delivered in between January and March 1982, will be called the 1982 course.

3 See CF82: 7–10, and also the course outline (*ibid.*: 473).

4 It is contained in the first hour of the third lecture of 1984, 15 February 1984. The first two lectures only reviewed material discussed in the past year.

5 In this second part of the lecture Foucault relies on the interpretation recently given by Georges Dumézil on the last words of Socrates. The subject matter, the tone and

style of delivery, and the place of the course in Foucault's work and life each clearly indicate that this analysis is highly autobiographical, even testamentary.

6 See, e.g., the Egyptian '*ma'at*', analysed in Chapter 5, or the Persian '*asha*'. But even a contemporary language like Hungarian can be evoked, as the word '*igaz*' originally stood for both 'true' and 'just', and it is only relatively recently that the word '*igazságos*' (literally 'truthful', but meaning 'just') emerged to differentiate between the two meanings.

7 See the lecture of 2 February 1983, first hour.

8 See the pioneering work of Thorkild Jacobsen, as referred to in Frankfort (1948: 215–21).

9 Still within the context of foundation, this evokes comparisons with Zeus's rape of Europa.

10 It is worthwhile recalling here that the Book of Job, composed around the same time, poses the same problem of an increasing 'self-consciousness' of God(s), related to human suffering, as opposed to the previous attitude of ignorance, or cruel innocence.

11 See also Meier (1987).

12 See the first hour of the fifth lecture of 1983.

13 See the very end of the second hour of the fifth lecture of 1983.

14 In fact, one of the most important definitions of the concept of problematisation by Foucault was given exactly at this juncture of the 1983 Berkeley seminars (DV: 48–9).

15 See the 1982 Toronto lectures in the Foucault Archives.

16 Vernant here uses the work of Rohde, one of Nietzsche's childhood friends; and of Cornford, a major source for Voegelin.

17 Affinities with these ideas can be seen in the Hermes and Orpheus myths, both central for the links between Greek mythology and philosophy.

18 To close the circle, about the Indian parallels of the Cynics with the Pasupatas, and their joint shamanistic origins, see Ingalls (1962), an article mentioned by Foucault in his 1984 lectures.

19 As the English version is based on the 1987 second edition, I will mostly use the French third edition of Hadot (1993).

20 In this respect it is important to point out that all four thinkers discussed in the paragraphs above belong to the same great World War Two generation, being born between 1920 and 1927 (Hadot in 1922, Voelke in 1925, Foucault in 1926 and Domanski in 1927). They also had a strong awareness of the contemporary relevance of their work and approach. In his inaugural lecture Voelke defined philosophy as 'an activity that aims to give an account of our experience', using rational discourse (Voelke 1993: 18), while in the 1997 Postface to his first book Hadot draws parallels between the Absolute, its Presence and the present moment (1997 [1963]: 201).

21 It should be added here that just a few pages previously Hadot provides an emphatic interpretation of the figure of the philosopher, referring to the same *Symposium*, that 'for Diotima, Eros is thus a philo-sopher, because his is half-way between (*mi-chemin*) *sophia* and ignorance' (Hadot 1995a: 77), referring exactly to the passage where Voegelin found the metaxy.

22 It is rather typical, though deplorable, of French academic life that in the work of Hadot no reference is made to Patocka, introduced in France by Paul Ricoeur.

23 It should be noted here that, while the seminars were given in the summer of 1973 in Prague, at a new height of the Cold War, Patocka repeatedly alludes to the interpretation of Girard, published just the year before, showing the remarkable intellectual curiosity of the then 66-year-old philosopher.

24 Though not mentioned again, this is also central for Kerenyi's perspective on myths. Kerenyi's work is discussed in some detail in Chapter 9.

25 Unfortunately, it is not possible here to continue a discussion of Patocka's ideas. We can only signal that his discussion of Democritus lays the basis of a thorough reassess-

ment of the link between the question of the knowledge of nature and the care of the self among the phusiologists, integrating the various hypotheses on the origins of the spiritual exercises in shamanism or in yoga; and also the question of the axial age. This latter is all the more plausible as Patocka identifies the specificity of Athenian philosophy in the principle of freedom, as developed in the context of the Persian Wars, thus close to the Foucaldian concern with parrhesia and the perspective developed in Chapters 6 and 8 of this book.

26 See Hadot (1993: 77–116), and (1995a: 46–85). The first version, originally delivered in 1974 for the Eranos circle, is much more powerful, due to its organisation and also to the more systematic references to Kierkegaard and Nietzsche. Hadot evidently was adversely affected by the lack of a proper recognition for this work by the audience (Hadot 2001: 66), and quite rightly, as the paper is a major *tour de force*, and the Jungian circle should have been the audience to recognise its merits.

27 This has close affinities with Foucauldian methodology.

28 About this, see Kerenyi (1984: 104–8).

29 The Greek *kore* and the Latin *pupilla* both mean 'little girl', 'daughter' and 'doll'.

30 The book was printed on 5 January 1984.

31 Increasing the suspense, in a letter to the editor published in the book Dumézil claims that the first part should really be entitled 'System of the World, Volume One'.

32 We should not forget that *Phaedo* is the dialogue where Socrates (or Plato) formulated his doctrine about the immortality of the soul.

33 Just before his death, in June 1985, Dumézil listened to this lecture on tape and was then interviewed by Eliane Allo (Dumézil 1986). While in his first impressions he expressed some doubts about the connections made by Foucault, he then improvised an etymological analysis of the Indo-European root 'mel', revising immediately his first judgement and supporting Foucault's intuition. The original meaning of 'care' would lie in the experience when somebody suddenly discovers that a thing that previously was external to him becomes important, a member (*melos*) or part of himself. Taking the point further, this experience is complementary with the experience of participation, singled out as central by Voegelin, Turner and Colin Turnbull.

34 It is worth mentioning that Foucault got loud applause after this lecture, which was not at all a practice of the Collège de France.

35 The Sophists were not discussed separately, though Foucault's repeated and valorised contrast between parrhesia and rhetoric also implies a position taken up, quite similarly to Voegelin, for the parrhesiastic philosopher and against the rhetorician Sophist.

36 See Paquet (1992: 108). The expression was quoted by Nietzsche (1999: 69) and Hadot (1993: 101, fn. 92).

37 One can argue that under such conditions a democratic assembly is transformed into a persecuting crowd (Szakolczai 2001a: 380).

38 This is actually postponed until the last lecture.

39 This point is also discussed by Gadamer and Voegelin.

40 These concerns are also repeated at the start of Letter Seven.

41 The term repeatedly used by Foucault is *frottement*, or the 'rubbing' of ideas upon each other.

42 This is the end of side A of tape C68 (10), and its obverse, side B, is empty. However, at the start of the lecture Foucault complained that he still had the flu, and it might be that the lecture was finished earlier than usual.

43 For a rare exception, see Rajchman (1985).

44 This may have been the first time Foucault used the term that would later identify his entire approach. One could add that Foucault may have been influenced here by Weber's categorisation of the three modes of *Wertrationalität*: religious, ethical and aesthetical.

45 From an Eliasian perspective, this hostility to the sense of shame shows at once their anti-civilisational and 'modern' character. In fact, this same point shows for Ingalls (1962: 297) the shamanistic or 'uncivilised' origins of the Cynics.

46 This also recalls Cartesian thought, where the problem is not simply the dualism of body and mind, but rather the omission of soul, spirit or beauty.

47 See the lecture of 2 February 1984, end of first hour, Foucault Archives, tape C69 (6).

48 It is striking how the figure of Georg Lukács, rendered timeless by Thomas Mann as Naphta in *The Magic Mountain*, unites the three figures: the Heidelberg aesthete, becoming a Bolshevik revolutionary, yet nevertheless extolling the virtues of the most extreme forms of medieval asceticism.

49 This theme would be taken up and elaborated in detail in HS2.

50 This served the purpose of showing a similar 'pedigree' for Diogenes as for Socrates.

51 Examples include the performance of all bodily functions in public, and writing two tragedies in praise of incest and cannibalism.

52 One should keep in mind that not a single saying or act of Diogenes can be considered as authentic, thus he is a 'truly mythical figure' (Klassen 1996: 254, fn. 101).

53 End of the first hour of the lecture of 21 March 1984.

54 At this point, one might wonder why Foucault could not simply spell out the obvious: that he fully adheres here to Weber's interpretation of 'inner-worldly asceticism'.

55 This can be taken as a reinterpretation, within philosophy, of the idea of *Discipline and Punish*, that war is politics waged by other means.

56 The parallels between this idea and the self-characterisation of members of the Communist Party apparatus are remarkable (Horvath and Szakolczai 1992).

9 Hellenistic–Roman parrhesia

1 In this sense, the religious equivalents of the Stoics are the Gnostics. It is a great pity that neither Foucault, nor Voegelin, made a sustained attempt to study the joint emergence of these types of thought in the early Hellenistic period.

2 See in this regard Foucault's discussion of Philon on the Therapeutes, identified with the Essenes (CF82: 112–13).

3 Foucault also discussed briefly the Cynics. This, however, has been integrated in Chapter 8.

4 Kerenyi (1897–1973) is widely considered as having written a classic in the field of mythology. He was strongly influenced by the work of C.G. Jung, and the correspondence between Jung, Kerenyi and Thomas Mann is a most fascinating document of the intellectual history of the period. Kerenyi belongs to the same great World War One generation, being born in the same year as Elias or Frankfurt and a year before Dumézil or Schutz. Together with his friend, Béla Hamvas (1897–1968), they founded in 1935 in Budapest a journal entitled *Sziget* (Island), in which they attempted to revitalise and reinvigorate Hungarian cultural life, in the general situation of crisis in the Central Europe of the mid-1930s. Several of the most important figures of Hungarian intellectual life of the period contributed to the journal which, however, foundered after the first two volumes. After this, their lives were separated. Kerenyi became increasingly detached from Hungarian intellectual life, decided to publish only abroad, and in 1943 left the country forever, settling down in Switzerland. Hamvas, however, opted for an internal emigration, first becoming a librarian, and with the Communist takeover forced to work as a stock-keeper in the plants of a desolate new 'socialist town'. Kerenyi's book appeared in 1942, thus in a highly liminal moment: during World War Two, and at the time that Kerenyi was finalising his exit from Hungary. It was at precisely this same moment that Hamvas

finished the first version of his *Scientia Sacra*, which began with his own account of the axial age, and then gave a *tour de force* systematic analysis of the wisdom contained in the sacred books of the world, especially the archaic ones – a work that can only be compared in its depth and scope to the work of the Rumanian Mircea Eliade (1907–97), who finished his first major work, *The Myth of the Eternal Return*, at the same time; and who gained a position in Paris, in 1945, and through the assistance of Georges Dumézil. In my reading of Kerenyi I was greatly assisted by the work of Agnes Horvath (1997,1998, 2000).

5 Nietzsche was a decisive formative influence upon both Kerenyi and Hamvas.
6 Kerenyi also compares and contrasts Hermes with Prometheus, concerning their relationship to sacrifices (Kerenyi 1984: 41), or – implicitly – in the role of enlightening (*ibid.*: 104). We should note here that books devoted to these four figures take up the main junctures of Kerenyi's work, marking the inner dynamics of the oeuvre. His work on Apollo, published in 1937, just after the foundering of *Sziget*, was his first book; he published a book devoted to Prometheus in 1946, just after World War Two; while *Dionysus*, his last book, appeared posthumously in 1974.
7 In a book devoted to modernity one should mention here that, on the basis of all these concerns, Hermes could well be nominated as the god of modernity, as his various tasks present a complete inventory of the values of modernity: science, commerce (especially enterprise), the communicative and mediatic use of language, and the emphasis on comfort. The only exception is the last, and most central, of the Hermetic tasks. One may wonder, though, whether *all* the previous aspects, taken together, in modernity, do not perform exactly the function of the 'stealing of the soul'.
8 The etymology of door (*porta*) is traced to the same root 'per'.
9 The text was discussed in the tenth course of 1980, introducing the crucial concept of *exagoreusis*; in the last lecture of 1982, to indicate the links to Christianity; and also in the 1982 Vermont seminars (Foucault 1988).
10 This language in itself immediately suggests interesting modern parallels, with the close affinity between 'enlightening' and commercial marketing strategies, explaining why a most lethal and intolerable form of modern life is at the same time the most difficult, evidently impossible, to be got rid of.
11 As the very term 'Cynic', developed as an insult but characteristically accepted by the Cynics as a self-designation, meant dog-like, the term 'barking' is not at all out of place here.
12 Foucault uses Letter 52 of Seneca, but argues that this was a philosophical commonplace at the time. One should also note the particular significance of the term for Foucault, given starting from the 'ship of fools', or *Stultifera navis*, in *Histoire de folie*.
13 See also Noica (1993), another major East European dissident thinker practising philosophy as a way of life, a university friend of Eliade.
14 As the comments on parrhesia have already been integrated into this chapter, this is the place to insert the more detailed remarks on *paraskeue*.
15 Just as Hadot used Goethe to analyse spirituality, Foucault refers here to Faust (CF82: 296–7). See also the end of the lecture of 7 March 1984, Foucault Archives, C69 (7).
16 This point would be inserted into and elaborated in HS3.
17 One may wonder here whether we are actually living in the period where the possession of these skills could no longer be taken for granted, due to TV, video, etc.
18 This theme was already discussed in detail in the first hour of the eighth lecture, alluding again to the intermediate position between classical philosophy and Christianity. Of particular importance is the metaphor of the money-changer, discussed in the detail in Foucault's lectures on the Cynics in 1984, and on Cassian in 1980.

19 As this lecture was not available in the Foucault Archives, I was not able to use these ideas when developing my concept of 'permanent liminality' (Szakolczai 2000).
20 The project to which Foucault alludes here is identical with the project sketched by Weber in the 'Anticritical Last Word' (Weber 1978).
21 For the text, see Penella (2000: 107). For an insightful interpretation that will be closely followed here, see Konstan (1996: 16–19).
22 Here I rely on the works of Monica Greco (1998) and Knut Mittendorfer (2000).

10 Christian parrhesia

1 At the start of his presentation Foucault states that his account will be largely based on Schlier (1954) and Marrow (1982).
2 The identity with the Weberian definition of charisma is striking.
3 This is image central for seventeenth-century Protestants and Jansenists, singled out for attention by Weber and Borkenau.
4 For the following discussion, see especially Jaeger (1957: 223–5), Klassen (1996: 234–9), and Scarpat (2001 [1964]: 89–93).
5 The exact Hebrew word meant 'to rise up' (Jaeger 1957: 223).
6 The yoke would become a fundamental 'living metaphor' for later prophets, exactly to chastise the overconfidence of the 'people' and its 'leaders' (see especially Jer. 27:2, 28:10–13). The etymology of the word 'yoga' is yoke.
7 One could conjecture here that perhaps the short way of this transfer lay through the trips of Plato to the courts of Sicily.
8 One should note here that this passage was written more recently than the New Testament (Scarpat 2001 [1964]: 104).
9 The mythical centrality of this anti-Babel theme in the Abraham story, that immediately follows the Babel Tower episode, was already emphasised in Chapter 5.
10 According to Winter, the 'strange emphasis on David's burial…suggests an allusion to Pericles' funeral oration' (1996: 189); a conjecture all the more likely as at another place in Acts a reference to the text of Thucydides is even incorporated in the standard edition of the Greek New Testament (*ibid.*).
11 See here Klassen 1996: 243, fn. 61.
12 This is not surprising, as it corresponds to the general characteristics of Johannine thought, i.e. the use of triads instead of dichotomies.
13 This is of considerable importance, as it is a main source of eschatological expectations, indicating a tight connection between parrhesia and eschatology, brought out in the Johannine works.
14 In German, both meanings are expressed with the same root ('offen' and 'öffentlich'), together with the much-related term 'evidently' ('offensichtlich'). It should be noted that according to Foucault, it was exactly the parrhesiastic game that was substituted by Descartes in philosophy with the search for 'evidence' (see the end of the last lecture of 1983).
15 See van Unnik (1962) vs Winter (1996).
16 With the exception of John (11:14), translated by the similar term *manifeste*.
17 Among the other four cases of *palam*, the most significant is its appearance in the very first sentence of the Book of Revelations.
18 The success of this parrhesiastic speech is immediately vindicated: at 26:28 king Agrippa assures Paul that he almost made him a Christian.
19 One should add here that Foucault's analysis of the New Testament in the last 1984 lecture also ends with the last word of this Letter.
20 Here I will closely follow the excellent analysis of Mitchell (1996).
21 As another indication of the neglect of the significance of parrhesia, it is worthwhile pointing out that Lindars failed to pay attention to the term parrhesia, though according to Mitchell this would have helpfully complemented his argument (Mitchell 1996: 225).

22 The significance can even be extended in time: Heraclitus, the philosopher who was widely credited to have 'discovered' the soul in the context of Greek thought, was also from Ephesus, and the Johannine community is often identified as a main source of Gnostic perfectionism.

23 One could argue that even such a preference has its own significance as, apart from Foucault, both Voegelin and – even more surprisingly – Weber expressed a clear inclination towards mysticism.

Conclusion

1 Following hints from Victor Turner, this concept was introduced in Szakolczai (2000: 215–26). For similar contemporary approaches, see Bauman (2000) and Sennett (1998).

References

Agamben, G. (1998) *Homo Sacer*, Stanford: Stanford University Press.

Assmann, J. (1997) *Moses the Egyptian: The Memory of Egypt in Western Monotheism*, Cambridge, MA: Harvard University Press.

—— (2001 [1990]) *Ma'at: Gerechtigkeit und Unsterblichkeit im Alten Ägypten*, Munich: Beck.

—— (2001) ' "Axial" Breakthroughs and Semantic "Transactions" in Ancient Egypt and Israel'. Paper presented for the Conference on the 'Axial Age', 17–18 December 2001, European University Institute, Florence.

Barth, M.K. (1993) 'The Letter of Paul to the Ephesians'. In B.M. Metzger and M.D. Coogan (eds) *The Oxford Companion to the Bible*, Oxford: Oxford University Press.

Bauman, Z. (2000) *Liquid Modernity*, Cambridge: Polity Press.

Benedict, R. (1934) *The Patterns of Culture*, New York: New American Library.

Betz, H.D. (1994) 'Jesus and the Cynics: Survey and Analysis of a Hypothesis'. *The Journal of Religion* 453–75.

Blasius, M. (1993) 'Introductory Note'. *Political Theory* 21: 198–200.

Blumenberg, H. (1983) *The Legitimacy of Modernity*, Cambridge, MA: The MIT Press.

Borkenau, F. (1981) *End and Beginning: On the Generations of Cultures and the Origins of the West*, New York: Columbia University Press.

Burkert, W. (1983) *Homo Necans: The Anthropology of Ancient Greek Sacrificial Ritual and Myth*, Berkeley: University of California Press.

Camic, C. (1992) 'Reputation and Predecessor Selection: Parsons and the Institutionalists'. *American Sociological Review* 57, 4: 421–45.

Clark, T. (ed.) (1969) *Gabriel Tarde on Communication and Social Influence*, Chicago: University of Chicago Press.

Clavel, M. (1975) *Ce que je crois*, Paris: Grasset.

Cohn, N. (1970) *The Pursuit of the Millenium*, London: Paladin.

—— (1993) *Cosmos, Chaos and the World to Come: The Ancient Roots of Apocalyptic Faith*, New Haven: Yale University Press.

Couliano, I.P. (1992) *The Tree of Gnosis*, San Francisco: HarperCollins.

d'Hauterive, R.G. (1948) *Dictionnaire des racines des langues européennes*, Paris: Larousse.

Davidson, A. (1995) 'Introduction: Pierre Hadot and the Spiritual Phenomenon of Ancient Philosophy'. In P. Hadot *Philosophy as a Way of Life*, Cambridge: Cambridge University Press.

Della Porta, D., Greco, M. and Szakolczai, A. (eds) (2000) *Identità, riconoscimento e scambio: Saggi in onore di Alessandro Pizzorno*, Bari: Laterza.

Diamond, J. (1998) *Guns, Germs and Steel: A Short History of Everybody for the Last 13,000 Years*, London: Vintage.

Diogenes Laertius (1925) *The Lives of Eminent Philosophers*, London: Heinemann.

Domanski, J. (1996) *La philosophie, théorie ou manière de vivre?*, Fribourg: Editions Universitaires Fribourg.

Dreyfus, H.L. and Rabinow, P. (1983) *Michel Foucault: Beyond Structuralism and Hermeneutics*, Chicago: University of Chicago Press.

Dumézil, G. (1958) *L'idéologie tripartie des Indo-Européens*, Bruxelles: Latomus.

—— (1970) *Archaic Roman Religion*, Chicago: University of Chicago Press.

—— (1984) *Divertissement sur les dernières paroles de Socrate*, Paris: Gallimard.

—— (1986) 'Entretien'. *Actes de la recherche en sciences sociales*, 83–8.

—— (1987) *Entretiens avec Didier Eribon*, Paris: Gallimard.

—— (1992) *Mythes et dieux des indo-européens*, Paris: Flammarion.

—— (1995) *Mythe et épopée*, Paris: Hachette.

Dupront, A. (1987) *Du sacré: croisades et pèlerinages*, Paris: Gallimard.

Dutripon, F. P. (1976) *Bibliorum Sacrorum Concordantiae*. Hildesheim: Georg Olms.

Eisenstadt, S.N. (1963) *The Political Systems of Empires*, New York: The Free Press.

—— (ed.) (1986) *The Origins and Diversity of Axial Age Civilisations*, New York: The SUNY Press.

—— (1995) *Power, Trust and Meaning*, Chicago: University of Chicago Press.

—— (1999) *Fundamentalism, Sectarianism and Revolution*, Cambridge: Cambridge University Press.

—— (2000) 'Multiple Modernities'. *Daedalus* 129: 1–29.

Eliade, M. (1954 [1949]) *The Myth of the Eternal Return, or, Cosmos and History*, Princeton: Princeton University Press.

—— (1969 [1954]) *Yoga, Immortality and Freedom*, Princeton: Princeton University Press.

Elias, N. (1983 [1969]) *The Court Society*, Oxford: Blackwell.

—— (1987a) *Involvement and Detachment*, Oxford: Blackwell.

—— (1987b) 'The Retreat of Sociologists into the Present'. *Theory, Culture and Society* 4: 223–47.

—— (1987c) 'The Changing Balance of Power between the Sexes – A Process–Sociological Study: The Example of the Ancient Roman State'. *Theory, Culture and Society* 4: 287–317.

—— (2000 [1939]) *The Civilising Process*, Oxford: Blackwell.

Engberg-Pedersen, T. (1996) 'Plutarch to Prince Philopappus on How to Tell a Flatterer from a Friend'. In J.T. Fitzgerald (ed.) *Friendship, Flattery and Freedom of Speech: Studies on Friendship in the New Testament World*, Leiden: E.J. Brill.

Eribon, D. (1991) *Michel Foucault*, Cambridge, MA: Harvard University Press.

Fitzgerald, J.T. (1996) 'Philippians in the Light of Some Ancient Discussions of Friendship'. In J.T. Fitzgerald (ed.) *Friendship, Flattery and Freedom of Speech: Studies on Friendship in the New Testament World*, Leiden: E.J. Brill.

Foucault, M. (1972 [1961]) *Histoire de la folie à l'âge classique*, Paris: Gallimard.

—— (1981) 'Sexuality and Solitude'. *New York Review of Books*, 3–7.

—— (1988) *Technologies of the Self*, London: Tavistock.

—— (1993) 'About the Beginning of the Hermeneutics of the Self'. *Political Theory* 21, 198–227.

Frankfort, H. (1948) *Kingship and the Gods*, Chicago: The University of Chicago Press.

—— et al (1949) *Before Philosophy*, Harmondsworth: Penguin.

Fredrickson, D.E. (1996) 'Parrhesia in the Pauline Epistles'. In J.T. Fitzgerald (ed.) *Friendship, Flattery and Freedom of Speech: Studies on Friendship in the New Testament World*, Leiden: E.J. Brill.

Fritz, K. von (1954) *The Theory of the Mixed Constitution in Antiquity: A Critical Analysis of Polybios' Political Ideas*, New York: Columbia University Press.

Gadamer, H.-G. (1975 [1959]) *Truth and Method*, London: Sheed and Ward.
—— (1976) 'The Universality of the Hermeneutical Problem'. In H.-G. Gadamer, *Philosophical Hermeneutics*, Berkeley: University of California Press.
Gernet, L. (2001 [1917]) *Recherches sur le développement de la pensée juridique et morale en Grèce*, Paris: Albin Michel.
Giesen, B. (2002) *Trauma and Triumph*, Chicago: University of Chicago Press.
Girard, R. (1972) *Violence et le sacré*, Paris: Grasset.
—— (1978) *Double Business Bound*, Baltimore: The Johns Hopkins University Press.
—— (1982) *Le bouc émissaire*, Paris: Grasset.
—— (1994) *Quand ces choses commenceront*, Paris: Arlea.
—— (1996) *The Girard Reader*, New York: Crossroad.
Glad, C.E. (1996) 'Frank Speech, Flattery, and Friendship in Philodemus'. In J.T. Fitzgerald (ed.) *Friendship, Flattery and Freedom of Speech: Studies on Friendship in the New Testament World*, Leiden: E.J. Brill.
Goldman, H. (1988) *Max Weber and Thomas Mann: Calling and the Shaping of the Self*, Berkeley: University of California Press.
—— (1992) *Politics, Death and the Devil: Self and Power in Max Weber and Thomas Mann*, Berkeley: University of California Press.
Gordon, C. (1991) 'Introduction'. In G. Burchell, C. Gordon and P. Miller (eds) *The Foucault Effect: Studies in Governmentality, with two lectures by and an interview with Michel Foucault*, London: Harvester Wheatsheaf.
Greco, M. (1998) *Illness as a Work of Thought: A Foucauldian Perspective on Psychosomatics*, London: Routledge.
Guenther, M. (1999) *Tricksters and Trancers: Bushman Religion and Society*, Bloomington: Indiana University Press.
Hadot, P. (1993) *Exercices spirituels et philosophie antique*, Paris: Institut d'études Augustiniennes.
—— (1995a) *Philosophy as a Way of Life*, Cambridge: Cambridge University Press.
—— (1995b) *Qu'est-ce que la philosophie antique?*, Paris: Gallimard.
—— (1997 [1963]) *Plotin ou la simplicité du regard*, Paris: Gallimard.
—— (2001) *La philosophie comme manière de vivre: Entretiens avec Jeannie Carlier et Arnold Davidson*, Paris: Albin Michel.
Hamvas, B. (1995) *Scientia Sacra*, 3 vols, Szentendre: Medio.
Hänsch, A. (2000) 'Symbolic Orders of Childbirth'. PhD thesis, European University Institute, Florence, Italy.
Heidegger, M. (1977) *Basic Writings*, New York: Harper and Row.
Hennis, W. (1988) *Max Weber: Essays in Reconstruction*, London: Allen and Unwin.
Herlihy, D. (1997) *The Black Death and the Transformation of the West*, Cambridge, MA: Harvard University Press.
Hirschman, A.O. (1977) *The Passions and the Interests*, Princeton: Princeton University Press.
Hollweck, T.A. and Caringella, P. (1990) 'Editors' Introduction'. In E. Voegelin *What Is History? And Other Late Unpublished Writings*, Baton Rouge: LSU Press.
Homer (1924–25) *The Iliad and the Odyssey*, London: Heinemann.
Horvath, A. (1997) 'The Political Psychology of Trickster-Clown: An Analytical Experiment Around Communism as a Myth'. Working Papers, SPS Department, Florence.
—— (1998) 'Tricking into the Position of the Outcast'. *Political Psychology* 19: 331–47.
—— (2000) 'The Nature of the Trickster's Game: An Interpretive Understanding of Communism'. PhD thesis, European University Institute, Florence, Italy.
Horvath, A. and Szakolczai, A. (1992) *The Dissolution of Communist Power: The Case of Hungary*, London: Routledge.

Hubert, H. and Mauss, M. (1968 [1902]) 'Essai sur la nature et la fonction du sacrifice'. In M. Mauss *Oeuvres I*, Paris, Minuit.

Huizinga, J. (1955) *Homo Ludens*, Boston: Beacon Press.

—— (1968) *Dutch Civilisation in the Seventeenth Century and Other Essays*, London: Collins.

—— (1990 [1924]) *The Waning of the Middle Ages*, Harmondsworth: Penguin.

Ingalls, D. (1962) 'Cynics and Pasupatas: The Seeking of Dishonor'. *Harvard Theological Review* 55: 281–98.

Jaeger, H. (1957) 'Parrésia et fiducia'. *Studia Patristica* 1: 221–39.

Jaspers, K. (1951 [1931]) *Man in the Modern Age*, London: Routledge.

—— (1953 [1949]) *The Origin and Goal of History*, New Haven: Yale University Press.

Jebb, R.C. (1887) 'Introduction'. In Sophocles, *Oedipus King*, Cambridge: Cambridge University Press.

Jonas, H. (1958) *The Gnostic Religion*, Boston: Beacon Press.

Kerenyi, K. (1984 [1942]) *Hermész, a lélekvezető: Az élet férfi eredetének mitologémája* (Hermes, the guide of the souls: The mythologem of the male origins of life), Budapest: Európa.

Klassen, W. (1996) 'Parrhesia in the Johannine Corpus'. In J.T. Fitzgerald (ed.) *Friendship, Flattery and Freedom of Speech: Studies on Friendship in the New Testament World*, Leiden: E.J. Brill.

Knemeyer, F.L. (1980) 'Police'. *Economy and Society* 9: 172–96.

Knox, B. (1957) *Oedipus at Thebes*, London: Oxford University Press.

Konstan, D. (1996) 'Friendship, Frankness and Flattery'. In J.T. Fitzgerald (ed.) *Friendship, Flattery and Freedom of Speech: Studies on Friendship in the New Testament World*, Leiden: E.J. Brill.

Koselleck, R. (1985) *Futures Past: On the Semantics of Historical Time*, Cambridge, MA: The MIT Press.

—— (1988 [1959]) *Critique and Crisis*, Oxford: Berg.

Landes, D. (1969) *The unbound Prometheus: Technological Change and Industrial Development in Western Europe from 1750 to the Present*, London: Cambridge University Press.

Liddell, H.G. and Scott, R. (1961) *A Greek–English Lexicon*, Oxford: Clarendon Press.

Lowith, K. (1949) *Meaning in History*, Chicago: University of Chicago Press.

—— (1988) *La mia vita in Germania prima e dopo il 1933*, Milan: Il Saggiatore.

Marrow, S.B. (1982) 'Parrhésia and the New Testament'. *The Catholic Biblical Quarterly* 44: 431–46.

Mauss, M. (1986) 'A Category of the Human Mind: The Notion of Person; the Notion of Self'. In M. Carrithers, S. Collins and S. Lukes (eds) *The Category of the Person: Anthropology, Philosophy, History*, Cambridge: Cambridge University Press.

Meier, C. (1987) *La politique et la grace: anthropologie politique de la beauté grecque*, Paris: Seuil.

Mennell, S. (1992) *Norbert Elias: An Introduction*, Oxford: Blackwell.

Milbank, J. (1995) 'Stories of Sacrifice: From Wellhausen to Girard'. *Theory, Culture and Society* 12: 15–46.

Mitchell, A.C. (1996) 'Holding on to Confidence: Parrhesia in Hebrews'. In J.T. Fitzgerald (ed.) *Friendship, Flattery and Freedom of Speech: Studies on Friendship in the New Testament World*, Leiden: E.J. Brill.

Mittendorfer, K. (2000) 'Mimesis and Christian Spirituality'. PhD thesis, European University Institute, Florence, Italy.

Momigliano, A. (1973) 'Freedom of Speech in Antiquity'. In P.P. Weiner (ed.) *Dictionary of the History of Ideas*, pp. 752–63, New York: Charles Scribner's Sons.

Mumford, L. (1956) *The Transformations of Man*, New York: Collier.

—— (1961) *The City in History*, London: Secker and Warburg.

Neher, A. (1961) *Jérémie*, Paris: Plon.

Nelson, B. (1976) 'Orient and Occident in Max Weber'. *Social Research* 43: 114–29.

Nietzsche, F. (1966) *Beyond Good and Evil*, New York: Vintage.

—— (1967) *On the Genealogy of Morals*, New York: Vintage.

—— (1968) *The Will to Power*, New York: Vintage.

—— (1974) *The Gay Science*, New York: Vintage.

—— (1982) *Daybreak*, Cambridge: Cambridge University Press.

—— (1986) *Human, All-Too Human*, Cambridge: Cambridge University Press.

—— (1999) *The Birth of Tragedy*, Cambridge: Cambridge University Press.

Noica, C. (1993) *Sei malattie dello spirito contemporaneo*, Bologna: Il Mulino.

Nygren, A. (1953) *Agape and Eros*, London: SPCK.

Oestreich, G. (1982) *Neostoicism and the Early Modern State*, Cambridge: Cambridge University Press.

Opitz, P.J. (1993) 'Max Weber e Eric Voegelin'. *Filosofia Politica* 7: 109–27.

—— (1996) 'Eric Voegelin's Nietzsche – eine Forschungsnotiz'. *Nietzsche-Studien* 25: 172–90.

Orihara, H. (1994) 'Eine Grundlegung zur Rekonstruktion von Max Webers "Wirtschaft und Gesellschaft"'. *Kölner Zeitschrift zur Soziologie und Sozialpsychologie* 46: 103–21.

Oughourlian, J.-M. (1982) *Un même nommé désir*, Paris: Flammarion.

Pagels, E. (1982) *The Gnostic Gospels*, Harmondsworth: Pelican.

Paquet, L. (1992) *Les cyniques grecs: fragments et témoignages*, Paris: Libraire Générale Française.

Patocka, J. (1976–77) 'Wars of the 20th Century and the 20th Century as War'. *Telos* 116–26.

—— (1981) *Essais hérétiques sur la philosophie de l'histoire*, Paris: Verdier.

—— (1983) *Platon et l'Europe*, Paris: Verdier.

Pels, D. (1993) 'Missionary Sociology between Left and Right: A Critical Introduction to Mannheim'. *Theory, Culture and Society* 10: 45-68.

Penella, R. (2000) *The Private Orations of Themistius*, Berkeley: University of California Press.

Pirenne, H. (1925) *Medieval Cities*, Princeton: Princeton University Press.

—— (1939) *Mohammed and Charlemagne*, London: Allen and Unwin.

Pizzorno, A. (1987) 'Politics Unbound'. In C.S. Maier (ed.) *Changing Boundaries of the Political*, Cambridge: Cambridge University Press.

—— (1991) 'On the Individualistic Theory of Social Order'. In. P. Bourdieu and J.S. Coleman (eds) *Social Theory for a Changing Society*, Boulder and Oxford: Westview Press.

—— (2000) 'Risposte e proposte'. In D. della Porta, M. Greco and A. Szakolczai (eds) *Identità, riconoscimento e scambio: Saggi in onore di Alessandro Pizzorno*, Bari: Laterza.

Plato (1914–35) *Plato in Twelve Volumes*, London: Heinemann.

Polybius (1922) *The Histories*, London: Heinemann.

Price, G.L. (2000) *Eric Voegelin: International Bibliography, 1921–2000*, Munich: Fink.

Rajchman, J. (1985) *Michel Foucault: The Freedom of Philosophy*, New York: Columbia University Press.

Riley, A.T. (1999) 'Whence Durkheim's Nietzschean Grandchildren?', *Archives européennes de sociologie* 40, 2: 304–30.

Rossbach, S. (1999) *Gnostic Wars: The Cold War in the Context of a History of Western Spirituality*. Edinburgh: Edinburgh University Press.

--- (2001) '"Gnosis" in Eric Voegelin's philosophy', paper presented at the August 2001 meeting of the *American Political Science Association*.

268   *References*

Sayre, F. (1938) *Diogenes of Sinope: A Study of Greek Cynicism*, Baltimore: J.H. Furst Co.

Scaff, L. (1984) 'Weber before Weberian Sociology'. *The British Journal of Sociology* 35: 190–215.

Scarpat, G. (1977) *Il pensiero religioso di Seneca e l'ambiente ebraico e cristiano*, Brescia: Paideia.

—— (2001 [1964]) *Parrhesia greca, parrhesia cristiana*, Brescia: Paideia.

Schlier, H. (1954) 'Parrhesia, parrhesiadzomai'. In G. Kittel and G. Friedrich *Theologisches Wörterbuch zum Neuen Testament*, Stuttgart: ZZZ.

Schluchter, W. (1989) *Rationalism, Religion and Domination: A Weberian Perspective*, Berkeley: University of California Press.

Segal, C. (1981) *Tragedy and Civilization*, Cambridge, MA: Harvard University Press.

Sennett, R. (1998) *The Corrosion of Character*, New York: W.W. Norton.

Smolders, D. (1958) 'L'audace de l'apôtre selon saint Paul: le thème de la parrésia'. *Collectanea Mechliniensia* 43: 117–33.

Szakolczai, A. (1994) 'Thinking Beyond the East West Divide: Foucault, Patocka, and the Care of the Self'. *Social Research* 61: 297–323.

—— (1998) *Max Weber and Michel Foucault: Parallel Life-Works*, London: Routledge.

—— (1999) 'The Spiritual Character of Modernity: Preemption, Crisis and Return'. In E. Hankiss (ed.) *Europe after 1989: A Culture in Crisis?*, Washington, D.C.: Georgetown University Press.

—— (2000) *Reflexive Historical Sociology*, London: Routledge.

—— (2001a) 'Civilization and Its Sources'. *International Sociology* 16: 371–88.

—— (2001b) 'Stages of a Quest: Reconstructing the Outline Structure of the *History of Political Ideas*', No. XXV in the 'Occasional Papers' of the *Eric-Voegelin-Archiv*. Ludwig Maximilians Universität, Munich.

Tarde, G. (1989 [1904]) *L'Opinion et la foule*, Paris: P.U.F.

Taylor, C. (1989) *Sources of the Self*, Cambridge: Cambridge University Press.

Tenbruck, F.H. (1980) 'The problem of thematic unity in the works of Max Weber'. *British Journal of Sociology* 31: 316–51.

Thrower, N. (1996 [1972]) *Maps and Civilization: Cartography in Culture and Society*, Chicago: University of Chicago Press.

Thucydides (1919–23) *The History of the Peloponnesian War*, London: Heinemann.

Tribe, K. (1989) 'The *Geschichtliche Grundbegriffe* Project: From History of Ideas to Conceptual History'. *Comparative Study of Society and History* 13: 180–4.

Tully, J. (1988) *Meaning and Context: Quentin Skinner and his Critics*, Cambridge: Polity Press.

Turnbull, C.M. (1968 [1961]) *The Forest People*, New York: Simon and Schuster.

—— (1973) *The Mountain People*, London: Jonathan Cape.

Turner, V. (1967) 'Betwixt and Between: The Liminal Period in *Rites de Passage*', New York: Cornell University Press.

—— (1969) *The Ritual Process*, Chicago: Aldine.

—— (1982) *From Ritual to Theatre: The Human Seriousness of Play*, New York: PAJ Publications.

—— (1985) 'Experience and Performance: Towards a New Processual Anthropology'. In E. Turner (ed.) *On the Edge of the Bush*, Tucson: The University of Arizona Press.

—— (1992) 'Morality and Liminality'. In E. Turner (ed.) *Blazing the Trail: Way Marks in the Exploration of Symbols*, Tucson: The University of Arizona Press.

Turner, V. and Turner, E. (1978) *Image and Pilgrimage in Christian Culture*, New York: Columbia University Press.

van Gennep, A. (1960 [1909]) *The Rites of Passage*, Chicago: The University of Chicago Press.

van Krieken, R. (1990) 'The organization of the soul: Elias and Foucault on discipline and the self'. *Archives européennes de sociologie* 31: 353–71.

—— (1998) *Norbert Elias*, London: Routledge.

van Unnik, W.C. (1962) 'The Christian's Freedom of Speech in the New Testament'. *Bulletin of the John Ryland's Library* 44: 466–88.

Vernant, J.-P. (1990 [1965]) *Mythe et pensée chez les grecques*, Paris: Découverte.

—— (1990) *Mythe et religion en Gréce ancienne*, Paris: Seuil.

Voegelin, E. (1944) 'Nietzsche, the Crisis and the War'. *Journal of Politics* 6: 177–212.

—— (1962) 'World-Empire and the Unity of Mankind'. *International Affairs* 38: 170–88.

—— (1990) 'What Is History?' In E. Voegelin, *What Is History? And Other Late Unpublished Writings*, Baton Rouge: LSU Press.

Voelke, A.-J. (1993) *La philosophie comme thérapie de l'âme*, Fribourg: Editions Universitaires Fribourg.

Waddell, H. (1987) *The Desert Fathers*, London: Constable.

Waley, D. (1969) *Le città-repubblica dell'Italia medioevale*, Milan: Mondadori.

Wallerstein, I. (1979) *The Modern World System*, New York: Academic.

Weber, M. (1978) 'Anticritical Last Word on The Spirit of Capitalism'. *American Journal of Sociology* 83: 1105–31.

Weiss, G. (2000) *Theorie, Relevanz und Wahrheit*, Munich: Fink.

Wengrow, D. (1999) 'The Intellectual Adventure of Henri Frankfort: A Missing Chapter in the History of Archaeological Thought'. *American Journal of Archaeology* 103: 597–613.

Winter, S.C. (1996) 'Parrhesia in Acts'. In J.T. Fitzgerald (ed.) *Friendship, Flattery and Freedom of Speech: Studies on Friendship in the New Testament World*, Leiden: E.J. Brill.

Zeitlin, I.M. (1984) *Ancient Judaism*, Cambridge: Polity Press.

Name Index

Subject Index